Using

Macromedia

Dreamweaver

1.2

Rick Darnell

Timothy Webster

A Division of Macmillan Computer Publishing, USA
201 W. 103rd Street
Indianapolis, Indiana 46290

MW01490050

Con...

Using Macromedia Dreamweaver 1.2

International Standard Book Number: 0-7897-1626-7

Library of Congress Catalog Card Number: 97-81455

Printed in the United States of America

First Printing: May, 1998

00 99 98   4 3 2 1

Trademarks

Executive Editor
Mark Taber

Acquisitions Editor
Randi Roger

Development Editor
Scott D. Meyers

Managing Editor
Patrick Kanouse

Senior Project Editor
Elizabeth A. Bruns

Copy Editor
Patricia Kinyon

Indexer
Bruce Clingaman

Technical Editor
Dan Giordan

Production
Mike Henry
Linda Knose
Tim Osborn
Staci Somers
Mark Walchle

Table of Contents

About the Authors

Rick Darnell (darnell@montana.com) hails from the rolling hills of eastern Kansas, although he currently finds his view blocked by a bunch of mountains while living with his wife and two daughters in western Montana. He graduated from Kansas State University with a degree in broadcasting, became confused, and started writing for two small energy industry magazines and a local weekly newspaper. Spending time as a freelance journalist and writer, Rick has seen the full gamut of personal computers since starting out with a Radio Shack Model I in the late 1970s. He has contributed to many Web-related publications from Macmillan Computer Publishing. Recent titles include *HTML 4 Unleashed*, *Sams Teach Yourself Dynamic HTML In a Week*, and the *JavaScript Quick Reference*. In real life, Rick is a certified candidate for ordination in the United Methodist Church, and holds certifications as an Emergency Medical Technician and a Hazardous Materials Technician.

Timothy Webster (tim@orbis-tertius.com) is a freelance writer and the principal designer of Timothy Webster Design & Consulting, Inc. His previous books for Macmillan include *Web Designer's Guide to NetObjects Fusion 2*, *Web Designer's Guide to PNG, GIF, and JPEG*, and *Teach Yourself Java in 21 Days for Macintosh* (with Lemay and Perkins). You can find Tim's chronically unfinished Web site at http://www.orbis-tertius.com. Tim lives on the south side of Chicago—the baddest part of town.

Contributing Author

Daniel Giordan is an artist, author, and lecturer who works in both digital and conventional artistic media. He is the author of *Dynamic Photoshop* (MIS Press 1997), and a contributing author for *The Whole Mac* (Hayden Books 1996).

Dedication

To Jane, Margaret, and Elizabeth.

—Rick Darnell

To my readers and students.

—Timothy Webster

Acknowledgments

One of the most gratifying aspects of working on a book like this is the people you meet along the way, beginning with the fine editors at Macmillan Computer Publishing. After all, writers are pretty pointless without editors, and vice versa. It's one of those mutually dependent relationships that can be a bit stressful at times, but can also lead to another fine finished product like the one you're holding.

Acquisitions Editor Randi Roger was the motivating force who reviewed the book proposals from Tim and me, presented them to the powers-that-be, arbitrated six weeks of table-of-contents discussions, negotiated the contracts, set the deadlines, and hounded us to make sure we delivered the goods in a timely manner. A book like this seems pretty cut and dried, but that's only because of the work someone like Randi puts into it.

Scott Meyers kept all of us focused on you, our beloved paying audience. He worked with us to make sure we fit within the scope of the *Using* series, and did a great deal of work to help interpret who our audience was and how to present the material.

Dan Giordan was our Technical Editor. He works with a Macintosh, I work with a PC. Because Dreamweaver works on both, it was very helpful to have someone who could give a little more balance to the book so it covers Dreamweaver, and not Dreamweaver for Windows.

Creating a table of contents for this book was not the easiest thing I've ever done, and there was a great deal of frustration involved for both co-author Tim Webster and myself. Probably the only thing that got us through that six-week period was the fact that we were frustrated and suffering together. I didn't get to have much contact with Tim once the actual writing was under way, but it was still good to be able to share the load with someone else.

Lots of other folks at Macmillan make these projects happen, from editorial boards and publishers, to lawyers and accountants, to copy and project editors, to designers, secretaries, custodians, and many others I have never met. Although I don't know everyone's name, everyone makes a contribution to the finished product. Many thanks to you all.

In addition to the folks who worked directly on this project, there are many people who have fostered me during my early attempts at writing, giving me the guidance needed to learn how to put the right words in the right order. This list includes Bonnie Montgall, David MacFarland, John Braden, and influences such as Edward Abbey, Kenneth Grahame, and A.A. Milne.

Last in this list of acknowledgments, but certainly not least, is you, the reader. Your investment in this book just made my bank account a few cents bigger. I hope you find the book useful and worth the money you shelled out for it. If it makes working with Dreamweaver easier, and hence, eases the task of communicating with the rest of humanity through the Web, then we've done our jobs right on this end. Thank you.

Rick Darnell

Jane Chuey and Steve Shannon at Macromedia.

Scott Meyers and Randi Roger at Macmillan Computer Publishing, with special thanks for their extraordinary patience.

University Publications, for good company and the use of the workstation.

Mike O'Neal and Jason Ulane, who did much of my real-world work during writing crunches.

Dan Talayco, Jen Burton, Rodolfo Celis, and Colette Speakman, for crisis management.

Joe Gallagher, for the ginchy home page.

Chris Corcoran, who continued to surprise me.

My co-author, Rick Darnell, who wrote the best parts of the book.

And, as always, my parents, for their continued love and support.

Timothy Webster

We'd Like to Hear from You!

Que Corporation has a long-standing reputation for high-quality books and products. To ensure your continued satisfaction, we also understand the importance of customer service and support.

Orders, Catalogs, and Customer Service

To order other Que or Macmillan Computer Publishing books, catalogs, or products, please contact our Customer Service Department:

Phone: 1-800-428-5331
Fax: 1-800-835-3202
International Fax: 1-317-228-4400

or visit our online bookstore:

http://www.mcp.com/

Comments and Suggestions

We want you to let us know what you like or dislike most about this book or other Que products. Your comments will help us to continue publishing the best books available on computer topics in today's market.

Mark Taber
Executive Editor
Macmillan Computer Publishing
201 West 103rd Street
Indianapolis, IN 46290 USA
Fax: 317-817-7070
Email: mtaber@mcp.com

Please be sure to include this book's title and author as well as your name and phone number or fax number.

We will carefully review your comments and share them with the author. Please note that due to the high volume of mail we receive, we might not be able to reply to every message.

Thank you for using Que!

Welcome to *Using Macromedia Dreamweaver 1.2*—the best guide to creating dynamic Web pages with the latest tool from Macromedia.

Why should you be interested in another HTML editor, let alone another book about one? There are a two important reasons why we think the combination of Dreamweaver and *Using Macromedia Dreamweaver 1.2* is important for serious Web authors and developers.

- Dreamweaver is specifically designed to take advantage of the current interaction of Web pages and scripting known as Dynamic HTML (DHTML). This is no small feat, given the differences in DHTML between Netscape and Microsoft.

- This book was written with Web designers and authors in mind. It's our goal to show you how to take advantage of Dreamweaver to achieve the design goals you require for your sites. To help keep the professional designer in mind, we used a technical editor with a very strong background in Web page design.

Dreamweaver is certainly not the be-all-end-all of HTML editors, but we feel it's the best tool available to work within the existing realm of Dynamic HTML.

There are a few things we're expecting from you, the reader. Because we're concentrating on using Dreamweaver to create Web pages, we have to assume there's a few things you already know:

- *HTML.* Like most visual Web editors, Dreamweaver does a fine job of creating the necessary HTML to create Web pages out of sight. However, to fully optimize a page or create special effects, you may need to tweak the source code of the page by hand. A knowledge of HTML, specifically the current HTML 4 recommendation, is very important. A good combination of resources includes the HTML 4.0 quick reference in the back of this book, the official HTML 4.0 Recommendation from the World Wide Web Consortium (http://www.w3.org), and a comprehensive reference book such as *HTML 4 Unleashed, Professional Reference Edition.*

- *Cascading Style Sheets.* Style sheets are an integral part of the new HTML standard. They offer an entire new dimension of control over the appearance of your page. There's an appendix at the back of this book that outlines the various attributes and values which are used within style sheets. There is a good introductory section on style sheets in the *HTML 4 Unleashed* book, or you can use a more in-depth resource such as *Web Designer's Guide to Style Sheets.*

- *JavaScript.* The guiding force behind dynamic and interactive behavior on a Web page is a solid scripting language. Currently, JavaScript is the choice of languages. It helps to have a background in programming, since JavaScript is in fact a programming language, albeit a lightweight one. A good introduction is *Sams Teach Yourself JavaScript in a Week,* although you may prefer something like *JavaScript Unleashed.*

- *Dynamic HTML.* Dynamic HTML is the combination of HTML, style sheets, and scripting that results in pages that change without any need for CGI scripts or other server interaction. It's not a terribly clear-cut technology, being still in its infancy in its various implementations. Check out *Sams Teach Yourself Dynamic HTML in a Week* or *Dynamic HTML Unleashed.*

In short, this book is not a tutorial in HTML, style sheets, JavaScript, or Dynamic HTML. To take full advantage of

Dreamweaver and this book, you need to have a firm background in the Web technologies it uses to create advanced and interactive Web pages.

How This Book Is Organized

This book is divided into five different sections, plus several appendixes. The book begins by working with Dreamweaver as an HTML editor. You'll see how to use the various property palettes to create and customize a basic HTML Page. From there, you'll work into multimedia content, and advanced page creation with tables, frames and layers. After the details of creating a page are covered, you'll get to dive into the real strength of Dreamweaver—creating cross-browser compatible dynamic pages. This is followed by some housekeeping details on site management, troubleshooting, and targeting your pages for various browsers.

Here's a section-by-section look at what's in store:

I. **Basic Page Creation**   This section covers how to create and edit Web pages with Dreamweaver. This includes coverage of the various tools for adding and formatting text, creating reusable libraries of Web pages, plus Dreamweaver's site management tools.

II. **Multimedia with Dreamweaver**   An important part of modern Web pages are various types of multimedia. Into this pot we include the various types of traditional multimedia content, such as Shockwave and Java. For the purposes of this book, we also include forms and imagemaps.

III. **Structuring Pages with Tables, Frames, and Layers**   An important part of page design is its organization. This section covers the three major organizational tools available to Web designers through Dreamweaver, including the more mundane tables, to the latest advancements in layers.

IV. **Adding Interactivity and Scripts**   This is the bread and butter of Dreamweaver. Through a series of dialog boxes and tools such as timelines, you can create moving and flashing images, expanding and collapsing outlines, and rollovers. This is where Dreamweaver really struts its stuff, and these are some of the most exciting chapters of the book.

V. **Site Management and Troubleshooting**   You can also call this, "Doesn't really fit in any of the other categories." This section includes some tips and guidance on maintaining sanity across your site, and strategies for tracing problems when things go wrong. There are also two chapters on using Dreamweaver's browser-targeting feature to help determine how your pages may or may not react on a particular browser.

The appendixes in the back of the book include more reference information to augment your use of Dreamweaver. There are appendixes to give you a quick guide to the text-based HTML editors that are packaged with Dreamweaver (HomeSite for Windows and BBEdit for Macintosh), an HTML 4 and Cascading Style Sheet quick reference, and a guide to installing and configuring Dreamweaver.

We hope the combination of information in the chapters and appendixes makes *Using Macromedia Dreamweaver 1.2* the most useful guide to creating dynamic Web pages with this exciting new tool.

Conventions Used in This Book

Sams.net has spent many years developing and publishing computer books designed for ease of use and containing the most up-to-date information available. With that experience, we've learned what features help you the most. Look for these features throughout the book to help enhance your learning experience and get the most out of HTML.

Sidenote

Sidebars are where you'll find information that might be useful or interesting, but isn't necessarily crucial to your understanding of using Dreamweaver. This includes useful or interesting information that isn't necessarily essential to the current discussion but might help you understand with background information or advice that relates to the topic. It also includes short advice on overlooked procedures or workarounds for specific problems.

- Screen messages, HTML tags, and code examples appear in `monospace type`.
- Commands the reader is instructed to use are in **bold type**.
- Uniform Resource Locators (URLs) used to identify pages on the Web and values for HTML attributes appear in `monospace type`.

Often, there is more than one way to use a tool or start a procedure. This includes using menus, function keys, or combinations of special keys. Wherever possible, we've included all the options in a list like this, beginning with what we feel is the quickest or easiest method:

- Press **F10**.
- Press **Ctrl+G** (Windows) or **Option+G** (Macintosh).
- Select **Tools**, choose **Obscure**, and then choose **Garbonzo**.

Where an option is universal for Macintosh or Windows, no mention of either platform is made. Where the method is the same, but keys are different, the combination of keys are given, followed by the platform in parentheses. Menu choices are listed in order of options chosen, beginning with the title on the menu bar.

Who Should Read This Book?

This book is geared towards professional Web designers and authors who are using Macromedia Dreamweaver. The approach is geared towards those people who are building Web pages as a regular part of their jobs.

By the same token, we've also worked within the popular *Using* series so this book will work as very usable reference by most people who have any experience with creating Web pages.

Novice or first-time Web authors will want to work through the book in a sequential fashion. This will give you a taste of everything Dreamweaver has to offer. Working through the examples in the beginning sections will have you comfortable with Web page creation and the Dreamweaver interface, so you'll be ready to tackle the concepts of frames, layers, interactivity, and scripting in the latter part of the book.

Intermediate users will probably want to skip around, based on their familiarity with the types of tasks Dreamweaver can accomplish and their experience with other HTML editors. For those who are used to working within a visual interface, such as FrontPage, PageMill, or similar products, Dreamweaver should be fairly intuitive. On the other hand, if you've spent all your time with text-based editors such as HomeSite, BBEdit, HotDog, or one of the many others, you'll probably take a quick tour through the first section to get acquainted with Dreamweaver's interface.

Advanced Web designers and authors will want to be sure to begin with Chapter 2, "Working with Files," and Chapter 8, "Reusable Parts for Web Pages." These two chapters in the first section explain two of the unique features of Dreamweaver that are not immediately intuitive. Chapter 1, "Jump Start to Creating Pages in Dreamweaver," introduces the Dreamweaver interface through a quick overview of basic tasks, including adding and formatting text, adding multimedia content, and working with the scripting controls.

We've worked hard to put together the best book for Web authors and designers who use Dreamweaver. We think you'll agree that it's a valuable companion to getting the most out of this powerful product for creating dynamic and exciting Web pages.

From Tim and me, and our devoted and hard-working editors, thank you for choosing *Using Macromedia Dreamweaver 1.2*.

Rick Darnell

(darnell@montana.com)

PART
I

Basic Page Creation

Jump Start to Creating Pages with Dreamweaver

Work with the Site window

Add and format text

Create style sheets

Edit the HTML source code

Add images and multimedia content

Create interactive scripts

Preview your work in a browser

The Dreamweaver Fast-Track

Working with Dreamweaver to create Web pages is an intuitive process. If you've ever used a What-You-See-Is-What-You-Get (WYSIWYG) Web page editor before, you'll be right at home working with Dreamweaver. This chapter is for those of you in that category—you have a background in working with Web editors or are otherwise familiar with this kind of software.

I'll hit the high points of Dreamweaver in this chapter and walk you quickly through the specific ways Dreamweaver creates Web pages. I'm not going to spend a lot of time on explanation or background—that's covered in the other chapters where each task is covered in detail.

For those of you unfamiliar with creating Web pages, this is a good place to get a quick feel for what's going on, but I'd still recommend you look at the other chapters in a little more depth. Your questions about HTML, FTP, JavaScript, and some of the other details of Web page creation are covered in the rest of the book.

Working with Files

If you're going to create a page with Dreamweaver (or any other editor, for that matter), you'll need a place to put your work. First, you'll need space on your local computer to put files you're currently working on. Then, you'll need access to the Web site where the files will be seen by the rest of the browsing public. Working with files in remote and local locations is covered in Chapter 2, "Working with Files."

All of this is accomplished in Dreamweaver using the Site window (see Figure 1.1) that is accessed in following ways:

- Select the **Site** icon from the launcher.
- Select **Window** and choose **Sites.**
- Press **F5**

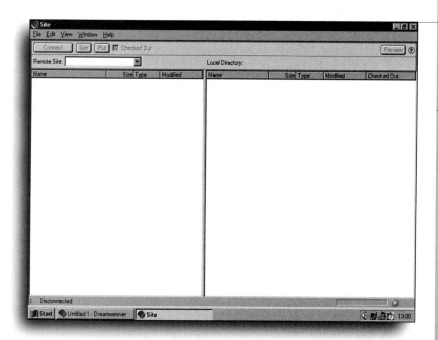

FIGURE 1.1

The Site window allows you to manage both the local and remote components of a Web site.

Defining the space for pages

1. From the Site window, select the arrow by the Remote List box, and select **Edit Sites**.

2. Click the **New Site** button in the Site Information window.

3. Click in the Site Name field and type a name for your site.

4. Next, tell Dreamweaver where the root directory for this site should be on your computer by clicking the **Choose** button (for Macintosh) or **Browse** button (for Windows).

5. Any new documents for this site are automatically placed in this folder if the **Default site root for new documents** option is selected. New files for a different site are placed in the default directory for that site.

6. For the **FTP Host**, enter the URL used to access the host where your files are placed for general consumption by your public. Dreamweaver automatically treats anything in this field as an FTP site, you can leave off the `ftp://` portion of the address.

7. Next, include the home directory at the remote host.

8. This is followed by the **Login** name and the **Password**. The password is masked with asterisks (*) to hide it from prying eyes. An example of finished site information is shown in Figure 1.2.

FIGURE 1.2

Completed site information for my personal Web site.

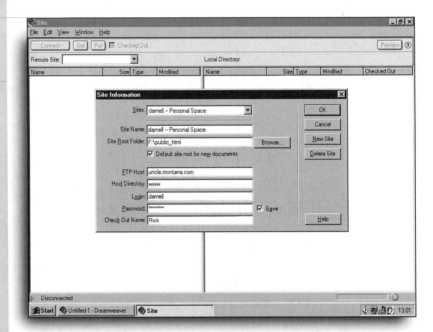

9. Click **OK** to save the information and return to the Site window.

The Site window now holds the name of our new site. The right side of the screen shows the contents of the site as it exists on the local computer, and the left side shows the contents of the site on the remote computer after you connect to it (see Figure 1.3). To see the remote site, make sure you have a connection to the Internet or your intranet (wherever your remote site is located):

- Click the **Connect** button.
- Select **File** and choose **Connect**.
- Select **Vie** and choose **Refresh Remote** (for Windows, press **Alt+F5**).

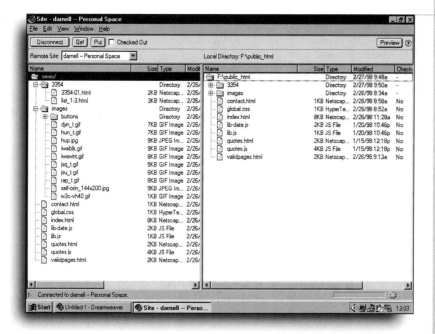

FIGURE 1.3

After connecting to a Remote
site, all of its files and directory
structure are displayed.

To open a page for editing from the Remote or Local portion of
a site, double-click the page. If you click a page from the
Remote site, Dreamweaver will mark it as checked out, so other
designers and Web authors won't attempt to edit the page at the
same time. The Remote file is updated when it's checked back in.

Checking in and saving pages

1. Select the page or pages to check in to the Remote site.
   They are identified with a green check-mark and a Yes in
   the Local Checked Out column.

2. Select the **Checked Out** box at the top of the Site window.

   If you just want to save the files and keep them checked out,
   click the **Put** button.

3. If you've created new files in the local site that should be
   placed on the Remote site, select the new files and click the
   Put button. This copies the files to the Remote site and
   marks them as checked out to you.

Under Windows, you can also select **File** and choose **Check In** to save the files and make them available for other people to edit. For Macintosh, the same results are achieved be selecting **File**, choosing **Site Window**, and then choosing **Check-In**.

Page management quickly becomes crucial when working with complex pages and complex sites. Dreamweaver has included these features to make your life easier in accomplishing this task.

Adding and Formatting Text

With a place to put pages, it's time to turn our attention to actually creating one. Dreamweaver opens with a blank slate for creating pages. Even though the page is blank, it's important to save the file as the name you'll be using within the proper Local site directory to make sure relative hyperlinks are interpreted properly.

You can open an existing page in two ways:

- Select **File,** choose **Open**, and select the appropriate folder and page.
- Double-click the file in the Site window.

Adding text to a new or existing page is the same as working with virtually any other Web page editor or word processor— just start typing. Text will automatically wrap at the end of the line. New paragraphs are started by pressing the Enter key.

Formatting the text into other elements, including headings, lists and hyperlinks, is accomplished with the Properties palette (see Figure 1.4), opened by selecting **Window** and choosing **Properties**.

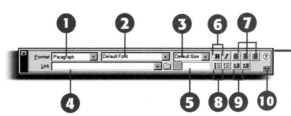

Before you can format text, it must be selected. Place the cursor or mouse pointer at the beginning of the text to begin selecting the desired text:

- Click and drag the mouse to the end of the line to highlight the text, and then release the mouse button.
- Double-click a word to select the entire word, and then continue to drag the mouse to select a word at a time.
- Place the mouse pointer to the left of a line where the pointer changes from an I-beam to an arrow. Click once to select the line, or click and drag to select multiple lines.
- Hold down the **Shift** key while pressing the **arrow keys** to select a letter or line at a time.

There are a wide range of options to format text from the Properties palette:

- To make the text a new paragraph, preformatted text, or a heading, select an option from the Format drop-down list.
- To select a different set of fonts, select an option from the Font drop-down list.
- To turn the text into a hyperlink:
  - Type a URL into the **Link** box.
  - Select a previously used address from the drop-down list.
  - Click the **Browse** button to select a page from the current local site.

- For a custom color:
  - Select a predefined color by clicking the color swatch to view a palette of choices, or create your own color by selecting the **Paint Palette** icon below the color swatches.
  - Type an HTML color name into the box, such as **red**, **blue**, or **silver**.
  - Type the hexadecimal triplet value for the color, preceded by a pound sign (**#**).
- Add and remove bold or italics features by selecting or deselecting the appropriate button.
- Select a default alignment by clicking one of three alignment buttons.
- Clicking the **Indent** button encases the text in <BLOCKQUOTE> tags, which indents it from both sides. Clicking the **Outdent** button removes the tags. If the text isn't already indented, the **Outdent** button has no effect.
- Turn the selection into a list by selecting one of the list buttons. Your choice is bulleted (unordered) or numbered (ordered). If multiple lines of text are selected, each paragraph within the selection is converted into one bullet or numbered item within the list.

In addition to the Properties palette, there are an additional set of formatting options available by selecting **Text** and choosing **Style**. This selection includes Underline, Emphasis (italic), Strong Emphasis (bold), Teletype (monospace).

Working with Style Sheets

The Properties palette uses methods to change text that depend on specific HTML tags within your text. This method is passing into obsolescence in favor of style sheets, which provide more formatting options and are less likely to cause problems with older browsers. Style sheets are managed and applied to your text from the Styles palette (see Figure 1.5):

- Select the **Styles** icon from the launcher.
- Click the **Plug-in** icon in the Object palette.

- Select **Window** and choose **Styles**.
- Press **F7**.

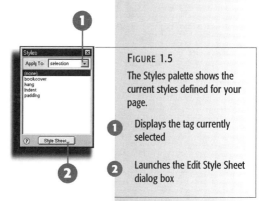

FIGURE 1.5

The Styles palette shows the current styles defined for your page.

1. Displays the tag currently selected

2. Launches the Edit Style Sheet dialog box

Read more about creating and using style sheets in Chapter 6, "Formatting Text with Style Sheets."

To create or edit a new style or HTML tag, click the **Style Sheet** button at the bottom of the Styles palette to view the Edit Style Sheet dialog box (see Figure 1.6).

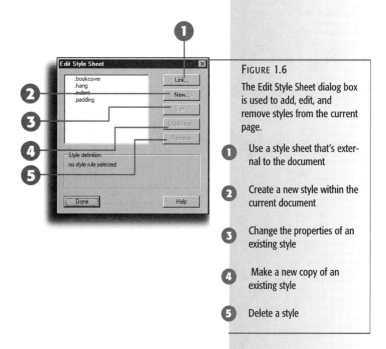

FIGURE 1.6

The Edit Style Sheet dialog box is used to add, edit, and remove styles from the current page.

1. Use a style sheet that's external to the document

2. Create a new style within the current document

3. Change the properties of an existing style

4. Make a new copy of an existing style

5. Delete a style

Creating a style sheet

1. From the Edit Style Sheet Dialog box, click **New** to create a new style.

2. This displays the New Style box (see Figure 1.7).

   - **Make Custom Style (class)**: Create a style definition that can be applied to any tag. Type a name for the class in the box, including the leading period, or select an existing class from the drop-down list.

   - **Redefine HTML Tag:** Change the default appearance for a standard HTML tag. For example, you can make all headings align to the right. Select an HTML tag from the drop down-list.

   - **Use CSS Selector:** This creates a style for one of three states for hyperlink anchor tags (active, link, visited). Select the selector from the drop-down list.

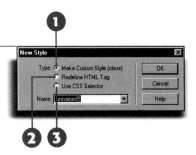

FIGURE 1.7

The New Style dialog box lets you choose what kind of style to make.

1 Create a style that can be applied to any tag

2 Change the default appearance of a tag

3 Create a style for the various states of a hyperlink

3. After selecting the type of style and style name, Dreamweaver provides you with a dialog box that includes a series of tabs which set the appearance of the style (see Figure 1.8).

   Select a category on the left side to display a set of style choices on the right. For most text items, the first three will hold all the choices needed. You'll find a quick reference to style options in Appendix D, "CSS Quick Reference."

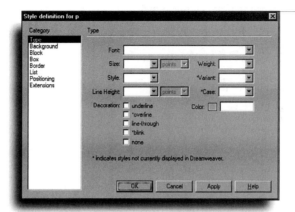

FIGURE 1.8
You can decide how the style
affects its text in the tabs of the
Style definition dialog box.

5. Once the style definition is completed, click **OK**. Any
attribute you don't define will revert to the default set by the
user's browser. The new style appears in the Edit Style,
along with the HTML definition of your selections at the
bottom.

To apply a style class, highlight the desired text and click the
style name in the Styles palette. If you're dealing with a set of
nested tags, such as an <EM> within a <P> within a <DIV>, you can
select the specific tag from the **Apply to** drop-down list in the
Styles palette.

Editing the Page Source

WYSIWYG is great for getting started editing pages, but most
Web authors and designers find that it becomes necessary to
tweak and adjust the page by altering the base HTML code.

Dreamweaver accommodates this group of people in two ways.
The first is the HTML Inspector (see Figure 1.9):

- Click the **HTML Inspector** icon on the launcher bar.
- Select **Window** and choose **HTML**.

FIGURE 1.9

The HTML inspector lets you view and edit the underlying source of a Web page.

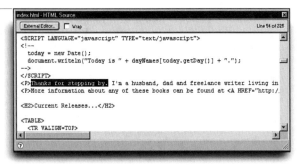

You can edit the source code directly in this window, adding tags, attributes, or text to the page. The results are immediately mirrored in Dreamweaver's graphical editing window. If any tags are entered that aren't recognized by Dreamweaver or are entered incorrectly (such as an end tag without a beginning tag), they appear in the graphical window highlighted in yellow.

The second method of editing the HTML source is by using a different HTML editor. Dreamweaver comes packaged with BBEdit (for Macintosh) and HomeSite (for Windows) for greater control over creating and editing pages. You can launch an external editor with the current page in Dreamweaver:

- Select **Edit** and choose **Launch External Editor**.
- Press **Ctrl+E** (in Windows) or ⌘**+E** (for Macintosh).
- From the HTML inspector, click the **External Editor** button at the top of the window.

For more information on configuring Dreamweaver to work with external editors, see Chapter 3, "Using Text Editors and Dreamweaver."

Inserting Images, Applets, and Other Items

Image and multimedia features are common additions to most Web pages. Dreamweaver includes an Objects palette (see Figure 1.10) to facilitate including these features on your Web page. Select **Window** and choose **Objects** to display the palette for use.

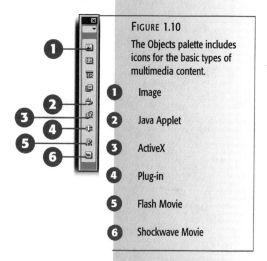

FIGURE 1.10

The Objects palette includes icons for the basic types of multimedia content.

1 Image

2 Java Applet

3 ActiveX

4 Plug-in

5 Flash Movie

6 Shockwave Movie

Adding an Image

Adding an image to your page is a straightforward task. First, position the cursor where you want the image to appear, then follow these steps:

Adding an image

1. Insert the image onto the page:

   • Click the **Image** icon in the Objects palette.

   • Select **Insert** and choose **Image**.

   • Press **Ctrl+Alt+I** (in Windows) or **Option+⌘+I** (for the Macintosh).

2. You're prompted for the location and filename of the image. Click on **Browse** to if you're not for sure exactly where to find it.

   If the image is outside the current site, Dreamweaver will prompt you to copy the file to a location in the current site.

3. After inserting, you're returned to the editing window. The image appears on the page and is selected for further manipulation if needed.

You can use the Properties palette to change the various features of an image, including its size, hyperlink status, and alignment. The boxes of the Properties palette are changed to reflect the available attributes for an image.

Adding a Plug-in

Inserting a plug-in is a rather generic process, since plug-ins cover such a wide range of content. Place the cursor where the plug-in should appear on the page, and then follow these steps:

Adding a plug-in

1. Add the plug-in to the page:
   - Click the **Plug-in** icon in the Object palette.
   - Select **Insert** and choose **Plug-in**.

2. A dialog box appears that prompts you for the filename and extension of the plug-in source file. Enter the name, or use the Browse button to locate the file by hand. Click **OK** when you've selected the file.

3. Make any changes to the plug-in through the Properties inspector. The Plg URL field tells the browser where to go looking if the necessary plug-in support files aren't installed to run the plug-in. If this isn't included, the user receives a generic prompt to search the Netscape Plug-in site. You also have the option of including an alternate image for browsers that don't support plug-ins.

SEE ALSO

➤ *Learn more about inserting and adjusting Shockwave Flash and Director movies, page 129*

Adding Java Applets

Inserting a Java applet is very similar to adding a plug-in. First, position the cursor where the applet should appear, and then follow these steps:

Adding a Java applet

1. Add the applet to the page:

   - Click the **Java** icon from the Object palette.
   - Click the **Plug-in** icon in the Object palette.
   - Select **Insert** and choose **Applet**.

2. A dialog box appears that prompts you for the name of the plug-in source file, which should always end with a .class extension. Enter the name, or use the Browse button to locate the file by hand. Click **OK** when you've selected the file.

3. Make any changes to the plug-in through the Properties inspector. The basic settings are similar to a plug-in, including an alternate image for incompatible browsers.

SEE ALSO

➤ *For more information on inserting and adjusting applets, page 131*

Adding ActiveX Content

ActiveX content is inserted the same as plug-ins and applets. The difference is in the properties for ActiveX, which are much more involved than the other two. The first step is the same—position the cursor where the ActiveX content should appear. Then follow these steps:

Adding ActiveX content

1. Insert ActiveX content on the page:

   - Click the **ActiveX** icon from the Object palette.
   - Click the **Plug-in** icon in the Object palette.
   - Select **Insert** and choose **ActiveX**.

2. Dreamweaver places an ActiveX icon on the page, and then changes the Properties Inspector to its ActiveX display (see Figure 1.11).

FIGURE 1.11

The Properties inspector for ActiveX content.

1 The unique code that identifies the type of ActiveX control used

2 Where to find the ActiveX control if it's not installed on the user's computer

3 Specifies the data file that holds the ActiveX content. Depending on the type of ActiveX control, this may not be used

4 Information for a plug-in version of the ActiveX content

5 An image to display if the browser doesn't support plug-ins

3. Since ActiveX uses the HTML <OBJECT> tag, you can also opt to include an optional plug-in through the Embed and Src fields within the ActiveX control, so you have the option of reach users of both browser.

SEE ALSO

➤ *For more information on inserting and adjusting ActiveX content, page 133*

Previewing Your Work

Dreamweaver can automatically load your page into any browser that is currently installed on your computer. However, before this works, you'll need to configure Dreamweaver with one or more preview browsers. A preview browser is typically installed automatically during Dreamweaver installation. For more information about installing Dreamweaver, see Appendix F, "Installing Dreamweaver and Accessories."

If a preview browser wasn't configured, you can still add a browser now.

Configuring a preview browser

1. To begin, open the Preferences dialog box:
   - Select **Edit** and choose **Preferences**.
   - Press **Ctrl+U** (in Windows) or **Option+U** (for the Macintosh).

2. Select **Preview in Browser** from the Category list (see Figure 1.12).

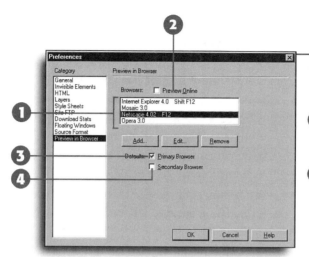

FIGURE 1.12

The Preview in Browser pane
of the Preferences dialog box.

1 Browsers currently available
for preview within
Dreamweaver

2 In Windows, this feature
loads the file using a local
Web server (if installed). Use
these buttons to add, change
or delete a browser from the
list

3 Sets the selected browser as
the default preview browser,
F12 in Windows

4 Sets the selected browser as
the secondary preview
browser, Shift+F12 in
Windows

3. If there are no browsers on the list, click the **Add** button.
Find the browser program on your computer, edit the name
as necessary, and select whether or not it's primary or secondary. Click **OK** when you're done.

4. After you've added all the browsers you require to your
browser list, click **OK** to return to Dreamweaver's editing
window.

With at least one preview browser in place, you're ready to
check your page within a real browser. Select **File,** choose
Preview in Browser, and then select the desired browser from
the list. Dreamweaver will display the current contents of the
editing window in the browser so you can see how it will appear
to your users.

From Here...

- Working with files, sites, and check-in policies is covered in
  Chapter 2, "Working with Files."
- Configuring the properties of a page, including background
  colors, images and default text colors, is covered in Chapter
  4, "Starting with a Blank Page."

- Adding and formatting text is shown in Chapter 5, "Adding Text to a Page."
- Creating and modifying style sheets for additional formatting options is discussed in Chapter 6, "Formatting Text with Style Sheets."
- Adding and modifying images and multimedia content is discussed in two chapters—Chapter 7, "Adding and Changing Images," and Chapter 9, "Working with Multimedia Content."
- Creating a library of Web page parts for easy reuse and updating is explained in Chapter 8, "Reusable Parts for Web Pages."
- Scripting and HTML-based interactive content is the topic of Part IV, "Adding Interactivity and Scripts."

Working with Files

Setting aside space on your computer

Defining local and remote sites

Adding placeholder files and folders

Put and get files from a remote site

Check in and check out for editing sanity

Creating a Home on Your Desk for Web Pages

Creating a Web site is a lot like building a closet—you create some space, and then start filling it up with stuff. The problem with closets is the same as for a Web site—if you don't begin with some basic organization, you just end up with a big pile where it's hard to tell the good stuff from the junk.

Dreamweaver comes equipped with a tool to help organize your Web closet, called the Site Manager. It does several things for you to make your life easier:

- It transfers files back and forth between your Web site and your local hard drive for editing and publishing.

- It allows you to create an entire Web site on your local drive before ever moving one page to the actual Web site.

- It lets you create, move, and delete directories and files to help keep your site organized.

- For sites where there's more than one person who can edit Web pages, it implements a check-out, check-in system to make sure no more than one person has access to a page at any given time.

With a little forethought on your part, you can use Dreamweaver to keep the neatest closet on the Web.

Before you can put a page on your Web site, you'll need some space on your computer to store it. Where you do this on your computer is a matter of personal preference and the specific requirements of your situation. If you're on a network, you may be using both space on your own computer and shared space on a network or workgroup drive somewhere. In my own case, I have a directory called wwork (short for "Web Work") on my local drive, where I create mirrors of the various sites I work on. I also have space called /~darnell/public_html on a network drive for a personal Web site, and additional space called /~public/public_html for shared workgroup files.

For the examples in this chapter, I'm going to create and manage files for a fictitious search and rescue organization. They log in to our network with the name sar, so that's what I'll call their local directory under wwork.

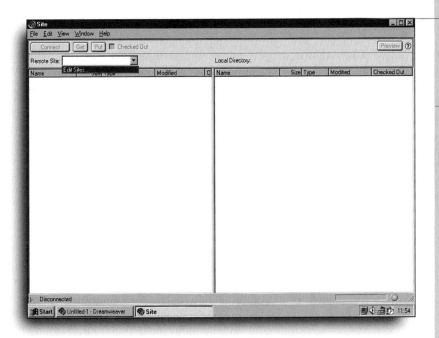 To get started, start Dreamweaver, open the Site window by clicking the **Site** button on the Launcher tool bar. Since this is our first experience with the Dreamweaver Site window, there are no sites available. We'll have to change that.

Adding a new local site

1. Select the arrow by the Remote Sites list box, and select **Edit Sites** (see Figure 2.1). You can also select **File**, and choose **Open Site.** Then select **Edit Sites** from the sub-menu.

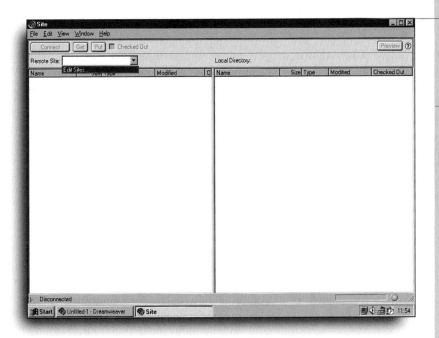

FIGURE 2.1

Initially the Remote Sites box has only one choice—Edit Sites—which is used to add and change sites.

2. The Site Information dialog box (see Figure 2.2) is used to add, edit, and delete sites. To get started, click the **New Site** button.

FIGURE 2.2

The Site Information dialog box sets where your pages are stored locally and on the remote location.

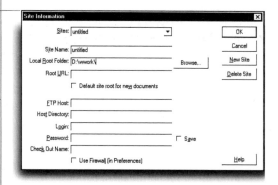

3. Now, all the fields are available for editing. Click in the Site Name field and type a name for your site. We'll call this one Search and Rescue.

4. Next, tell Dreamweaver where the root directory for this site should be on your computer, called amazingly enough the Site Root Folder. Click the **Browse** (Windows) or **Choose** (Macintosh) button and navigate to the wwork directory, and then add a new directory called sar. I'll select sar, and then click **OK** to return to the Site Information dialog box, where the new directory has been entered in the Site Root Directory field.

5. If you want any new documents you create with Dreamweaver to be placed in this directory automatically, select the **Default site root for new documents** option. This option only affects files for this site. New files for a different site are placed in the default directory for that site.

6. Click **OK** to finish the process for now. We'll take care of the FTP portion of the site later in this chapter. For the time being, we're just working on the local side of a site.

SEE ALSO

➤ *Configuring the remote side of a site, page 33*

The Site window now holds the name of our new site, Search and Rescue. The right side of the screen shows the contents of the site as it exists on the local computer (we just created it, so it's empty). The left side will show the contents of the site on the remote computer, which we'll connect to later in this chapter.

Macintosh users: A browsing bug

For some reason, perhaps a design bug, there is no button to create a new folder in the Browse dialog box. Macintosh users may have to switch to the Finder to create the folder they want before browsing for it. This isn't the way Macintosh is supposed to work, but it's what we have to deal with in Dreamweaver for now.

At this point, you can close the Site window to return to the main Dreamweaver window. Feel free to create and edit files to your heart's delight.

SEE ALSO

➤ *Learn how to create a basic page with text, page 67*

Adding Pages Without Editing

Let's return to the Site window once more to see a quick and dirty way of building a Web site without actually editing pages. Dreamweaver allows you to build the structure of your site by creating placeholder directories and files.

Placeholders are just empty files that mark where you're going to want real files later on. Give them the real names the files are going to have, and then open and edit the empty file when it's time to actually add content.

I'll create four files in the root directory. These four files are: index.html (the home page), Contact.html (for contact information), History.html (history of search and rescue), and Legalities.html (for copyright, disclaimers, and other stuff lawyers make us say).

Adding pages to a site

1. Right-click (Windows) or Control-click (Macintosh) with the mouse on the local pane (right side) of the Site window (see Figure 2.3).

2. Select **New File**. A new page, untitled.htm, is added to the current folder in the Site window. This file is created using Dreamweaver's default template. You can also create new pages in two other ways:
   * Press **Command+Option+Shift+N** (Macintosh) or **Ctrl+Alt+Shift+N** (Windows).
   * From the **File** menu, choose **New File.**

3. Click the file name, and type a new name for it. You'll need to make sure to preserve an .htm or .html to make sure Dreamweaver recognizes the file as a Web page.

One view at a time

The tasks in this section are easier for some folks if the Site window isn't cluttered. You can focus exclusively on the Local side by hiding the unused Remote side. Select **View** and choose **Show Local**, and the Remote side goes away for a time. If you want to see both again, from the **View** menu, choose **Show Both**.

FIGURE 2.3

The first choice in this list allows you to add files to a site without editing.

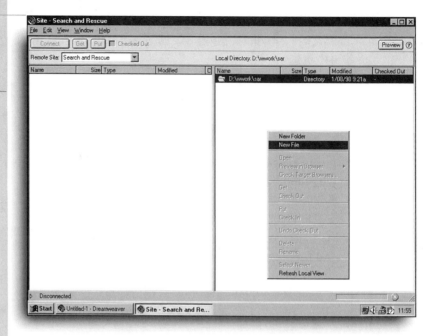

4. Repeat steps 1 through 3 for any additional pages you need to add.

SEE ALSO

➤ *Modifying the default page template, page 52*

➤ *For using a different page template, page 56*

We'll continue the process on the Search and Rescue site by also creating a basic directory structure. This includes a folder for information about past searches, and one about the dogs used by the Search and Rescue team. The steps are essentially the same as adding a new file.

Adding folders to a site

1. Right-click with the mouse on the local pane (right side) of the Site window.

2. Select **New Folder**. A new folder, untitled, is added to the current folder in the Site window. You can also create a new folder in two other ways:

   • Press **Option+Shift+N** (Macintosh) or **Ctrl+Shift+N** (Windows).

   • From the **File** menu, choose **New Folder.**

3. Click the folder name, and type a new name for it. Don't use spaces in the folder's name or some Web servers and browsers may have a hard time accessing it.

4. Repeat steps 1 through 3 for any additional folders you need to add.

By repeating the process of adding files and folders to a local site, you can completely build the framework for a Web site without actually editing any Web pages. Once the folders and pages are in place, you can use Dreamweaver to edit the pages and add content.

Getting Files to and from a Web Site

Now that you've created your masterpiece, it's time to share it with the world. This involves getting the page (or pages) from your computer on to your Web site. You'll need some important information before you go any further.

- The URL of the FTP server that leads to your Web site. You can get this from your Internet Service Provider or system administrator, depending upon your own particular circumstance. For a commercial site, it usually looks similar to the URL of a Web site, such as `ftp://www.bigbusiness.com/`. If it's a personal page, it may look something like `ftp://uncle.peon.com/`. Either way, it should begin with `ftp` to ensure acceptance.

- Your login name.

- Your password.

- Any additional directory information to get to your home base on the Web. For instance, sometimes you may find yourself in the htdocs directory when you log in to the site, when your actual home is in htdocs/big_eddie.

For our example, the URL of the FTP site is `ftp://ftp.darnells.com`, the login name is SAR, the password is good-dog!, and the directory is public_html. With these bits of information in hand, you can go back to the Site window once again by clicking the **Site** button on the Launcher toolbar.

File Transfer Protocol

FTP stands for File Transfer Protocol, and is the prescribed way to move any kind of file around on the Internet. It's much different than HTTP (Hypertext Transfer Protocol) which is used for Web pages, and the two are not interchangeable. That's really about all you need to know about either one, since anything else falls under the category of "incredibly irrelevant technical detail."

Since there's only one site we've defined so far, it shows up as the default in the site list. We'll need to edit this site to add the FTP information.

Adding remote site information

1. Select **Open Site**, and then choose **Edit Sites**.

2. For the FTP host, enter the name of the FTP site. In our example, it's `linux.darnells.com`. Since Dreamweaver automatically treats anything in this field as an FTP site, you can leave off the `ftp://` portion of the address.

3. Next, include the home directory, in our example `public_html`.

4. This is followed by the Login name `sar` and the Password `gooddog!`. You'll notice that no matter what you type for the password, Dreamweaver displays asterisks (*). This keeps honest people honest by hiding your password from prying eyes. Our finished site information is shown in Figure 2.4.

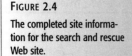
FIGURE 2.4

The completed site information for the search and rescue Web site.

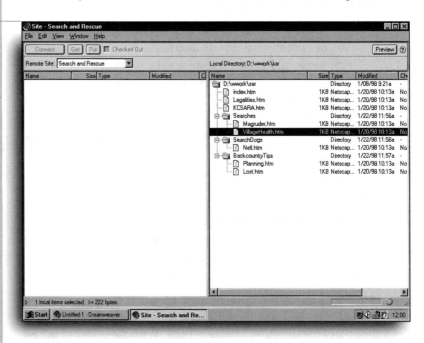

5. Leave the **Check Out Name** blank. We'll come back to it in the next section.

6. If you're on an internal network that reaches the outside world through a firewall or proxy, check the Firewall option at the bottom of the box. You'll also need to configure this information through the Perferences dailog. Check with your system administrator for help.

7. Click **OK** to save the new information and return to the Site window, which doesn't look much different than it did before.

To make magic happen, you'll need to make sure you have a connection to the Internet. Then, click the **Connect** button. Dreamweaver will connect you to the FTP site and display its contents on the left side of the screen (see Figure 2.5). In our example, you can see that we're in the public_html directory underneath /home/sar, and that there's already one file in this directory called index.html.

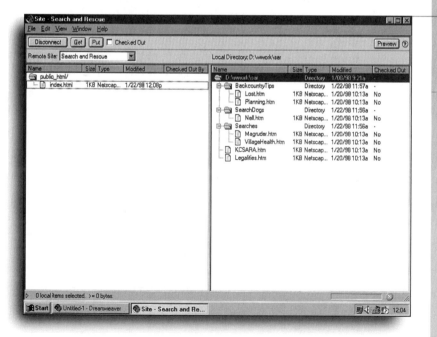

FIGURE 2.5

Once connected to the remote site, its directory structure and all the files are displayed.

Differences in what you see at log on

The actual details of what you'll see when you log on are apt to be quite different, depending on your network or Internet Service Provider. The system in this example automatically creates a public_html directory with a generic index.html file for every new account. This directory is reached by using the account name preceded by a tilde (~), such as `http://www.darnells.com/~sar/`.

For a commercial account on an ISP, chances are you would find yourself by default in your specific directory, which is usually a subdirectory of htdocs. The htdocs directory is the home directory accessed by using just the address of the ISP, such as `http://www.darnells.com`.

To make the left (remote) side of the screen look like the right (local) side, click the **Put** button at the top of the screen. There will be a great flurry of activity on the screen as the files for your site are transferred from the local drive to the remote site. When the dust clears, the remote site will look just like the local site.

Isn't life just amazing sometimes?

Many People and One Web Page: Check in and Check Out

One problem that is new to the electronic era of editing is the issue of several people editing the same file. Back in the olden days of publishing books and magazines, there was usually one copy of a document that was passed around and edited by various people in turn.

With the advent of electronic documents, now many people can get access to the same document at the same time. This creates a dilemma—what happens when Joe and Jill both want to edit the same document? Joe makes some changes while Jill makes other changes. How is the computer supposed to know what to do?

Dreamweaver has tackled this problem through the use of a system that resembles your local public library.

Check Out a File

All files on the local site are saved as read-only. This means you can look at them, but not make any changes to them. If you want to edit a file, you need to check it out from the remote site.

There are two ways to do this. The first is the "double-click check-out." With the files on the remote site in view (whether you're connected or not), double-click the file you want to edit. Dreamweaver will copy the file to your local hard drive, mark it as checked out to you, and open it into Dreamweaver for editing. No muss, no fuss.

However, if you're checking out files to work on over the weekend or evening, you can accomplish the same results and bypass the step of automatically loading the pages into the Dreamweaver editor.

Checking out files

1. After opening the Site window, select the site you're working on and click the **Connect** button.

2. Click the page or pages you want to check out. In this case, it's Legalities.html.

   If you want to select a range of contiguous pages, click the first one in the group, hold down the Shift key, and click the last one. Everything in between and including the two you clicked are selected.

   To select several files that may not be next to each other, click the first file, and then Ctrl+Click for the rest.

3. Select the **Checked Out** box at the top of the window (next to the **Put** button).

4. There will be some activity in the status bar as Dreamweaver makes sure you have the most recent version of Legalities.html, and then marks it as checked out on the Remote site (see Figure 2.6).

Although it's hard to see in Figure 2.6, there is a green check mark on the file icon for Legalities.html in both the Remote and Local site views. In addition, the Checked Out By column in the Remote window says "Jill (sar)." This indicates that Jill currently has the file checked out, and used the user name sar for the FTP site. Likewise, the Local window also shows a green check mark on the file icon, and the Checked Out column says "Yes."

If Joe decides he needs to work on the file, he'll log in to the site, and the file will be marked with a red check mark in the Remote window, and Jill's name will appear by it in the Checked Out By column. This essentially tells Joe, "Jill is working on this file, so don't make any changes until Jill is done with it," (see Figure 2.7).

FIGURE 2.6

Legalities.html now has a
green check mark to note that
it's currently checked out.

FIGURE 2.6

Legalities.html now has a
green check mark to note that
it's currently checked out.

FIGURE 2.7

Dreamweaver posts a warning
when attempting to check out
a file already in use by someone else.

Check In a Page

When Jill is done working on the Web page, she can check it back into the Remote site.

Checking in a file

1. Make sure the file is saved.
2. Select the Remote Site, and highlight the file to check in.
3. Deselect the **Checked Out** box at the top of the window.

When this happens, Dreamweaver will automatically post the revised file back to the Remote Site, mark it as available for editing by others, and turn Jill's local copy into a read-only file.

You can have as many people working on the site as you want, and this system helps keep some organization to the mess by controlling who has access to a file at any given time. As with most things in life, there is an important exception to this check out, check in process.

The Big Check Out Loophole

There is one more exception. Let's say that Jill is still working on the Legalities.html file. Joe has something he feels he needs to add to the page right away. So, he opens the site and sees that Jill still has the file checked out. Joe clicks the file, and selects the **Checked Out** box at the top of the screen. In a perfect world, Dreamweaver would tell Joe to go sit on a pin, and work it out with Jill if he really needs the file that badly. In the world we live in, Dreamweaver gives Joe the option to override Jill's check-out. If he chooses to do this, the file is marked with Joe's name. Jill is now sitting out in the cold with her changes while Joe works his voodoo on the file.

As you might guess, this loophole could potentially create some real problems with keeping the file current, not to mention causing all sorts of bad blood between Jill and Joe. Therefore, I strongly recommend that you respect the check out status of other people's Web pages.

Warning

File check-in and check-out is a Dreamweaver feature not recognized or supported by other editing or FTP software. If someone is using file management software other than Dreamweaver, such as FTP Explorer, CuteFTP, or HomeSite, they'll be able to overwrite and change files on the remote site irregardless of their check out status.

Someone using other software to get and put files from the remote site will only see an additional file with the same name and an LCK extension to correspond with each file that's currently checked out.

Respecting check out status

If you really need to check out a file, contact the person who has access and make arrangements for them to check in the file long enough for you to make your changes.

From Here...

- To begin a new Web page, see Chapter 4, "Starting with a Blank Page."

- To edit and add content to a Web page, see Chapter 5, "Adding Text to a Page."

- For more information on maintaining your site, see Chapter 26, "Making Your Site Work."

- For help in figuring out why your site may be having problems, see Chapter 27, "Troubleshooting Dreamweaver."

Using Text Editors
with Dreamweaver

Dreamweaver and Text Editors

I realize it's still fairly early in the book and I've said a great many positive things about Dreamweaver, but it's time for a confession—Dreamweaver is not the be-all and end-all HTML editor.

Dreamweaver was primarily designed as a tool to integrate dynamic, interactive features and effects within a Web page. The tools you'll learn about in Part IV, "Adding Interactivity and Scripts," will show you how to create various forms of HTML-based animation and interaction with the user. As a side benefit, that means Dreamweaver includes two other features—a WYSIWYG environment and an HTML editor.

But, most of the focus of Dreamweaver's design went into the creation of Dynamic HTML features. Yes, Dreamweaver can create a basic HTML page, and you could get by without using any other HTML editor. But, creating and fine-tuning basic HTML pages is not Dreamweaver's strong suit. For example, Dreamweaver doesn't support cutting and pasting HTML source code, link checking or validation, drag-and-drop hyperlink creation, or color-coded HTML syntax. There are other HTML editors on the market that do a much better job of building and editing HTML, giving page authors and designers much finer control over their pages.

Here's the positive side to my confession—Macromedia recognizes Dreamweavers strengths and weaknesses, and has made allowances for you to use your favorite HTML editor to augment Dreamweaver's capabilities. So, if you've been using HotDog, Windows Notepad, HomeSite, or any other program as your main tool to build Web pages, you can still use it almost seamlessly with Dreamweaver.

Just to show what good sports they are, Macromedia has included fully licensed versions (serial numbers and all) of HomeSite for Windows and BBEdit for Macintosh with its release of Dreamweaver. HomeSite and BBEdit are considered the best and most popular text-based HTML editors for their respective platforms. Macromedia is working hard to make sure you have a complete package of solutions for creating Web pages, and not have to rely just on their product.

Using Dreamweaver with HomeSite

You can read more about using Allaire HomeSite in Appendix B, "HomeSite Quick Reference." Suffice it to say that HomeSite is a "people's choice" kind of HTML editor. It was developed in the great American "guy and an idea" style, and then acquired and further improved and marketed by Allaire Corporation. If you went out to a store or purchased HomeSite from Allaire's Web site, it would cost you approximately $100 for a full-featured licensed copy. Macromedia includes the same full-featured, final-release, non-demo version as part of the purchase price for Dreamweaver.

Since Dreamweaver was designed to work hand-in-hand with other HTML editors, Dreamweaver's configuration for HomeSite is a straightforward process.

Configuring Dreamweaver for HomeSite

1. Select **Edit** and choose **Preferences (Ctrl+U)** to view the Preferences dialog box shown in Figure 3.1.

2. The first field to check is marked On Launch. It controls what happens with the page that is active in the Dreamweaver editing window when HomeSite is launched. There are three choices:

    • **Always**   This automatically saves the current page before launching HomeSite. When HomeSite begins, it is ensured of loading the most recent changes to your document.

    • **Never**   Dreamweaver will not save your document before launching HomeSite. HomeSite will have to work with whatever your page looked like the last time you saved it. Any changes you've made to the page since you saved it last will not appear in HomeSite.

Roundtrip HTML

One of the big features of Dreamweaver touted by Macromedia is Roundtrip HTML. This really isn't so much something that Dreamweaver does, as what it doesn't. One of the big drawbacks of visual HTML editors in the past is their habitual rewriting of HTML source code. If there are tags or attributes they don't like, they'll get rid of them automatically without asking you. They'll format the source code the way they want it, ignoring your preferences for making HTML readable.

Dreamweaver doesn't do this. It deals with what you give it. So, if you create a page in another HTML editor and then open it with Dreamweaver, your original source code remains untouched, right down to whether you use four spaces or five to indent lines.

This feature may not sound like much, but having fought with the likes of FrontPage, PageMill, and Backstage, I soon learned to really appreciate it. I'm sure you will, too.

- **Prompt to**   Select this option to have Dreamweaver ask you if you want to save the document before launching HomeSite. This option gives you the most flexibility. Of course, it's also the slowest and most tedious because you must answer the question every time you launch the external editor.

FIGURE 3.1

The Preferences dialog box includes two fields at the bottom that define how HomeSite is used.

❶ Where to find HomeSite

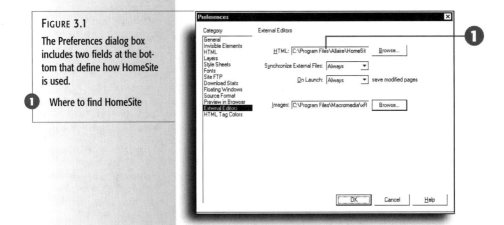

3. The next option sets the location of HomeSite. By default, this location is C:\Allaire\HomeSite\homesite3.exe. If you're using an earlier or later version of HomeSite, the filename will reflect the current version. For example, version 2 of HomeSite is homesite2.exe.

If you can't find HomeSite at this location, you can click the **Browse** button and locate \Allaire\HomeSite directory by hand. If you don't specify a valid path and filename, Dreamweaver will let you know and require you to correct the situation before moving on (see Figure 3.2).

4. When you've finished setting these two options, click **OK** to close the Preferences dialog box.

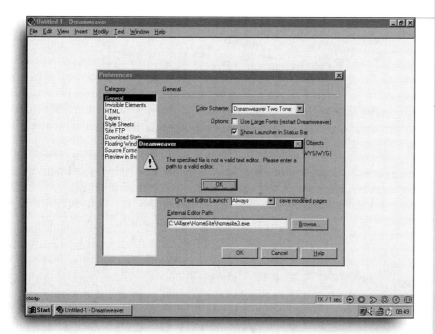

FIGURE 3.2

A path and/or filename was listed that doesn't match reality. Dreamweaver protests and sends me back to try again.

Once you've given Dreamweaver the correct information about the location of HomeSite, you can launch HomeSite from Dreamweaver:

- Press **Ctrl+E** (in Windows) or **Option+E** (for theMacintosh).

- Select **Edit** and then choose **Launch External Editor**.

- Select the **External Editor** button at the top of the HTML inspector window.

To learn more about the HTML Inspector window, see Chapter 5, "Adding Text to a Page."

The version of HomeSite that is shipped with Dreamweaver has one extra item added to its feature list—you can launch Dreamweaver directly from HomeSite. The HomeSite bundled with Dreamweaver automatically includes this feature, and you don't have to do anything special to enable it. To start Dreamweaver from HomeSite:

- Click the Dreamweaver icon at the bottom of the vertical toolbar.
- Press **Ctrl+D**.
- Select **View** and then choose **Macromedia Dreamweaver**.

If you begin your pages in HomeSite, this enables you to easily launch Dreamweaver to add multimedia and Dynamic HTML effects. However, I don't recommend using these methods to switch between Dreamweaver and HomeSite, as you'll end up with multiple sessions and editing windows for both, which will only lead to confusion and corrupted pages. When switching between applications, the recommended method is to use the Windows 95 task bar or **Alt+Tab**.

Using Dreamweaver with BBEdit

If you've spent much time writing HTML by hand on a Macintosh, you probably have used, tried, or heard about BBEdit. The "BB" stands for bare bones, and BBEdit was originally designed to be a powerful text editor free of the RAM-hogging features of a word-processing program. BBEdit is really a programmer's editor at heart, and when zillions of folks started programming HTML, BBEdit really took off. (See Appendix A, "BBEdit Quick Reference," for the skinny on what makes BBEdit such a great tool for HTML editing, and how you can get the most out it.)

It's quite possible that you will develop your site using only Dreamweaver's WYSIWYG tools. After all, Dreamweaver can add just about any kind of Web page object to your page for you, and (in most cases) allows you to customize the object however you like. However, there are still times when you may want to roll up yer sleeves and work on the HTML directly:

- When you want to add a special tag that Dreamweaver doesn't support, like Microsoft's `<scriptlet>` tag, or SSI tags used by some server packages

- When you want to add <meta> information (such as a list of search terms) to your pages

- When you're developing custom scripts for your pages

- When you're troubleshooting Dreamweaver-created pages that have strange appearance or behavior

- When you're a cranky old thing that can't stand the idea of letting a WYSIWYG program do all the work

Of course, you can use any old text editor—from the oldest version of TeachText to a gargantuan installation of Microsoft Word—to edit HTML files. However, BBEdit offers some nice features that make HTML writing and scripting most pleasant. BBEdit offers such features as:

- Very sophisticated search-and-replace features, including support for regular-expression matching and a pop-up list of all of the JavaScript functions in the document

- HTML syntax checking and color-coding

- Parenthesis-balancing and syntax-coloring for script development

- Automatic structuring of HTML code

And that's just scratching the surface. If you're a real Macintosh rocket scientist, you'll find that BBEdit is very AppleScript- and MacPerl-friendly.

Using Dreamweaver with BBEdit

1. Select **Edit** and choose **Preferences**, or press **Ctrl+U**. Dreamweaver presents the Preferences dialog box, shown in Figure 3.3.

2. Make sure that **General** is highlighted in the list on the left side of the Preferences dialog box.

3. Make sure that the Enable BBEdit Integration checkbox is checked. If it's not checked, click it with the mouse to check it.

FIGURE 3.3

Use the Preferences dialog box to control the way that Dreamweaver interacts with BBEdit.

1 Click here to enable BBEdit Integration

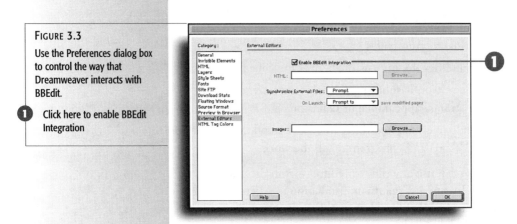

4. Take a look at the Synchronize External Files pop-up menu. This menu allows you to specify what, if anything, Dreamweaver does to save the files you send to BBEdit for processing. Your choices are:

- **Always** Specifies that Dreamweaver saves the file you're working on in Dreamweaver before the file is sent along to BBEdit. Dreamweaver will save the file quietly and automatically, without asking or making any announcements.

- **Never** Specifies that Dreamweaver sends BBEdit the latest saved version of the page you're currently working on in Dreamweaver. If you've made any changes to your page between the time you saved it with Dreamweaver and the time you send the page to BBEdit, BBEdit will not see the changes. (I'm not sure there's really a good reason to choose the **Never** option!)

- **Prompt** Specifies that Dreamweaver asks you whether you want to save the current page before sending it to Dreamweaver, or to send the latest saved version instead. This option is the most annoying (if you hate dialog boxes), but it also offers the most flexibility.

5. Click **OK** to dismiss the dialog box.

Once you have configured Dreamweaver to work with BBEdit, you can launch BBEdit by selecting **Edit** and then choosing (**Ctrl+E**).

Configuring Dreamweaver for Other Editors

Although HomeSite and BBEdit are two of the most popular HTML editors on the market for Windows and Macintosh, not everyone uses these products or is willing to install them just because they were shipped with Dreamweaver. Have no fear. Dreamweaver is just as happy working with other HTML editors.

Using Dreamweaver with any editor

1. Select **Edit** and choose **Preferences** (**Ctrl+U**) to view the Preferences dialog box (refer back to Figure 3.1).

2. The first field to check is the same as for the two favorite editors: On Launch. It controls what happens with the page that is active in the Dreamweaver editing window when the HTML editor is launched. Refer to step 2 of Configuring Dreamweaver with HomeSite to review the options for this field.

3. The next option sets the location of your editor. This will vary depending on which editor you plan on using. Some editors install their files in a subdirectory of C:\Program Files, some create their own directory structure in the root of C:, and some may be configured to reside on different drives. You'll need the specific information for your specific situation.

   If you plan on using Windows Notepad (still a favorite for tweaking HTML among many Windows Web authors), the path is C:\Windows\notepad.exe.

   If you don't specify a valid path and filename for your editor, Dreamweaver won't let you leave the Preferences dialog box until you provide one, or erase the field completely.

4. The last option on the screen allows you to select a default image editor. Enter the path to your favorite paint program, wheather it's xRes, Photoshop, or whatever. This option is used when the external editor option is selected while an image is chosen.

5. When you've finished setting these two options, click **OK** to close the Preferences dialog box.

With Dreamweaver and the HTML editor of your choice, you have a powerful combination for creating Web pages. Any deficiencies in Dreamweaver are compensated for by the features of your favorite HTML editor. It's as close as we're going to get to a perfect world in the realm of Web page creation.

From Here...

- To start a Web page with Dreamweaver, see Chapter 4, "Starting with a Blank Page."

- For information on creating a basic Web page with text, hyperlinks, lists, and headings, see Chapter 5, "Adding Text to a Page."

Starting with a Blank Page

Using page templates

Editing and creating templates

Setting page properties: title and colors

Using Page Templates to Get Started

Here's the story of your efforts so far: You've created a place for your site on your computer and you've enabled Dreamweaver to work with your favorite editor (HomeSite, BBEdit, Notepad, or whatever). Now, it's time to actually begin the basics of creating a Web page with Dreamweaver.

Before we actually begin adding text and images to the page, we'll need to set up some preliminaries first.

Dreamweaver includes a selection of templates to make starting a new Web page a little easier. The most important template is called Default.html. This is the template that's used every time you begin a new Web page.

What does the Default.html page look like? Not much. The source code is found in Listing 4.1, and Figure 4.1 shows the resulting page as it appears in Dreamweaver.

LISTING 4.1   **The Dreamweaver default template for creating Web pages.**

```
1   <HTML>
2   <HEAD>
3   <TITLE>Untitled Document</TITLE>
4   <meta http-equiv="Content-Type" content="text/html; charset=">
5   </HEAD>
6
7   <BODY BGCOLOR="#FFFFFF">
8
9   </BODY>
10  </HTML>
```

SEE ALSO

➤ *Explanation of HTML source code and the HTML inspector, page 87*

In a nutshell, the Default.html page contains the basic skeleton of a Web page—a head, body, title, and identifying wrapper. If you want your shell to be a little (or a lot) different, you can change the template, just like any other Web page.

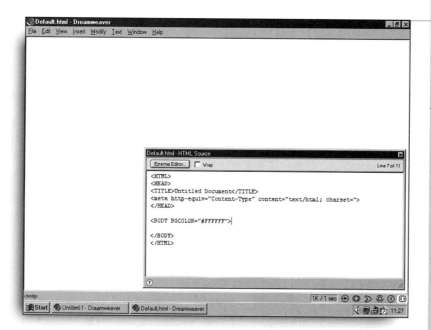

FIGURE 4.1

Default.htm as it appears in Dreamweaver. The HTML inspector shows the source code behind the page.

Open it into Dreamweaver, HomeSite, BBEdit, or whatever you're using for your favorite Web page editor, and make the appropriate changes. For example, I changed my Default.html to make it more useful for the Search and Rescue site. It includes a document type declaration, a basic style sheet, and a little more useful title. It also includes the default links that lead to the copyright and legal information. It's found in Listing 4.2 and displayed in Figure 4.2. Changing the page title, background color, and other page-wide attributes are covered later in this chapter in the "Changing the Page Title," "Colors for Every Purpose," and "Setting Properties for Your Page" sections, respectively. To learn about style sheets, see Chapter 6, "Formatting Text with Style Sheets."

LISTING 4.2 **A different Default.html for creating Web pages.**

```
1  <!DOCTYPE HTML PUBLIC "-//W3C//DTD HTML 4.0 Final//EN">
2  <HTML>
3  <HEAD>
4  <TITLE>Search and Rescue</TITLE>
```

continues...

Starting with a Blank Page

LISTING 4.2 **Continued**

```
 5  <meta http-equiv="Content-Type" content="text/html">
 6
 7  <STYLE type="text/css">
 8  BODY {background:white}
 9  </STYLE>
10  </HEAD>
11
12  <BODY BGCOLOR="#FFFFFF">
13
14  <SMALL>
15    <A href="copyright.html">Copyright 1998 Knockneed County SAR
      </A><BR>
16    <STRONG><A href="legalities.html">Important Information</A>
      </STRONG>
17  </SMALL>
18  </BODY>
19  </HTML>
```

FIGURE 4.2

My new default page, which was loaded when I started a new page.

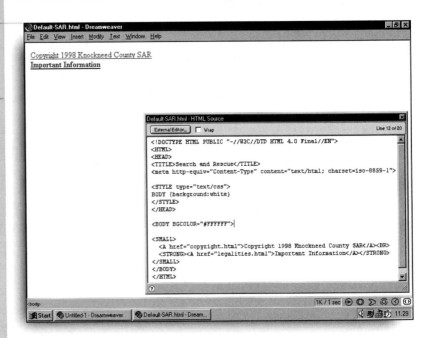

This generic Web page is loaded into Dreamweaver every time I start a new document. It has taken care of the housekeeping details I used to insert by hand into each page when it was created, usually with varying degrees of accuracy. Now that it's part of the default template, all I have to worry about is adding the content.

In a perfect world, every document would begin with a document type definition. At least, that's what the folks at the World Wide Web Consortium (W3C) say. The document type declaration tells browsers, validators, and other technical bits of software what flavor of HTML was used to create the page.

In the real world, `<!DOCTYPE>` is kind of hard to implement. There are enough differences in the HTML supported by the major players, including Netscape, Microsoft, W3C and the National Center for Supercomputing Applications (NCSA, who created Mosaic), that it's getting harder and harder to exclusively use one narrow definition of HTML to create a Web page.

The three current document types endorsed by the W3C are:

- `<!DOCTYPE HTML PUBLIC "-//W3C//DTD HTML 4.0//EN"`
  `"http://www.w3.org/TR/REC-html40/strict.dtd">` for the strict definition of HTML 4.0 (no deprecated elements, attributes, or frames).

- `<!DOCTYPE HTML PUBLIC "-//W3C//DTD HTML 4.0`
  `Transitional//EN" "http://www.w3.org/TR/REC html40/`
  `loose.dtd">` for the entire HTML 4.0 standard, including deprecated elements and attributes. This helps for designers developing pages for older browsers.

- `<!DOCTYPE HTML PUBLIC "-//W3C//DTD HTML 4.0 Frameset//`
  `EN" "http://www.w3.org/TR/REC-html40/frameset.dtd">` for HTML 4.0 plus the frame tags.

So why do I include a `<!DOCTYPE>`? Well, I like to try and create documents which meet the official standards of HTML that W3C has worked hard to develop. This is purely a personal preference issue. There are also times I throw the standards out the window and just use what I need to build the page I want.

You'll find adamant people on both sides of the issue, whether it's the official-standards-only camp, or the damn-the-torpedoes-make-it-look-pretty camp. The bottom line is that it's your page and a free world, and you can create your page any way you want to for your readers. I'm certainly not going to come knocking on your door to bug you either way. There are way more important things to worry about.

Using and Creating Other Templates

This is one of those good-news-and-bad-news departments. The good news is that Dreamweaver ships with three other templates to make building various types of pages easier. For the bad news, there's not an easy way of using them. For Windows users, the templates are found in the same location as the Default.html template—/Program Files/Macromedia/Dreamweaver/Configuration/Templates. For Macintosh users, this is Dreamweaver:Configuration:Templates.

When you start a new document (File, New), there is no way to select one of these other three templates. The standard Default.html is always selected by default.

The three templates in addition to Default.html are

- *basic_tables.html.* A two-column layout with a lime-green background image running down the left side (see Figure 4.3). It's suggested for navigation in the left column, and content in the right.

- *company_profile.html.* Another two-column layout designed with a company home page in mind (see Figure 4.4).

- *story_column.html.* This template creates a single column of text down the middle of the page which is a consistent 10–15 words wide, depending on the user's screen resolution and how big your words are (see Figure 4.5). It uses techniques from the early days of the Web that are still valid today to create the space, so it's compatible with everyone's browser, whether it's the venerable old Lynx or the latest copy of Netscape Navigator 4.0.

In order to use one of these alternate templates as your standard default, you need to rename the pages.

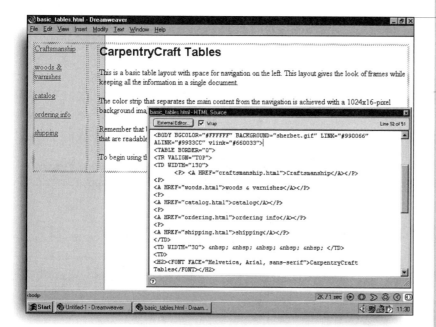

FIGURE 4.3

The basic_tables.html template creates a page with two columns.

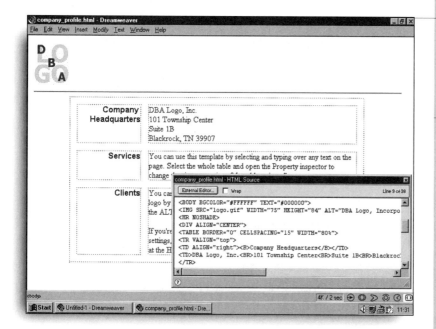

FIGURE 4.4

company_profile.html is another two column layout, yet this one is designed for a more businesslike look and feel.

FIGURE 4.5

`story_column.html` cre-ates a basic layout with ample whitespace on each side. This is very effective for text-heavy pages like a story or article.

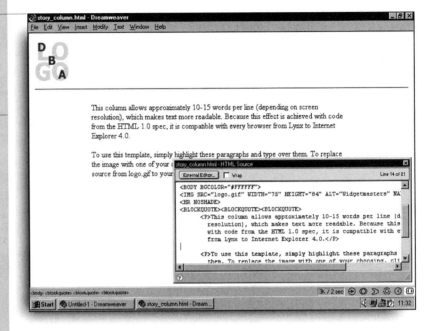

Easier access to templates

The engineers at Macromedia say they plan on creating easier ways to use templates in a future revision of Dreamweaver. Until such time, here's a way to work around the problem.

Create a new site called Templates in the Site window. The path should point to where your template files are located. By default, this is C:/Program Files/Macromedia/ Dreamweaver/Configuration/ Templates (Windows) or Dreamweaver:Configuration: Templates (Macintosh). Now, you can use the Site window to create, edit, and rename template files with-out crawling through your folder structure every time.

Renaming templates for automatic use

1. Navigate to the folder that holds the Dreamweaver tem-plates.

2. Rename the file Default.html to something else imaginative, like Generic.html.

3. Rename the template file you want to use to Default.html.

Once these steps are completed, return to Dreamweaver and select **File**, **New**. The file you renamed Default.html is used as the basis of your new page. If you're not careful, the other option is a little more risky.

Opening templates directly

1. Make sure you remember where you want to save the new file when it's completed.

2. From Dreamweaver, select **File**, and then choose **Open**. Navigate down to the folder that holds all of the template files.

3. Double-click the template you want to use to open it into Dreamweaver.

4. Before you do anything else, select **File**, and then **Save As**, and navigate back to the folder to hold the finished file.

5. Type a new name for the page and click the **Save** button.

Either of these two methods will let you use the Dreamweaver templates, albeit neither method is the easiest way to do things. In the meantime, we'll have to wait for Macromedia to finish ironing out the kinks.

Creating a template is as simple as creating other pages.

Creating a new template

1. Begin with the basic page, including title, tables, standard text, and other information.

2. Select **File**, choose **Save As**, and navigate back down to /Program Files/Macromedia/Dreamweaver/ Configuration/Templates.

3. Type a name for the template that describes its use.

4. Finish by clicking **Save**.

Now that your template is tucked away in a safe place, you can use it as a shortcut to creating new Web pages with Dreamweaver.

Setting Properties for Your Page

Now that you have the basic skeleton of your page in place, it's time to work with a few other properties that affect how your page is seen by the rest of the world. These properties include the page title, background image, colors, and document encoding.

All of these page-wide settings are accessed through the Page Properties dialog box (see Figure 4.6). Select **Modify**, and then choose **Page Properties** to view the box.

Be sure to rename first

If you don't follow the renaming step right away, chances are you'll forget you're working directly on the template and overwrite it with your new page as your fingers select **Ctrl+S** to save the file without even thinking. Save it in a different place under a different name now, or don't come crying to me when you've ruined the original template.

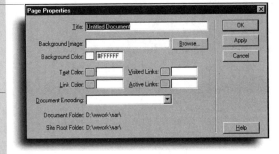

Changing the Page Title

The first order of business is the page title. This is, by default, Untitled Document, which has to be one of the most unimaginative titles since Brand X. There's a fine art to picking a title to a page, and like the use or non-use of <!DOCTYPE>, it varies from person to person.

A convention I like to use is a short description (one or two words, or initials) of the site, followed by the purpose of the page. For example, a page for the Search and Rescue site with their copyright information could be SAR—Copyright. Other people like to just use the purpose of the page, such as Copyright Information. Other folks leave it blank.

The page we're preparing in this chapter will be added to in the next chapter—a page for search and rescue legal disclaimers—so I'll use my favorite convention and type SAR—Legal Stuff in the Title field.

Adding Background Images

One of the great mysteries of the universe is why computers in general, and browsers in particular, insist on displaying black text on a gray background when we're used to black letters on white pages. Luckily, Dreamweaver has an easy way of changing this situation. In this section, we're going to learn how to change the color of the background of the page to something you like better.

There are three options for tweaking the background of your page. The first and easiest is to do nothing—the user's browser will use its own default (usually gray or white) for the background behind your page.

The second option is to use a background image. This is a graphic that is tiled across the background, and is usually some light-colored abstract design or pattern. Other popular choices are textures (such as marble or basket weave) or logos.

Choosing a background image

1. Click on the **Browse** (Windows) or **Choose** (Macintosh) button next to the Background Image field.

2. Dreamweaver opens a file dialog box beginning at the local root of your current site.

3. Navigate to the image you want to use for a background and double-click it. The file will probably have a .gif, .jpeg, or .jpg extension.

4. When you click **OK** to leave the Page Properties dialog box, the background image is automatically tiled into the background of your page.

There is one more method to create a custom background for your Web page, and you can use it to change the color of your text too. Read on in the next section for details.

Colors for Every Purpose

The third and most-used option is to change the background color. This is like choosing the color of paper you use in your printer. Although choices like hot pink may seem like a good idea at the time, they typically wear thin and become abrasive to the eyes very quickly. The best choice is good old white, unless you have some compelling reason to use something different.

For stark effect, some designers make the background of their first page black, and put white text on it. Others opt for the good old days of WordPerfect for DOS and its yellow text on a blue background. Whatever you choose, remember that not everyone has a Super Mega VGA display with eleven thousand megabytes of RAM and eleven million colors. Keep it to reliable colors—black, white, blue, yellow, red, green, and so on—and you'll be in good shape for the vast majority of your readers.

Changing the background color

1. To change the background color, click and hold on the swatch of color next to the Background Color field. A palette of choices appears (see Figure 4.7).

FIGURE 4.7

Select from a broad selection of colors by clicking the color swatch.

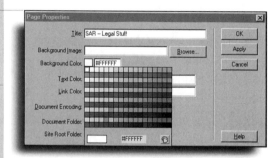

2. While holding down the mouse button, move the mouse pointer to the background color you desire. As you move the mouse around over the palette, you'll notice the Background Color field with letters and numbers changing. This is the value that is actually passed to the browser to let it know what color to use.

3. Release the mouse button when the pointer is over the color of your choice.

What does the # mean?

The pound sign (#) preceding the value in the Background Color field indicates that this is a number and not a word or some other type of value.

4. If you don't find anything that strikes your fancy from Dreamweaver's default choices, you can click the little artist's mixing palette near the bottom-right corner of the swatches. This displays the Color dialog box (see Figure 4.8).

5. You can mix colors to your heart's content here, by changing the way colors are mixed. You can click in the big color wheel to select a color directly, or you can set the values of its various components directly.

6. When you're done being artistic, click **OK** until you return to your document with the background of your choosing.

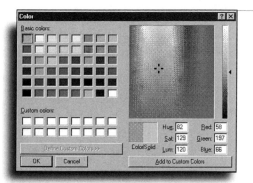

FIGURE 4.8

If a premixed color doesn't catch your eye, you can also mix your own from the Color dialog box.

Of course, now that we've taken you through this process of picking colors by their actual color, there is one more way to do it. There are fifteen names of colors recognized by Dreamweaver. If you include one of these names, Dreamweaver will automatically know what you mean and include the right digits. The choices are:

- black
- silver
- gray
- white
- maroon
- red
- purple
- fuchsia
- green
- lime
- olive
- navy
- blue
- teal
- aqua

To use one of the color names, select the Background Color field, and overwrite the hexadecimal digits (pound sign and all) with the name of the color you want to use.

Beware the shades of mauve

Not all browsers and platforms support all colors. Some browser/platform/monitor combinations only support a limited set of colors, and some have no color at all. So, as you go throwing colors into the bucket, keep in mind that not everyone will see the exact shade you see, and some may not see the color at all.

For the safest bet, stick to one of the sixteen standard colors listed later in this section.

Colors, computers, and six little digits

What does a combination of six letters and numbers have to do with color? Here's one of the pieces of bad news about defining color for a Web page—it was designed by guys who work with computers for a living, and not by people who work with color.

The fancy name for the color value is a "hexadecimal triplet." Before we can talk about the triplet, we need to talk about the hexadecimal. A hexadecimal number can be from 0 through F, like this: 0, 1, 2, 3, 4, 5, 6, 7, 8, 9, A, B, C, D, E, F. This allows people who work deep in the bowels of a computer to represent a number from 0 to 15 with one letter. The next hexadecimal number after F is 10 hexadecimal, which is the same as 16 decimal. Putting two hexadecimal digits together allows you to represent a number from 00 (0 in our decimal system) to FF (255 in our decimal system).

Now, to the triplet part. The six digit hexadecimal number represents the mix of red, green, and blue. It does this by dividing itself into three two-digit hexadecimal numbers. So, the default value of FFFFFF becomes FF (255 out of 255 parts of red), FF (255 out of 255 parts of green), and FF (255 out of 255 parts of blue). This combination of complete saturation of all three colors results in white on the screen. A value of 000000 would mean no red, no green, and no blue—in other words, black.

In case you haven't figured it out by looking at the Page Properties dialog box, you can also set the colors for four different types of text—regular, links, active links, and visited links.

The text color is just that, the standard color of text on the screen. Odds are really, really good that the default is black on the user's browser. Unless you have a reason to change it, like going to the good old yellow-on-blue DOS WordPerfect scheme, you can just leave it alone.

The next three colors control how hyperlinks appear. The basic link color is used for any link that hasn't been visited recently by the user's browser. The common default is blue. An active link is a hyperlink the user has just clicked, but not yet released the mouse button. It's color is very temporary (usually red), since it lasts only a mouse-click. The last option is visited link, which is a link that the user has clicked recently. Common defaults are green or purple, although this choice varies much more widely among browsers than the other text colors.

You set the color of the four text items in the same way as you change the background color. You can type one of the sixteen standard color names directly into the color field, or you can perform the following steps.

Setting default text colors

1. Click and hold on the swatch next to the type of text you're changing.

2. Select the color from the default choices or click the artist palette for free-form choices.

3. Release the mouse button, and then click **OK** to finalize the choice.

The text and hyperlink colors are the last of the properties you can set for your Web page. Like changing other default settings, make sure any choices you make here have a good reason. Having pink text on a red background may seem like a good idea at the time, but your readers will probably not thank you for your choice.

From Here...

- To further customize page appearance, see Chapter 6, "Formatting Text with Style Sheets."
- To create a basic page with text, see Chapter 5, "Adding Text to a Page."
- To add images and graphics to the foreground of a page, see Chapter 7, "Adding and Changing Images."

What is this hyperlink thing?

We'll talk more about hyperlinks (links for short) later, but here's a quick definition. A hyperlink is a piece of text you click to jump to another page on the Web.

Adding Text to a Page

Add text and format it

Create headings and lists

Turn text into hyperlinks

Work directly with your source code

Adding Text

In the previous chapter, we spent all our time working on the behind-the-scenes portion of your Web page. Now it's time to take the next big leap and work on the stuff that your readers see—the text.

Yes, it's true. Lots of sites are graphics and multimedia intensive, and many are even constructed exclusively of specialized content. But at the heart of the Web, most people still work with the written word. And that's where we'll start our page.

With all the preamble out of the way, let's get down to brass tacks. You have your page, and you have something to say. It's as easy as using your favorite word processor.

First, you'll need to open the file you're going to work on. To make your life easier, you'll want to begin at the Site window. Open the site you want to work on ("Search and Rescue" in our example), and then double-click the file you want to edit ("Legalities.html" in our example). Chapter 2, "Working with Files," contains more information about opening and managing files from within the Site window.

Adding text

1. Make sure you're in the Dreamweaver editing window. The name of the file is visible in the top-left corner.
2. Put your fingers on the keyboard.
3. Start typing. When you're ready to start a new paragraph, press Enter.
4. When you've said enough, stop typing.

OK, so it looks pretty simple. But that's only because it is. As an alternative, you can also cut and paste out of other open documents on your computer. The page I've been working on is shown in Figure 5.1. It doesn't look like much, but we'll work on it some more as we work through this chapter.

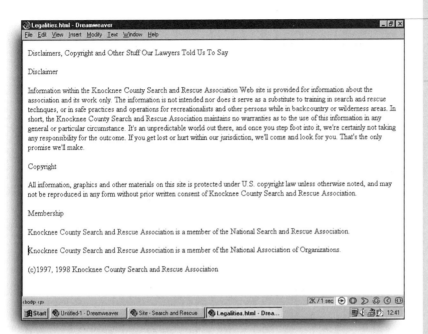

FIGURE 5.1

The legal disclaimer page as I've typed it so far.

Formatting Text

Now that there's some text on the screen, let's see if we can't make it look a little more palatable and appealing. You'll need the Properties Palette (see Figure 5.2) for this and the following sections. In case it's not already a part of your Dreamweaver environment, select **Window** and then choose **Properties**.

FIGURE 5.2

The Properties Palette is the main point of contact for formatting text.

As you can see on our page so far, there's a fair amount of text, including stuff that reads like headings and other organizational snippets. But, right now there's no way to infer any meaning from the appearance of the text. Everything is the same size.

Let's change all that. We'll begin with the main heading on the page, "Disclaimers, Copyright and Other Stuff Our Lawyers Told Us To Say."

Turning text into headings

1. Place the mouse pointer at the beginning of the text. Click and drag the mouse to the end of the line to highlight the text, and then release the mouse button.

2. To turn the text into an **H1** heading (the biggest)

   - Select **Heading 1** from the Format drop-down list in the Properties palette (see Figure 5.3).

   - Press **Ctrl+1** (or Ctrl+ the number of another heading size through 6).

   - From the **Text** menu, select **Format** and then choose **Heading 1**.

FIGURE 5.3

The drop-down list for formatting includes the basic styles of Web page text.

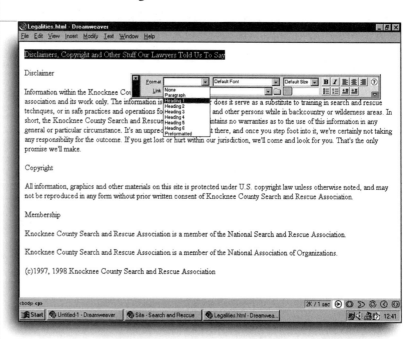

3. The highlighted text is changed immediately to reflect its new style (see Figure 5.4).

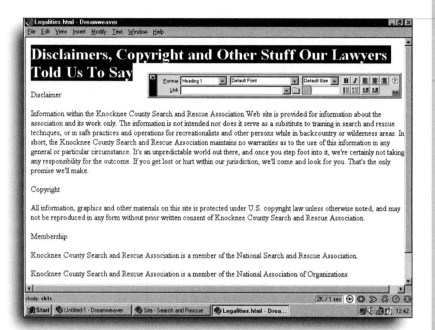

FIGURE 5.4

Our line of plain text is
changed to big heading text.

Congratulations, you've now mastered the fine art of basic text
formatting with Dreamweaver. We'll repeat this process by
selecting the lines of text for the subheadings and format them as
H2. Paragraphs were automatically added when the Enter key
was pressed at the end of a line while typing the base document.
The result of the typing and formatting is seen in Figure 5.5.

But let's face it, there's more to building a Web page than throwing around a little text and headings. Let's move on to some
other things we can do with text.

There are a few items on this page that I'd like to emphasize a
little more, such as the name of the organization and the exhor-
tation that readers can use the information within the site at
their own risk.

We'll begin by making the name of the organization bold.

FIGURE 5.5

The page with its basic formatting in place, including headings, subheadings, and
paragaphs.

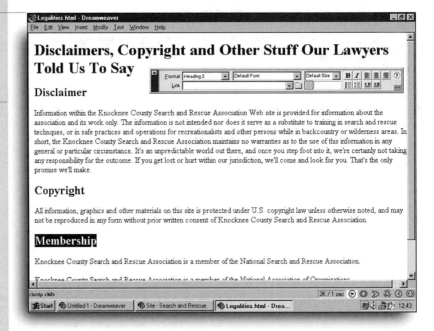

Making text bold

1. Make sure the Properties Palette is currently visible. You do this by selecting **Window** and then choosing **Properties**.

2. Click and drag over the desired text. In this example, I high-lighted the first occurrence of "Knocknee Search and Rescue."

3. Click the bold button in the Properties Palette. This is a bold-faced **B**. The text is immediately formatted to appear bold.

There's another way to make text bold using a special format called "Strong Emphasis." Formatting text this way is a little different than the first way, because it doesn't use the Properties Palette.

Making text bold with strong emphasis

1. Click and drag over the desired text. In this example, I high-lighted the second occurrence of "Knocknee Search and Rescue."

2. Select **Text** from the menu bar, choose **Style**, and then choose **Strong Emphasis** (see Figure 5.6). You'll notice that there are several other styles available. You can select any of the available styles to format your text.

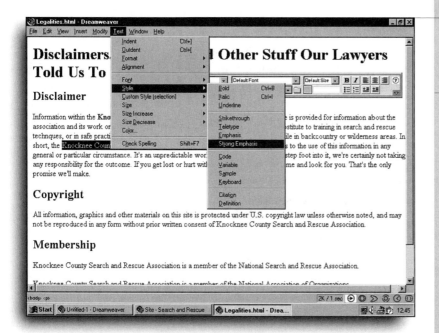

FIGURE 5.6

The menu under **Text, Style** includes a variety of ways to format your text.

So what's the real difference between these two methods? Other than the first is easier, not much. The second set of steps includes a wider variety of styles than is available through the Properties Palette, so you may need to go the menu route if you need something other than headings or bold text.

The outcome, however, may be different depending on what combination of browser and computer the user has. Using the strong emphasis tag implies a special meaning—this bit of text is really important, and should stand out. It doesn't suggest a visual representation, although tradition and usage has dictated bold-face. On the other hand is the bold tag. This doesn't imply any meaning—it only gives direction for the physical appearance.

The difference between <STRONG> and <B>

The former–<STRONG>–hearkens to the roots and purpose of HTML. HTML was originally designed for, and appears to be leading back to, structure and meaning-based markup. This type of markup leaves it up to the browser to determine how to represent the text to the user. As browsers for people with disabilities become more common, it becomes more important. A browser for a blind person may need to display strong emphasis formatting differently than for someone who is deaf.

You'll see other HTML tags similar to <STRONG>, including <CITE> for citation, <CODE> for a listing of programming code, or <DFN> for definition.

The same steps apply for applying italic text. If you're using the first method, click the italicized **I** from the Properties Palette. If you opt for the second method, select **Emphasis** from the **Text, Style** submenu.

Changing Text Alignment

Another way to change the appearance of text on your page is to adjust whether it's flush against the left or right side of the browser, or centered in the window. For example, some people like to center all their headings. This is accomplished by using buttons in the Properties Palette.

SEE ALSO

➤ *Learn how to justify text and headings using style sheets, page 94*

➤ *Learn how to position text with style sheets and layers, page 255*

Centering text in your Web page

1. Click and drag to the text to change. In my example, I'll select the first heading on the page.

2. Next to the **B** and **I** buttons in the Properties Palette are three buttons that control alignment. Select the middle button for centering.

3. The text is now centered at the top of the page (see Figure 5.7). Like a heading, this type of formatting is also applied to the entire paragraph. It would be a bit difficult just to center one part of a line and leave the rest of it untouched.

Changing Text Fonts and Colors

The last bit of formatting we'll cover in this section allows you to change the default font and color used to display sections, words, or individual letters. Again, this is accomplished from the Properties Palette accessed by selecting **Window** and then choosing **Properties**. We'll begin by changing the text size.

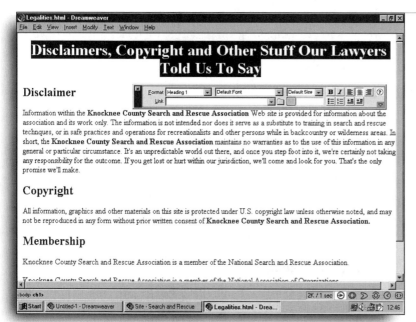

FIGURE 5.7

The first heading is now centered at the top of the page.

Text size on a Web page is defined by using a number from 1 to 6. This number doesn't correspond directly to an actual size. Rather, it simply represents an incremental set of sizes that are actually determined by the browser. So, instead of thinking of "size 1," think "really small." Likewise, at the other end of the scale think of size 6 as "really big." The default font size is 3, which you can think of as "medium."

Changing text size

1. Click and drag the mouse to select the text to change.

2. On the Properties Palette, click the drop-down list for size. If you haven't changed this field previously, it will say Default Size.

3. Select a number from the list to represent how big the text should be.

4. The change is immediately reflected in the text.

Now that we've learned how to justify text and change its size relative to everything else on the page, we'll tackle the last two big formatting options—color and typeface. The first is changing text color.

Changing text color

1. Click and drag to select the desired text.

2. Click the swatch of color to display a default palette of colors.

3. Select the color from the palette, or click the artist's palette at the bottom-right corner to mix your own color.

SEE ALSO

➤ *Learn more about options for selecting color, page 61*

Changing Typefaces

The last item, as promised, is changing the typeface. I saved this item for last because it is usually the least effective way to change text on your page. Why? Because your choices are limited to the typefaces available on your computer. And, if you choose a seldom used face such as Ad Lib or Berthold Oblique, there's a very good chance your readers will just see plain old Times (or whatever their browsers use as a default). So, change the typeface if you want, but not everyone can see the joy you've created.

SEE ALSO

➤ *Using style sheets to define font selection, page 94*

Changing the typeface

1. Click and drag with the mouse to select the text to change.

2. Click the drop-down list for fonts. If you haven't changed this, the name will still appear as `Default Font`.

3. Select a list of typefaces.

Why is there a list? It gives the reader's browser a few more chances to find a match with a name you've listed. For example, the first choice on the font list is `Arial, Helvetica, sans-serif`. This tells the browser, "Use the typeface called Arial. If you don't have it, try Helvetica. If all else fails, use any sans-serif typeface you have lying around." If all three choices fail, the browser will use whatever default it uses for all other text.

This helps when dealing with differences in typeface names across platforms. Why do names change? Because they're covered under copyright, although the details of the alphabet aren't. So, Windows calls its version of Helvetica (a simple block alphabet) by the name Arial. Including both names and the general category of type they belong to increases the odds that the user's browser will find a match.

You can create your own list of preferred typefaces by selecting the last item in the font list, **Add Font List**. This displays the Font List dialog box (see Figure 5.8). To edit an existing list, select it from the Font list and then add or remove fonts from the Chosen Fonts list. To add a new list select the last choice in the Font List and then add fonts from the Available Fonts list in the order you want to use them.

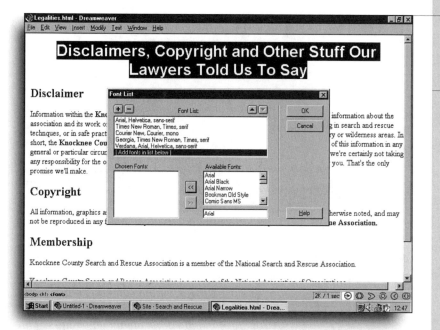

Creating Lists

We'll begin the following sections by creating a new page. Select **File**, and then choose **New** to get a blank Web page ready to start. This is another page for our Search and Rescue site. This one is an explanation and list of items needed for a 24-hour pack.

I've started off by giving the page a title, and adding a heading and text (see Figure 5.9).

FIGURE 5.9

The basic page, before the addition of a list.

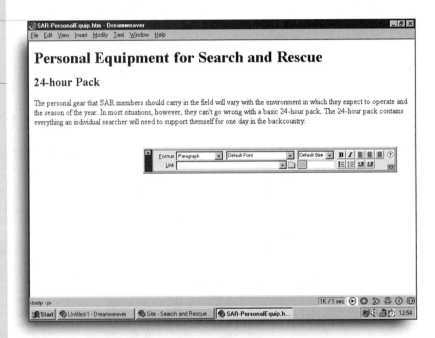

At this point, it's time to add the list of items that should be in the pack. This will be an unordered list—no item in the list is more important than any other, and the items don't have to appear in any particular order.

Creating an unordered list

1. Make sure the Properties Palette is visible by selecting **Window**, and then choosing **Properties**.

2. Click the Unordered List button (underneath the **B** button). A list is started with a bullet next to it.

3. Type the items in your list, pressing **Enter** after each item.

4. After entering the last item, press **Enter** one more time (see Figure 5.10).

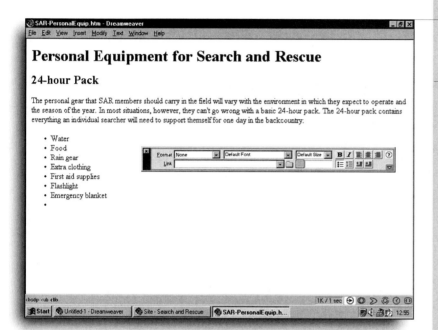

5. Click the Unordered List button again to end the list.

An alternative method is to type each of the items in the list while you're typing the rest of the text, again with each item on its own line. Then, click and drag to select the text, and click the Unordered List button.

The process to create an ordered list is the same, only you use the Ordered List button instead (go figure). An ordered list is automatically numbered so you can indicate a series of steps, an order of preference among items, or similar structuring.

The last kind of list you can create is called a definition list. A definition list is composed of two pieces for each list item—a term and a definition separated by a hard return. In HTML it looks like this:

```
<P>Moo</P>
<P>What a cow says</P>
```

Let's continue with our current list, and add descriptions to each of the items (see Figure 5.11). Each of the descriptions just looks like another item on the list, and the effect is a little confusing.

FIGURE 5.11

I've added descriptions under each of the items on the list.

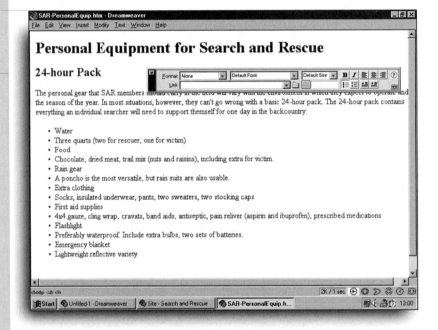

Click and drag to select all the text that will be part of the definition list. Select **Text**, choose **Format**, and then select **Definition List**. Beginning with the first item, the list is formatted into pairs of items, with the first being a term and the second a definition. The definitions are indented below the terms so the relationship between the two is apparent (see Figure 5.12).

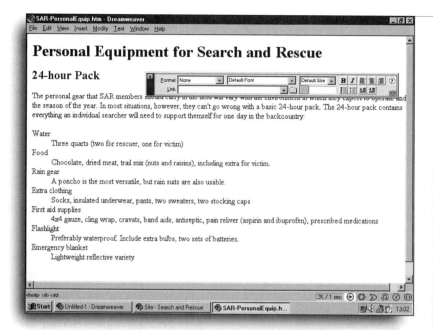

FIGURE 5.12

Our unordered list is now a definition list, with pairs of terms and definitions.

Creating Hyperlinks and Anchors

For the last bit of trickery with our text, we're going to add some hyperlinks and anchors. But first, a word about the two.

A hyperlink, in a nutshell, is what makes the Web so easy to navigate. It is a piece of text that, when clicked by the reader, tells the browser to load a new page. An anchor is similar to a hyperlink, but it marks a specific spot within a page, like a bookmark. I'll begin with hyperlinks, since they're more commonly used than anchors.

We're going to use Legalities.html again, so open it into Dreamweaver. To do this select **File** and choose **Open**. Then select Legalities.html from the list of available pages.

Formatting text as a hyperlink

1. Make sure the Properties Palette is visible by selecting **Window** and then choosing **Properties**.

2. Click and drag over the desired text. In this example, I high-lighted the first occurrence of "National Search and Rescue Association."

3. In the Link field of the Properties Palette, type the address of the hyperlink (see Figure 5.13). This can be in three forms—absolute, server-relative, or document-relative.

   You can define a document-relative URL with Dreamweaver by selecting the folder icon next to the Link field, and navigating to the file on your computer.

FIGURE 5.13

By typing an Internet address (URL) in the Link field, the selected text becomes a hyper-link.

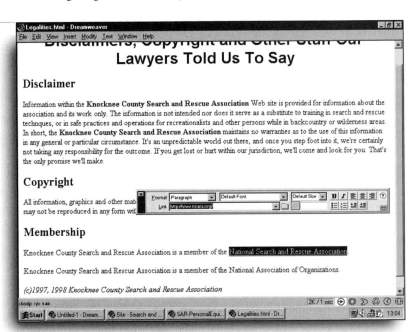

4. The text is formatted in blue with an underline to indicate that it's a hyperlink.

A URL for Hyperlinks

A few terms are in order to help you understand hyperlinks. First is an Uniform Resource Locator, called a URL (pro-nounced by saying each letter, not as "Earl"). A URL is to the

Internet what a street address and zip code are to the Post Office
—it defines a specific place.

There are three ways to write a URL. The first is as an absolute
URL. This includes a protocol (Web pages use HTTP), a server
name, a path, and possibly a file name. The pages we've been
working on are located on the server called `www.darnells.com` in
the sar directory. Let's add some information, and say we're
going to link to a file called nell.html in the SearchDog subdirectory of the sar site. The absolute URL that describes this is
`http://www.darnells.com/sar/SearchDog/nell.html`. Absolute
URLs are most useful when you're entering a hyperlink that
leads away from the server where your pages are located. Using
an absolute URL for pages within the same site or directory will
add a lot of typing for yourself.

A server-relative URL doesn't include the protocol and server
name. It begins with a forward slash, indicating the root directory of the server where the current page is located, followed by
the rest of the path information for the address. The server-
relative URL that corresponds to our example is `/sar/SearchDog/`
`nell.html`.

The last type of URL is called document-relative. This is usually
the shortest type of URL. If we're looking at a document that's
currently located in the sar directory, the document-relative
URL to our example is `SearchDog/nell.html`.

You can also use two dots to indicate the directory located above
the current document. If we're at the page `http://`
`www.darnells.com/sar/SearchDog/nell.html`, the document-
relative URL for `http://www.darnells.com/sar/Legalities.html`
would be `../Legalities.html`.

Verifying Hyperlinks

Once you've created a hyperlink, one of the most important
issues is making sure the link stays valid. Nothing is more frustrating for users than to click on a hyperlink and be greeted with
the dreaded, "Error 404: Document Not Found," message on

their browser. Dreamweaver won't fix the links for you, but it will identify which ones are broken. To verify all the links in the current document in the Dreamweaver window:

- For the current document in , press **Ctrl+F7** (Windows) or **Option+F7** (Macintosh).
- Select **File, Check Links, This Document**.

You can also run the Link Checker on individual files or groups of files from the Site window. Select which documents or folders you want to check, then:

- For the current document in, press **Ctrl+F7** (Windows) or **Option+F7** (Macintosh).
- Select **File, Check Links, Selected Files/Folders**.

As a last option, you can check all of the hyperlinks within a site. This is available with the same methods from both the Dreamweaver editing window and the Site window:

- Press **Ctrl+F8** (Windows) or **Option+F8** (Macintosh).
- Select **File, Check Links, Entire Site**.

Using any of the above methods invokes the Link Checker dialog (see Figure 5.14) to display the results.

FIGURE 5.14
The Link Checker displays the results of its search for broken hyperlinks.

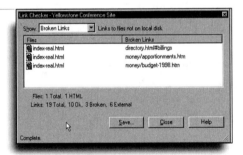

Select the type of errors you want to see from the Show list at the top of the page. Your choices are

- Broken Links (default): Any link to a file that doesn't exist within the current site.
- External Links: Links to files outside of the current site that weren't checked. This includes files in other sites, or on the Web at large.

- Orphaned Files: Files on your site that aren't referenced in a hyperlink in any other file. Someone would have to type the exact URL to access these documents. This option is only used when you check an entire site.

Double-clicking on an entry in the Link Checker will highlight the offending line in your page so you can change the reference in the Properties Palette.

Adding a Named Anchor

Now, we're going to place an anchor on the page. An anchor is to a hyperlink what a gun is to a target—the hyperlink is the starting point, the anchor is the destination.

Creating an anchor uses a new window, called Objects (see Figure 5.15). If this window isn't currently visible, select **Window** and then choose **Objects**. The default view for the Objects window includes icons for common objects, such as images, tables, horizontal rules, and similar items. We need the selection of hidden objects. This is chosen by clicking the black arrow at the top of the window, and then selecting **Invisibles** from the drop-down list. The Objects window should now look like Figure 5.16.

Adding an anchor

1. Place the cursor at the place where you want to place the bookmark. In this example, I placed it before the words, "Copyright notice."

2. Click the Anchor icon in the Objects window. A window appears to name the anchor (see Figure 5.17).

3. Type a unique name for the anchor in the Anchor Name field. It should not duplicate the name of any other anchor on the page. Just to keep life simple, I'll call this one Copyright.

4. Click **OK**. An anchor icon should appear at the spot where the cursor was positioned.

Now you have a point in your page that you can jump to directly, without scrolling through the entire page—an especially handy feature for long documents.

Where's the anchor icon?

Can't see the anchor icon? You may have the view of invisible objects blocked. Select **View**, and then choose **Invisible Elements**, or press **Ctrl+Shift+I**.

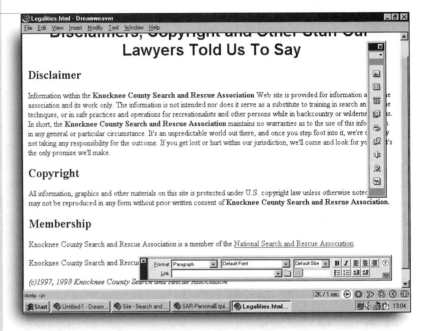

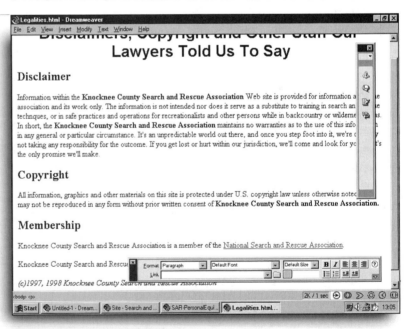

FIGURE 5.17

Enter a unique name for the anchor in this window.

To use this nifty feature, add a hash mark (#) and the name of the anchor to the end of the appropriate URL.

- If you're accessing a page and anchor beyond the current page, you must include the file name of the Web page the anchor is included in, such as `Legalities.html#Copyright`.

- If you want to use the anchor to jump around within the current page, the URL only needs the hash mark and the anchor name, such as `#Copyright`.

With hyperlinks and anchors, you'll be able to tie your pages to each other and the rest of the World Wide Web, where one-click navigation can get your readers anywhere they need to go.

Working with HTML Source Code

It's time to take a brief respite from the buttons and boxes of Dreamweaver's visual interface to take a look directly at the HTML source code. Although Dreamweaver offers a very fine front-end for creating Web pages, there comes a time in every page author's life when you need to work directly with the HTML code underneath the page. Dreamweaver supports this with the HTML Inspector (see Figure 5.18). You can open this window in one of several ways:

- [⟨⟩] Press the HTML source icon from the launcher.
- Press **F10** (Windows).
- Select **Window** and then choose **HTML**.

You can edit your page directly from the HTML Inspector, and any changes are immediately reflected in the visual portion of Dreamweaver's editing window. Your HTML source is color-coded in Dreamweaver with the same defaults used by BBEdit or

HomeSite, depending on which platform you're working from. If you want to change the color scheme, including default background colors, select **Edit, Preferences, HTML Tag Colors**. The only real shortcoming in this window is that you can't cut or paste blocks of text—the HTML Inspector is primarily for minor changes and alterations to your page. For more extensive changes to your page from a source-code level, you'll need to use an external HTML editor such as HomeSite or BBEdit.

FIGURE 5.18

The HTML Inspector window shows the source code underneath the visual page.

1 External Editor: Launches a user-specified HTML or text editor

2 Wrap: Enables/disables word wrapping for long lines

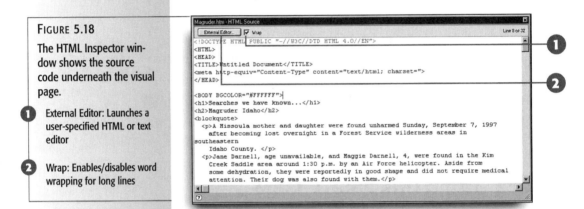

From Here...

- To use style sheets to format text, see Chapter 6, "Formatting Text with Style Sheets."

- To add images to your page, see Chapter 7, "Adding and Changing Images."

- To create reusable parts for often-used page elements, see Chapter 8, "Reusable Parts for Web Pages."

- To add Shockwave, Java applets, plug-ins, ActiveX, and other multimedia content to your page, see Chapter 9, "Working with Multimedia Content."

- For advanced techniques to format and structure pages, see Part III, "Structuring Pages with Tables, Frames, and Layers."

- To create and include other interactive features, see Part IV, "Adding Interactivity and Scripts.

Formatting Text with Style Sheets

Working with Cascading Style Sheets

Cascading Style Sheets are one of the new additions to the world of Web pages. For newcomers and old-timers alike, there remains a bit of confusion. What is a style sheet and what does it do?

It's a lot like defining a set of styles with a publishing program such as QuarkXPress or PageMaker. You can create definitions for how a page looks—margins and default typeface—and then create a set of more specific styles—heading and headline size, indents and outdents for introduction and conclusion paragraphs, lists with numbers or letters, and footnote typeface and size.

I'll spare you a lot of history and philosophy and boil it down to this. Style sheets put all the information about appearance in one place on the Web page, making it easier to change the appearance of the Web page. Do you want hyperlinks to be purple with no underline? You can make it happen with a style sheet. Do you want all your headings flush right? You can make it happen with a style sheet. Do you want to indent all paragraphs a half inch? Well, you get the idea.

Before we actually work through the process of creating a style sheet with Dreamweaver, it's good to take some time to look at the different forms of a style sheet.

The first form of a style sheet is inline. This most closely resembles the <FONT> tag, except that it's an attribute that can be applied to any tag. For example, if you wanted to make the following heading red

```
<H1>Eat at Joe's</H1>
```

the <FONT> option would work this way:

```
<H1><FONT color="red">Eat at Joe's</FONT></H1>
```

An inline style sheet does away with the need for the <FONT> tag, and applies the style directly to the affected tag.

```
<H1 style="color:red">Eat at Joe's</H1>
```

If you wanted every heading displayed in red, this could get to be a bit tedious. Which brings us to the next form of a style sheet—embedded. An embedded style sheet is a collection of definitions within the head of the document that are then applied automatically to the rest of the document.

```
<STYLE type="text/css">
H1 { color: red }
H1.green { color: green }
.yellowblue { color: yellow; background-color: blue }
</STYLE>
```

The definitions within an embedded style sheet take on two basic forms—new definitions for existing tags, and style classes that can apply to any tag. Class names begin with a period. You can also create a subclass within an existing element by including a tag name, followed by a period and the class name.

Once the style definitions are created, you can apply them to various parts of your Web page. In the previous example, a Heading 1 element now appears in red on style sheet-compatible browsers. A Heading 1 element with the class name green appears in green. Any element using the class yellowblue displays in yellow text on a blue background. The actual HTML syntax looks like the following:

```
<H1>Eat at Joe's</H1> <!-- This line in red -->
<H1 class="green">I really mean it</H1> <!-- This line in
green -->
<H1 class="yellowblue">No, I'm not kidding</H1> <!--
...yellow on blue -->
<H2 class="green">But you have to be hungry</H2> <!--
...black text -->
<H2 class="yellowblue">And have a lot of money</H2> <!--
...yellow on blue -->
```

Everything looks as expected, except for the first Heading 2. It says class="green" but it appears in black? Remember the style definitions. The green class only applies to Heading 1 elements. It's inoperable on anything else. We'll cover this behavior in a little more detail later in the section on cascading.

The last type of style sheet is a linked style sheet. To create a linked style sheet, you take a set of style definitions in the same format as an embedded style sheet and save it in a file all by itself, such as style.css. Using our embedded style sheet, my style.css looks like the following:

```
H1 { color: red }
H1.green { color: green }
.yellowblue { color: yellow; background-color: blue }
```

Including this style sheet in your Web page makes use of the <LINK> tag (hence the name) in the head of the document.

```
<LINK rel="stylesheet" href="style.css" type="text/css">
```

With this line in place, you can use the style sheet just as if it were embedded into your document.

Resolving Style Conflicts with Cascading

This brings up the issue of cascading. The term "cascading" refers to the orderly application of one or more types of style sheets. To see how the conflicts between different style definitions are resolved, we'll use an example.

```
<LINK rel="stylesheet" href="style.css" type="text/css">
<STYLE type="text/css">
H1 { color: white; background-color: black }
</STYLE>
...
<H1>Eat at Joe's</H1>
<H1 class="yellowblue">Eat at Joe's right now</H1>
<H1 class="yellowblue" style="background-color: teal">Eat at
Joe's or else</H1>
...
```

Here's what's going to happen:

1. The browser loads style.css with its style definitions. Normally, a heading (and virtually all other text) is displayed in black. The new definition for H1 overrides this, and specifies red text for an H1 element, and yellow text on a blue background for the yellowblue class.

2. Next, the browser evaluates the embedded style sheet. It also includes a definition for H1. Because the embedded style is more specific by virtue of the fact that it's local to the document, the new definition of H1 becomes white text on a black background.

3. When the document is loaded, the first <H1> appears in black on white.

4. In the second heading, the class yellowblue is applied. Since the class has been applied directly to the tag, it's more local to the tag than the default definition of H1. The tag appears in yellow on blue.

5. The last tag begins with the default definition of H1—white on black. The class tag forces it to the yellow on blue style class. The inline style takes the whole process one step deeper, and specifies a new background color. Since the inline style is even more specific than the class definition, the text is displayed in yellow on teal.

In short, a Cascading Style Sheet begins with the most general and distant style definitions—the defaults set by the browser. Any browser defaults are overridden by definitions in the linked style sheet. Then it moves to an embedded style sheet. Any duplicate definitions between the linked and embedded style sheets default to the embedded style sheets. From here, it moves down to the tag level. A class definition overrides any default presentation for the tag, and an inline style overrides everything else.

Although it sounds a bit convoluted, the logic is really quite simple. You can start with a generic style sheet for your entire site. This style sheet can be linked to every page you create. You can then create a custom style for special pages by embedding a style sheet, knowing that you don't have to disassociate your page from the linked style sheet—where there are conflicts, the embedded style sheet takes precedence. Then, as you apply the style to your document, you can tweak the style and appearance even further by applying classes and inline styles as necessary.

Using Cascading Style Sheets with this hierarchy in mind gives you the most flexibility and power in controlling the appearance of your Web pages.

Creating a Style Sheet

Now that we have a firm background about how style sheets work, we can actually work on creating one. For this section, we're going to need that fine old Legalities.html file again (we created it in Chapter 4, "Starting with a Blank Page"). Remember some of the changes we made to it? We centered headings and changed typefaces, backgrounds, and text colors. Style sheets let us do all that and more, and it's actually a little easier.

Let's say I want to center all the headings on my page and display them in Helvetica or some other sans-serif face, just like the first heading. Using the methods in the last chapter, I could click-and-drag to select each heading, and then click the appropriate buttons in the Properties window. But, I'm going to use a style sheet instead.

Before we get started, we'll need the Styles palette. Select the Styles icon from the Launcher, or select **Window**, and then choose **Styles** (see Figure 6.1). Then, click the Style Sheet button at the bottom of the Styles palette to view the Edit Style Sheet dialog box (see Figure 6.2).

Creating a style sheet

1. From the Edit Style Sheet Dialog box, click **New** to create a new style.

2. This displays the New Style box (see Figure 6.3). We want the second choice, **Redefine HTML Tag**. We'll take a look at the other options later on.

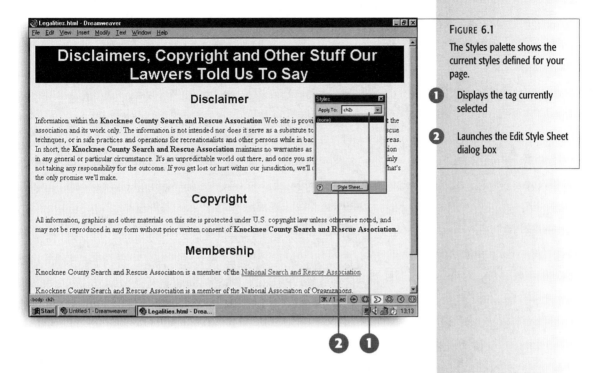

FIGURE 6.1

The Styles palette shows the current styles defined for your page.

1 Displays the tag currently selected

2 Launches the Edit Style Sheet dialog box

FIGURE 6.2

The Edit Style Sheet dialog box is used to add, edit, and remove styles from the current page.

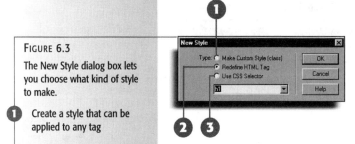

FIGURE 6.3

The New Style dialog box lets
you choose what kind of style
to make.

1 Create a style that can be
applied to any tag

2 Change the default appearance of a tag

3 Create a subclass of a tag,
such as the various states of
a hyperlink

3. The drop-down list is now loaded with a bunch of tag
names. Select the tag name, in our case **H1**.

4. After selecting the tag name, Dreamweaver brings up the
style definition for the tag in question (see Figure 6.4).

Selecting a category on the left side of the window allows a
different set of choices about the appearance of the style on
the right. For most text items, the first three will hold all the
choices needed.

FIGURE 6.4

You can decide how the style
affects its text in the Style definition for h1 dialog box.

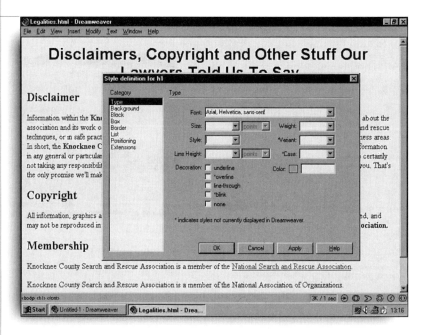

- **Type** This covers all the basic choices for the text style, including font selection, color, size, italics, bold, and so on. For our heading style, I want the Helvetica font in white.

- **Background** The background affects the choice of background colors and images for the selected style. You can set the background for an item independent of the page it's on and its surrounding items. To make our white type appear, we'll give the heading a black background.

- **Block** These options cover basic alignment and spacing of the text. As before, we want the heading centered, so we'll select **center** from **Text Align**.

There are a lot of possibilities for controlling the appearance of text with a style sheet. You'll find a complete listing in Appendix D, "CSS Quick Reference."

5. With the style definition out of the way, click **OK**. This creates a style section in the head of your document that includes the definition line for your new style.

```
<style type="text/css">
<!--
h1 {  font-family: Arial, Helvetica, sans-serif; color:
#FFFFFF; background-color: #000000<style type="text/css">
<!--
h1 {  font-family: Arial, Helvetica, sans-serif; color:
#FFFFFF; background-color: #000000; background-position:
center}
-->
</style>}
-->
</style>
```

The <STYLE> tags mark the beginning and end of the definition. The comment tags hide the style sheet from incompatible browsers, such as Mosaic, that are still prone to

The tag names correspond to different types of text. For example, H1 is used to mark a heading (the first and biggest). H6 is also a heading (the last and smallest). The A is used for hyperlinks and anchors. The P marks paragraphs.

You'll find an HTML quick reference that tells about the different tags and their uses in Appendix C, "HTML 4 Quick Reference."

displaying this material as part of the document. As you can remember from your choices, this style definition sets the default font for a Heading 1 element (Arial, Helvetica, or any sans-serif face). The text color is white with a black background. The background should be centered in relation to the element.

Any attribute you don't define is set by the browser according to the browser defaults. The new style appears in the Edit Style Sheet dialog box (see Figure 6.5), along with the nitty gritty details of its definition at the bottom. The style itself is applied to the current page—the first heading is white on black, centered, using a sans-serif type face.

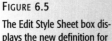

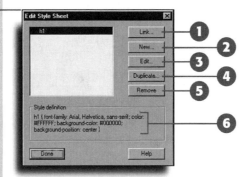

FIGURE 6.5

The Edit Style Sheet box displays the new definition for the heading tag.

1 Use a style sheet in a different document

2 Create a new style with the New Style dialog

3 Edit the current style

4 Make a copy of the current style

5 Delete the current style

6 The style syntax as it will appear to the browser

Congratulations, you've created your first style with Dreamweaver. If you want to look at it firsthand, you can use the HTML inspector to view the source of the document, including the style sheet in the head of the document.

At this point, we'll take a break to address a few other points on style sheets. First is the issue of what happens to style sheets on browsers that don't style. This is an easy one—nothing. The style sheet is ignored, and the text is displayed according to the browser's defaults.

The second issue concerns what a tag would normally look like, if styles weren't being used. Take our H1, for example. What would happen if we set the background color to black without changing the default text color? Style sheets won't second-guess your intentions. Instead, they'll follow your rules right out the window. In this case, you would display black text (the default) on a black background (your choice).

Now, let's go back to the Edit Style Sheet dialog box to finish up our work. I want to use the H1 style as the basis for the way the next heading style (H2) is displayed.

Copying a style

1. Select the **H1** style in the Edit Style Sheet box.

2. Click the **Duplicate** button to create a copy.

3. Select the tag that should look like the first. In this case, you can select **H2** from the drop-down list, or just type the tag name directly into the box.

4. Click **OK**. The same style definition is now copied to H2, and the result is also displayed in the Dreamweaver editing area.

5. To change the attributes for the new style, click the **Edit** button. Follow the previous directions to make any changes to the style. For mine, I changed the text color and background color back to their default values.

From the Edit Style Sheet dialog box, click **Done** to return to the view of the Styles window. You'll notice after adding two styles, nothing shows up here. What gives?

So far, we've worked on changing the appearance of pre-existing styles. If you'll recall, making a piece of text a heading changed its appearance. This is a type of style already built into browsers. All we've done so far is change what that default style looks like. We can also create our own brand new styles, completely independent of the tags. Adding style tags without changing the tag's default appearance is discussed in "Adding Style to Text: A Method with Class," later in this chapter.

Now that you've changed some of the elements within a page, it's time to let you in another secret of the universe—you can set all of the same attributes for the entire document at once, just like you did in Chapter 4 with the page properties.

Follow the same steps for creating a new style for an HTML tag, but for the name of the tag, choose BODY. The <BODY> tag is a special tag that holds all of the content on your Web page. Any changes to the style for BODY become the default style for your page, just as if you were setting the page properties. This includes items like background colors, images, default typefaces, margins, text size, text alignment, and just about anything else you can set with a style sheet.

Adding Style to Text: A Method with Class

One of the things I've run into on occasion is the need to do two different things with the same tag. Take our headings for example. Sometimes for effect, I'll set every other heading and the paragraphs below it to right-justification. There's a problem, though. If I change the heading and paragraph in a style sheet to be right-justified, all of those headings will be right-justified, not just the ones I want.

To get around this problem, I define special styles, called classes, that hold the special formatting I need. To take care of formatting every other heading and its following paragraphs, I might have one called `left` and one called `right` to force left and right-justification as needed. We'll start this section by creating a class, and then see how to apply it to the page.

Creating a style class

1. From the Edit Style Sheet dialog (click the Style Sheet button in the Styles window), click **New** to create a new style.

2. Select the first type, **Make Custom Style (class)**. Dreamweaver fills in the name with .unnamed1. Type your own name for the style, but be sure to leave the period. The period is what tells the browser that this is a style class and not a tag name. It's a good idea to keep the name short and free of spaces and special characters.

3. Click **OK**, and then edit the style definition to meet your tastes.

4. Select **OK** to finish and **Done** to return to your document. When you view the Styles window again, the new style class appears on the list.

I created two new styles for my style sheet called right and left. Now, I want to apply these styles to the first two paragraphs in my document and their headings.

Applying a style class to text

1. Make sure the Style window is in view by selecting **Window** and then choosing **Styles**.

2. Click the text to which you want to apply the style. In this case, I'm going to apply the right style to the second paragraph and its respective heading, so I'll begin by clicking the heading.

3. Next, click the style name in the Styles window. The style is automatically applied to the heading and it moves to right justification.

4. Repeat the process for the paragraph under the heading. First, click the paragraph, and then click the style.

That's all there is to it. Click, click, and the style is applied. The downside is that you can't apply the style to more than one paragraph at a time. You have to click each one individually, then click the appropriate style. If you're applying a lot of style to a page, this can get a bit tedious, but there's really no way around it.

There is one more option to consider when applying a style class to a piece of text. Look at this bit of HTML (see Figure 6.6).

```
<DIV name="example">
<P>A six line stanza is called a sextet or sestet. Here is an
    example:</P>
<BLOCKQUOTE><P>Fear no more the heat o' the sun<BR>
Nor the furious winter's rages;<BR>
Thou thy world task hast done,<BR>
Home art gone and ta'en thy wages:<BR>
Golden lads and girls all must,<BR>
As chimney-sweepers, come to dust.</P>
```

```
<P><CITE>Dirge</CITE> from <CITE>Cymbeline</CITE>, William
    Shakespeare</P></BLOCKQUOTE>
<P>The trochaic pattern here is four-foot lines. One of the
    favorite stanzas of Robert Burns has the iambic pattern of
4, 4, 4, 2, 4, 2...</P>
</DIV>
```

FIGURE 6.6

This paragraph of text includes a variety of nested tags.

Before you decide which style to apply, you need to decide which part of the paragraph it will apply to—the entire division, the block quote, a specific paragraph within the block quote, the citations, or some subset thereof.

For example, if I select a few letters from the title of the sextet, *Dirge*, the HTML guide at the bottom lets me know that the hierarchy of tags, from the body to the current cursor position is

`<body><div><blockquote><p><cite>`

Now, when I apply a style, I can apply it to any one of these elements, or just the selected text. This is accomplished by selecting a style, and then clicking the Apply To drop-down list at the top of the Styles box (see Figure 6.7), where you can select which element the style should apply to. The default is the current selection.

FIGURE 6.7

The Apply To box of the Styles palette includes a choice for each element that could be affected by the style.

From Here...

- For other text formatting methods, see Chapter 5, "Adding Text to a Page."

- Creating reusable library items is covered in Chapter 8, "Reusable Parts for Web Pages."

- Additional page formatting is possible with tables, covered in Chapter 12, "Building Tables," and Chapter 14, "Refining Page Layouts Using Tables."

- Frames are yet another way to control the appearance of pages in a browser window. See Chapter 15, "Creating Frames," and Chapter 17, "Creating a Frame-Based Navigation System."

- Last but not least, layers are related to style sheets in their ability to customize the appearance of a page, and are covered in Chapter 18, "Working with Layers."

Adding and Changing Images

Add an image to a Web page

Change image alignment

Identify quick-loading, low-resolution images

Create a seamless image from smaller images

Adding Images

Virtually no Web page is complete without a picture of some sort. Whether it's a picture of a favorite cat on a personal home page, or a flashy company logo at a corporate site, people use images everywhere. They're also used for lots of other purposes. Many navigation icons, such as bullets and arrows, are also images. Whatever the use, an image is an image, and it's put on the page in the same way.

In this chapter, we'll take a look at how to put an image on your page with Dreamweaver, tweak it so it fits with the rest of the page, and also give some pointers on how to be a good Web neighbor when placing graphics on your site.

Adding images to your site is a fairly simple process. You'll need two basic things—your Web page and the graphic you want to add. The Web page probably already exists on your local site. The image can be anywhere on your hard drive. If it's sitting on your remote site, you'll want to go get it and put it on your local site.

SEE ALSO

➤ *Learn more about getting files from remote Web sites, page 33*

For this exercise, we're starting a new page for our search and rescue site. It includes stories about a previous search operation, with pictures of searchers and the person they found. Figure 7.1 shows the page as it exists so far.

The easiest way to add images is to use the Objects palette. To view the palette, select **Window**, and then choose **Objects**. The default Objects palette includes an icon for selecting images at the very top.

Putting an image on a Web page

1. Position the cursor in the page where the image should appear. In my page, I want a picture appearing at the beginning of the last paragraph.

2. Click the **Image** icon on the Objects palette. In the box, type the filename of the image to use if it's contained within your site, or click **Browse** to navigate to another location.

3. My picture is located outside the current site, so I had to browse to it. Since Dreamweaver likes to keep birds of a feather together, it prompts to copy the file to the current site (see Figure 7.2). The original file is left in place.

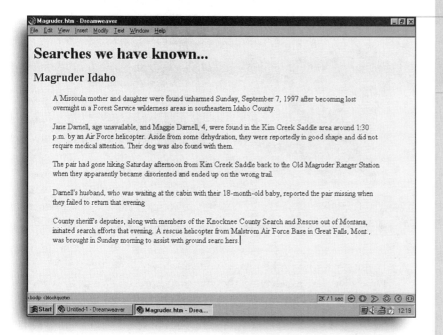

4. If you have to copy the file, you'll be given the opportunity to pick the specific location and filename within the site where it will be located. When you've made these choices, click **OK** in the Insert Image dialog box to finish.

5. The image is inserted into the page and selected for further manipulation if needed (see Figure 7.3).

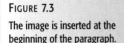

FIGURE 7.3

The image is inserted at the
beginning of the paragraph.

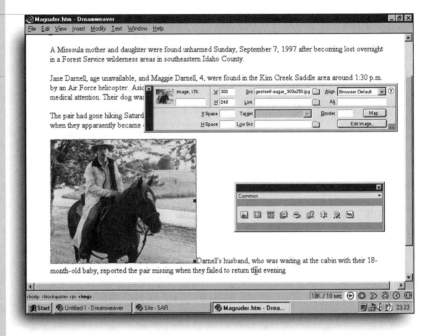

If you need to edit the image, you can do so directly from
Dreamweaver by selecting the image and pressing **Ctrl+E**
(Windows) or **Option+E** (Macintosh) to launch the current
image editor defined in your External Editor Preferences.
Inserting an image was easy enough. But, as you can see, its
placement leaves a bit to be desired. The image is kind of big,
and hangs out like a sore thumb at the beginning of the paragraph. Let's see if we can make it look any better.

Aligning Images

One of the biggest tricks in making images look better with their
surrounding text is to change how the image is arranged in relation to the surrounding text. As a default, images are displayed
inline. That means that the bottom of the image is lined up with
the bottom of the line of text where it appears. The results can
look a little odd if the image is very large, as seen in
Figure 7.3.

Forcing the image to left or right justification can result in a
more aesthetically pleasing page.

Aligning images

1. Make sure the Properties window is in view by selecting **Window**, and then choosing **Properties**).

2. Click the image to select it. It will appear to get darker.

3. Click the drop-down list in the Properties window for **Align**. The common three choices are **Browser Default**, **Left**, and **Right**. Left alignment forces the image to the left margin of the browser window, and the text wraps around the right side. The opposite is true for Right alignment. For our example, I'm choosing Right alignment.

4. The image is moved to its new position (see Figure 7.4).

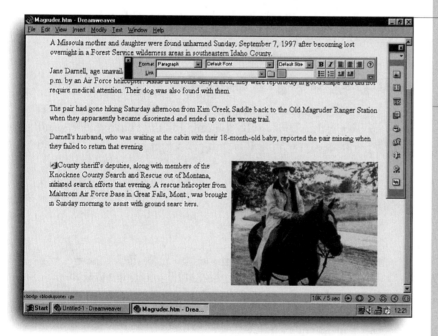

FIGURE 7.4

The image is now aligned against the right edge of the browser window with text flowing to the left.

One of the things you'll notice in Figure 7.4 is a small icon at the left margin opposite the image. Where did it come from? This is one of the helpful features of Dreamweaver—it marks where the actual tag for the image is located. Even though the formatting has placed it visually at the right margin, the tag is still located at the beginning of the paragraph. If you were to look at the source code for that part of the page, it would like this:

```
<p>Darnell's husband, who was waiting at the cabin with
their 18-month-old baby, reported the pair missing when they
failed to return that evening</p>
<p><img src="../self-sugar_300x250.jpg" width="300"
height="249"
    name="buddy" align="RIGHT">County sheriff's deputies,
along with members of the Knocknee County Search and Rescue
out of Montana, initiated search efforts that evening. A
rescue helicopter from Malstrom Air Force Base in Great
Falls, Mont., was brought in Sunday morning to assist with
ground searchers.</p>
```

Sometimes, it's a bit confusing to figure out where the tag is actually located in relation to the text, especially with visual editors. This feature of Dreamweaver removes that guesswork.

Changing Image Features

There are a few more things you can do with the images, other than hang them on a wall. You can also assign names, sizes and hyperlinks to the image. Turning an image into a basic hyperlink is the same as turning a piece of text into a hyperlink. We'll cover a special type of image hyperlink, called an imagemap, later in this chapter.

SEE ALSO

➤ *Learn how to create a hyperlink, page 81*

All of these features are controlled through the Properties window for images (Figure 7.5), viewed by selecting **Window**, choosing **Properties**, and then clicking the image. To view all the options for an image, click the expander arrow to view the entire properties window.

Several of these fields are worth noting in more detail.

"...that annoying blue line around link images in Netscape..."

One of the common questions in HTML newsgroups concerns removing the border around images defined as hyperlinks (in all fairness, Netscape isn't the only browser that displays this feature). You can control this behavior using the Border field.

This field defines the width in pixels of a border to display around the image. For non-hyperlink images, the default is 0. For hyperlink images, the default is usually 1 or 2.

However, a lot of page authors and designers, myself included, don't like a border around images, even when they are hyperlinks. To avoid this annoying little trait, enter a 0 in the Border field to force the image to never have a border.

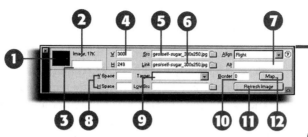

FIGURE 7.5

The Properties window for images includes a thumbnail of the image and fields to change other image properties.

❶ Thumbnail: Miniature representation of the image.

❷ Size: Image size in kilobytes.

❸ Name: A name for the image, used for interactive effects and scripting.

❹ Dimensions: Image size in pixels (width by height).

❺ Src: Location of the image, relative to the current document.

❻ Link: Enter a hyperlink target if the image is clickable. Align: Image alignment in relation to the surrounding text.

❼ Alt: Alternate text content for browsers that don't show the picture.

❽ V Space, H Space: Additional padding for space around the image.

❾ Target: Name of a frame or window to load a link into. Low Src: Low resolution (smaller file size) image to load first.

❿ Border: Width of border around image, primarily used for hyperlinks.

⓫ Refresh Image: Reload image from file.

⓬ Map: Create image map information.

Adding a Name and Alternate Content

A name is given to an image to identify it for scripts. The scripts can then move the image around on the screen or otherwise manipulate it in response to the user. To learn how to add interactivity to you Web page, see Chapter 21, "Creating Animations: Moving Objects."

The field to hold a name for the image is unmarked on the Properties window. It's located next to the thumbnail of the image at the left of the window. Click the field, and type a unique name for the image.

Another option is to enter a line of text to use if the user's browser doesn't support images (such as the venerable Lynx) or if the user has images turned off (to speed up page download and display). In most browsers, the text is displayed in an empty box where the image would have appeared. It is also used in some browsers as a "tool tip" when the mouse pointer is placed over the image. A small box appears with the alternate text to give the reader an extra clue as to what the image is.

The text for this purpose is entered into the Alt (for "Alternate content") field on the right of the window. Keep the text short and descriptive. For the image we've been using, something like "SAR Ranger Doug" would work well.

Setting the Image Size

Image size is filled in automatically by Dreamweaver when it's placed on the page. This serves an important purpose. When the reader's browser loads the page and comes across the image, it knows how much space to set aside in the browser window. If the browser wasn't given the dimensions, it would have to download the entire image before it could begin to accurately render the page.

The size also has another use, although it's not recommended. If you have a large image that you want to fit in a smaller space, you can enter different values in the W and H fields for width and height or click and drag one of the handles on the image (located on the right and bottom sides and bottom-right corner). Most browsers, including those from Microsoft and Netscape, will resize the image to fit in the space you've defined. The downside is that the browser still has to download the entire large image. So, if you're displaying a large graphic as a thumbnail, it will still need to download the entire large graphic. You're better off resizing the large graphic into a separate, smaller image for this use. By the same token, if you're displaying a small graphic in a bigger space, there is a corresponding loss of image quality.

The moral of the story is to use images at their original size whenever possible. Resizing an image on the Web page is an ineffective use of the browser, and should only be considered a temporary fix.

Quick-Downloading Images

Another important field is Low Src. This is a good attribute to use with large images. It specifies another copy of the same image, only in a low-resolution (read, small file size). It is downloaded first, followed by other Low Src images on the page. Then, when everything else on the page is loaded, the browser goes back to download the "real" image. This decreases the time needed for the user to view a page with images, while still giving the browser a chance to retrieve all the content.

Another option is pre-loading the image. While there's nothing the user can do but wait for images on the current page, you can pre-load images that will be used on subsequent pages into the browser cache. This is accomplished through the Behaviors palette (**F8** or **Window**, **Behaviors**).

Preloading an image

1. Position the cursor at the top of the document (you may have to use the HTML Inspector) so that Event side of the Behaviors palette says **<body> Events**.

2. Select **4.0 Browsers** from the drop-down list.

3. Click on the plus (+) button, and select **onLoad** from the list of events that appears.

4. On the Actions side of the Behaviors palette, click on the plus (+) button and select **Preload Images** from the list of available behaviors. This displays the Preload Images dialog (see Figure 7.6).

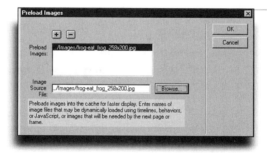

FIGURE 7.6

Enter the filenames of images into the Preload Images dialog box so they're ready and waiting in the cache the next time they're needed.

5. Enter the path to an image, or use the **Browse/Choose** button to navigate to it.

6. To add additional images, click on the plus (+) button. To remove an image, select the image from the list, and click on the minus (-) button.

When the page is finished loading, a compatible browser will begin to load the named images into its cache. The next time the pre-loaded image is referenced, its display is virtually instant since it comes from the user's hard drive, and not from the network connection.

Seamless Image Placement

One of the concerns of both page authors and users is how long it takes for a page to load, especially when it includes a large image. It can seem like forever for an entire big picture to download in a user's browser.

An increasingly common way of dealing with this problem is to break apart images into a set of smaller pieces. In essence, one big image becomes a puzzle that you reassemble with image tags on the Web page.

Assembling a seamless image

1. Begin with your set of images. You'll probably have at least two rows of at least two images. Depending on the size of your final image and how its broken apart, there could easily be more.

2. Start a new line by creating a hard return.

3. Insert the top-left image at the beginning of the line. Set its properties to 0 H Space and a 0 Border.

4. Insert the next and subsequent images for that line, using the same horizontal space and border properties as the first. When you reach the end of the line, insert a line break (<BR>).

5. Repeat steps 3 and 4 until you've included all the pieces of your image.

This technique can also work to assemble button bars for the user. If you want a seamless row of buttons for the browser, start a new paragraph and add each of the images in turn. Then, adjust the properties on each image so they are forced to a 0 H Space and a 0 Border.

From Here...

- Learn how to create reusable parts for your Web pages and store them in a library in Chapter 8, "Reusable Parts for Web Pages."

- Learn how to add Java applets, ActiveX controls, and Shockwave movies in Chapter 9, "Working with Multimedia Content."

- Learn how to turn an image into an imagemap in Chapter 11, "Setting up Imagemaps."
- Learn how to use tables to layout your images and text in Chapter 14, "Refining Page Layouts Using Tables."

Reusable Parts for Web Pages

Create and edit a library of reusable page segments

Insert a library item on your page

Update all library items on all site pages

Creating Web Page Parts

One of the things you'll see stressed in many design books, whether they're geared towards a print or electronic medium, is consistency. Use the same elements in the same way, and your reader will be happy. Library Web parts help in this goal, allowing you to create a page element once, and then insert it as needed in your other pages.

The best part about using the Dreamweaver library feature is that it doesn't require any extra software on the Web server to function. Dreamweaver inserts a copy of the library part directly into your page, along with a reference to the library file. This also allows you to update the page automatically if you edit the library part after it's inserted on a Web page.

If you can create a Web page, you can create a library item for your Web page. As a matter of fact, the easiest way to create a library item is to use a piece of an existing page. I'm going to create a library item out of the copyright statement on the Legalities.htm Web page.

Creating a library item

1. Open the Web page you're going to copy from, or create and save a new page with the content. Libraries are linked with sites, so you must work from a page on an existing site for any of this to work.

2. Open the Library palette by selecting **Window**, and choosing **Library** (see Figure 8.1).

FIGURE 8.1

The Library Palette is used to manage the various parts in your site's collection.

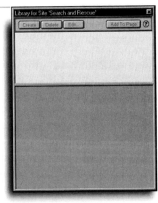

3. Click and drag the mouse to select a portion of the page to use as a library item. It can include text, images, and multimedia content (Java, plug-ins, ActiveX, and so on).

4. Hold down the Control key and drag your selection to the Library palette. A new entry is created with the name untitled. This retains the original in the document. If you don't hold down the Control key, the selection is replaced with a library item, albeit, it's the same as the library item you created.

5. Type a name for the library item. I'll call mine copyright (see Figure 8.2). Note that you don't need to add an .htm or .html extension to the name. Library items are handled in their own special way by Dreamweaver.

A note of caution

Be careful when using any content such as images or multimedia content. If you move the source files for this content from its position, it won't show up in the library item.

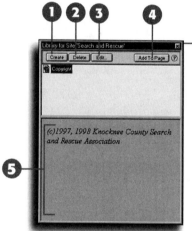

FIGURE 8.2

The Library palette now includes our copyright item.

1 Create button: After highlighting text, click this button to create a new library item.

2 Delete: Select a library item and click this button to remove it.

3 Edit: Click this button to edit the current library item.

4 Add to Page: This button adds the library item at the current cursor position.

5 Preview pane: Displays what the library item contains.

That's all there is to it. There are lots of things that lend themselves to storing in the library, including copyright and other legal notices that should appear on every page, contact information, navigation bars, company logos, and anything else you use a lot.

Editing a Library Item

Once you create a library part for your Web page, chances are it will need changing at some point. This is especially true if the library item includes hyperlinks to other pages on the Web, or even within your own site. Lucky for you, editing a library item is as easy as creating it.

Editing a library item

1. Select **Window**, choose **Library**, and then select the desired item from the Library palette.

2. Click the **Edit** button at the top of the Library palette. A new editing window is opened with the contents of the item.

3. Make any changes as you would for a normal Web page, including adding or removing text, images, hyperlinks, and other items.

4. When finished, select **File** and choose **Close**. Dreamweaver will prompt you to save your changes and close the editing window.

5. As the library item closes, Dreamweaver will prompt you to update any pages in your site that contain this item. If you're only making changes to one item, this is a quick and easy way to accomplish the task. Otherwise, if you're changing several items and the site has more than 20 or 30 pages, you can say no and update all the pages at once later. To update all the library items in a site at the same time, see the "Many Pages, One Part, One Update" section later in this chapter.

6. The library item will now appear, changes and all, in the Library palette.

This process makes it easy to keep your library items up-to-date. As you add these parts to many different Web pages, you'll appreciate the efficiency of only having to edit one small piece of a page, instead of many different pages. The chances of making a typo are greatly reduced.

Adding a Library Part to Your Page

Now that we've created a library item, let's add it to a page. I'm going to add my copyright notice to the bottom of the page about the Old Magruder Ranger Station search that we created in Chapter 7, "Adding and Changing Images." Again, you'll need to open the Library palette by selecting **Window**, and then choosing **Library**.

Adding parts to pages

1. Select the library item you want to add to the page. Clicking a library part also displays it in a small preview window below the list of items.

2. Drag the desired library part from the Library palette to the appropriate location on the page.

3. The item is inserted on the page and highlighted in yellow to indicate it's a linked selection from the library.

Again, that's all there is to it. Save your page, and the part is saved along with it. How does all this magic happen? For our example with the copyright, Dreamweaver inserts all the content from the library item created in the previous section, plus a little bit more:

```
<p><!-- #BeginLibraryItem "/Library/Copyright.lbi" -->
<i>1997, 1998 Knocknee County Search and Rescue
Association</i>
<!-- #EndLibraryItem --></p>
```

The library item is bracketed by a set of comment tags (marked by an opening <!-- and a closing -->) that mark the beginning and end of the item. These comment tags are ignored by the user's browser and aren't displayed (unless they choose to look at the source). Dreamweaver includes the items so that it knows what to look for when you update the library item later down the road.

There are two more options available for library items. You'll need to open the Properties palette, and then click a library item. There are only two buttons on the palette—one to make the library item editable, and the other to re-create it.

- **Make Editable**—This button removes the comment tags that mark the beginning and ending of the item. In Dreamweaver's eyes, the item is just a part of the page. Any attempt to update library items on a page will ignore it, since it appears as if it's just part of the page. Once you've done this, you can't undo it. You have to go back and reinsert the part.

- **Recreate**—This creates a new item in the library with the same name as the currently selected item on the page. This is useful in case someone accidentally removes an item from the library. Dreamweaver will still look at the part on your page as an item, it just doesn't have any way to update it. Clicking **Recreate** will put the item back into your library.

Many Pages, One Part, One Update

As you've seen so far in this chapter, library items are easy to create and insert on a Web page. The parts are even easy to edit once they're created. But here's the rub—just editing a library item doesn't automatically update all the pages where the item is inserted. That takes one extra step. In my example, I've added some additional information to the copyright notice, and now all the pages with the copyright need to be updated.

Updating pages with parts

1. From the Dreamweaver editor, select **Modify**, choose **Library**, and then choose **Update Entire Site**. This displays the Update Site dialog box (see Figure 8.3).

2. Select which site to update from the drop-down list at the top of the box.

3. Click **Start** to begin the update. Dreamweaver searches through the pages on your site for library items, and updates any it finds with the current contents from the library. As it works, it generates a log in the bottom window so you can view its progress (if the Show Log box is selected).

Get it before you update it

Before Dreamweaver will update a page for you with revised library items, you will need to check out the files. Basically, you'll need to check out all the files for a site (see Chapter 2, "Working with Files," for more information), and then run the update. If you can't get access to all the files because other people have them checked out, you'll need to make sure that everyone updates their sites periodically, or you'll have out-of-date content on your pages.

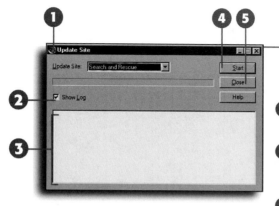

FIGURE 8.3
The undate Site box controls which site is updated.

1 Update Site: Pick which site to update from this list.

2 Show Log: Select this to display the progress of the update.

3 Log window: Displays the update log as it's generated.

4 Start: Start the library update process for the selected site.

5 Close: Close the Update Site dialog box.

If there are several people working on a site, you'll need to update the entire site periodically using this method to make sure everyone is working with the same content. Part of using the Dreamweaver library is making sure that the library items stay current on the page.

From Here...

- For more information on managing files in a site, see Chapter 2, "Working with Files."
- For more information on creating Web pages, see Chapter 5, "Adding Text to a Page."
- For more information on fixing problems with the library, see Chapter 27, "Troubleshooting Dreamweaver."

Multimedia with Dreamweaver

Working with Multimedia Content

Why Multimedia?

Multimedia content is extending its flashy tendrils to every corner of the World Wide Web. Web sites are increasingly divided by the type of content they contain. It's either dad's old olive green Buick with text and a couple of images, or, a cherry '68 Mustang with Java, ActiveX, and the plethora of plug-ins currently available.

So what's the big deal? For the most part, multimedia content is still a spectator sport for the viewer. They'll get to see a neat little movie or other animation, listen to some cool sounds, or watch the latest animated PowerPoint presentation showing the steady decline of your investment portfolio.

Some multimedia, beginning a few years ago with Shockwave (another fine invention from Macromedia), actually allows the user to interact with the show. Users can click, type, move the mouse around, and otherwise affect how the show is presented (see Figure 9.1).

FIGURE 9.1

One of the more worthwhile endeavors of Shockwave developers is animating "Dilbert" comic strips.

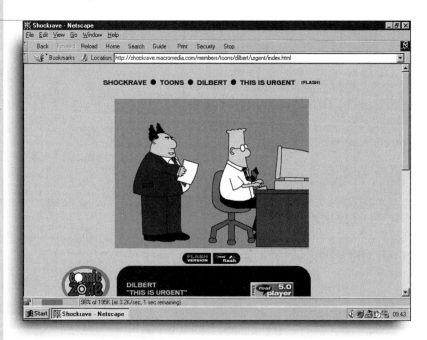

In this chapter, we'll show you how to include a wide variety of content to your Web pages.

Adding Shockwave Movies

This section will focus on adding a Shockwave Netscape plug-in. The same steps apply to any of the other plug-ins available for Netscape Navigator browsers, including plug-ins for specialized graphics and sound formats.

To make these steps easier, you'll need the Objects palette (select **Window** and then choose **Objects**). Shockwave now comes in two flavors, Director and Flash, both represented with individual icons at the bottom of the palette. You'll also need the expanded Properties Inspector which can be accessed by selecting **Window** and then choosing **Properties**.

Adding a Shockwave movie

1. Place the cursor where the movie should appear on the page.

2. Click the appropriate icon for the type of Shockwave movie you're adding—Director or Flash. Other methods include:
   * Select **Insert** and then choose **Shockwave Director**.
   * For Director, press **Ctrl+Alt+D** (in Windows) or **Option+Command+D** (for the Macintosh).
   * Select **Insert** and then choose **Flash Movie**.
   * For Flash, press **Ctrl+Ald+F** (in Windows) or **Option+Command+F** (for the Macintosh).

3. A dialog box appears that prompts you for the name of the source file for the movie. Enter the name, or use the **Browse** button to locate the file by hand. Click **OK** when you've selected the file.

4. Make any changes to the movie in the Properties Inspector (see Figure 9.2). There is a variety of settings here, some of which apply to all Shockwave movies, and others that only

---

What this chapter isn't

Since this is a book about Dreamweaver, I'm not going to spend any time discussing how to build a Java applet or a Netscape plug-in. You can find that sort of information in any of the fine Web publishing books on the market today, like *HTML 4 Unleashed* from Macmillan Computer Publishing.

Shockwaves for two worlds

The software that plays Shockwave movies is available as both a plug-in, for Netscape Navigator, and as an ActiveX control, for Microsoft Internet Explorer. Dreamweaver uses the tags necessary for both browsers to make sure your user has the best chance of experiencing your special content.

The process is same whether you're inserting a Shockwave or Flash movie (or any content that comes in both a plug-in or ActiveX flavor). First, Dreamweaver inserts the ActiveX version using the `<OBJECT>` tag, and any necessary parameters using the `<PARAM>` tag. Then, the plug-in version is included using the `<EMBED>` tag and any accompanying `<PARAM>` tags. Then comes the closing `</EMBED>` and `</OBJECT>` tags.

The page ends up with the plug-in tags nested inside the ActiveX tags. When Internet Explorer loads the page, it sees the ActiveX control, loads it, and ignores the `<EMBED>` tag. When Navigator loads the page, it ignores the ActiveX tag and the loads the plug-in.

apply to Shockwave Flash. You'll need to consult documentation for your specific movie to see what is required for your content.

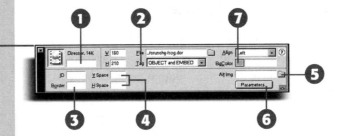

Once the movie is embedded, it appears on the page as a gray box surrounding a movie camera icon (see Figure 9.3). When this page is loaded by a compatible browser such as Netscape Navigator or Microsoft Internet Explorer, the movie is loaded along with the appropriate controls to start, stop, and pause the action. For incompatible browsers, nothing appears unless an alternate image is specified.

Adding a Plug-in

Inserting a Netscape plug-in is similar to inserting a Shockwave movie, except it's a bit more generic because a plug-in covers a wider range of content. As with inserting a Shockwave movie, you'll need to use the Objects palette accessed by selecting **Window** and then choosing **Objects**), and the Properties Inspector accessed by selecting **Window** and then choosing **Properties**.

Adding a plug-in

1. Place the cursor where the plug-in should appear on the page.

 2. Click on the plug-in icon from the Objects palette, or select **Insert** and then choose **Plug-in**.

3. A dialog box appears that prompts you for the name of the plug-in source file. The filename and extension (letters after the dot) depend on what kind of plug-in it is, so you'll need to check your specific situation on what to type here. Enter the name, or use the **Browse** button to locate the file by hand. Click **OK** when you've selected the file.

4. Make any changes to the plug-in through the Properties Inspector (see Figure 9.3). The basic settings are similar to a Shockwave movie, with a couple of differences. One important field is Plg URL, which tells the browser where to go looking if the necessary files aren't installed to run the plug-in. As with the Shockwave movies, including an alternate image is a good idea for incompatible browsers.

> **Remember the little people**
>
> Using an alternate image is a good idea, since not everyone is using the latest and greatest browsers from the "Big Two." There are still a lot of old versions of Navigator and Internet Explorer surfing out there, along with other products such as Opera, Mosaic, Lynx, and others that don't support ActiveX or plug-ins. It's good manners and good etiquette to help these folks see something other than a blank spot on the page.

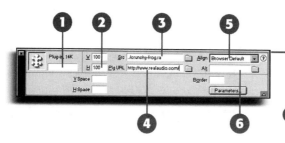

FIGURE 9.3

The Properties Inspector for Netscape plug-ins.

❶ Name: An identifier to use for scripting

❷ The width and height (in pixels) of the plug-in (or use the control panels)

❸ Where the plug-in content is located

❹ Where to find the software to install support for the plug-in content on the browser

❺ How to align the plug-in in relation to the surrounding text

❻ An image to display if the browser doesn't support plug-ins

Netscape plug-ins were the first attempt to extend the capability of a browser without releasing a new version of the browser. By including this type of content on your page, you can introduce the user to all sorts of new experiences, from interactive spreadsheets to arcade games.

Adding Java Applets

A Java applet is an odd duck in the world of multimedia content for Web pages. Java is platform-independent programming language that has a wide variety of uses. In its earlier days, it was primarily used for including animations, scrolling marquees, and

Choose a plug-in, any plug-in

Plug-ins are add-on bits of software that help Netscape Navigator do things that it wasn't designed for, including movies, special image formats, and other items. There are a whole bunch of plug-in applications floating around the Web, and which types a user has installed for his browser is a pretty personal choice. For that reason, it's a good idea to include a URL to the place where the user can install support for your content.

other simple special effects. Applets have now matured to the point where they can handle forms processing, database interactivity, and other actions that require a give-and-take of information between the server and the user's computer.

By working with a programmer or commercial software vendor, you can find applets for a wide range of uses, including database access, guest book management, electronic commerce, and a whole host of other applications. By combining the powerful and flexible Java programming language with Web page scripting, virtually anything is possible.

There are several sources for Java applets on the Web, including the comprehensive resource through the Gamelan directories at the Professional Developer's Resource (http://www.developer.com). This has extensive directories of applets by category of use.

Adding a Java applet

1. Place the cursor where the Java content should appear on the page.

2. Click the **Java** icon from the Objects palette, or select **Insert** and then choose **Applet**.

3. A dialog box appears that prompts you for the name of the plug-in source file (see Figure 9.4), which should always end with a .class extension. If it ends with .java, it's very likely to be the source code for the applet, and it won't work in the user's browser. Enter the name, or use the **Browse** button to locate the file by hand. Click **OK** when you've selected the file.

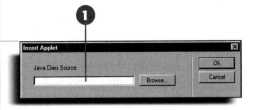

FIGURE 9.4

The Insert Applet dialog box for Java applets.

① The applet's class file

4. Make any changes to the plug-in through the Properties Inspector (see Figure 9.5). The basic settings are similar to a Shockwave movie, with a couple of differences. As with the Shockwave movies, including an alternate image is a good idea for incompatible browsers.

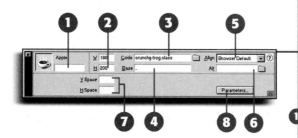

FIGURE 9.5
The Java applet Properties Inspector.

1. Name: A name to use for scripting applications

2. The size of the applet on the page (required)

3. The name of the Java applet class file

4. Path to the class file

5. Alignment of the applet in relation to surrounding text

6. An alternate image for browsers that don't support applets

7. Extra space for padding around the applet

8. Click this button to define additional parameters, depending on the applet

Adding ActiveX Content

ActiveX controls are Microsoft's answer to plug-ins, except their use is generally limited to Microsoft Internet Explorer on Windows 95/NT computers. There is some ActiveX content available for the Macintosh version of Internet Explorer, but it is by far in the minority. Essentially, ActiveX serves the same purpose as a plug-in—it extends the capability of a browser without releasing a new version of the browser. An ActiveX control is different from a plug-in in one important aspect, however. If someone loads a page with an ActiveX control not supported by her browser, the browser will automatically install the needed software. This is compared to plug-ins, where the user must seek out and install the software by hand.

Other than the convenience issue, the two items essentially serve the same purpose, and are installed in essentially the same way.

Adding ActiveX content

1. Place the cursor where the ActiveX content should appear on the page.

 2. Click the **ActiveX** icon from the Objects palette, or select **Insert** and choose **ActiveX**.

3. Unlike a Shockwave movie, Netscape plug-in, or Java applet, you're not prompted for a source file. This is because ActiveX works in a slightly different manner, which also makes your life a little harder. Dreamweaver places an ActiveX icon on the page, and then changes the Properties Inspector to its ActiveX display (see Figure 9.6).

FIGURE 9.6

The Properties Inspector for ActiveX content.

❶ The unique code that identifies the type of ActiveX control used

❷ Where to find the ActiveX control if it's not installed on the user's computer

❸ Specifies the data file that holds the ActiveX content; depending on the type of ActiveX control, this may not be used

❹ Information for a plug-in version of the ActiveX content

❺ An image to display if the browser doesn't support plug-ins

4. The first and most important piece of information is the ClassID. This code uniquely identifies the type of ActiveX content used. Three class ids are predefined for Dreamweaver—the two types of Shockwave movies and one for RealAudio. If you're using another type of control, you'll need to enter the code by hand.

5. The Base field is similar to the PlgSrc field for plug-ins. If the ActiveX control isn't installed on the user's computer, the browser will automatically attempt to install the control at the location specified in Base.

6. If your content uses a data file, then enter its location in the Data field. Some ActiveX content, such as Shockwave movies, doesn't use this field, and instead uses a generic parameter to send the data to the control. You'll need to check your specific situation for the type of content you're using.

7. The Embed and Src fields are used to supply optional information for a plug-in. If your special content is available as both a plug-in or ActiveX, you enter the content as ActiveX, include the plug-in information in these two fields, and the user will get the picture whether he or she is using Internet Explorer or Navigator.

ActiveX content and the controls that make it work are a unique and convenient way for your readers to experience multimedia content. Their only downside is their relative complexity to include on the Web page. You'll need to decide for yourself whether you want to use plug-ins, ActiveX, or both.

Other Methods of Adding Multimedia Content

Some forms of multimedia and specialized content, such as animated GIF images, are easy to add—it's the same as adding an image.

Adding an image

1. Position the cursor in the page where the image should appear. In my page, I want a picture appearing at the beginning of the last paragraph.

2. Click the **Image** icon on the Objects palette. In the box, type the filename of the image to use if it's contained within your site, or click **Browse** to navigate to another location.

3. My picture is located outside the current site, so I had to browse to it. Since Dreamweaver likes to keep birds of a feather together, it prompts to copy the file to the current site. The original file is left in place.

4. If you have to copy the file, you'll be given the opportunity to pick the specific location and filename within the site where it will be located. When you've made these choices, click **OK** at the Insert Image dialog box to finish.

5. The image is inserted into the page and selected for further manipulation if needed.

For more information on adding and formatting images, see Chapter 7, "Adding and Changing Images."

There are other items that like to consume the entire browser at once, or actually launch an application external to the browser.

Examples of these include some of the specialty document viewers like Adobe Acrobat, and some movie viewers such as QuickTime.

Loading this type of content into your Web page is similar to creating a hyperlink, with one important nuance—the name of the file. Check out step 2 below.

SEE ALSO
➤ *Learn how to create hyperlinks, page 81*

Working with multimedia outside the page

1. Click and drag over the text that will become the link to the special content.
2. In the Link field of the Properties window, type the path and filename of the content. Note that the content won't have an .html or .htm file extension, but whatever extension is appropriate for the type of file it is.
3. The text is formatted in blue with an underline to indicate it as a hyperlink. You may want to include some explanation with the hyperlink to indicate that it's pointing to special content and not to another HTML page.

However you include multimedia and other specialized content, the extra pizzazz should provide a special attraction to keep your reader's attention at your site.

From Here...

- Adding static pictures to your page is covered in Chapter 7, "Adding and Changing Images."
- Learn how to reuse any part of a Web page, including multimedia, in Chapter 8, "Reusable Parts for Web Pages."
- Learn to create an imagemap from your images in Chapter 11, "Setting up Imagemaps."
- Learn how to add multimedia and interactivity without specialized plug-ins, controls, or applets in the seven chapters of Part IV, "Adding Interactivity and Scripts."

What happens when a user clicks on the hyperlink?

There are two possible outcomes, depending on the browser. First, if the browser doesn't recognize the content, it will probably generate an error message that says so. Older browsers may also try to display the contents of the file as text, which could lead to a lot of garbage on the user's screen.

If the browser does recognize the content, the content will completely occupy the browser without any of the trappings of a normal HTML page. For some content, such as VRML, there are even additional buttons and controls that can be added. For other types, such as portable documents like Adobe Acrobat, the browser becomes a special document viewer.

If the content doesn't provide a method to move on to a regular HTML page, the user will probably have to use the **Back** button on his browser to get out of it.

Using Forms

How to add a blank form to your page

How to configure your form to work with your server

How to add components (like text fields and buttons) to your pages

What Are Forms?

A form is a collection of user interface elements in a Web page. What's a user interface element? Basically, it's something on the page with which the user can interact: text fields that the user can use to type out a message, boxes that users can check (or not check) in response to true-or-false questions, pop-up menus that offer the user a list of choices, buttons that the user can push, and so on.

Under ordinary circumstances, forms are used to gather feedback from visitors to a Web site. The visitor enters some data into the form, or checks a few boxes, and clicks a button to submit the information in the form to a form-handling CGI program Web server. The CGI processes the information by zinging it off in an email message or storing it in a database, and the user moves on to a new page. Figure 10.1 shows this kind of data-gathering form: visitors to a printer's Web site fill out a questionnaire-style form and send the results to the printer's marketing department.

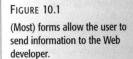

FIGURE 10.1

(Most) forms allow the user to send information to the Web developer.

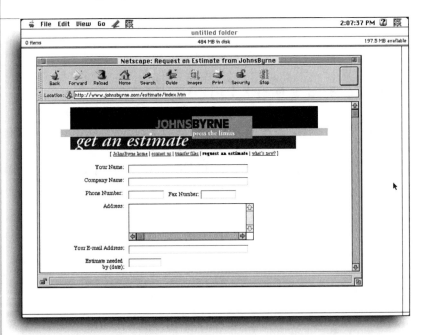

There are a few special uses for forms that don't necessarily involve sending information to the server. Because form elements were designed for interactions with users, they make a very handy "front end," or user interface, for JavaScripts and VBScripts that require user input. One common example of a form that doesn't send data is shown in Figure 10.2. The Fitness Online (http://www.fitnessonline.com) site uses drop-down list form elements as a navigation tool; the user simply picks an area of the site from the drop-down list, and a JavaScript redirects the browser to the new page based that selection. (This approach allows the developer to add and remove items from the navigation tool without redesigning a navigation bar with every change. It's also a very compact little navigation system compared to an ordinary navigation bar.)

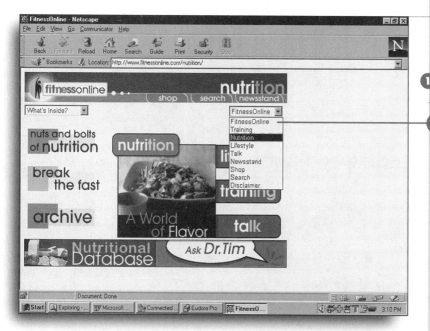

FIGURE 10.2

Some forms act as an interface between users and scripts.

1 Drop-down list form element

Dreamweaver isn't particular about how you use your form; you can use it to send data, or attach scripts to form elements as you like. In either case, form elements are added to the page in pretty much the same way that images, applets, and other page elements are added. Form elements are objects with properties that can be adjusted via the Properties palette. If the form will transmit data to the server, an invisible framework (called simply a "form") must be added to organize the form elements.

Understanding the Forms Palette

Because Dreamweaver treats form elements like other kinds of page elements, it's not too surprising to find that the basic form tools are found in the Objects palette.

Putting the Objects palette into form-building mode

1. Make sure that the Objects palette is visible. If not, choose **Windows** and then select **Objects**. (If you're not sure, pull down the Windows menu and make sure that Windows, Objects is checked. If it is checked, the window is on your screen somewhere.)

2. Click the palette mode pop-up menu at the top of the Objects palette. (See Figure 10.3 to see what the menu looks like.) Chose **Forms** from the pop-up menu.

When you're finished, the Objects palette should like the screen in Figure 10.3.

Adding an Empty Form to Your Page

Sending data the hard way

It's not completely impossible to transfer form data to a server without a form object; for instance, you could use the JavaScript `submit()` method to send data to an address that's decided on-the-fly.

Dreamweaver uses form objects to store information about where the form's data is to be sent. It's possible to add form objects (like text boxes and buttons) to a page that doesn't contain an empty form, but it is difficult and impractical to send form data to a server when there is no form object on the page.

Adding a blank form to the page

1. Click the **Insert Form** tool in the Tools palette.

2. Make sure that the Properties palette is in Forms mode—it should display the form label and icon on its left side, as it does in Figure 10.3. If the palette isn't in Forms mode, click inside the form's red dashed border.

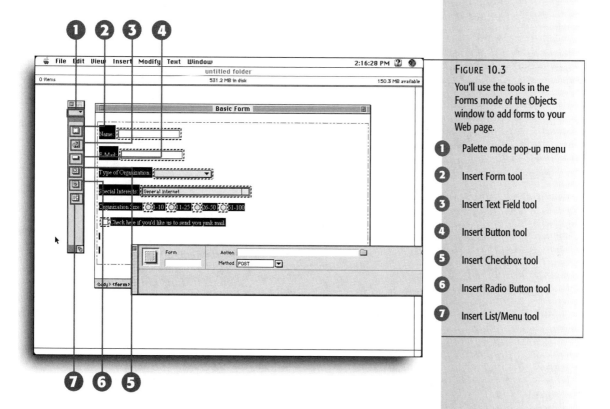

FIGURE 10.3

You'll use the tools in the Forms mode of the Objects window to add forms to your Web page.

❶ Palette mode pop-up menu

❷ Insert Form tool

❸ Insert Text Field tool

❹ Insert Button tool

❺ Insert Checkbox tool

❻ Insert Radio Button tool

❼ Insert List/Menu tool

3. Enter `http://hoohoo.ncsa.uiuc.edu/cgi-bin/query` in the Action field of the Properties palette. You'll replace this URL with a URL specific to your site in the "Configuring the Form" section later in this chapter.

4. Make sure that the Method field is set to GET. If necessary, you'll adjust this value in the "Configuring the Form" section.

Dreamweaver uses a red dashed-border box (like the one in Figure 10.4) to designate form objects. The box is for your editing convenience only; it will not appear in the final HTML page.

Remember, URLs are always subject to change

`http://hoohoo.ncsa.uiuc.edu/cgi-bin/query` is the URL of an NCSA-sponsored CGI that anyone can use to test forms. The CGI has remained at the same address for years, but it's possible that it may move or cease to exist.

FIGURE 10.4

Dreamweaver uses a dashed red line to show the borders of a form.

1 Form border

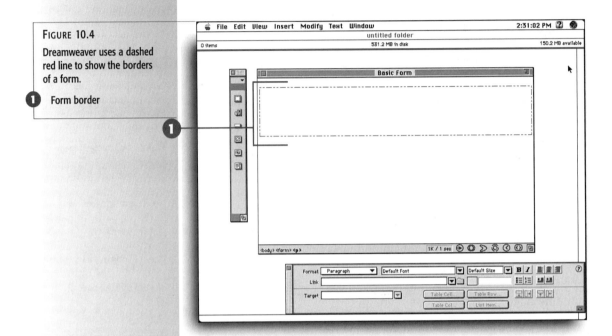

You can put just about anything inside the boundaries of a form object: form elements, of course, as well as text, images, tables, and just about every other kind of object. Simply position the cursor inside the form object and add the element as you normally would—start typing to add text, use Insert, Image to add a picture, and so on. The boundaries of the form object will expand to accommodate anything that you add.

There is one object you can't put inside a form—another form. You can't nest one form inside another, just as you shouldn't nest <form></form> tags when you're writing HTML by hand.

Adding Buttons to the Form

There are three basic flavors of form element buttons:

- Submit buttons send the content of the form that contains the button to the address specified in the form's ACTION parameter.

- Reset buttons cause the values of all of the form elements in the button's form to revert to the values that the elements had when the form was loaded.

- Generic buttons have no built-in behavior. Generic buttons are useful as triggers for scripts.

Ordinarily, buttons are added to the bottom of a form. We're going to add the buttons first, though, so that we can test the other form elements as we add them to the page.

Adding buttons to your form

1. Click inside the form's red-dashed border. (You'll know you're inside when the Properties palette displays the Form label and icon on its left side.)

2. Click the **Insert Button** tool in the Objects palette. Dreamweaver adds a new button at the insertion point.

3. Make sure the **New** button is selected. If the button isn't selected, select it.

4. Take a look at the Action field in the Properties palette. By default, the Submit form radio button is selected. Click **Reset form** to change the button to a reset button. (Traditionally, reset buttons are laid out to the left of submit buttons.)

5. Note the button's name in the field in the bottom-left corner of the Properties palette. By default, the button is named Reset. That's a fine, descriptive name for the button; unless you have a compelling reason to name it something else, leave this value as it is.

6. Note that the button's Label field in the Properties palette is set to Reset. Select the contents of this field, and type in a new label: Clear, or, if you're feeling creative, a name of your own devising. As soon as you press the **Enter** (on Macintosh, **Return**) key, or click in another field or window, Dreamweaver updates the button with the new label.

7. Click inside the form object's border to the right of the button you just created.

8. Click the **Insert Button** tool in the Objects palette. Dreamweaver adds a second button, labeled submit, to the right of the first button. Make sure that the button is selected.

9. Note the button's name—Submit—displayed in the bottom-left corner of the Properties palette. Again, this is a perfect name as is. Don't change the name without a good reason.

10. Check the button's Label field in the Properties palette. (If all is well, it should contain the word Submit.) Replace this with Send Data, or a label of your own.

   At this point, your page should look pretty much like Figure 10.5. It's not very interesting, but it actually works.

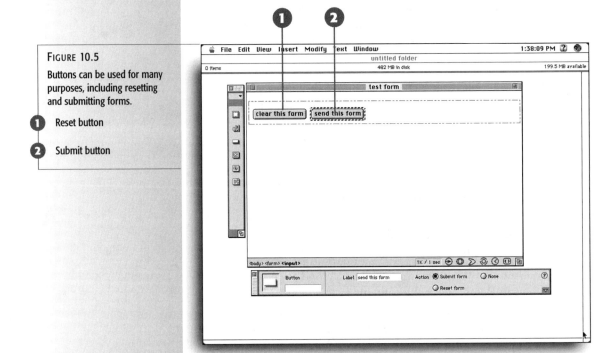

FIGURE 10.5

Buttons can be used for many purposes, including resetting and submitting forms.

❶ Reset button

❷ Submit button

11. Save your work.

12. Preview the form in a browser. Press **F12** to see the page in your preferred browser, or pick a browser by selecting **File**, and then choosing the **Preview** submenu.

13. Click the **Send** button in the browser window. (I'm referring to the Submit button you just created as part of your form, not one of the browser's own built-in buttons.) The browser will connect to the NCSA URL that you set up in the previous section, "Adding an Empty Form to Your Page." (If you didn't work through the previous section, this form test won't work.)

It may take a minute or two for the test CGI at NCSA to reply to your request. Once your request has been processed, your browser will be redirected to a follow-up page that looks something like Figure 10.6. NCSA's test CGI creates a simple page that reports what the browser submitted. You can see that the browser sends a value for the Submit button—specifically, the button's label—and ignores the Reset button completely.

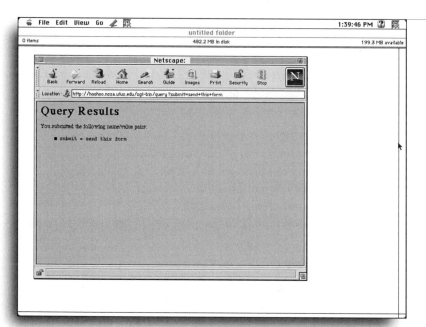

FIGURE 10.6

NCSA's test CGI returns a simple report that shows the form data sent by the browser.

Adding Text Fields to the Form

A text field is simply an empty box that accepts text. Text fields can contain just about any kind of text data, from short strings—like names and credit card numbers—to long blocks of text, such as guest book entries.

The labels in Figure 10.7 (Name, Credit Card Number, and Postal Address) are not really part of the text field form objects. Rather, they are ordinary text I added in the ordinary way—by typing them in at the insertion point. Also notice that I have used a table to make everything line up neatly; the table is there for purely aesthetic reasons, and is not necessary for the proper functioning of the form. To find out more about using tables to organize your forms, see Chapter 14, "Refining Page Layout Using Tables."

There are three basic flavors of text boxes:

- Single-line boxes, such as the name field in Figure 10.7, which accept a single line of text.
- Password boxes, such as the credit card field in Figure 10.7, also contain a single line of text. When the user enters information into a password box in the browser, the contents of the password box are hidden, so that any hooligans walking by can't read the password.
- Multi-line boxes, such as the credit card field in Figure 10.7, are large rectangular text fields equipped with scroll bars. The user can type as much information as desired in a multi-line box.

Let's add some text boxes to the form. In order to stay focused on the mechanics of text boxes, we'll skip the table, but you can certainly structure your form with a table, if you like. (Be sure to start with the form that you created in the previous sections of this tutorial, so that you can test your text boxes once you've created them.)

Adding text boxes

1. Click with the cursor to position the insertion point to the left of the buttons you created in the previous steps in this chapter.
2. Type a label for your text box. I've used "Name:" in the figures. Style the label as desired.
3. Click the **Insert Text Field** tool in the Objects palette. Dreamweaver adds a new text field at the insertion point.

4. Make sure that the new text field is selected. If the field isn't selected, click it with the mouse.

5. Note the text field's name in the bottom-left corner of the Properties palette. By default, the field will be named Textfield; this is a bad, non-descriptive name that should be replaced with a name that describes the contents of the field. Select the contents of this field, and replace it with userName.

6. Take a look at the Char Width and Max Chars fields in the Properties palette. Char Width sets the size of the text box, but does not affect the number of characters the user can type into the box. Max Chars sets a limit on the number of characters the user can enter into the box, but does not affect the box's size. You can experiment with these values if you like, but the default settings are perfectly appropriate for the form's Name field.

7. If you like, enter a value (such as "Your name here.") into the Init Val field of the Properties palette. The message in the Init Val field will be displayed in the field when the form is loaded, and will be restored if the user resets the form with the reset button.

8. Click to the right of the new text field to position the insertion point. Press **Enter** (on a Macintosh, **Return**) to start a new line, and type a label for the second text box. I've used "Credit Card Number:" as the label in the figures.

9. Click the **Insert Text Field** tool in the Objects palette. Dreamweaver adds a new text field at the insertion point. Make sure that the new text field is selected.

10. Enter a descriptive name for the new text field in the Name field at the bottom-left of the Properties palette. I suggest cardNumber.

11. Click the **Password** radio button in the Properties palette. There's no immediate feedback that shows you that the text field is now in password mode; you'll check it in the browser later.

12. Click to the right of the new text field to position the insertion point. Press **Enter** (on a Macintosh, **Return**) to start a new line, and type a label for the third and final text box. I've used "Postal Address:" as the label for this box.

Naming form elements

In theory, you can give a text field a name that consists of two or more words: user name, visitor name, or whatever. Dreamweaver won't stop you from giving a form element a multi-word name. However, it may cause problems for the CGI program that processes the form. Just to be on the safe side, it's best to remove the spaces from form element names: use userName or username, rather than user name.

13. Click the **Insert Text Field** tool in the Objects palette. Dreamweaver adds a new text field at the insertion point. Make sure that the new text field is selected.

14. Enter a descriptive name for the new text field in the name field at the bottom left of the Properties palette. I suggest `postalAddress`.

15. Click the **Multi Line** radio button in the Objects palatte. Dreaweaver will resize the text box and add scrollbars to its top and right sides.

At this point, your page should look roughly like Figure 10.7. (Remember, however, that you didn't add a table, so the alignment of the boxes won't look quite the same.) Now, let's test the results in the browser.

16. Save your work.

17. Press **F12** to preview the form in your primary browser, or or pick a browser by selecting **File**, and then choosing the **Preview** submenu.

18. Fill out the form: type in a name, a made-up credit card number (not your real credit card number!), and an address. When you're done, the results should look something like Figure 10.8. Use the submit button to send your form data to the browser.

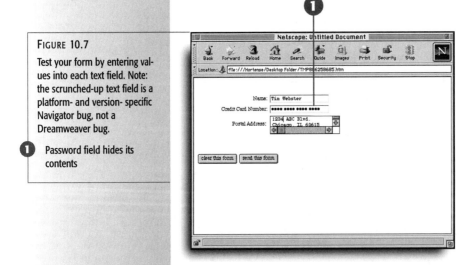

Again, it may take a minute or two before the test CGI responds. When it does, the results should look like Figure 10.8. The CGI returns a summary of everything the user (in this case, you) typed into the form's text boxes.

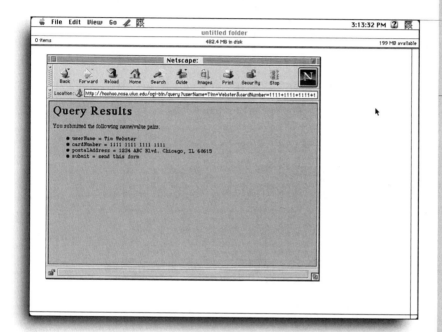

FIGURE 10.8

Once again, the NCSA CGI returns a simple report showing the data from the form.

Adding Lists or Menus to the Form

Both lists and pop-up menus allow the user to select values from a limited set of choices. Lists display many items from the list all at once, and allow the user to pick more than one item from the list. Menus display one item at a time, and allow the user to select only one item from the list. Figure 10.9 shows how lists and menus appear in Dreamweaver.

Lists and menus share a common insertion tool in the Objects palette, because the core procedure for creating a set of options is exactly the same for both kinds of objects. In this section, we will start by creating two option sets, and then configure the first set as a list, and the second set as a menu. Be sure to build on the form that you've already started, so you can test the new form elements after you've added them.

FIGURE 10.9

Both menus and lists allow the
user to pick values from a limited set. Menus allow the user
to pick one item from the set;
lists allow the user to pick
multiple items.

1 Menu element

2 List element

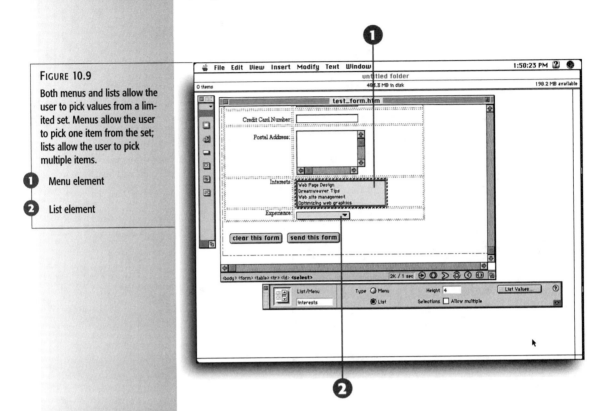

Adding lists and menus

1. Position the cursor to the right of the last form element you
   created, and press **Return** (**Enter** on a PC) to start a new
   line in the layout.

2. Click the **Insert List/Menu** tool in the Objects palette.
   Dreamweaver adds a new menu element at the insertion
   point.

3. Make sure the new menu element is selected. The menu
   should have a black dashed border, and the Properties
   palette should display a List/Menu label and icon. If the
   menu isn't selected, click it with the mouse.

4. Take a look at the menu's name in the bottom-left of the
   Properties palette. By default, the name is select:—replace
   this with a sensible name that describes the contents of the
   set of choices that the form component will contain. In this
   example, I've used the name "interests."

5. Click the **List Values...** button in the Properties palette. Dreamweaver displays the Initial List Values dialog box, shown in Figure 10.10.

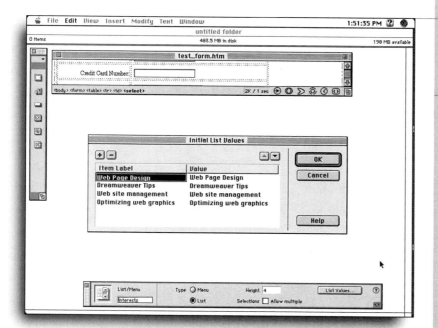

FIGURE 10.10

Use the Initial List Values dialog box to add user choices to the element.

6. Notice that the first line of the Item Label column is highlighted. Each entry in this column will appear in the list or menu element exactly as it appears here. I've used "Web Page Design" as the first label in the example list in the figure.

7. Press the **Tab** key. Dreamweaver highlights the first line in the Value column. The value entries won't show up when the form element is displayed; however, it is this value setting—rather than the label that appears in the display— that is sent as data when the form is submitted. Enter a value in the Value column; I've used "Web Page Design" for the Value column of the first line.

8. Click the plus button (**+**) to add a new line to the set of user choices.

9. Repeat steps 6 through 8 to add more items to the set of user choices. I've used the following values in the example:

```
Label     Value
Dreamweaver Tips     Dreamweaver Tips
Web Site Management     Web Site Management
Optimizing Web Graphics     Optimizing Web Graphics
```

10. Repeat steps 1 through 10 to create a second list/menu item. Give it the label Experience and the name experience, and use the following label/value pairs:

```
Label     Value
None     0
Some     1
Intermediate     2
Advanced     3
```

At this point, you've got two menu items on the your page. Next, you'll configure the first item as a list.

11. Click the item to select it.

12. Select the **List** radio button in the Properties palette.

13. Enter a value in the Height field. Because the set of user options you've built for this example contains four choices, enter 4 in this field.

14. Click the **Allow multiple** check box to activate it.

Once the list and menu are in place, you can test them using the same basic technique that you learned to test the text fields: save your work, preview the page in the browser, and submit the form.

Adding Radio Buttons to the Form

Functionally, radio buttons act just like menus; they allow the user to select a single item from a group of choices. Radio buttons are always added in sets of two or more; only one button in a given group can be selected at any time. Figure 10.11 shows one of many typical uses for radio buttons.

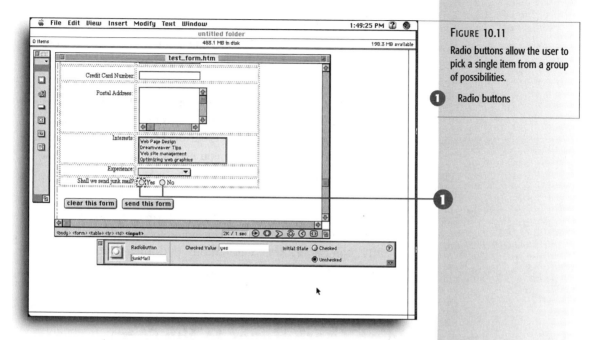

FIGURE 10.11

Radio buttons allow the user to pick a single item from a group of possibilities.

1 Radio buttons

Adding radio buttons to the form

1. Click with the mouse to position the insertion point where you'd like the radio button to appear.

2. Click the **Insert Radio Button** tool in the Objects palette to add the radio button at the insertion point.

3. Make sure that the new radio button is selected.

4. Give the radio button group a name by typing the name into the field at the bottom-left corner of the Properties palette. It's important that this name be descriptive of the entire group of radio buttons that the individual button belongs in; the name should not describe the individual button. In the sample form, I've used the name junkmail, rather a name like true or yes.

5. Enter a value in the radio button's Checked Value field in the Properties palette. The Checked Value is the text that will be sent to the CGI on the server-side if the button is checked when the form is submitted; thus, the Checked Value should describe the individual button, rather than the button's group. I've used true as the value in the example form.

Naming radio button groups

Always give the same name to all of the radio buttons within a particular group.

6. Type a label for the radio button at the insertion point. Style the text as you like. (If you prefer to have the button's label appear to the left of the radio button, perform this step before step 2.)

7. Repeat steps 1 through 6 as necessary to add buttons to the group. Be sure to give all the buttons in the group the same name (step 4), and give each button a unique Checked Value (step 5). For this example, you need only add one more button to the group—give it the name `junkmail` and the value `false`.

After adding two radio buttons to your form (with two passes through the previous), your form should look similar to Figure 10.11. You can test the radio buttons' performance in the usual way: save your work, preview the form in the browser, and submit the form to the NCSA test server.

Adding Check Boxes to the Form

Check boxes look a little bit like radio buttons, but they're quite different in the way that they behave. Individual check boxes are free agents; checking (or un-checking) one box won't affect any other check boxes (or anything else) in the same form. Check boxes are mostly useful for soliciting true/false- and yes/no-style answers from users.

Adding a check box

1. Position the insertion point where you'd like to add the check box.

2. Click the **Insert CheckBox** tool in the Objects palette.

3. Make sure that the new check box is selected. It should have a dashed border around it, and the Objects palette should display a CheckBox label and icon.

4. Give the check box a descriptive name by typing the name in the field at the bottom-left corner of the Properties palette. In the example, I've given the check box the name receipt.

5. Take a look at the Checked Value field; this is the text that
will be submitted to the form-processing software on the
server side if the check box is checked when the form is submitted. Give it a sensible value. (I've used true in the example.)

At this point, your form should look similar to Figure 10.12.
After you've added your check box, test the form in the usual
way: save, preview the form in a browser, and submit the form to
the NCSA test CGI.

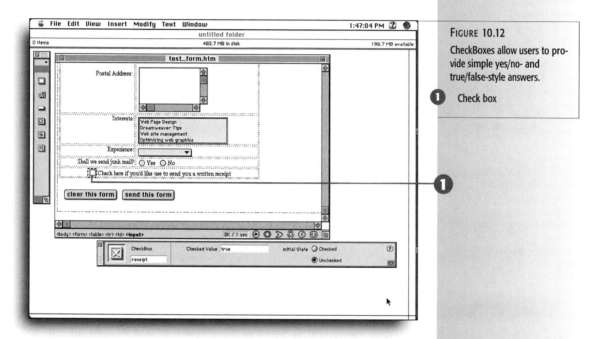

Configuring the Form

At this point, all of the components in your form are in place,
but the form isn't especially useful to you—all that it does is send
the user's data to a test CGI at a university somewhere in down-
state Illinois.

In order to send form data to a server-side machine for processing, the Web browser needs two important pieces of information:

- *The address to which the data should be sent.* The address that receives the data is ordinarily different from the address of the page that contains the form, although most often the two addresses are within the same domain, and often on the same machine.

- *The encoding method that's used to package the data.* The HTML standard provides two methods for packaging data to be sent from the browser to the server. Each method has its own advantages; we'll look at the details later in this section.

Most ISPs offer one or more form-handling CGI programs as part of their basic Web site hosting services; ask your Webmaster for the address that your form should use, and whether you should use GET or POST to encode form data.

There are two methods for sending data from a Web browser to a data-handling program on the server side: GET, which packs up the data as an extension to the program's URL address, and POST, which sends the data in a separate package.

You really don't need to know too much about the difference between these two methods, as long as you know which one the CGI program on your server uses. Check your software's documentation, or ask your Webmaster or ISP technical support staff. (If your program is a Perl script, the documentation may be inside the script itself, rather than in a separate documentation file. Open up the script with a text editor, and be sure to close the script without saving any changes.)

For the record, most folks agree that POST is the preferred method for sending data. GET imposes some limitations on the amount of form data that can be sent, and so isn't well-suited for long forms with lots of data.

Configuring the form for your site

1. Contact your Webmaster or ISP technical support staff, and ask for the URL of any ready-to-use CGI software on the server. If there's no ready-to-use software, ask for help in finding a package that's safe and compatible with your server.

2. Ask the technical support representative whether the CGI software (or the package that he or she recommends you install) accepts POST- or GET-encoded form data.

3. Ask your technical support representative if the form requires the use of any hidden fields. (If he or she doesn't know, take a look at the program's documentation.) If so, you'll want to read the following section, "Adding Hidden Fields."

4. Select your form by clicking the form's red-dashed border. When the form is selected, the Properties palette will display a Form icon and label.

5. Enter the URL you obtained in step 1 in the Properties palette's Action field. Be sure to type it in just as your tech person instructs.

6. Check the Method pop-up menu in the Properties palette, and make sure that it agrees with the advice that you received in step 2.

Once you've configured your form, you can go ahead and test it. However, it's unlikely that your form-handling CGI will simply return a summary of form data, as the NCSA CGI did; your CGI will probably send the form data to a particular email address, or stash it in a database. You'll need to know what your CGI is supposed to do before you can evaluate its performance.

Handling complicated URLs the easy way

If the URL of your CGI program is really complicated, have your technical support person email the address to you. Copy the URL from your email program's text window, and paste it into the Action field in the Dreamweaver Properties palette.

Adding Hidden Fields

Some form-handling CGIs require that your form contain information about the way the form data is to be processed. For instance, many programs that bundle form data into an email message will want to know the email address that will receive the data.

HTML offers a special kind of form component, called a hidden field. Hidden fields have names and values, just like other form components. However, the value of a hidden field is fixed and can't be changed by the reader. As their names suggest, hidden fields are invisible, and don't appear in the form. When the form is submitted by the user, the browser sends along the hidden field names and values with the rest of the form data.

The last selection on the Forms Object palette is used to add hidden fields to forms. Let's say that your form requires that you include a hidden field with the name RECIPIENT_ADDRESS and an email address as a value. We'll use the fictitious address `bitbucket@null.com` as our email address value.

Click on the Insert Hidden Field, or select Insert, Form Object, Hidden Field. The Properties plaette has two fields—one for the name, and one for the value. Using my example, Dreamweaver will generate this HTML for the hidden field :

```
<input TYPE = "hidden" NAME = "RECIPIENT_ADDRESS" VALUE =
"bitbucket@null.com">
```

A hidden field can occur anywhere in the form, and is marked with a yellow shield with an "H" for the crest. You can also use Dreamweaver to insert form elements that may be custom to your system, or perhaps haven't been invented yet.

Adding a custom field

1. Open the HTML window by selecting **Window**, and then choosing **HTML**, or press **F10**.

2. Find the opening <FORM> tag. If the form has been configured, it probably has NAME, ACTION, and METHOD parameters, so it's more than just the word <FORM>.

3. Insert the HTML for the input within the <FORM> tag. The format is the same as the HTML for the hidden field, but will have a different value for type.

4. Close the HTML window.

Finding the <FORM> tag

If you can't find the **<FORM>** tag right away, launch your external editor with the HTML window's **External Editor...** button, and use your editor's search function.

Once the custom element is added to the HTML, you can edit with a Dreamweaver Properties palette by clicking on the element on the form. The palette will include a new field to handle the custom input type, plus fields for the name and default value. Additional attributes are added through the Parameter buttom.

Providing Your Own Form-Handling CGI

If your ISP doesn't have some sort of form-handling CGI set up already, ask your Webmaster or technical support representative for advice about how to proceed. There are a lot of details to figure out.

There are plenty of freeware, shareware, and inexpensive-ware form-handling CGI scripts and programs available for download on the Web. In most cases, scripts and programs are platform specific; even Perl scripts, which are fairly portable between platforms, will probably need some adjustments before they can be used on a Windows- or MacOS-based server.

If you're a programmer, or you've got money for a consultant, retrofitting CGI scripts isn't too tough or time-consuming. It's also possible to write your own scripts from scratch, although doing so is probably an enormous waste of time, unless you have special needs (like a custom database) that ready-made scripts can't address.

Your ISP probably has some policy about what kind of software you can run on the server-side, and, in any case, you'll need to know some details—the operating system platform of the server, for instance, whether or not the server has a Perl interpreter, and so on. Understand that running a CGI script can affect the performance and security of the server, and that there may be very compelling reasons for seemingly restrictive ISP policies about CGI programs.

From Here...

- To add a script that validates the form (checks it for errors), see Chapter 20, "Validating Forms."

Setting up Imagemaps

What an imagemap is

The difference between server-side and client-side imagemaps

How to add hotspots to an imagemap

How to set up links between imagemaps and URLs

How to create a server-side imagemap with Dreamweaver

What Is an Imagemap?

Hypertext—the technology that is the soul of the Web—allows the developer to connect words or characters on one Web page with other pages, addresses, or resources. An imagemap is a kind of hyperimage: imagemaps allow you to connect portions of an image on a Web page to other pages, addresses, or resources. The important word in the previous sentence is "portions"— within a single image, different parts of the image may point to different resources.

Figure 11.1 shows an imagemap from the widely used Infoseek search engine page, http://www.infoseek.com. The page's navigation toolbar, which looks like a set of adjacent buttons, is really a single wide GIF image. Even though the navigation bar is built from a single piece, clicking different parts of the bar—specifically, on the different buttons—sends the browser to different parts of the Infoseek site.

FIGURE 11.1

Imagemaps are often used to create navigation tools, like this navigation bar on the Infoseek home page.

1 Imagemap-based navigation bar

Imagemaps don't necessarily need to be an orderly array of rectangular buttons. For instance, take a look at Figure 11.2, which shows an imagemap from the Internet Underground Music Archive site. (You can find the page shown at http://www.iuma.com/IUMA-2.0/brew/; of course, the image or the whole page may change or disappear before you read this.) The buttons on the IUMA imagemap are elliptical, and arranged in an irregular pattern.

FIGURE 11.2
Imagemaps can include
elliptical or complex shapes.

Reckoning Imagemap Coordinates

All imagemaps are based on the concept of hotspots. A hotspot is merely a geometrical description of a region within an image—for instance, the coordinates of the top-left and bottom-right corners of a rectangular region, or a list of the coordinates of all the vertices of a polygonal region—and a URL associated with region.

To see how this works, take a look at Figure 11.3. The outer rectangle represents an image that is 400 pixels wide by 200 pixels tall. The image contains a square hotspot that's 100 pixels long on each side. We measure coordinates within the image using the top-left corner as the (0,0) point; x and y values (horizontal and vertical distances) increase from left-to-right and top-to-bottom. Thus, the top-left corner of the square hotspot in the figure has the coordinates (200,50), and the bottom-right corner of the hotspot has the coordinates (300,150).

FIGURE 11.3

Hotspots are described using the geometrical coordinates of the hotspot's vertices.

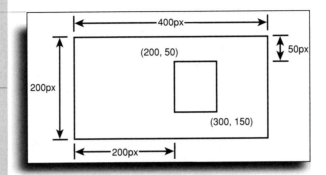

Similar coordinate-based systems are used to define round and polygonal hotspots. You don't really need to know how to define hotspot regions by hand; most folks don't. You can use Dreamweaver to create hotspots with simple Adobe Illustrator/Macromedia Freehand-style drawing tools, and Dreamweaver will create the coordinate hotspot sets for you.

Server-Side Versus Client-Side Imagemaps

The current version of the HTML standard defines two different kinds of imagemaps: server-side and client-side. From the perspective of a visitor to your site, there's not much difference between the two kinds of imagemaps, but from the developer's point of view, there are a few important differences.

Server-Side Imagemaps

Server-side imagemaps were the first "official" implementation of imagemaps, and it's the only kind of map that certain early browsers support. There probably aren't a lot of folks out surfing with Netscape Navigator 1.1 or Mosaic 1.0, but be aware that there is a small segment of the Internet audience that can only read server-side maps.

As the name suggests, server-side imagemaps rely on resources running on a Web server to function. When a user clicks the imagemap, the user's Web browser sends the coordinates of the mouse click to a URL specified within the image's <IMG> tag. The program or script at the URL compares the click coordinates with a map file that contains geometric descriptions of the image's hotspots. If the map-handling program on the server-side calculates that the mouse click falls within one of the image's hotspots, it sends the browser instructions to load a new page.

In a server-side imagemap system, the coordinate definitions are stored on the server, rather than within the HTML document that contains the image. Also, most of computing horsepower is supplied by a machine on the server end; the computer running the Web browser doesn't need to figure out whether or not the mouse click falls within a hotspot. This system isn't the most efficient use of resources, because the machine the browser is running on is usually a perfectly good computer that can do geometry on its own. Furthermore, the server-side system requires two small transfers over the network that aren't necessary if the browser does its own figuring.

Because client-side imagemaps are much more efficient, they are more widely used than server-side maps. In fact, Dreamweaver does not directly support the use of server-side maps. Unfortunately, there are still a fair number of folks out there who are still using browsers that can only handle server-side maps, so if you want to guarantee that your pages are compatible with Lynx and the first few versions of Netscape and MSIE, you must use a server-side map. You can add server-side maps to your pages using Dreamweaver's HTML-editing features, but there are no handy WYSIWYG tools for server-side maps.

Client-Side Imagemaps

Client-side imagemaps were introduced to provide snappier imagemap performance on the user end, and reduce loads on the server end. There's very little reason for a modern desktop computer to ship off a geometry problem to another machine to solve, especially when the other machine may receive hundreds of such requests every minute.

In a client-side imagemap system, the geometrical data that describes an imagemap's hotspots is stored in the HTML file that contains the map. When the user clicks with the mouse inside the imagemap, the browser calculates which hotspot, if any, encompasses the click. If the browser finds a matching hotspot, it loads the associated URL immediately.

Adding a Map to Your Page

You can make an imagemap from any GIF or JPEG file you like. You can find the GIF image file I used in this chapter at www.mcp.com/info.

Download the image file using Netscape Navigator or Internet Explorer

1. Load the page www.mcp.com/info or the mirror page at http://www.orbis-tertius.com/dreamweaver/ch11step.htm.

2. If you're using a Macintosh, click the image and hold the mouse down until a contextual menu appears. If you're using a Windows machine, right-click the image.

3. If you're using Netscape, choose **Save Image As** from the contextual menu. If you're using Internet Explorer, choose **Save Picture As**.

4. Your browser will present a standard file dialog box. Save the file in a convenient place on your hard disk. I named the file HXO.gif, but you may name it as desired.

5. Use the **Add Image** tool in Dreamweaver's Object palette to add the image to your layout.

6. Click the newly-added image to select it.

7. Click the **Map** button in the Properties palette. Dreamweaver presents the Image Map Editor dialog box.

If you're working with the sample image from the Web site, you should see something very much like Figure 11.4 on your screen.

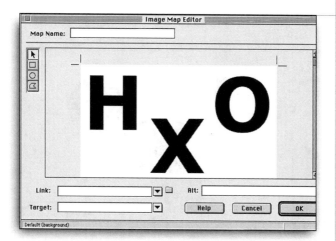

FIGURE 11.4
Use the Image Map Editor dialog box to add imagemaps to your Web site.

Drawing and Editing Hotspots

Once you have your image open in the Image Map Editor, you can start drawing hotspots for the image. There are three basic kinds of hotspot shapes: rectangle, circle, and polygon. Each basic shape has its own drawing tool in the Image Map Editor window.

Let's draw shapes for each of the letterforms in HXO.gif. The letter H is pretty square, so we'll use the rectangle tool to draw the H's hotspot.

Draw a rectangular hotspot

1. Click the rectangle tool at the left side of the dialog box to select the tool.

2. Note that the arrow pointer cursor has turned into a pair of crosshairs. Position the crosshairs at the top-left corner of the letter H.

3. Drag the mouse from the top-left corner of the H to the bottom-right corner. Dreamweaver will display a thin border around the hotspot as you draw, and, when you release the mouse, Dreamweaver reverses the colors within the hotspot. (See Figure 11.5)

FIGURE 11.5

Use the rectangle tool to draw square hotspots.

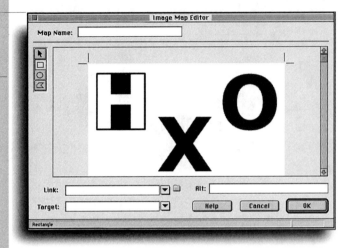

A little cushion room

It's usually a good idea to add a few extra pixels of hotspot around the button's shape in the image.

Naturally, the circle tool is most appropriate for shapes like the O letterform.

Draw a round hotspot

1. Select the circle tool from the left-side of the dialog box window.

2. Dreamweaver turns the arrow cursor into a crosshairs cursor. Position the crosshairs right in the center of the letter O.

3. Drag the mouse down in any direction you like. (You can change directions in mid-drag, if necessary.) Dreamweaver draws a border around the hotspot as you drag. Stop when the hotspot covers the whole letter. The results should look something like Figure 11.6.

FIGURE 11.6
Use the circle tool to draw round hotspots.

The polygon tool is best for irregular shapes, like the letter X.

Draw a polygon hotspot

1. Select the polygon tool from the left side of the dialog box window.

2. Dreamweaver replaces the arrow cursor with a pair of crosshairs. Position the crosshairs at the top-left edge of the X, right above and to the left its top left vertex.

3. Click the mouse button and release.

4. Move the crosshairs clockwise towards the next vertex of the X. You'll see that Dreamweaver draws a thin border between the point where you first clicked and the crosshairs; as you move the mouse, the line moves with it.

5. When the mouse is over the next vertex, click the mouse button. Dreamweaver sets down an anchor at the point where you click; the first segment of the polygon will be fixed in place.

6. Move the mouse pointer to the next vertex. Note that the current segment of the polygon follows the cursor. Click when the crosshairs are over the next vertex of the X's shape.

7. Continue tracing the X's shape, clicking each vertex.

What if you want an oval?

Unfortunately, it's the *circle* tool, not the *oval* tool. Very often you an use the rectangle tool to handle an oval button—after all, who cares if the user clicks slightly outside the button's border? (Now that I think about it, I probably know a few people who would care.)

If you have several oval buttons all in close proximity, you may not be able to use rectangles to define the buttons' hotspots. You can use the polygon tool (described later) to create a pretty good approximation of an oval.

You don't need to follow the line exactly

You don't need to move the mouse along the edge of the X's shape; as long as the cursor finds its way over the next vertex of the polygon, it doesn't matter where the cursor goes along the way.

8. When you have added an anchor on each vertex, position the cursor at the starting point. (Unless you're really fussy, you don't need to put the cursor exactly where you started. As long as you're within 5 or 10 pixels of the start, you're fine.

9. Double-click to finish the polygon.

When you're done, the results should look like Figure 11.7.

FIGURE 11.7
Use the polygon tool to draw hotspots with complex shapes.

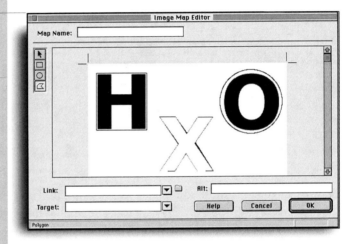

A blue border when viewed in browser

Most browsers add an ugly blue border around imagemaps. Unfortunately, you won't see the border until you preview the page in a browser; Dreamweaver doesn't show the blue border in the layout. To remove the border, select the image, and then enter 0 in the Border field of the Properties palette.

Editing and Removing Hotspot Shapes

Surprisingly, Dreamweaver 1.0 allows you very little control over hotspot shapes once you have drawn them. You can't reshape or resize rectangles or circles, for instance, and you can't reposition a polygon's individual vertices. It's likely that a future implementation of Dreamweaver will offer some sort of shape-editing features.

In the meantime, you can make two basic changes to a hotspot's geometry: you can move the whole hotspot without changing its shape or size, or you can delete it.

Editing hotspots

1. Select the arrow tool from the left side of the Image Map Editor window.

2. Click the shape to select it.

3. To move a shape, drag it with the mouse.

4. To remove a shape, press the **Delete** key while the shape is selected.

Assigning URLs and Targets to Hotspots

Once you have set a hotspot's shape, you're ready to set up a relationship between the hotspot and a URL. You can connect a hotspot to any kind of resource that can be described by a URL: a Web page, a CGI or database that creates dynamic pages, a mailto: address, a newsgroup, or whatever you like. As with an ordinary hypertext link, you can provide a target for the URL so that the resulting page is displayed in a particular frame or window.

Linking hotspots to URLs

1. Select the arrow tool at the left side of the Image Map Editor dialog box.

2. Click the hotspot over the letter H with the arrow tool to select the hotspot.

3. Enter the URL `http://www.dreamweaver.com` in the Image Map Editor dialog box's Link field.

4. Select **_blank** from the Target pop-up menu to cause the Dreamweaver home page to open in a new window.

5. Click the hotspot over the letter O with the arrow tool to select the hotspot.

6. Enter the URL `news://forums.macromedia.com/ macromedia.dreamweaver` in the Image Map Editor dialog box's Link field.

7. Click the hotspot over the letter X with the arrow tool to select the hotspot.

8. Enter the URL `mailto:bitbucket@alt.null` in the Image Map Editor dialog box's Link field.

Linking to a local page

You can use the folder-shaped browse button to quickly specify a page that's local to your site, just as you would if you were creating a hypertext link.

Creating a Server-Side Imagemap

Dreamweaver does not provide any handy visual tools for creating server-side imagemaps, but it's easy enough to do using Dreamweaver's HTML editor.

Before you start working with Dreamweaver, you'll need to prepare a .map file for the image. A .map file is simply a text file that describes the shape and URL for each hotspot in the map.

If you're a masochist, you can create your .map file by hand using a text editor. For a clear and concise description of the syntax of a .map file, see `http://hoohoo.ncsa.uiuc.edu/docs/tutorials/imagemapping.html`. There's no advantage to creating an imagemap by hand. Most folks prefer to use a .map-generating program. I've always liked mapedit, which you can find at `http://www.boutell.com/mapedit/`. Mapedit's interface is very similar to Dreamweaver's Image Map Editor dialog box described previously.

After you've created your map file, you're ready to create a server-side imagemap with Dreamweaver.

Creating a server-side imagemap

1. Ask your Webmaster or technical support person where the .map file is to be stored on the server. (The specifics vary widely, depending on the server software package.) Make a note of the map file's URL.

2. FTP the .map file to the address you received in step 1, using your preferred FTP software. Ask your Webmaster or techical support person if you need help with your FTP software.

3. In Dreamweaver, add the image to your Web page. Use the Add Image tool in the Object palette.

4. Click the image to select it.

5. Find the Link field in the Properties palette. Enter the URL you received in step 1 into the field.

6. Select **Window** and choose **HTML**, or press **F10**.

7. Find the `<img>` tag of the imagemap image. (The whole tag should be selected in the HTML window, as long as the image was selected in the Dreamweaver window when you executed step 6.

8. Add the parameter `ismap` to the image tag; simply type the word `ismap` in the tag's parameter list. The parameter does not take a value. As with any tag parameter, you may add `ismap` at any point in the list of parameters for the image tag; just make sure that you don't put it between another parameter and the parameter's value.

9. Close the HTML window.

Testing a server-side imagemap

You'll need an Internet connection and a running server to test a server-side imagemap; there's simply no way to test it on a local machine.

Structuring Pages with Tables, Frames, and Layers

CHAPTER 12

Building Tables

How to add a basic table to your page

How to figure and set the number of rows and columns
in a table

How to figure and set the width of a table

What is a Table?

When the <TABLE> tag was first introduced as a Netscape-sponsored HTML extension, its purpose seemed fairly narrow; <TABLE> (and its assistants <TR> and <TD>) would be used to display tabular data, such as the timetable shown in Figure 12.1. By "tabular data," we mean data—numbers, words, or whatever—structured in a set of regular rows and columns.

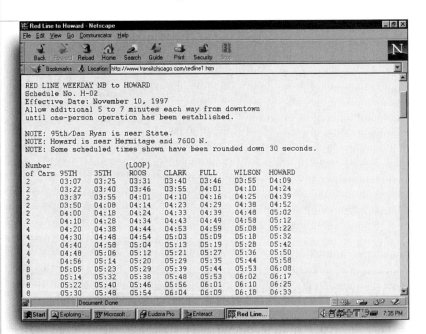

In the real world, tables are used for more than just tabular data. Many graphic designers soon discovered that tables could be used to refine page layout, too. HTML—especially early versions of the standard—offers very few tools to control the layout of a Web page; page elements simply flow from the left edge of the browser window to the right, and from the top edge to the bottom, like text in a word processor. Graphic designers discovered that tables could be used to create structural aids, such as page margins, columns, and to precisely align page elements.

Figure 12.2 shows a typical modern page that relies on tables to structure the page. At first glance, the page looks like a single huge GIF file; in fact, it consists of a set of many small GIFs and other elements created with HTML. The various parts of the page are aligned using <TABLE>.

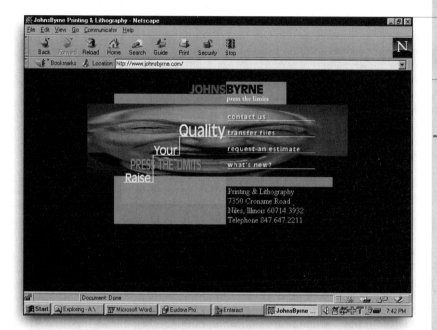

FIGURE 12.2

This complex layout looks like one big GIF image.

By showing the table borders, we can see the individual components that make up the layout. The precise alignment of this page isn't possible if we simply plunk down the page elements one after another; if the viewer resizes the browser window, the layout will fall apart. The <TABLE> tag holds the elements in their relative positions, no matter what size the browser window may be.

The dark side of tables

Some HTML experts feel that using tables to control layout is inappropriate. They argue that HTML should be used to structure documents that will display legibly on any Web-capable machine, from a PalmPilot with a tiny LCD screen to a cutting-edge Macintosh with a crisp 20-inch monitor. Unfortunately the complex use of tables is not compatible with all of these devices.

This is one of those endless, Kirk-versus-Picard debates that will be argued forever on the net, and we're not going to take sides. We will show you how to use Dreamweaver to structure your layout with <TABLE>, but it's up to you to decide whether you want to use tables or CSS. See Chapter 6, "Formatting Text with Style Sheets," for more information about formatting text with CSS.

As a kind of compromise, the Cascading Style Sheet specification promises to allow developers to tweak the page's layout without using HTML extensions like <TABLE>. Unfortunately, the majority of users just aren't ready for CSS, so tables are still widely used.

Understanding Basic Table Behavior

There are a few simple rules to remember when you put a table on your page:

- *Tables can nest.* In theory, you can put anything in a table cell, including another table. In practice, putting tables inside tables can cause some older browsers to crash. Nowadays, very few visitors to your site will have problems with nested tables, but don't say you weren't warned.

- *Tables are block items.* Most browsers treat tables as block, rather than inline items; this is really just a geeky way to say that browsers will put space above and below the table in the layout. Even if you don't specify a break in the text (with something like <br> or <p>), the browser will put the table on its own "line" in the browser window.

- *Tables resize.* Both tables and the individual cells that make up tables will grow to accommodate any content you put in them. If the table contains two side-by-side JPEGs that are each 500 pixels wide, your table will be at least 1000 pixels wide, even if you specified a smaller size for your table.

- *Tables affect perceived performance.* Some browsers (like Netscape Navigator 3.0) may wait until all of a table's contents are in transit from the server before displaying the table at all, especially if the table contains subtables or images without size parameters. As a result, improperly created table pages can seem to load very slowly. (Fortunately, Dreamweaver automatically adds size tags to any images it adds to the page.)

Adding a Simple Table to Your Page

Adding a table to your layout with Dreamweaver is as simple as adding an image or a rule.

Adding a basic table

1. Click the **Insert Table** tool in the Objects palette. Dreamweaver presents the Insert Table dialog box shown in Figure 12.3.

2. Adjust the values in the Rows and Columns fields of the Insert dialog box, if necessary. If you're not sure how many rows and columns you'll need, use the default values; you can change the number of rows and columns later, if you like. If you're not sure how to count the rows and columns of your table, see the "Specifying the Number of Rows and Columns in a Table" section later in this chapter.

3. Adjust the value in the Width field, if necessary. If you're not sure how wide you'd like the table to be, don't worry about it. You can fix it later. If you're not sure how the width specification works, see "Specifying the Size of a Table," later in this chapter.

4. Click **OK**. Dreamweaver adds the table to your layout at the insertion point.

Other ways to add tables

There's more than one way to bring up the Insert Table dialog box. The following methods are exactly equivalent to clicking the **Insert Table** tool:

- Choose **Insert** and choose **Table**.

- Press **Ctrl+Alt+T** (in Windows) or **[Cmd]+Shift+T** (for the Macintosh).

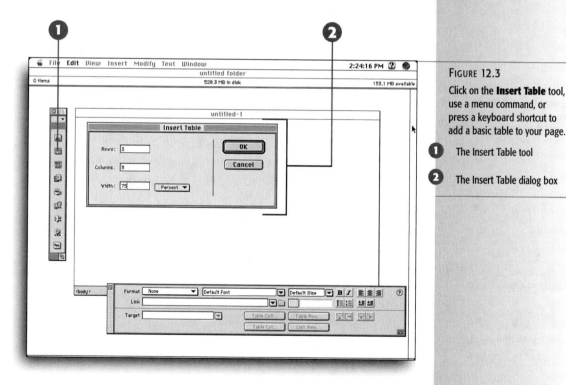

FIGURE 12.3

Click on the **Insert Table** tool, use a menu command, or press a keyboard shortcut to add a basic table to your page.

❶ The Insert Table tool

❷ The Insert Table dialog box

Working with Tables

Once you've got the table on your page, it's easy to add content or to change the table's appearance and behavior.

Adding Content

To enter data into a table cell, just click inside the cell with the cursor. Dreamweaver shows you that you're working on an individual cell by putting the insertion point inside the cell.

Don't fret about the size of the cell. If it's too small for your content, Dreamweaver (and the Web browser) will expand the cell and, if necessary, the table, to accommodate whatever you put into the cell.

Selecting a Table

How to select a table

1. Position the cursor over the left edge of the table. You'll know you're in the right place when the cursor changes from an I-beam/Insertion Point style cursor to an arrow-style cursor.

2. Click the left edge or top of the table with the arrow cursor.

There are several cues that will show you that the whole table (rather than part of the table) has been selected:

- The whole table, border and all, will be highlighted. (On most, but not all, machines, the highlights will be black and the table's colors will be reversed.) If only part of the table is selected, only the selected cell (and none of the border) will be highlighted.

- The Property palette will show a table icon on its left side, labeled with the word Table.

- The <table> tag in the readout at the bottom of the main window will be bolded.

Alternate table selecting techniques

There's more than one way to select a table. You may find it more convenient to select the table the same way you select characters of text: drag the cursor over the table with the mouse, or hold down the Shift key and use the arrows to move the cursor over the table.

If the cursor is already inside the table, you can select the table by clicking the <table> tag in the readout at the bottom of the window. Or, if it's handier, you can right-click the table (on a Macintosh, **Control+click**) and pick **Select Table** from the contextual menu that appears.

Altering Table Properties

The Dreamweaver Property palette provides a thorough list of table attributes. In most cases, if you want to change a table's appearance or behavior, it's easiest and most precise to simply enter the desired value in the appropriate field.

Figure 12.4 shows a close-up of an expanded Property palette in Table mode. Suppose you wish to change the three-row-by-three-column table in the example into a four-by-four table.

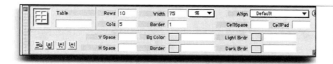

FIGURE 12.4

The Property palette allows you to alter many characteristics of a table.

Changing the numbers of rows and columns in a table

1. Select the number **3** in the Property palette's Rows field.
2. Enter the new value—in this example, 4—replacing the old value.
3. Select the number **3** in the Property palette's Columns field.
4. Enter the new value—in this example, 4—replacing the old value.

There's quite a bit more that you can change using Property palette fields; we'll look at the specifics in the following sections and in Chapter 13, "Customizing Table Appearance." In most cases, the results are self-explanatory, or at least easy to see; feel free to experiment.

Reducing can mean deleting

You can reduce the number of rows and columns in the table by entering a smaller value in the appropriate field. Be aware that Dreamweaver will simply throw away the right-most columns and bottom-most rows, and anything that you've entered in such rows or columns will be thrown away too. You can regain your lost material by selecting **Edit** and choosing **Undo**, but, for some bizarre reason, you can't regain lost material using the **Ctrl+Z** (in Windows) or ⌘**+Z** (for the Macintosh) shortcut. Weird, huh?

Specifying the Number of Rows and Columns in a Table

Clearly, specifying rows and columns in the Insert Table dialog box or the Property palette isn't rocket science. In this section, we'll take a quick look at how rows and columns are reckoned in simple and complex tables.

The simplest and most common kind of table is "regular"—each row in the table has the same number of column cells, and each column has the same number of row sells. Take a look at Figure 12.5; each row has five columns, and each column has ten rows. You'll notice that the Properties palette displays these row and column values on the left side of the palette. (Again, you can change the number of rows or columns in the table by entering a new value directly into the appropriate field.)

FIGURE 12.5

A regular table contains the same number of cells in each row, and the same number of cells in each column.

Sometimes, though, you'll want to create tables that vary from row-to-row or from column-to-column. You might want to create one big cell that stretches across the top of your whole table, for instance, or combine two table cells into one. Figure 12.6 is an extreme example of the kind of funky Mondrian-esque results that are possible if you're really in the mood to do strange things with tables.

FIGURE 12.6

Some tables aren't as regular as others: in this table, it's hard to tell where the individual rows and columns begin and end.

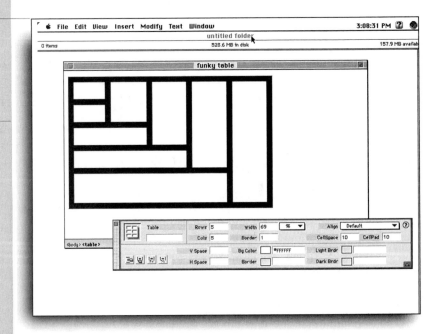

Even in this complex case, however, it's easy to determine the number of rows and columns for the whole table. Here's the rule: Use the row with the maximum number of columns, and the column with the maximum number of rows. If we count along the top edge of Figure 12.6, we can make out five distinct columns. Other rows (like the bottom one) contain fewer cells, but you would count five columns for the purposes of entering a value into the Insert Table dialog box. Similarly, if we count along the left edge of the table, we can make out five separate rows, so that's the number we'd use in the Row field of the dialog box. Remember, you can always add or remove rows later if you miscount.

Specifying the Size of a Table

There are two yardsticks that can be used to specify the size of tables: you can specify an absolute width in pixels, or a relative width represented by a percentage of the width of the browser window. By default, Dreamweaver uses the relative-width system. You don't need to commit to either measuring system; it's easy to change your table from one system or another.

Specifying table size using absolute width in pixels is exactly like specifying the size of images, Java applets, or plug-in content. When you use the absolute system to measure your table width, the tables size will stay (approximately) the same size, no matter how the user's browser window may be set.

To specify a fixed width for the table, simply select **Pixels**, from the pop-up menu at the bottom of the Insert Table dialog box, and enter the estimated size on the Width field. Web browsers will display the table at the specified size, no matter what the width of the browser window.

Specifying table size by using relative width causes the browser to use the size of the browser window to determine the size of the table. Let's say that you create a table using the default value of a relative width of 75%. If the browser window is 640 pixels wide, the table will be 640×.75 = 480 pixels wide; if the browser window is 800 pixels wide, the table will be 800×.75 = 600 pixels wide, and so on.

Draw your table first

When you're planning a complex table, like the ones in Figures 12.1 and 12.6, it helps to draw the table on paper before you start building the table with Dreamweaver. Count the number of rows and columns in your drawing, and use these numbers in the Insert Table dialog box.

Absolute doesn't always mean absolute

Remember, "absolute" is a relative term when you're building Web pages. Specifying the width of a table in pixels does not guarantee that the table will have a fixed physical size, or that the table will look exactly the same as it does when you look at the table on your monitor. In most cases, however, what you see on your monitor is a pretty good representation of what most users will see..

Let's see these two different measurement systems in action. Figure 12.7 shows two tables. The dark gray table on top has an absolute width of 300 pixels, and the light gray table at the bottom has a relative width of 75% of the width of the browser window. Because the browser window happens to be about 400 pixels wide at the moment, the bottom table is 400×.75 = 300 pixels wide—just about the same width as the top table.

FIGURE 12.7

These two tables look the same when the browser window is set to just the right width.

❶ Absolute width table

❷ Relative width table

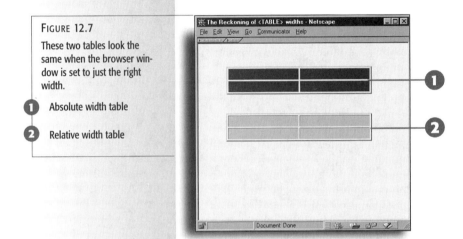

In Figure 12.8, the browser window has been opened up to nearly twice its previous width. The top table, which was specified using absolute width, remains unchanged; the bottom table, which uses relative width, is now nearly twice as wide as the top table.

Changing the Width of a Table

There are two simple ways to change the width of a table. If you like to work by eyeball, you can resize your table by dragging its edges around with the mouse. If you want to set your table to a precise size, you can enter a width value in the Width field of the Property palette.

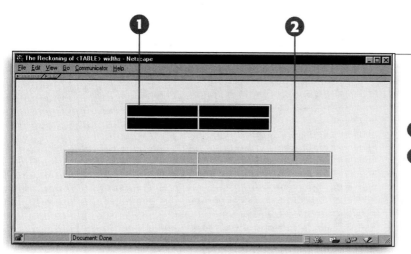

To resize the table using WYSIWYG tools, position the mouse over the right edge of the table. (You'll know you're in the right place when the cursor changes from an I-beam/Insertion Point cursor to a double-headed arrow cursor. Drag the right edge of the table left or right as desired. Notice that when you resize the table manually, the Property palette updates itself manually to reflect the new size.

If you have a fairly good idea what size you'd like the table to be, you can simply enter the desired size directly into the Width field. For instance, in Figure 12.9, we'd like to size the one-column-wide table so that it's exactly the same width as an image.

Create a perfect match between an image and a text block

1. Click the image with the cursor to select it.

2. Make a note of the image's width: it's in the field labeled "W" in the Property palette. (In this example, the GIF is 125 pixels wide.)

3. Click the left edge of the table to select the entire table.

4. Make sure that the pop-up menu next to the Width field in the Property palette is set to pixels. Don't worry if the table changes size when you change the pop-up menu—we'll fix that in the next step.

FIGURE 12.9

To resize this table to the width of the GIF above it, we'll enter an exact width in the Property palette.

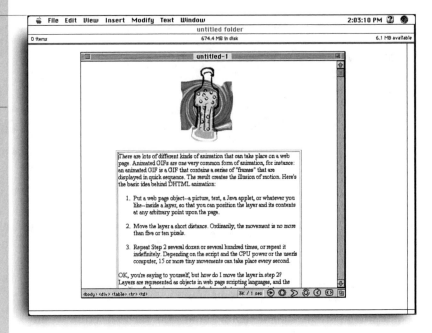

5. Take the size of the image you figured out in step 2 (in this example, 125), and enter this value in the Width field of the Property palette.

Figure 12.10 shows the results of this procedure; the table is exactly the same width as the GIF.

Converting Between Measurement Systems

Sometimes, you'll want to change measuring systems without changing the size of your table. Dreamweaver provides special tools to make this conversion as painless as possible.

Let's say that you've created your table using the default setting of 75% of the browser window's width. The Dreamweaver window is about 400 pixels wide, so the table is 300 pixels wide. You decide that 300 pixels is just about right no matter how wide the window is set, so you should use the absolute measuring system.

If you simply change the pop-up menu in the Property palette from pixels to %, you'll get an unwelcome surprise:

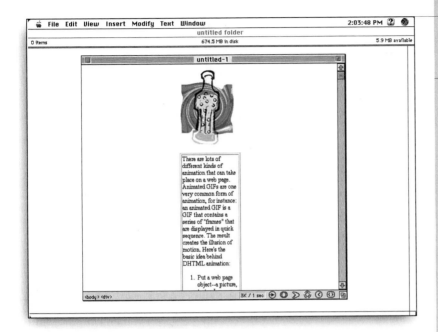

FIGURE 12.10

We've resized this table to line up the image and table.

Dreamweaver will change the measuring system, but it won't change that value of 75 in the Width field. Thus, your table will have an absolute size of 75 pixels—about a quarter of the size you had in mind.

Of course, you could change the value in the Width field from 75 to 300, but this isn't always easy. If the Dreamweaver window is, say, 523 pixels wide, you'd need to lug out your calculator (or fire up your calculator software) to figure out 75% of 523. (I'd need to fire up the calculator, anyway.) In any case, there isn't an easy way to gauge the width of a Dreamweaver window unless the window fills the screen or is the same size as an object of known dimensions.

Dreamweaver makes converting between measuring systems easy by providing two special buttons on the Property palette. Figure 12.11 shows where you can find these time-saving tools:

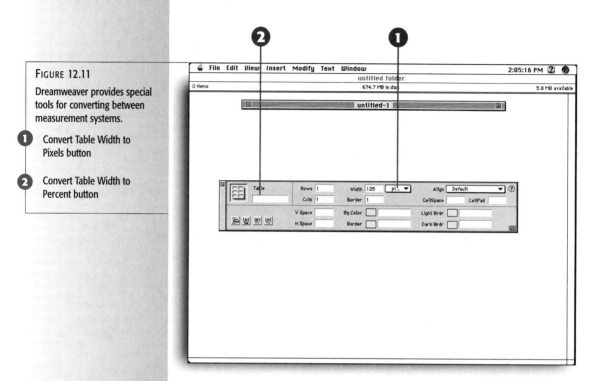

FIGURE 12.11

Dreamweaver provides special tools for converting between measurement systems.

1 Convert Table Width to Pixels button

2 Convert Table Width to Percent button

I'm sure you can figure out how these buttons work from their names:

- The **Convert Table Width to Pixels** button changes tables measured in percentage terms to absolute-sized tables. For instance, if the Dreamweaver window is 523 pixels wide, the button changes a default 75% table to a 392 pixels absolute-size table.

- The **Convert Table Width to Percent** button changes a table measured in absolute size to a table measured as a percentage of the browser (or Dreamweaver) window. For instance, if the Dreamweaver window is 600 pixels wide, the button changes a 300 pixel, absolute-size table to a 50% table.

From Here...

- To see the finer points of presenting tabular data, see Chapter 13, "Customizing Table Appearance."
- To see an alternate use of tables, control of a page's layout, see Chapter 14, "Refining Page Layouts Using Tables."

Customizing Table Appearance

How to align table cell content horizontally and vertically

How to add color to your table

How to knock out table cell walls

How to change the table's cell padding, cell spacing, and border weight

Creating a Timetable

Transportation schedules, like bus and train timetables, are my notion of the archetypal presentation of tabular data. In this chapter, you'll start with one of the clunky cage-like tables that Web browsers create by default, and finesse the table's appearance—fix the alignment, add some color, and so on—so the table doesn't look out of place in an elegant layout.

The ordering of sections in this chapter isn't especially important. There's no reason why you should adjust the horizontal alignment before the vertical alignment, and no reason why you can't add some color, if you like, before you even think about alignment issues. I do suggest that you save the last section, "Removing the Table Border," as the last step of table customization. It's convenient to be able to see the table borders when you're making other changes to the table's appearance.

Sketch Out a Plan for the Table

Dreamweaver is a great tool that can help you implement your ideas quickly and accurately. Unfortunately, Dreamweaver can't come up with ideas for you, or design pages automatically. Good graphic design is really about thinking things through before you invest a lot of time building your pages.

I find that it's very helpful to sketch out tables before I start to work on the table in Dreamweaver. You don't need to work at a drafting table or create elaborate diagrams that show the contents of every cell in the table; drawing a few lines on a lunch napkin works just fine, and may make your lunch tax deductible. If you prefer to work on a whiteboard, or an etch-a-sketch, or by pure visualization, please do.

Figure 13.1 shows what you're shooting for here: the train's schedule information is organized into a neat grid. Every row and every column has its own individual label, and the horizontal and vertical axes are also labeled. The table doesn't have border lines, which (to my over-sensitive eyes) make it hard to read across on the table, and otherwise clutter up the page. In order to make it easy for the eye to track the horizontal rows, I've given alternating rows a light background color.

FIGURE 13.1

Dreamweaver allows you to customize the colors, alignment, spacing, and other aspects of a table's appearance.

Create the Basic Table

Start by adding a basic table to your page. Your table should have five rows and five columns; the default width of 75% is fine. See Chapter 12, "Building Tables," for information about adding basic tables to the page.

Enter the data as shown in Figure 13.2. (You can use your own station names and times if you like, but make sure that you follow the basic pattern.) Notice that all of the cells in the first row, all of the cells in the first column, and the second cell in the second row are all empty.

If you don't want to type the schedule

If you like, you can cut and paste the table data from the Chapter 13 page on the book's site, or from the mirror page at http://www.orbis-tertius.com/dreamweaver/ch13step.htm. You'll need to copy and paste cell by cell, but you may find it easier than typing. If you're really lazy, save the page to disk, open it with Dreamweaver, and start with the basic table in the step 2 section of the page.

FIGURE 13.2

Add a basic 5-by-5 table to your page, and add data as shown here.

In the so-called real world, most train schedules would be quite a bit more complex than the three train, three station system that I've created for this example. I assume that you'd prefer to spend your time learning about tables, rather than typing up an imaginary train schedule.

Adjust Horizontal Alignment

Horizontal alignment in a table is pretty easy to understand: the contents of a particular table cell can be aligned with the left or right edge of the cell, or centered in the middle. It's the same basic idea behind aligning text in Dreamweaver or in a word processing or page layout program.

It's easy to set the alignment of table cells. Let's say that we want to set the station names in the second column of the sample table so that they're flush right.

Adjusting horizontal alignment

1. If you're using a Macintosh, Control-click the cell. If you're using a PC, right-click the cell.
2. Select **Cell Properties** from the Contextual menu that appears. Dreamweaver presents the Table Cell Properties dialog box shown in Figure 13.3.

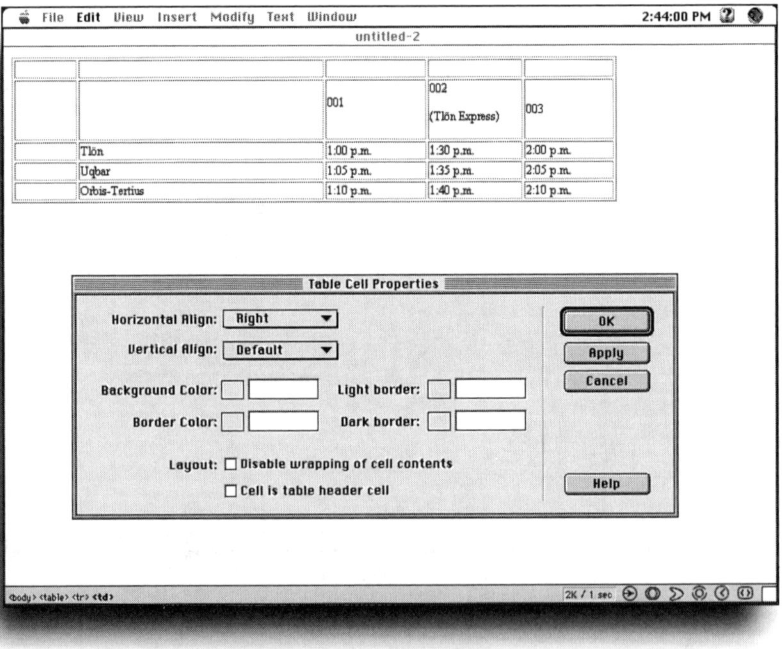

FIGURE 13.3

Set the alignment of individual cells with the Table Cell Properties dialog box.

You can use style sheets instead

It's a real pain to individually format the typography of each entry in this kind of entry. To save yourself a lot of grief, create a CSS-style sheet for the `<table>` tag; the style will be applied to each table entry. See Chapter 6, "Formatting text with Style Sheets," for an introduction to Dreamweaver's excellent support for CSS.

Aligning content in a cell

By default, Dreamweaver displays a table cell's content at the left edge of the cell. If you look at the HTML that Dreamweaver generates, you'll see that the `<td>` tag that defines the table cell does not explicitly specify `alignment = "LEFT"`. In fact, Dreamweaver does not add an alignment parameter at all when it creates a simple table. Without an alignment parameter, the browser will simply use its default alignment for table cells. In the case of the major browsers (and most of the minors), the default is to put the cell contents on the left edge of the cell.

3. Select **Right** from the Horizontal Alignment pop-up menu in the Table Cell Properties dialog box, and click **OK**.

Dreamweaver moves the word Tlön so that it aligns with the right edge of the cell.

Very often, you'll want to use the same kind of horizontal alignment for every cell in a particular column. For instance, in our example table, all of the station names in the second column should be right-aligned. Fortunately, you don't need to set the alignment of each of the cells in the column one by one. Dreamweaver offers a shortcut that allows you to set the alignment of all of the cells in the column with one dialog box.

Set the whole column flush right

1. If you're using a PC, right-click the Tlön cell. If you're using a Macintosh, Control-click. (Actually, you can click any of the cells in the column.)

2. Select **Column Properties** from the contextual menu that appears. Dreamweaver presents the Table Column Properties dialog box.

3. Select **Right** from the Horizontal Alignment pop-up menu.

Yes, the Column Properties dialog box does look remarkably like the Cell Properties dialog box. In general, any property that you adjust at the cellular level can be applied to all of the cells in a column via the Column Properties dialog box.

I've chosen to center each of the captions and times in the three Trains columns on the right. Go ahead and select these columns one by one, and set the horizontal alignment of each to **Centered**. At this point, your table should look like Figure 13.4.

Mixing alignment

If, for some crazy reason, you decide that you want to mix the alignment of the cells in a column—say, set two cells flush right and one cell centered—you can set the alignment of the whole column with Column Properties, and then go back and alter individual cells with Cell Properties. Changing single cells won't undo or otherwise undermine the column-level change.

FIGURE 13.4

Use the Table Column Properties dialog box to center the contents of each of the three Trains columns.

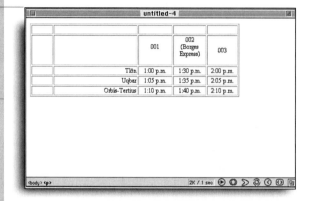

Adjust Vertical Alignment

Vertical alignment is just a tiny bit trickier than horizontal alignment. It's pretty obvious that vertical alignment sets the position of the cell content with respect to the cell's top and bottom. The tricky parts (and they're really not all that tricky) are

- There's a special vertical alignment setting, `baseline`.
- Table cells often stretch horizontally when they are displayed in the user's browser.
- The default vertical alignment—centered—isn't what page-layout veterans have been conditioned to expect.

"Baseline alignment" means that the contents of the table cells in a particular row are aligned using the baseline of the first line of text in the cell, rather than the top, bottom, or middle of the cell. (If the cell contains no text, the alignment is reckoned by where the text would be if the cell held text.) What's the baseline of a line of text? It's the bottom of those letters without descenders. Letters with descenders vary from font to font, but in most fonts, the lowercase letters g, p, q, y, the uppercase letter Q, and the italic form of *f* have descenders. (In most cases, Q is the only upper-case letter with a descender.) Figure 13.5 shows what baseline alignment looks like in a Web page table.

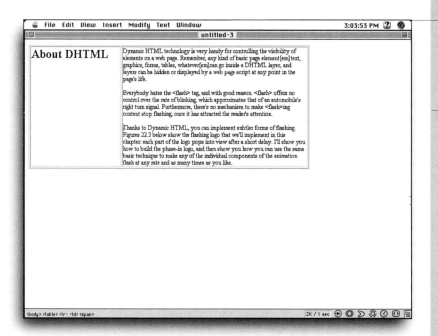

FIGURE 13.5

Baseline alignment uses the text inside a cell (rather than the cell itself) to align the cell contents.

Sometimes it's easy to forget that the user's machine may not necessarily have the same set of installed fonts as the machine you're using to create your Web pages. If fate is against you (and it always is), two columns that are equal in size when you build the page in Dreamweaver may have uneven lengths when loaded by a user. Because browsers vertically center cell content, uneven cell heights can make two adjacent columns look misaligned, or, as we say in the art room, "funny-looking." (Ordinarily, the user who sees the funny-looking page is your client or supervisor.)

To see what I mean, take look at Figure 13.6. The two side-by-side columns of text are lined up so that their baselines match. That's exactly what you want from two columns of text.

FIGURE 13.6

These columns are properly aligned.

FIGURE 13.6

These columns are properly aligned.

If the cell content is vertically centered within the cell, the baseline-to-baseline alignment is lost if one cell's content becomes longer than its partner. You can see the results in Figure 13.7; the baselines of the columns, and the tops, for that matter, don't line up.

FIGURE 13.7

These columns have lost their alignment.

This behavior isn't what Quark and PageMaker jockeys expect; they expect columns to stay lined up at the top, rather than in the center. Sadly, vertical centering is the standard on Web pages.

Let's fix the vertical alignment of the second row of our example table. I know that I'd feel a lot more comfortable if all of the train numbers in the second row lined up with each other, so that the baseline of 001 lines up with the baselines of 002 and 003.

Vertically align cell content with the tops of cells

1. If you're using a Macintosh, Control-click anywhere in the second row of the table. If you're using a PC, right-click.

2. Chose **Row Properties** from the contextual menu. Dreamweaver presents the Table Row Properties dialog box.

3. Chose **Top** from the Vertical alignment pop-up box.

At this point, your table should look like Figure 13.8.

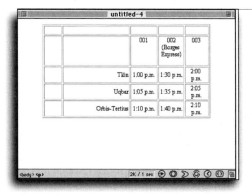

Can I set the vertical alignment of a column?

Of course, you can adjust the vertical alignment of individual cells with the Table Cell Properties dialog box, just as you used it to fix individual cells' horizontal alignment. Most of the time, however, you'll want to work on the vertical alignment of whole rows.

FIGURE 13.8

Use the Table Row Column dialog box to adjust the vertical alignment of a whole row of cells.

Alternate Row Colors

Color always makes a page look more…er…colorful, and good use of color can make a chart more legible. I think the vertical bars in Figure 13.1 make it easier for the eye to follow the row of each chart. (On a wider or longer chart, this kind of visual cue would be even more important.)

You can affect the color of tables in on four different levels:

- You can set the background color of the whole table.
- You can set the background color of individual cells. Setting the color of a cell overrides any global color for the table within the affected cell, but does not alter any other cells.

- You can set the color of the border, although only Internet Explorer will use this border color information.

- You can specify a pair of colors to be used for the border, although only Internet Explorer will use this border color information.

Figure 13.9 shows how Internet Explorer uses bordercolorlight and bordercolordark attributes. The black areas in the border are the dark border color, and the gray areas are the light border color.

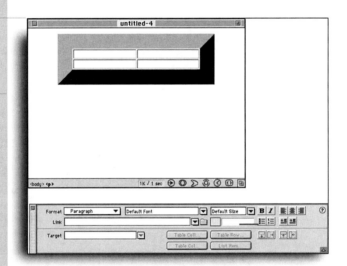

As with horizontal and vertical alignment, Dreamweaver provides some convenient shortcuts that allow you to change the color of a whole row or a whole column of table cells with one dialog box. In fact, you use the same Table Row Properties and Table Column Properties dialog boxes you used to set alignment in the previous sections.

Set the color of the first row of the timetable

1. If you're using a PC, right-click in the cell that contains the word Tlön, or anywhere in the same row. If you're using a Macintosh, Control-click.

2. Choose **Row Properties** from the contextual menu that appears. Dreamweaver presents the Table Row Properties dialog box.

3. Click the gray color swatch next to the Background Color label and pick a color from the pop-up swatch palette. Alternatively, you can type a color value into the Background Color field. (I used #ffff 99 on the example page.)

Use the same procedure to colorize the row labeled Orbis-Tertius. When you're done, your table should look like Figure 13.10.

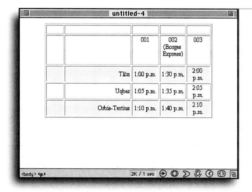

Coloring the whole table at one time

To colorize the whole table at once, use the Background Color swatch in the Properties palette while the table is

FIGURE 13.10
You can assign colors to individual cells of a table.

Knock Out Cell Walls

As you learned in Chapter 12, a table doesn't need to be perfectly regular; the number of cells per row can vary from row to row within the table. For instance, the first row of the example table contains a triple-wide cell that spans the width of the three train columns. Similarly, the first column contains a tall row that spans three rows of schedule entries.

To create this sort of complex table, you must remove borders between cells. It's a big hassle to set up this kind of table when you're coding by hand—I don't ever do it right the first time I try, anyway—but Dreamweaver makes this task fairly painless.

The basic tools for removing and restoring table cells can be found in the Properties palette when it is in Table mode. See Figure 13.11 for a rundown of the basic tools.

Older browsers and individual cell colors

The major browsers began support for individually colored table cells in NS 3.0 and MSIE 3.0. Older browsers won't add color to individual table cells; they'll use the table's background color, or, if no table background is specified, they will use the Web page's background color. (Unfortunately, I learned this the hard way. I built a page using white type that reversed out a dark table cell. When I showed my client the layout on the 2.0 browser in his office computer, the type was completely illegible against the page's white background.)

FIGURE 13.11

Use the tools in the Properties palette (when it's in table mode) to remove and restore table cell walls.

1 Increase row span tool

2 Increase column span tool

3 Decrease row span tool

4 Decrease column span tool

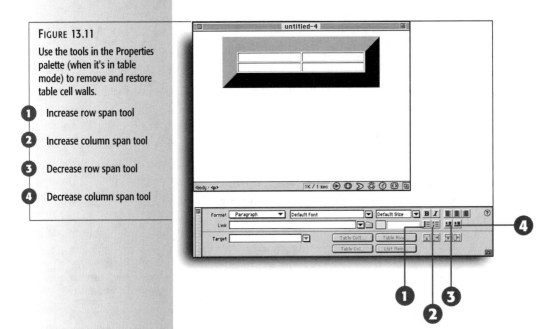

Let's start by knocking out the vertical walls in the first row.

Knock out vertical table walls

1. Click with the mouse to position the insertion point in the cell that's to the immediate left of the wall you wish to remove. In this case, start with the third cell of the first row, directly above the cell that contains the train number 001.

2. Click the **Increase Row Span** tool. Dreamweaver knocks out the wall to the right of the insertion point.

3. Click the **Increase Row Span** tool again to remove another cell wall; the large cell should now be three columns wide.

Now, we'll knock out the horizontal walls on the left edge of the table.

Knock out horizontal table walls

1. Click to position the insertion point in the cell that's above the wall you wish to remove. In the example table, click in the first cell of the third row, to the left of the cell that contains the word Tlön.

2. Click the **Increase Column Span** tool. Dreamweaver removes the wall below the insertion point.

3. Click the tool again to remove another wall; the large cell should now be three rows wide.

4. If you colored the Tlön row in a previous section, your large cell is now yellow (or whatever color you used). Control-click the cell (on a PC, right-click), select **Cell Properties** from the contextual menu, and correct the color of the cell in the Table Cell Properties dialog box.

When you're done, merge the four cells in the top-left corner.

Merge cells

1. Click in the first cell in the first row.

2. Click the **Increase Row Span** tool. Dreamweaver removes the wall to the left the insertion point. Let the insertion point remain in the new double-wide cell.

3. Click the **Increase Column Span** tool. Dreamweaver removes the walls separating the double-wide cell from the two cells below, and also removes the wall separating the two lower cells.

At this point, your table should look like Figure 13.12.

Restoring walls you've removed

To restore table walls that you have removed, use the Decrease Row Span and Decrease Column Span tools. These tools will put back any walls you removed, but they can't create a new wall where there was no wall before.

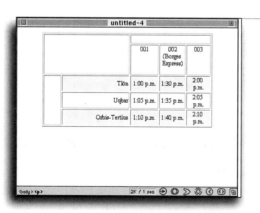

FIGURE 13.12

Use the Increase Row Span and Increase Column Span tools to knock out walls between table cells.

If you're menu-prone

If you prefer using menus, you can use the following menu commands to remove and restore cell walls:

Select **Modify**, choose **Table**, and then choose **Increase Row Span**.

Select **Modify**, choose **Table**, and choose **Increase Column Span**.

Select **Modify**, choose **Table**, and choose **Decrease Row Span**.

Select **Modify**, choose **Table**, and choose **Decrease Column Span**.

Each of these menu commands behaves in exactly the same way as the button with the same name.

Add Images or Text Labels

The next step is an easy one: we'll add labels to the extra-wide and extra-tall cells we created previously.

I used a slightly cryptic label, ST, on the left edge of the timetable. Basically, I didn't want to write out the word station because it would make the cell really tall, and I'd need to fatten up the other rows of the table to match. My old art director would hit me on the knuckles with a ruler for wasting so much space inside the table, so I'm inclined to use an abbreviation.

Actually, a real-world timetable would probably contain many more rows, and there would be plenty of room for a very tall cell in the first column.

Style the label however you like, using standard text-wrangling tools or CSS. When you've added the labels, your table should look like Figure 13.13.

FIGURE 13.13

Click inside a cell and start typing to add content to the cell.

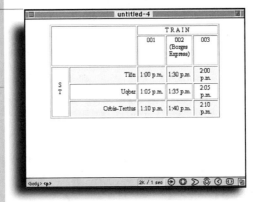

Experiment with Cell Padding and Cell Spacing

You may wish to add cell padding and cell spacing to your custom table. I don't think that the example table really needs anything in this department, but I've added a few points of cell padding for demonstration purposes.

Cell padding refers to extra space the browser adds between the contents of a cell and the edge of the cell. This extra space is added to all four sides. The distance between cells—say, the distance from the right edge of one cell to the left edge of its neighbor, or the distance from the bottom of one cell to the top of the cell below it—is not affected. Figure 13.14 shows what our example table looks like with an outrageous 25 points of cell padding added. (Don't add this much padding to the table!)

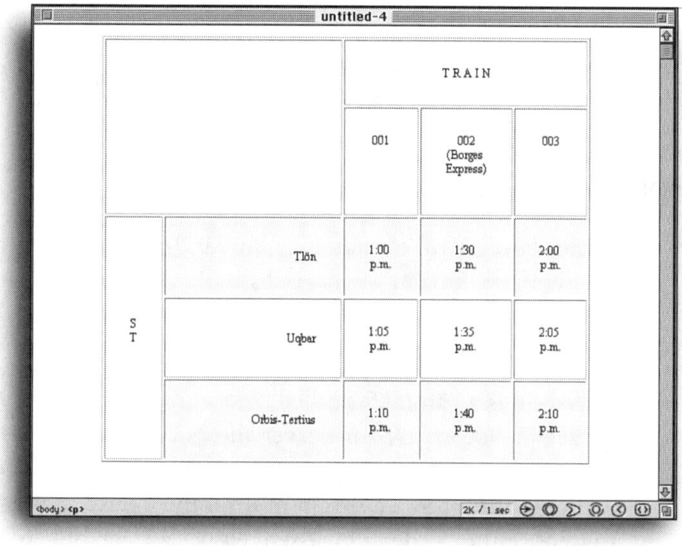

FIGURE 13.14

Cell padding adds space between a cell's content and the edge of the cell.

Cell spacing, on the other hand, adds space between cells but does not add any padding inside cells. Figure 13.15 shows what happens when we add 25 points of cell spacing to the table. (As you can see, I've removed the crazy cell padding that I added in the last illustration.)

I think just a touch of cell padding will take care of the example table.

Add cell padding

1. Select the table by clicking its left edge.
2. Enter the value 2 in the Cell Padding field in the Properties palette.

FIGURE 13.15

Cell padding adds space between a cell's content and the edge of the cell.

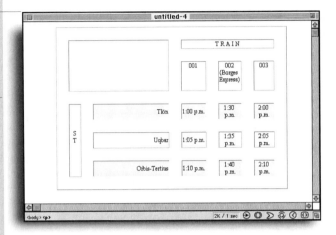

Expanding borders

When the table has a border, as does the table in 13.18, the table's border expands to fill the empty space between cells. If the table does not have a border, the Web page background shows through the space between cells.

Leave border setting for last

When you're building your page, it's handy to keep the table's borders going until the last minute. Often, when you preview your page in the browser, the table doesn't look quite like what you expect it to look like, and the position of the table borders is often a useful clue about what's going on.

Remove Table Borders

Finally, let's get rid of that table border. In my aesthetic universe, table borders are almost always bad; the vertical bars make it hard to read across the table, and they're just plain ugly. (I still respect you if you happen to prefer table borders.)

HTML uses a parameter called BORDER to specify the heaviness of a table's border. Dreamweaver allows you to set the value of BORDER via the Properties palette. The default value, 1, yields the kind of table border shown in most of the figures in this chapter. To remove the border, you assign BORDER a value of 0; to fatten up the border, you assign BORDER a higher value.

Remove the border from the example table

1. Click the left edge of the table to select it.
2. Enter 0 in the Border field of the Properties palette.

Dreamweaver displays a dashed-line border to show where the table's borders should be; these dashed lines will not appear when the table is loaded by a browser.

After you've removed the table borders, your table should look like Figure 13.16. (Yes, it's the same as Figure 13.1—I've repeated it here to save you the trouble of turning back to find it.)

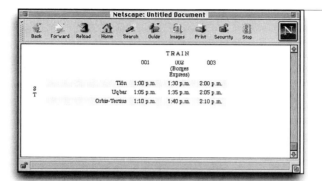

		TRAIN		
		001	002 (Borges Express)	003
S T	Tlön		1:00 p.m.	1:30 p.m.	2:00 p.m.
	Uqbar	1:05 p.m.	1:35 p.m.	2:05 p.m.
	Orbis-Tertius	1:10 p.m.	1:40 p.m.	2:10 p.m.

FIGURE 13.16

Use the Border field in the Properties palette to adjust the weight of the table's border.

From Here...

- For information about how to format table text (and other text) with CSS, see Chapter 6, "Formatting Text with Style Sheets."

- For remedial information on adding basic tables to your pages, see Chapter 12, "Building Tables."

- To see another common use of tables—structuring a page's layout—see Chapter 14. "Refining Page Layout Using Tables."

Refining Page Layout Using Tables

How to add margins to a page with tables

How to use tables to precisely position page elements

Plan Your Page

Remember, Dreamweaver implements your design ideas; it doesn't think them up for you. If you want to get the best results from Dreamweaver, it's best to have a plan for your page before you get started.

In this chapter, you'll create a simple page that demonstrates the kind of control over margins and positioning that's possible with the clever use of tables. Figure 14.1 shows what we're shooting for; the text block is a nice, readable width, and it lines up well with the logo at the top of the page. There are ample margins on both sides of the text, and a nice sidebar on the left side of the page.

FIGURE 14.1

In this chapter, you'll use tables to control the finer points of the page's layout.

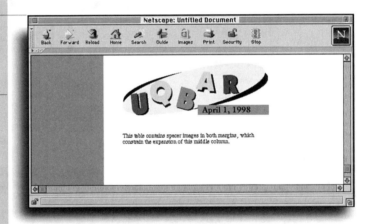

Add Sidebar

The first step is strictly for aesthetics and doesn't actually involve using table-handling tools. We're going to add a field of solid color to the left side of the page. The sidebar adds a little color to the page, balances the text column, and besides, corporate clients really seem to love color sidebars.

The easiest way to create this kind of sidebar is to create a really wide, really short image, and use it as the page's background. I've set up a GIF file that's ready for you to use, or you can create your own image, using my file as a model. The image is mostly white, with a tiny bit of the sidebar color on the left. (See Figure 14.2.)

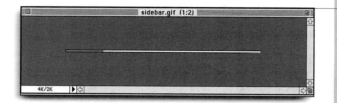

FIGURE 14.2

You'll use a tiling background image, rather than a table, to create the page's solid sidebar. Here's what the tile looks like in Photoshop.

Add a sidebar to your page

1. Use your Web browser to load the tile image from the book's Web site at www.mcp.com/info, or from the mirror site at http://www.orbis-tertius.com/dreamweaver/sidebar.GIF.

2. If you're using a PC, right-click the image in the browser window; if you're using a Macintosh, click and hold.

3. Choose **Save Image As** from the contextual menu that appears.

4. The browser presents a file dialog box. Save the background image to your hard disk in a convenient place.

5. Open a new Dreamweaver document. If you're using a Macintosh, Control-click the page's background. If you're using a PC, right-click.

6. Choose **Page Properties** from the contextual menu that appears.

7. Dreamweaver presents the Page Properties dialog box. Click the **Browse** button next to the Background Image dialog box, and use the file dialog box to navigate to the image you saved to disk in step 4.

Dreamweaver adds the image to the left side of the page. At this point, your page should look like Figure 14.3.

FIGURE 14.3

Once the sidebar is in place, we can use tables to create appropriate margins.

Background images versus tables

Why use a background image to create the solid sidebar? Why not use a big table cell as the sidebar, and give the cell a background color? Good question.

Unfortunately, a table won't butt up against the edge of the browser window; the browser will add just about 10 pixels of space as a margin between the edge of the window and the table cell. The resulting gap is just plain unsightly. (Try it and see if you don't believe me!)

Create Table for Margins

Now that the sidebar is in place, we can create a basic table to control the page's margins. (I'll refer to this basic table as the "master table" in the instructions below.)

Every page is a little different, and every page may need a slightly different table. Here's how I reasoned through the choices for the example page:

- We need a column for the left margin, a column for the text, and a column for the right margin. Thus, our table will have three columns.

- The page doesn't really need any kind of vertical organization. After all, there's nothing at all in the margin, and the column that contains the text is just an image and some text. (Actually, it's not just an image, but we can treat it like one when we're working out the details of the master table.) Because our needs are simple, a single row will do.

- We'll design for a screen that's 480 pixels tall by 640 pixels wide. There are smaller screens out there in cyberspace, but most users will have at least this many pixels available. I'll set up the table with a width of 600 pixels, to leave a little room for the browser window itself.

Add the master table to the layout

1. Click the **Insert Table** tool in the Objects palette. Dreamweaver presents the Insert Table dialog box.

2. Enter 3 in the Rows field.

3. Enter 1 in the Columns field.

4. Choose **Pixels** from the pop-up menu to the right of the Width field.

5. Enter 600 in the Width field.

After Dreamweaver adds the table to your page, the results should look like Figure 14.4.

FIGURE 14.4

Create a table to define the page's margins.

Set Column Widths and Insert dot.gif

Once the table is in place, it's time to set the widths of each column. How wide should each column be? Here's how I decided.

The sidebar is about 150 pixels wide, so the left margin should be a little wider than that—about 175 pixels or so. I'd like the text block to be about 300 pixels wide, which seems like a nice, readable length, and that leaves about 125 pixels for the right margin.

We can use the Column Properties dialog box to set the width of each column. As you shall see, setting column widths isn't an entirely adequate solution, but it's a good start.

Setting column widths

1. If you're using a Macintosh, Control-click in the left column. If you're using a PC, right-click in the column.

2. Choose **Column Properties** from the contextual menu that appears. Dreamweaver presents the Table Column Properties dialog box.

3. Select the **Pixels** radio button beneath the Column Width label. Enter 175 in the Pixels field. Click **OK** to close the dialog box.

4. Repeat steps 1 through 3 above to assign a width of 300 to the middle column, and a width of 125 to the right column.

Alas, the column widths that you set using this technique aren't terribly useful when you're trying to create a precise layout. Web browsers treat width values as suggestions, and may change column widths to accommodate the table's content.

To see this for yourself, click with the mouse to position the insertion point in the table's middle column and start typing. (If you're experiencing writer's block, cut and paste some text from an old word processor file.) The column widens to fit the new text, as you can see in Figure 14.5.

Dreamweaver's ever-changing moods

Be sure to change the width of all of the columns in the table. If some of the columns are set to pixel widths, and some are set to percentage widths, the width of the pixel-reckoned columns may shift.

FIGURE 14.5

Table cells can widen to fit content.

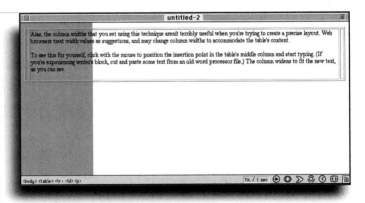

There's a fairly simple way to keep the middle column from growing larger: keep the left and right margins from getting smaller. To preserve the width of the margins, we'll put something that can't be reflowed—an image—in each margin.

The image that we use is very small—in fact, it's only one pixel—so the image downloads quickly. We'll make the image transparent, so that it doesn't clutter up the layout.

Add the spacer images to the table

1. Use your Web browser to load the spacer image from the book's Web site at www.mcp.com/info, or from the mirror site at http://www.orbis-tertius.com/dreamweaver/dot.gif.

2. If you're using a PC, right-click the image in the browser window; if you're using a Macintosh, click and hold. (It's pretty small, it may take a few clicks to find it.)

3. Choose **Save Image As** from the contextual menu that appears.

4. The browser presents a file dialog box. Save the spacer image to your hard disk in a convenient place.

5. Click in the table's left column to position the insertion point in the column.

6. Click the **Insert Image** tool in the Objects palette.

7. Dreamweaver presents a file dialog box, use it to navigate to the image file you saved to disk in step 4.

8. Click with the mouse to select the image you just placed. (When the image is selected, the Properties palette will display an Image label.)

9. Enter the desired width of the column—in this case, 175—in the Properties palette's W field.

10. Repeat steps 6 through 9 above to add the spacer image to the right column. Make this image 125 pixels wide.

Creating your own spacer GIFs

If you're comfortable with Adobe Photoshop or another image-editing application, you can create your own one-pixel transparent GIF, rather than downloading the GIF that we've put on the book's site.

Create Logo Sections

Sometimes, fairly simple-looking images are made from composites of more than one image. For example, the "Uqbar" logo in Figure 14.1 consists of three separate parts: the left side of the logo, the top of the right side of the logo, and the bottom of the right side. Figure 14.6 shows what these components look like when they are separated into individual files.

To make sure that these image components align correctly to form a single composite image, we use a table to "glue" the images together. Using a table also ensures that the images maintain their relative position; the right side of the logo won't reflow to a position underneath the left side of the logo, even if the user sets his browser window to a crazily narrow width. Finally, the table guarantees that the image sections butt up against each other—there are no tiny slivers of page background between the images.

Why cut up an image like this? Isn't it simpler to create a single image? Under ordinary circumstances, it is simpler (and thus better) to use a single image. What makes this particular image special is the bottom of the right side of the logo. This portion of the image contains a rectangular banner that displays the date of the current "issue" of the site; it's inevitable that this little corner of the logo will become obselete—maybe next month, maybe next week, maybe tomorrow. It makes sense to update this particular corner of the site's logo, rather than updating the whole logo on a weekly or monthly basis.

In the world of Dynamic HTML, fancy server-side tools, and other Web geegaws, there are plenty of things that can happen inside the date banner:

- A server-side program could generate a new GIF image with the current date every day, replacing the old file on the server.

- You could replace the dateline with a set of random motto lines: "The Magazine of Web Culture," "Another Cryptic Web Zine," "Baffling Readers Since 1994," or whatever, and use a Web page script to choose a motto line at random whenever the page is loaded.

- You could put HTML, rather than a GIF image, in this section of the logo. Changing the contents of the banner is as quick as editing the HTML file. You could also create a Web page script to generate HTML for this section of the logo automatically.

- You could use an animated GIF (or a Java or Shockwave animation, or whatever) to make the dateline more interesting.

Download the logo sections from the sample page

1. Load the page www.mcp.com/info or the mirror page
http://www.orbis-tertius.com/dreamweaver/ch14step.htm
with your Web browser.

2. If you're using a PC, right-click the left side of the logo. If
you're using a Macintosh, Control-click.

3. Choose **Save Image As** from the contextual menu that
appears.

4. The Web browser presents a file dialog box. Use it to save
the image to your disk.

5. Repeat steps 2 through 4 to download the top right and bottom right sections of the logo.

Create Mortise Table

Once you have all the parts for the composite logo, you'll need
to create a table to hold all of the parts. (I'll call this the mortise
table, because it mortises together all of the parts of the logo.)
The table needs two columns: the left column will contain one
row, and the right column will need two rows. We'll put the
mortise table inside the margin table.

Create mortise table

1. Click with the cursor to position the insertion point in the
middle column of the margin table.

2. Click the **Insert Table** tool in the Objects palette.
Dreamweaver presents the Insert Table dialog box.

3. Enter 2 in the Rows field of the Insert Table dialog box.

4. Enter 2 in the Columns field.

5. Make sure that the pop-up menu to the right of the Width
field is set to **Percent**.

6. Enter 100 in the width field. (Because the table that we're
adding is contained inside another table, the width of 100%
is measured relative to the width of the cell that contains the
new table, rather than relative to the width of the browser
window.)

7. Click with the mouse to position the insertion point in the top-left cell of the mortise table.

8. Click the **Increase Column Span** tool in the Properties palette to merge the two cells in the left column into a single cell.

Figure 14.6 shows what your page should look like at this stage.

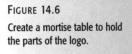

FIGURE 14.6

Create a mortise table to hold the parts of the logo.

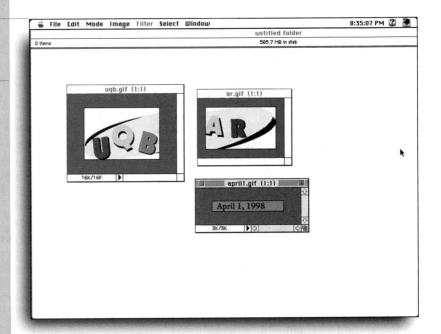

Add Sections to Mortise Table

After you've created the mortise table, you can fill it up with the logo parts. You'll need to make sure that each cell's alignment is set up correctly, so that the parts butt up against each other to create a seamless whole.

Add sections to the mortise table

1. If you're using a Macintosh, Control-click the single cell of the left column of the mortise table. If you're using a PC, right-click.

2. Choose **Column Properties** from the contextual menu that appears.

3. Choose **Right** from the Horizontal Alignment pop-up menu in the Table Column Properties dialog box.

4. Choose **Top** from the Vertical Alignment pop-up menu. Click **OK** to close the dialog box.

5. Click to position the insertion point in the left column of the mortise table.

6. Click the **Insert Image** tool in the Objects palette. Dreamweaver presents a file dialog box.

7. Use the file dialog box to navigate to the image that contains the left side of the image. (You downloaded this image in the previous section of this chapter; if you saved it with its original name, it's called uqb.gif.)

8. If you're using a Macintosh, Control-click the top cell of the right column of the mortise table. If you're using a PC, right-click.

9. Choose **Column Properties** from the contextual menu that appears.

10. In the Table Column dialog box, Choose **Left** from the Horizontal Alignment pop-up menu.

11. Pick **Top** from the Vertical Alignment pop-up menu.

12. Click to position the insertion point in the top cell of the right column.

13. Click the **Insert Image** tool in the Objects palette.

14. Use the file dialog box to navigate to the image file that contains the top right portion of the logo. (If you saved the file with its original name, it's called ar.gif.)

15. Click to position the insertion point in the bottom cell of the right column.

16. Click the **Insert Image** tool in the Objects palette.

17. Use the file dialog box to navigate to the image file that contains the bottom right portion of the logo. (If you saved the file with its original name, it's called date.gif.)

18. Make sure that the Properties palette is in table mode; if it's not, click the table's left edge to select the table. Click the **Clear Row Heights** button in the bottom left-hand corner of the Properties palette to remove any extra vertical space from the table.

Take a look at Figure 14.7 to see what your table should look like at this point. It's not quite done—you'll need to make some minor adjustments and replace the table border—but you can clearly see the composite logo taking shape.

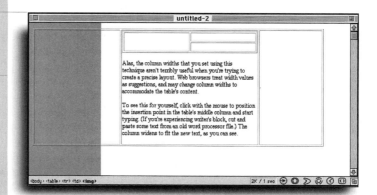

Remove Table Borders

As you saw in Figure 14.7, the mortise table's borders obviously prevent the logo components from joining together smoothly. You'll need to remove the table borders to make the composite logo work.

Remove table borders

1. Click the left edge of the mortise table to select the table. (Dreamweaver will reverse the colors of the table and display a table label and icon in the Properties palette when the table is selected.)

2. Enter 0 in the Border field of the Properties palette.

Once you've removed the table border, your page should look like Figure 14.8.

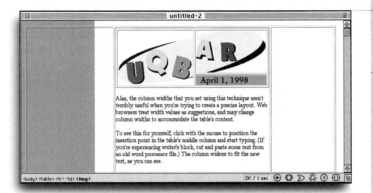

FIGURE 14.8
Remove the border from your mortise palette.

Adjust Cellspacing

Figure 14.8 looks pretty good; when you look at the table in Dreamweaver, the mortise table seems to be holding the logo sections firmly together. However, the dashed black line that Dreamweaver uses to indicate the edges of the table cell obscures the view, and it's hard to see exactly what's going on where the images meet. Figure 14.9 shows what you'll see if you preview the image in your browser; there's a tiny one-pixel gap between the cells of the table. (To preview the page with your browser, press **F12** or pick a browser by selecting **File** and choosing **Preview**.)

FIGURE 14.9
When you preview the mortise table in your Web browser, you'll see a tiny gap remains between the table cells.

Having trouble clicking the edge?

After you've removed the table's border and cellspacing, it can be hard to select the mortise table by clicking the left edge. Remember, you can always select the table by right-clicking (PC) or Control-clicking (Macintosh) anywhere in the table and selecting **Select Table** from the contextual menu that appears.

What's happening here? By default, browsers add one point of cell spacing between table cells. If you leave cell spacing untouched when you're building your page in Dreamweaver, this extra point of space will be added automatically. Now you want to remove that space.

Adjust cellspacing

1. Click the left edge of the mortise table to select it.
2. Enter 0 in the CellSpace field in the Properties palette.

Variations and Alternatives

The <table> tag can be used to solve many other Web page layout problems. That other WYSIWYG layout program, NetObjects Fusion, seems to create two or three new invisible tables every time you click the mouse. Other common <table> tricks include:

- Use a single-celled table to control the width (but not position) of a block of text, as in Figure 14.10.

FIGURE 14.10

Use a single-celled table to control the width (but not position) of a block of text.

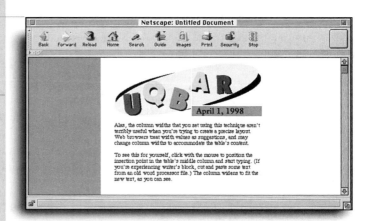

- Use a two-column table to organize forms. Put each form element's label flush right in the table's left column, and the element itself flush left in the right column. Figure 14.11 demonstrates a typical table-based form.

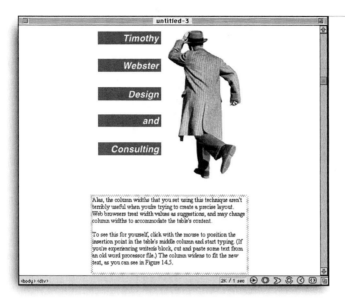

FIGURE 14.11

Use a two column table to organize forms.

- Use a single-column, multi-rowed table to add precise custom "drops" (vertical space) between heads and paragraphs, images, photographs, or anything else stacked vertically. See Figure 14.12 for an example of this technique.

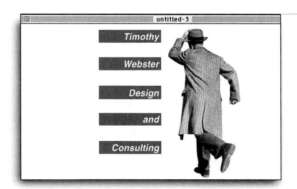

FIGURE 14.12

Use tables to add precise amounts of vertical space.

Many of the special effects that are created with the `<table>` tag, such as page margins, can be implemented using Cascading Style Sheets technology. I will spare you another rehash of the CSS versus HTML tricks debate here, but I should remind you that Dreamweaver offers excellent support for CSS. For more information about CSS, see Chapter 6, "Formatting Text with Style Sheets," and Appendix D, "CSS Quick Reference."

From Here...

- For information on adding a basic table to your page, see Chapter 12, "Building Tables."
- To see the traditional use of tables—structuring tabular data—see Chapter 13, "Customizing Table Appearance."

Creating Frames

Creating Frames

Frames are an interesting feature that is relatively new to the Web. Frames allow you to divide the browser window into sections, each of which can hold a different Web page. One frame can hold a table of contents, while another frame displays the material. This can make navigation and browsing easier for the reader because they're viewing the table of contents and the material at the same time, and don't have to constantly backtrack to the table of contents page each time they want to move on. There are other uses for frames, of course, which I'll touch on in later chapters. In this chapter, I'll just show you how to create basic frames and the content that goes in them.

One word of warning is in order here—frames are not universally adored and accepted by the Web community. Some Web authors have misused them, using frames for advertisements, and have neglected to provide content for browsers that don't support frames. Frames also slow down the user's browsing experience because there are several pages that must be loaded at once, instead of just one. If you're responsible and conscientious in your use of frames, you should be able to avoid the wrath of the vast majority of frame nay-sayers.

In this chapter, I'm going to create a new set of pages that utilize frames. In order to follow along as this happens, we're going to need to share two basic frame terms:

- *Frame.* A rectangular area within the Web browser that contains content independent of other frames on the page.
- *Frameset.* A special Web page that defines a set of frames, and the content that each frame contains.

Creating a page with frames means creating a frameset. Creating frames is a visual exercise, so I'm going to enable some visual tools in Dreamweaver. First, I want to see where the frame borders are, so I've selected **View**, and chosen **Frame borders** (see Figure 15.1). This adds an additional border to the inside of the Dreamweaver editing window that represents the outside borders of the frame. Since there are no frames defined yet, the border encompasses the entire page.

To get a continually updated picture of what's happening during the frame-creation process, you'll need to turn on the Frame Inspector window by selecting **Window** and then choosing **Frames**, as seen in Figure 15.1.

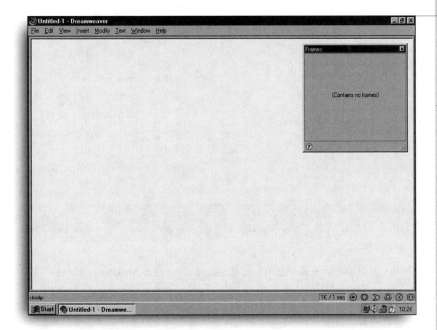

FIGURE 15.1
The editing window ready for frames, with frame borders visible and the Frame Inspector for our current document.

When it comes right down to it, every Web page has at least one frame, defined by the browser window. The frame borders view just highlights this fact. As you start to create additional frames, the HTML frame creation tags come into play to subdivide the screen. That comes next as we create a simple two-frame layout.

Creating a frame

1. Place the mouse pointer over the left or right frame border. Of course, if you're creating horizontal frames, you could use the top or bottom frame border.

2. Hold down the **Alt** key (in Windows) or **Option** key (for a Macintosh), and drag the border to the location of the dividing line for the new frame (see Figure 15.2). Alternately, you can drag from a corner to create four frames at once.

FIGURE 15.2

The mouse pointer changes to arrows as the property line for the new frame is dragged across the page.

If you'd rather not use the mouse, select **Modify**, choose **Frameset**, and then choose **Split Frame** along with one of the directions—up, down, left, or right.

3. The Frame Inspector window changes to illustrate the current frameset, which now consists of two vertical frames. Both are listed as "no name" because I haven't assigned a name to them yet.

SEE ALSO

➤ *Learn how to give your frame a name, page 238*

Clicking within a frame in the editing window selects the corresponding frame in the Frame Inspector (see Figure 15.3). Likewise, clicking a frame in the Inspector selects the corresponding frame in the editing window.

It may not look like much, but getting this far by creating HTML pages by hand was once the topic of a multi-page tutorial. If I wanted to add a further layer of complexity to my frame page, I could further subdivide one of the new frames. This is accomplished the same way you created the original two frames.

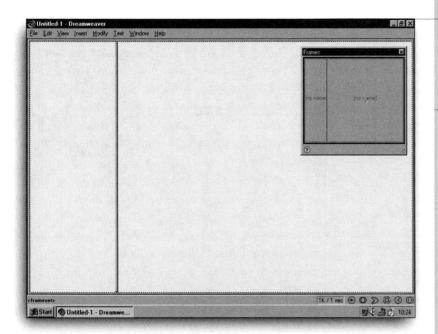

Creating a frame within a frame

1. Click within the frame to subdivide, by using either the editing window or the Frame Inspector.

2. Hold down the **Alt** key (in Windows) or **Option** key (for the Macintosh), and drag the border to the location of the dividing line for the new frame. Again, you can select **Modify**, choose **Frameset**, and then choose **Split Frame** along with one of the directions—up, down, left, or right.

3. The Frame Inspector window changes to illustrate the new subdivided frame (see Figure 15.4). The two new frames are "children" of the frame from which they were created, which is now referred to as the "parent."

You can create this process ad infinitum to create as many frames as you think are needed. However, as Benjamin Franklin advised, moderation is a virtue. The more frames, the less space each has to display its contents, and the more time required to load the content for each. As a general rule, three frames is a practical maximum, and five is an absolute.

FIGURE 15.4

The page now consists of one vertical and two horizontal frames, again reflected in the Frame Inspector.

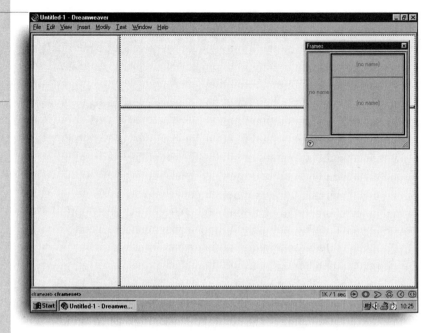

FIGURE 15.4

The page now consists of one vertical and two horizontal frames, again reflected in the Frame Inspector.

Watch that save!

If you just press Ctrl+S or select **File** and choose **Save**, you'll only save the file in the currently selected frame, and not the frameset. Then, when you exit Dreamweaver, you stand a good chance of losing all your work. There are no shortcuts to saving a frameset, so you'll need to make sure to select **File** and choose **Save Frameset**.

Additionally, you can save everything at once—the frameset and the content within each frame—by selecting **File** and choosing **Save All** (**Ctrl+Shift+S**). This is also necessary before you preview your work with an external browser. Otherwise, all you may see is the frameset without its content.

If you have too many frames and need to delete one, click and drag the frame border all the way off the page or to the border of its parent.

Once all the frames are created, you're ready to save the frameset. Select **File**, choose **Save Frameset**, and enter a filename (I've used index.html, because this page will be the default for its folder).

Editing Frame Content

Now that we have our frames, it's time to put something in them. The frame on the left will be used for an index to back-country travel tips, while the frame on the right will contain the content. Clicking a link in the left frame will display the results in the right frame, so the index is always available.

SEE ALSO

➤ *Learn how to control the content of one frame from another, page 240*

Essentially, editing content in a frame is the same as creating content in a normal page. After all, that's what you're creating—a normal page that just happens to be displayed within another page. To create a basic Web page, see Chapter 5, "Adding Text to a Page." To learn how to add multimedia content, such as plug-ins and ActiveX controls, see Chapter 9, "Working with Multimedia Content."

SEE ALSO
➤ *Adding images and graphics to your page, page 106*

In my example, I've created a list that will become a set of hyperlinks and named it tips-index.html. In the right frame, I'll add an existing page I've already created.

Adding an existing Web page to a frame

1. Click the frame to hold the Web page.

2. Open the file into the frame in one of the following ways:

   - Press **Ctrl+Shift+O** (Windows)
   - Press **Command+Shift+O** (Macintosh)
   - Select **File** and choose **Open in Frame**

3. From the Select HTML File dialog box (see Figure 15.5), select a page from the local directory, or you can specify a relative or absolute URL of another file on your site or on the Web.

4. Click **OK** to complete the process. The new page is loaded into the frame (see Figure 15.6), and can be edited as any other Web page.

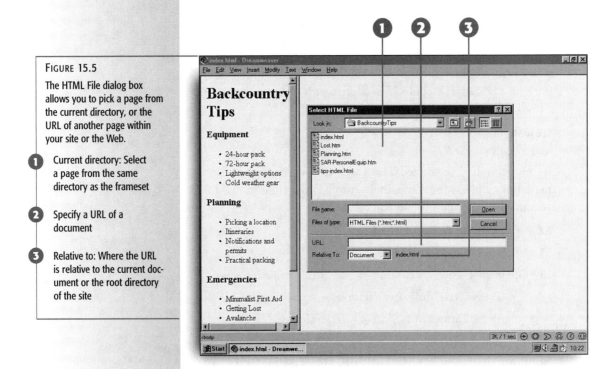

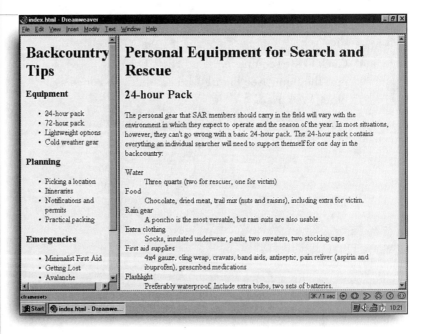

Now is a good time to select **File** and choose **Save All** (**Ctrl+Shift+S**), to save the current frameset and the content within all the frames. You can also save the content of each frame as you complete it by clicking in the frame and selecting **File** and choosing **Save** (**Ctrl+S**).

Once you've added content to a frame by creating a new page or adding an existing one, you can also change its properties just by right-clicking the frame and selecting **Page Properties** from the list that appears. You can adjust the page title, background color, default text colors, and other basic page information. For more information about changing the properties of a page, see Chapter 4, "Starting with a Blank Page."

Editing Content for Frame-less Browsers

It may be hard to believe, but not everyone who looks at your Web pages always has the latest and greatest Web browser. Frames are a perfect example. Earlier versions of Netscape Navigator and Microsoft Internet Explorer don't support frames, NCSA Mosaic never has, and text-only browsers such as Lynx never will.

So, in order to be a conscientious Web author and good Web citizen, you'll want to include content that these people can see when they load your page.

Creating NOFRAMES content

1. Select the frameset by clicking one of the frame borders.
2. View the HTML source by selecting the HTML Inspector. You can access the HTML Inspector in several ways:
   * Select the icon from the launcher.
   * Select **Window** and choose **HTML**.
   * Press **F10** (Windows).
3. In the HTML inspector window shown in Figure 15.7, there are three lines:
   ```
   <noframes><body bgcolor="#FFFFFF">

   </body></noframes>
   ```

What does frameset HTML look like?

As Dreamweaver works to create the frameset according to the addition and deletion of each frame, it is generating a bevy of HTML behind the scenes. If you happen to run across this set of HTML in other situations, it might be helpful to actually know what you're looking at.

```
<framese cols=
"200,588"rows="*">

<frame src="tips-
index.html">

<frame src="SAR-
PersonalEquip.htm">

</frameset>

<noframes><body
bgcolor="#FFFFFF">

</body></noframes>
```

The first line defines the basic frameset, including the size of each column or row in pixels. In this example, two columns are specified. Next is an entry for each column, including a file-name that tells the browser where to look for the frame content.

After the closing frameset tag (</FRAMESET>) comes a special set of tags for browsers that don't support frames. This is a good place to put a link to a version of your pages that doesn't require frames. In my example, this could be a link to the tips-index.html file. That process is covered in the section, "Editing Content for Frame-less Browsers."

FIGURE 15.7

Alternate content for browsers without frames is inserted from the HTML inspector window.

 Insert text and content for frame-less browsers here

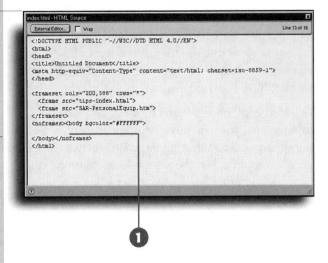

Got an editor? Use it!

If you'd prefer, this is a good time to use an external HTML editor such as HomeSite or BBEdit. Click the **External Editor** at the top of the HTML inspector window to launch the editor with a copy of your frameset. See Chapter 3, "Using Text Editors with Dreamweaver" for more information on configuring Dreamweaver to work with another editor.

4. Place the cursor on the blank line between the two, and begin entering your content. It's important to note that you're working with HTML source, which means you'll need to enter tags for hyperlinks, headings, and other items by hand. Unfortunately, Dreamweaver does not support visual editing of the alternate frame content.

With your frames happily in place and saved, and a bit of something for people who don't have browsers that support frames, you've got one of the hardest parts of working with frames out of the way. In the next few chapters, you'll learn how to further fine-tune your frames, including turning a set of frames into a navigation system.

From Here...

- Learn how to give your frames a name and how to create hyperlinks in one frame that control content in another in Chapter 16, "Working with Frames."

- With naming and hyperlinks in place, create an integrated wayt to view Web pages in Chapter 17, "Creating a Frame-Based Navigation System."

- Layers are another way to organize the content on your Web page. Read about them in Chapter 18, "Working with Layers."

16

Working with Frames

Give your frame a name

Aiming hyperlinks at other frames

We spent the last chapter looking at how to create and save frames, and then spent a bit of time loading them with content. The frameset I created for an example (see Figure 16.1) is designed for the user to click the left frame and have the content appear in the right frame.

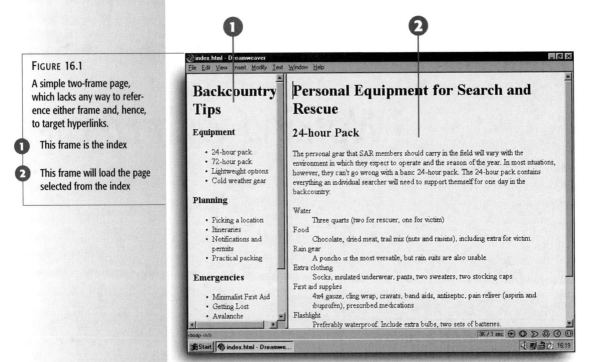

FIGURE 16.1

A simple two-frame page, which lacks any way to reference either frame and, hence, to target hyperlinks.

1 This frame is the index

2 This frame will load the page selected from the index

There's just one small problem—it doesn't work yet. The left frame doesn't know about the right frame, so there's no way to create the hyperlinks and have them work correctly.

Naming a Frame

There are some clever methods of referring to specific frames by relying on their relationships to each other and to the parent frameset. It's akin to referring to my sister as the boy's mother's daughter. Lucky for you, we're not going to talk about that method here.

We're going to give a name to our frames and refer to them as something meaningful, like Rick and Deliena. I'm going to use the index.html file created in the previous chapter. To see the results of my efforts, I'll also need the Frame Inspector (select **Window** and choose **Frames**) and the Properties palette (select **Window** and choose **Properties**).

Naming a frame

1. Select the frame to name by clicking its counterpart in the Frame Inspector. You can also **Alt+Click** (in Windows) or **Option+Click** (for the Macintosh). The Properties palette (see Figure 16.2) reflects the current state of the frame.

FIGURE 16.2

The Properties palette for a frame controls most of its features and attributes.

❶ Name field

❷ Source file for frame content

2. In the Name field next to the frame icon, enter a name for the frame. Since I'm working with the right frame, I'll call it `tip`. It's a good idea not to use spaces in your name, even though they're allowed technically. Instead, substitute underscores or dashes to keep the name neat and universally functional.

3. Repeat steps 1 and 2 for each frame in the frameset. I named the left frame `list`. Both frame names are now reflected in the Frame Inspector (see Figure 16.3).

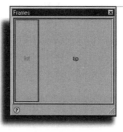

FIGURE 16.3

The Frame Inspector shows a representation of my frameset with their new names.

Giving a name to the frames might seem like a bit of frivolous behavior right now, but it will all make sense in the next section. Now that both frames are named, we can work on setting a hyperlink between the two.

Targeting a Frame in a Hyperlink

The process described in this section is the key to everything that happens in the next chapter, "Creating a Frame-Based Navigation System." You'll need to make sure the Properties palette is available for these steps (select **Window** and choose **Properties**).

SEE ALSO

➤ *For more information on creating hyperlinks, page 81*

Targeting a frame from a hyperlink

1. Click and drag the text for the hyperlink.

2. Using the browse button in the Link field, select the page to link.

3. Click the **expander arrow** in the bottom-right corner of the palette to view the Target field (see Figure 16.4).

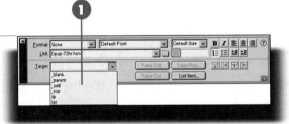

FIGURE 16.4

The expanded Properties palette reveals a field to define the hyperlink's target.

1 Target field

4. Click the arrow in the Target field to reveal a list of possible destinations for the hyperlink. These include generic destinations such as **_self** and **_parent**, and the object of our desire, **tip**. Advanced users can use the generic names (beginning with an underscore) for relative navigation, but we'll just select the name we need and call it good.

5. Repeat steps 1 through 4 for each hyperlink that needs to load its target into a different frame.

Once you've completed this process, clicking a hyperlink in the left frame will load the contents into the right frame, maintaining a constantly visible index for the reader. This method will work for any number of frames on a page—give each one a name, and then just select that name from the Target field. It's really that simple.

Fine-Tuning Frame Appearance

The Properties palette for frames also allows for control of other attributes (see Figure 16.5). Remember to select a frame, and not text or an element, to see the properties of a frame. Click the corresponding frame in the Frame Inspector, or click using the mouse and the **Alt** key (in Windows) or **Option** key (for the Macintosh).

First are frame borders. Traditional thinking says, yes, draw lines around your page so readers know where one page begins and another one ends. However, there are some sites that have stopped using borders, making the different frames appear as one seamless entity. The default behavior for most browsers is to display borders. You can override the default with **Yes** for always display borders and **No** for never display borders.

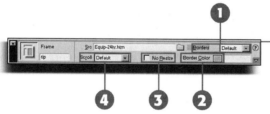

If you choose to use borders, you can also control their color. This attribute isn't supported by all browsers that support frames, so if it's crucial to your layout, you might start thinking of other solutions. Selecting a color for the border is the same as choosing a color for the background or text.

SEE ALSO

➤ *For more information on color, page 61*

Another option to decide is whether or not you want readers to be able to change the size of your frames. If your frame is housing a graphic of a specific size, or you're really particular about

---

No name city

If you type a name into the target field on the Properties palette without selecting it from the list, your users will experience an interesting phenomenon. In most browsers that support frames and targets, referencing a frame that doesn't exist launches a new instance of the browser. So, instead of one browser window, they'll have two. The first will hold the original file, and the second will have the page referenced in the hyperlink from the original.

This is an especially fun trick to use to create a free-floating navigation bar. As a matter of good manners, make sure you only create one or two extra windows—if each part of a navigation bar creates a new window, it quickly clutters the user's screen and resources to the point where nothing is useful.

FIGURE 16.5

The Properties palette controls several other aspects of frame behavior and appearance.

1. Controls whether or not borders are displayed between frames

2. Sets the color of the border between frames

3. Block readers from changing the size of frames

4. Controls use of scrollbars to view documents larger than the frame

controlling the appearance of your layout, you can select **No Resize**. If it really doesn't matter, you can leave the **No Resize** box alone and the reader can resize the frames to suit. This is helpful for vision-impaired readers who need to expand the readable area to accommodate larger fonts.

The last option controls the use of scrollbars. If the user is viewing a page that is wider and/or longer than the frame, most browsers automatically add scrollbars so he or she can move around and see the entire document. By selecting **Yes** in the Scroll field, you tell the browser to always use scrollbars, even if the entire document fits within the frame. Likewise, selecting **No** always blocks use of scrollbars, even if the document scrolls off the screen and isn't entirely visible.

There's one more Properties palette that is used for frames (see Figure 16.6). You access it by clicking the left border of a frameset in the editing window or on its outer border in the Frame Inspector. Click the **expander arrow** to see all of the properties.

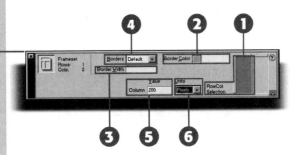

FIGURE 16.6

The frameset edition of the Properties palette controls common features of its frames, and is most useful when it's expanded.

1 Selects which frame to apply the setting to

2 Sets border color for the selected frame

3 Sets border width for the selected frame

4 Sets border for the selected frame

5 Sets the width (height) of the selected frame

6 Sets the units for the value in pixels, percent, or as a ratio to the other frames

This Properties palette is special because it includes an interactive thumbnail of the current frameset on the right side of the palette. You can click a frame in the thumbnail to make it the currently selected frame as you're applying settings.

The Border, Border Width, and Border Color fields are all identical to their counterparts discussed earlier in this section. The last two fields—Value and Units—control how the size of a frame is measured.

The two fields work in conjunction with each other. The setting for Units determines how the Value is interpreted. You can select **Pixels**, **Percent**, or **Ratio**. A pixel is a physical value, equal to one dot on your screen. It's very exact, but prone to unpredictable results when the page is viewed on browsers with different resolutions.

The second choice is **Percent**, which interprets the value as a percentage of available space. In my example, a value of 200 would mean 200 percent of the available space, or, a frame that scrolls off the right side of the screen.

The last choice is **Ratio**. It means that the value is treated as a portion of the whole. For example, say one column has a value of 2 and the other has a value of 3. That means the browser looks at the total of the two values (5), and assigns the first column two units of the available space, and the second three units. If there are three columns, and you want the first to have twice as much space as the other two, the values would be 2, 1, 1.

It is possible to mix and match values between frames. For example, let's say that you have a vertical frame that needs to hold an image that's 70 pixels wide, and the main frame will hold content. You can set the width of the frame to 70 pixels, and leave the width value for the other frame blank. The browser will allocate 70 pixels for the first, and the remainder of the window to the other.

You can also intermix the ability for resizing frames, although you'll want to think this through carefully. Let's say you have a three-frame system (one horizontal over two vertical). If you set either of the bottom two frames to block resizing, you've effectively blocked resizing for the entire frameset because resizing either of the other two frames would also affect the size of the locked frame. However, you could lock the top horizontal frame, and the bottom two frames could be resized by the users at will, since they wouldn't be affected by the top frame.

From Here...

- Review the ins and outs of setting the properties of a Web page in Chapter 4, "Starting with a Blank Page."
- Use tables to structure pages similar to frames in Chapter 14, "Refining Page Layouts Using Tables."

- Take the next step with frames and see how to build a three-frame navigation system in Chapter 17, "Creating a Frame-Based Navigation System."

- Are frames causing problems for you and your users? See Chapter 27, "Troubleshooting Dreamweaver."

Creating a Frame-Based Navigation System

Creating a header frame

Creating a navigation frame

Creating a content frame

Linking everything together

An ounce of preparation

Before the frames portion of this navigation system is started, we're going to assume a few things. First, that the book is written, converted to HTML, and the appropriate anchors are in place as targets for hyperlinks. Two, that an index page for each chapter has been created. The index page contains the chapter number, title, and section headings—all hyperlinked to the appropriate parts in the chapter. Last, that a table of contents page has also been created containing only the chapter numbers and titles, hyperlinked to the appropriate chapter index page.

Admittedly, there is a bit of work in the preparation, but it makes the work of creating the frame system much easier. Plus, the pages will stand on their own before the frame-based system is implemented, making the readers much happier people.

Getting the Workspace Ready

In this chapter, I'm going to create a navigation system with frames that would work with a book, such as this one, if it were placed in an online format. The system should make browsing the book a simple experience, whether the user has a frame-based browser or not.

To create this set of frames, I'll need the tools we've used so far in learning about frames—the Frame Inspector (accessed by selecting **Window** and then choosing **Frames**), the frame boundaries (accessed by selecting **View** and then choosing **Frame Borders**), and the Properties Inspector (accessed by selecting **Window** and then choosing **Properties**).

Creating a Header Frame

As I usually do with these projects, I'll start with a blank page. The first frame I want to create is at the top of the page—a header frame.

Create a header

1. Place the mouse pointer over the top frame border.

2. Hold down the **Alt** key (in Windows) or **Option** key (for the Macintosh), and drag the top border to the location of the dividing line for the new frame. If you'd rather not use the mouse, select **Modify**, choose **Frameset**, and then choose **Split Frame Up** (see Figure 17.1).

3. Select the top frame in the Frame Inspector, and then give it a name in the Properties Inspector. I'll call this one "header."

4. Save the frameset. I'm calling this frameset "dreamweaver.html."

5. Include the file for the header. The header is the top level of navigation, so I'm going to include dreamweaver-toc.html, which includes the chapter names and numbers for the book (see Figure 17.2).

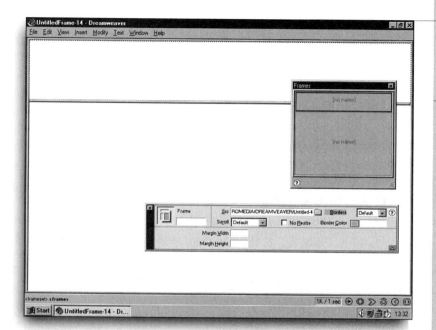

FIGURE 17.1

The first step is splitting the page into a header and footer frame.

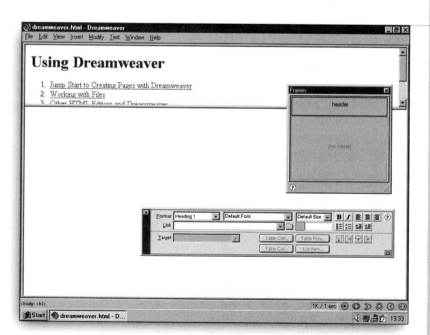

FIGURE 17.2

The header frame is named and its content is loaded.

Now that I've created the header and saved the frameset, I can move on to creating the two frames the user will interact with the most—the navigation and content frames.

Creating the Navigation Frame

After the header is in place, we're going to split the bottom frame into two vertical frames. The one on the left will become a navigation frame, and the other will hold the content.

Create a navigation frame

1. Click the bottom frame in the Frame Inspector.

2. Hold down the **Alt** key (in Windows) or **Option** key (for a Macintosh), and drag the left border of the bottom frame in the editing window to the location of the dividing line for the navigation frame. If you'd rather not use the mouse, select **Modify**, choose **Frameset**, and then select **Split Frame Left** (see Figure 17.3).

FIGURE 17.3

The footer frame is now split into two vertical frames. The one on the left is destined for use in navigation.

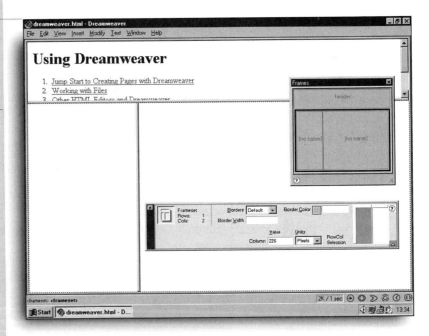

3. Select the bottom-left frame in the Frame Inspector, and then give it a name in the Properties Inspector. I'll call this one "navigation."

4. Include the default file for the navigation frame. Just to be unconventional, I'll include the Chapter 2 index (dreamweaver-2-index.html) as shown in Figure 17.4. This file includes the chapter number, name, and hyperlinks to the section titles within the chapter.

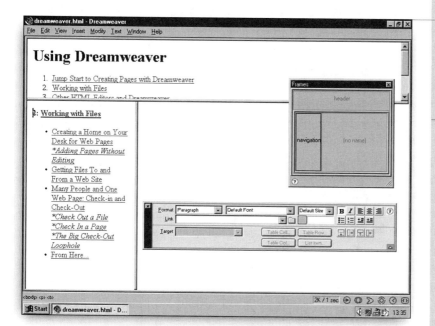

FIGURE 17.4

The header and navigation frames are named and loaded with content. The last construction step is to name and load the content frame.

5. Save the frameset.

With the header and navigation frames created and named, our attention now turns to the content frame. Since it was physically created in the process of creating the navigation frame, all that's left is to name it and load it with a default page.

Creating the Content Frame

The last construction step is naming the content frame and setting up a default page for it. To do this, follow the same steps used to create the navigation frame. The only difference is that we select the bottom-right frame in the Frame Inspector and name it "content." We will also use the actual text for Chapter 2 instead of just the index (see Figure 17.5).

FIGURE 17.5

The frameset construction is complete. Now, it's time to make the connections.

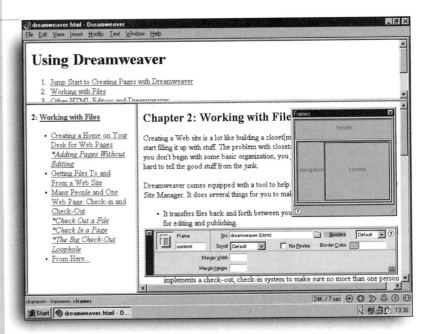

As you've seen in the last few pages, the construction of a navigation frameset is not terribly complicated—you don't even have to be a rocket scientist to get it done. The steps to link the frames together into a functional system are just as simple.

Linking Header and Navigation Anchors to the Content

The house is built, the walls are up, now all we need are a few doors to lead from one frame into another. To accomplish this, we need to use a special HTML tag in the header page and in each index page for the navigation frame.

There are two ways to accomplish this. The tedious way is to define a target for every hyperlink (see Figure 17.6). For example, every hyperlink in the header frame needs navigation as its target, and every hyperlink in the navigation frame needs content for a target.

FIGURE 17.6

For every hyperlink in the header frame, you would need to type `navigation` as the target–not much fun.

There's an easier method if you work directly from the HTML source code of the header frame (see Figure 17.7). Open the HTML Inspector by selecting **Window** and then choosing **HTML**, or clicking the HTML icon from the launcher.

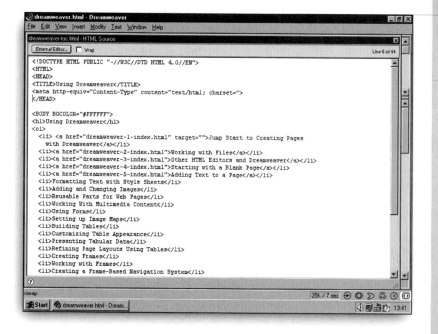

FIGURE 17.7

The HTML source of the header frame.

Linking header to navigation

1. After opening the HTML Inspector, move to the top of the document.

2. Position the cursor immediately before the `</HEAD>` tag.

3. Type the following:

   ```
   <BASE target="content">
   ```

   When you're done, the top few lines of your document should look like this in the Inspector:

   ```
   <!DOCTYPE HTML PUBLIC "-//W3C//DTD HTML 4.0//EN">
   <HTML>
   <HEAD>
   <TITLE>Using Dreamweaver</TITLE>
   <meta http-equiv="Content-Type" content="text/html;
   charset=">
   <BASE target="content">
   </HEAD>
   ```

4. Close the HTML Inspector and save the file.

What you've just done is inserted a special HTML tag that tells the browser how it should handle any hyperlinks on the page. Whenever the user clicks a hyperlink, the browser will automatically direct its content to the frame named in the `target` attribute of `<BASE>`. This process is repeated for each of the chapter index pages, only the target is set to `content`.

With everything in place, load the main frameset into your preview browser and try it out. Clicking a chapter name in the header loads its index into the navigation frame. Clicking a section in the navigation frame loads that chapter section into the content frame. It's quick, it's easy, it works.

From Here...

- Other methods of structuring multiple pages is possible with layers, covered in Chapter 18, "Working with Layers."

- You can also control frames with scripts, which are introduced in Chapter 19, "Adding Scripts to Pages."

- Try a different kind of index in your navigation frame by following the steps in Chapter 25, "Creating a Collapsible Outline."

- Make sure your pages are organized in a method that makes it easy to set up frame-to-frame relationships. See Chapter 26, "Making Your Site Work" for some site management pointers.

Working with Layers

What Are Layers?

"Layer" is a generic term for a variety of similar effects accomplished with different tricks, techniques, and a whole suite of proposed extensions to HTML.

Even though layers are implemented in many different ways, the basic ideas behind layers are pretty simple:

- *A Web page can be divided into as many parts or sections as desired.* This isn't a new, crazy, or controversial idea; in fact, it's an idea commonly used in HTML's ancestor SGML. Many documents consist of several different sections, and it makes sense to use HTML to mark where each section begins and ends. A layer, in its simplest sense, is simply one section of a Web page—usually, but not necessarily, a named section.

- *Each section of a page can be positioned independently. Under Netscape 4 and MSIE 4, any section of a page can be positioned anywhere in the layout. Thus, you can think of a layer as a page section that appears at a specific place on the page.* Here's where HTML purists start to get a little nervous; when you start to talk about positioning material, you are describing the document's appearance, rather than its logical structure. HTML isn't really about appearance, the purists say, and you shouldn't really use HTML to control the way a page looks—that's what style sheets are for. In fact, many layering techniques rely on a special extension to CSS, called CSS-P, where P stands for positioning.

- *Content can overlap.* Here's where layering makes a substantial break from The Way Things Have Always Been on the Web. If each section of the document can be positioned independently, why not put one section of the document on top of another section? That's exactly what some of the Web's crazier designers are doing.

- *Layers can move and change.* At this point, we are completely outside the universe of HTML and style sheets. Both Netscape Communicator/Navigator 4 and Microsoft

Internet Explorer 4 have expanded the power of scripts. Nowadays, scripts can alter the contents of a layer, or even reload the layer from a new URL, rather than reload the whole page. Scripts are also empowered to re-position web page objects, so that it's possible to animate and otherwise funk-i-fy the contents of a layer.

Examples of Layers in the Real World

There are many different ways that layer ideas can be applied to page design. Let's take a quick tour of some interesting layer-based sites.

One site that used layers-based animation at the dawn of the 4.0 browsers is the Macromedia-sponsored Dynamic HTML Zone site at `http://www.dhtmlzone.com`. (Tim Webster, the author of this chapter, developed this page with Macromedia alumnus Natalie Zee.) You can see a screen shot of the home page in Figure 18.1, but to get the full effect, it's best to load the page in your browser.

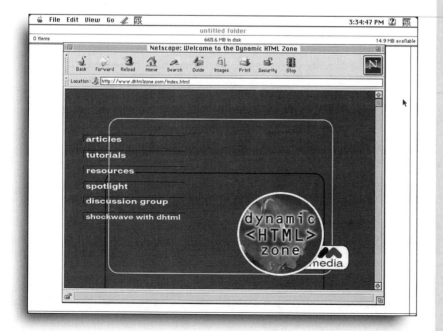

FIGURE 18.1

The Dynamic HTML Zone Web site uses layers technology for many special effects.

Each of the page's components—the logo, the table of anchors, both of the framing squares, and the copy—are in separate layers. The layers are carefully positioned and stacked on top of each other, so that the composite looks like a traditional `<table>`-based layout. Immediately after the page loads, each layer jumps a random distance and direction and then returns, via simple animation, to its proper position.

The Dynamic HTML Zone home page also uses layers technology for a less dramatic purpose: because the page contains several images, it takes a while to load. While the images are loading, the page displays a scrim—a nearly-empty layer with the message `loading`—that hides the action backstage until the animation is ready to start.

Layers are also handy for creating slide-show style presentations on a single page. Typically, layers are used to stack images on top of each other, and a script shuffles the images to bring a new image to the front when the user presses a button or otherwise attracts the script's attention.

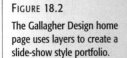

FIGURE 18.2
The Gallagher Design home page uses layers to create a slide-show style portfolio.

You can see an example of this use of layers on the Gallagher Design Web site at `http://www.cupofjoe.com`. Gallagher Design has created a layers-based portfolio in the bottom frame of the page; to navigate between site thumbnails, use the red arrow buttons on the left side of the frame.

Layer Caveats

There are a few important things to remember when you're working with layers:

- *Some layer tags are browser specific.* There are several different approaches to adding layers to your pages. (We'll look at the different flavors of layer tags in the "Layer Types" section later in this chapter.) Two of these tags, `<layer>` and `<ilayer>`, are Netscape extensions that are not currently supported (and may never be supported) by non-Netscape browsers.

- *Layers are cutting-edge technology.* Serious support for layers technology was introduced in Communicator/Navigator 4 and MSIE 4. There are plenty of users out there with older versions of Navigator or MSIE, users who use non-layer-savvy graphical browsers—such as the AOL browser or Sun's HotJava, and even some fossils and curmudgeons who use text-based browsers like Lynx. As of February, 1998, my reading of the client statistics at Browserwatch (`http://browserwatch.internet.com`) suggests that about 25% of MSIE users and 35-40% of Navigator/Explorer users have layers-compatible browsers, so about 30% of all browsers support frames.

It's possible to design pages that will satisfy users on both browser platforms, and even to design pages that will satisfy both layers-friendly and layers-blind browsers. In fact, one of Dreamweaver's great strengths is that it can help you juggle these issues. However, you need to be careful: it's easy to create pages that work well with layers-friendly browsers but fall apart when layers support is not available.

Problems usually arise when the page layout depends on overlapping content. For instance, in Figure 18.3, I've used Dreamweaver's layer support to create a drop shadow effect using HTML and only HTML. A layer containing red type overlaps a layer that contains the same type in black; by offsetting the red layer slightly, the black type shows through as a drop shadow.

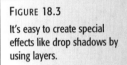

FIGURE 18.3

It's easy to create special effects like drop shadows by using layers.

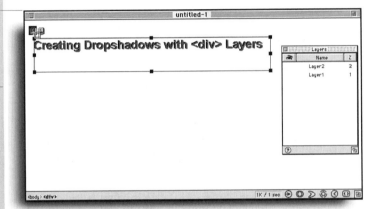

Although the drop shadow works brilliantly in the Dreamweaver window and in layer-compatible browsers, older browsers can't stack the two lines of text on top of each other. When we load Figure 18.3 in an older browser, the headline is separated from its shadow, creating the embarrassing results like the page shown in Figure 18.4.

FIGURE 18.4

The drop shadows effect may not survive in browsers that are not layer-compatible.

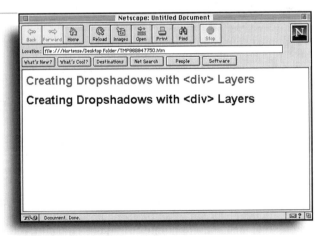

In general, when your layout depends on the precise positioning of individual layers, you'll have trouble with older browsers. The ordering of content may be jumbled, items meant to be hidden may be visible, and so on. For best results, use layers to enhance, rather than organize, a page that is meant to be universally compatible.

Layer Types: *div, span, layer, ilayer*

Dreamweaver supports four different kinds of layer tags: `<div>`, `<span>`, `<layer>`, and `<ilayer>`. The first two, `<div>` and `<span>`, are supported Navigator/Communicator 4 MSIE 4, and other CSS-P-compliant browsers, such as the W3C test browser Amaya. It's likely that other "minor" browsers, like HotJava and Mosaic, will eventually support these two tags. The `<layer>` and `<ilayer>` tags are a Netscape extension; although Netscape's open standards policy allows other developers to support these tags, it seems unlikely that `<layer>` and `<ilayer>` will be compatible with anything but Netscape-brand browsers.

Let's look at each of the tags in detail.

<div>

`<div>` has always had good standing with the HTML purist crowd; `div` is short for division, and the `<div>` tag is used to section a document into its logical parts. If this chapter were put into HTML format, for instance, the document's divisions would probably correspond to the major sections in the chapter, such as "What Are Layers?" and "Layer Caveats."

There are no innate layer features to `<div>`. It's merely a convenient way to group together all of the HTML that makes up the layer. The following shows the use of the `<div>` in its simplest form:

```
<div name = myFrame1>
<img src = myPicture.gif>
<p>CEO Mr. I. G. Farben</p>
</div>
```

Making peace between layers and older browsers

One solution to this kind of problem is to set up alternate pages for browsers that support layers and browsers that don't, and try to redirect readers to the appropriate page. There are many different ways to accomplish redirection: servers can send (or compose) different pages based on the client, Web page scripts can swap in new pages for the current page, or readers can be offered the choice between "hi-tech" and "low-tech" pages. Of course, creating alternate sets of pages means you need to build two or more pages for each; this can be a lot of work, especially on a large site.

The `<div>` tag doesn't say anything about where the image and its caption should be placed on the page; nor does it specify whether or not the material is to be visible or invisible. And there's no mention of the material's stacking order with respect to other page content. All the `<div>` tag really does is specify that the picture and text go together—they're one logical unit.

In order to specify the position and other display attributes of the material in the `<div>` layer, we use a CSS-P style sheet. As I mentioned earlier in the chapter, the P stands for positioning, and CSS-P is an extension of the proposed CSS standard. You don't need to know the details, really—Dreamweaver will take care of everything for you—but if you're interested, you can find W3C's authoritative documentation at `http://www.w3.org/TR/WD-positioning`.

By using CSS-P, we can specify position and display parameters for the contents of the `<div>` tag like the following:

```
<style>
#myLayer {
    position:absolute;
    left:100px;
    top:100px;
    width:100px;
    height:100px;
    z-index:1
}
</style>
```

or simply add the style as an inline element within the tag itself:

```
<div id="myLayer1" style="position:absolute; left:100px;
top:100px; width:100px; height:100px; z-index:1">
```

In fact, this is exactly how Dreamweaver generates layers using the `<div>` tag.

<span>

The `<span>` tag will be familiar to those readers who have experimented with CSS. Like the `<div>` tag, the `<span>` tag is used to mark off items into groups. However, `<div>` is used to create block-level groupings; while a `<span></span>` pair can contain a series of block-level elements, and it can also be used to mark elements inside a block item. For instance, we can set up a `<span>` within a single line of text:

```
Many years later, as he faced the firing squad, <span name =
character>Colonel Aureliano Buendña<span> was to remember
that distant afternoon when his father took him to discover
ice.
```

Ordinarily, the `<span>` tag is used when you want to leave the tagged material exactly where it is, rather than moving it into its own display block. For instance, in the passage from *One Hundred Years of Solitude*, we'd like the name Colonel Aureliano Buendña to remain inside the sentence that it's a part of, rather than floating over some other part of the page.

However, that's not the way that Dreamweaver treats the `<span>` tag. Dreamweaver automatically applies CSS positioning to the contents of a `<span>`-based layer, so that such layers behave in the same way that `<div>` layers do. (Dreamweaver does use the `<span>` tag in a more sensible way when it applies style sheets to text.)

<layer>

`<layer>` is a extension tag introduced by Netscape. It has not gained wide acceptance and is not supported by MSIE.

Functionally, the `<layer>` tag is very much like a `<div>` tag that has a CSS-P position attached to it. The difference is fairly subtle, but significant. A `<div>` tag without a CSS-P style sheet specifies the logical function of a block of HTML; it says nothing about how the block should be displayed. The `<layer>` tag, on the other hand, is used solely to specify where and how the block of text should be displayed.

`<layer>` does offer a few unique advantages: you can load the contents of a layer from an external source file, and you can re-load the layer from a new source file without disrupting any other elements of the page that contains the `<layer>`. If these features sound a little familiar, it's because this linking to external HTML files is very similar to what happens with garden-variety `<frame>`s.

<ilayer>

<ilayer> is also a Netscape extension tag; it was introduced as a companion to <layer>. Netscape brand browsers offer the only support for <ilayer>.

The <layer> tag, like <div>, is used to handle block-level items such as headlines, paragraphs, and tables. Like the <span> tag, <ilayer> tag is meant to handle inline items, such as images or a few words or lines within a paragraph.

To be honest, Dreamweaver just doesn't know what to do with <ilayer> tags, so it creates <ilayer>-based layers in exactly the same way that it creates <layer>-based layers—as an independent block. If you want to work with <ilayer>, it's best to add the tags by hand with the HTML editor, rather than by using Dreamweaver's WYSIWYG tools.

Adding a Layer to Your Page

Enough theory. Let's make some layers. In this chapter, we'll use layers to create a logo for a "magnetic poetry" site. Figure 18.5 shows the basic look we're shooting for.

FIGURE 18.5
You'll use layers to individually position each word in the logo.

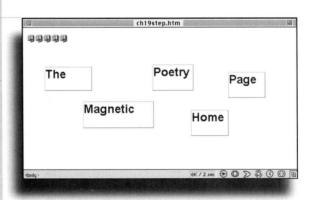

Adding a set of layers to the page

1. Start with a new, blank layout.

2. Click the **Marquee Layers** tool in the Objects palette. You'll notice that the arrow cursor turns into a crosshairs cursor. (See Figure 18.6)

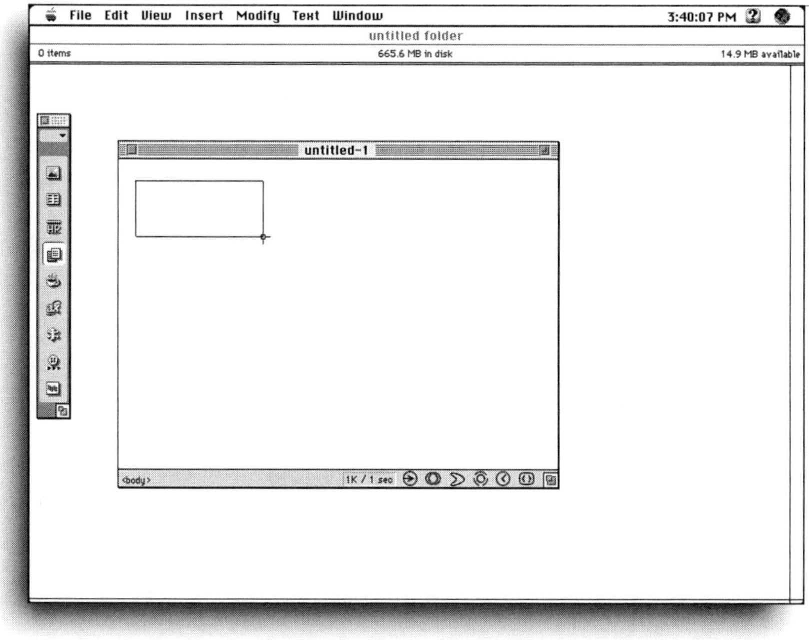

FIGURE 18.6

Dreamweaver displays a crosshairs cursor when you're drawing layers.

3. Use the crosshairs cursor to draw the first layer. Position the crosshairs where you'd like to put the top-left corner of the layer. Click and hold, and then drag the mouse down and to the right. You'll see the layer's outline appear as you draw. When the layer is about the right size to hold the word The, release the mouse.

4. Dreamweaver adds a layer anchor point to the layout (see Figure 18.7). The anchor and the layer border appear in Dreamweaver as an editing convenience; they won't appear in the final layout.

5. Click inside the layer's border to position the insertion point inside the layer.

6. Type the first word of the logo (The) at the insertion point. Size and style the type as desired, using Dreamweaver's standard text tools.

7. Click the Marquee Layer tool in the Objects palette. The arrow cursor turns into a crosshairs cursor.

8. Use the crosshairs cursor to draw a second layer box.

FIGURE 18.7

Dreamweaver adds an anchor point to the layout as an editing convenience.

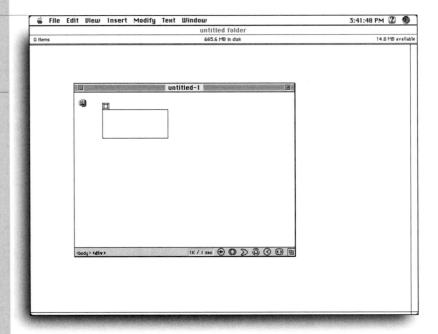

9. Click inside the new layer's border to position the insertion point inside the layer.

10. Type the second word of the logo (Magnetic) at the insertion point. Size and style the type as desired.

At this point, your layout should look something like Figure 18.8. (The size and position of your layers may be different—that's perfectly OK.) Notice that no matter where you position the layers on the page, the layers' anchor points are side-by-side in the top-left corner of the page—exactly where an ordinary object would appear if you added it to the layout.

In fact, those layer anchor points show you exactly where your layer content will appear if the page is viewed with a down-level browser. Figure 18.9 shows what the completed logo looks like when displayed by Netscape Navigator 3.1 for MacOS.

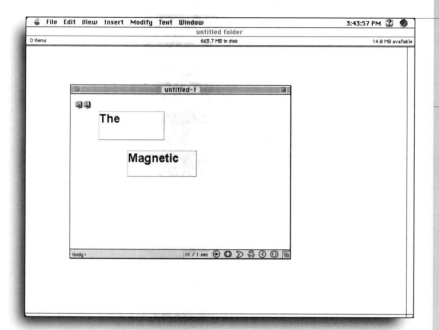

FIGURE 18.8

No matter where you position the layers on the page, the layers' anchor points appear side-by-side at the insertion point.

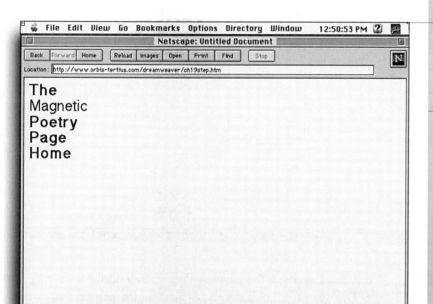

FIGURE 18.9

Dreamweaver's layer anchor points show where layer content will be displayed by a down-level browser.

Working with Layers

Why is the logo stacked?

If the layer anchors are in a horizontal row in the Dreamweaver layout, why are the layer contents in a vertical stack in Figure 18.9? Dreamweaver adds <p></p> tags around the content in each layer, just as it does with any text that you type at the insertion point. The <p> tags cause the line breaks between words.

11. Repeat steps 7-10 to add the remaining layers (Poetry, Home, and Page), positioning each layer as desired.

Understanding the Layers Palette

The Layers palette is an essential tool for managing complex pages with several layers. You can use the Layers palette to select layers, rename layers, and (as we shall see in a subsequent section of this chapter) control the stacking order of layers.

Naming the page's layers

1. To bring up the Layers palette, press **F11**, or select **Windows** and choose **Layers**. Figure 18.10 shows what your Layers palette should look like.

FIGURE 18.10.

Dreamweaver's Layers palette helps you manage the naming and stacking of layers.

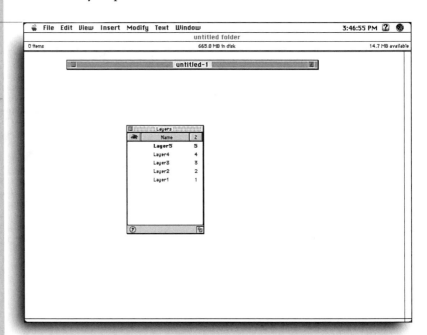

2. Click **Layer1** in the **Layers** palette. You'll notice that Dreamweaver bolds the layer's name in the palette, and selects the layer in the layout.

3. In the main Dreamweaver window, click the handle of the layer that contains the word Magnetic. (The handle is the little # nubby at the top-left corner of the layer's border.) Notice that Dreamweaver bolds the layer's name (Layer2) in the Layers palette.

4. Double-click the Layer's name in the Layers palette. Dreamweaver highlights the layer's name, to show that that the name can be edited. Change the name to The.

5. Repeat step 4 to name each of the layers in the layer palette, naming each layer after the word that it contains.

When you're done, your layout and Layers palette should look like Figure 18.11.

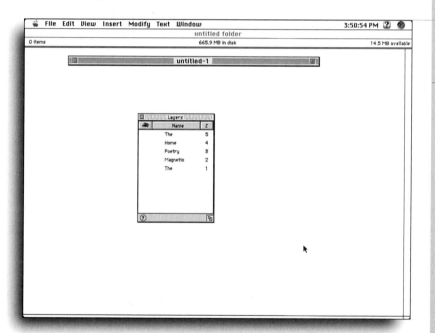

FIGURE 18.11
Give each of the layers in your page-sensible names.

Choosing a Layer Tag

Dreamweaver allows you to specify which of the four layer tags—<div>, <span>, <layer>, or <ilayer>—should be used to create the layer. See the "Layer Types" section for a detailed analysis.

In most cases, it's best to use the <div> tag, which is recognized by both Netscape Navigator 4 and MSIE 4. <div> is Dreamweaver's default.

Changing a layer's tag to the Netscape-only <*layer*> tag

1. Click the layer's anchor point (or the layer's name in the Layer dialog box) to select the layer.

2. In the Properties palette, choose **Layer** from the tag pop-up menu.

   When you change a layer's tag to <layer> or <ilayer>, Dreamweaver makes a slight change to the layer's anchor point. Ordinary anchor points are labeled with a "C" (for "cross browser"); Dreamweaver labels <layer> and <ilayer> anchor points with an "N" (for Netscape.) Figure 18.12 shows the two kinds of anchor points side-by-side.

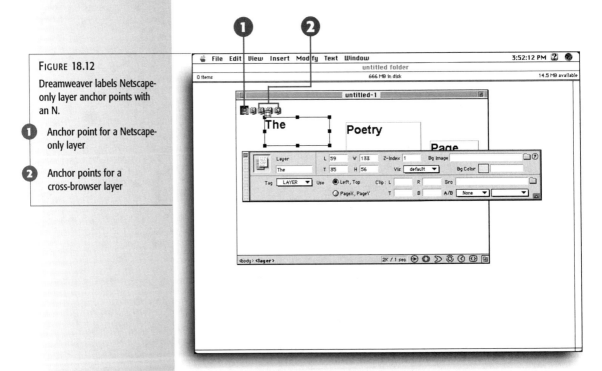

FIGURE 18.12

Dreamweaver labels Netscape-only layer anchor points with an N.

❶ Anchor point for a Netscape-only layer

❷ Anchor points for a cross-browser layer

3. Change the layer back to a <div> layer. There's no good reason to use <layer> in the magnetic poetry logo.

Sizing Layers

Dreamweaver's layer-sizing tools will seem familiar to those of you who have worked with page layout programs such as QuarkXpress and Adobe Pagemaker. To resize a layer, you simply move the handles that are positioned around the layer's border.

Resizing layers

1. Click the layer's name in the Layer palette (or the layer's anchor point) to select the layer. Dreamweaver highlights the layer and adds eight handles around the layer's edges (see Figure 18.13).

<table>
<tr><td>

You can reset the default to your favorite tag

If you find that you routinely use a layer tag other than `<div>`, you can reset Dreamweaver's default with the Preferences dialog box. First, select **Edit** and choose **Preferences** to bring up the dialog box. Click the **Layers** category in the list on the left, and choose your preferred tag (such as `<layer>` from the Tag pop-up menu.

</td></tr>
</table>

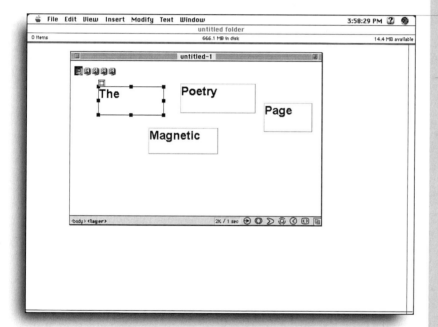

FIGURE 18.13

Use the layer's handles to resize the layer.

2. To change a layer's height without affecting its width, click and hold the layer's top or bottom handle and drag the handle.

3. To change a layer's width without changing its height, click and hold a side handle and drag the handle.

4. To change a layer's size freestyle (both width and height at once), click and hold any handle and drag the handle.

So, you want to be more precise?

You can size the layer precisely by adjusting the layer's H (for height) and W (for width) fields in the Properties palette.

So What's Clipping?

What happens if the size that you specify for your layer isn't big enough to accommodate the content for the layer? Does the layer get bigger, or does some of the content disappear? That's a good question. Unfortunately, there isn't a good answer.

In theory, this issue is handled by CLIP settings. CLIP is both a CSS-P style name (in the case of the <div> tag) and a tag parameter (in the case of the <layer> tag). When you specify CLIP settings, you specify limits on how much of the layer is displayed. If you don't specify a CLIP, the layer will expand to fit everything.

In practice, the implementation of CLIP is all over the place, and the same version of the same browser behaves differently on different platforms. Even within a single version and platform, whether or not CLIP actually behaves is unpredictable at best. Play with CLIP, if you like, but don't count on it.

Positioning Layers

I'm also pretty confident that you have figured out how to move layers around once you have added them to the layout. For the record, you perform the following steps.

Positioning layers

1. Click the layer's anchor or its name in the Properties palette to select the layer.

2. Click and hold the layer's handle (that # nubby thing at the top) and drag the layer.

To more precisely position a layer

If you want to precisely position a layer, use the L field in the Properties palette to specify the distance in pixels from the left edge of the browser window to the left edge of the layer. Use the T field to specify the distance between the top of the browser's window to the top edge of the layer.

Stacking Layers

One of the really cool thing about layers is that you can stack them on top of each other. For instance, you can create the kind of drop-shadow effect I demonstrated earlier in this chapter, create animated-GIF-style animations, or create any number of other special effects. Let's do a little experimenting to see how this works.

Stacking layers

1. Click the **The** layer's name in the Layers palette to select the layer.

2. In the Properties palette, use the bgColor swatch to assign a background color to the layer. Any color is fine.

3. Repeat steps 1-2 to give a different color to each layer in the layout. (Using different colors will make it easy to see the stacking order of the layers.)

4. Drag the layers so that they all overlap. (See Figure 18.14 for one example of what this might look like.)

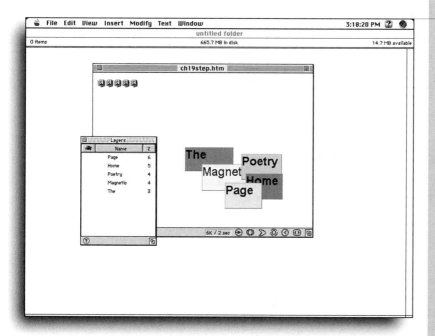

FIGURE 18.14

Stack the layers on top of each other.

Note that the ordering of the names layers in the Layers palette exactly reflects the stacking order of layers in the layout. "The" is at the bottom of the Layer palette, and it's at the bottom of the stack of layers.

5. In the Layers palette, drag the entry line for the "The" layer to the top of the list of names in the Layer palette. Dreamweaver brings the "The" layer to the top of the stack in the layout. (See Figure 18.15.)

FIGURE 18.15

Changing the stacking order in the Layers palette changes the stacking order of entries in the layout.

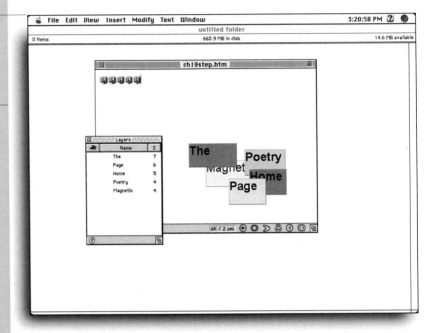

Z-order parameters

Web browsers use the layers' Z-order parameters to determine the layers' stacking order: the layer with the highest Z-order goes on the top of the stack, and the one with the lowest Z-order goes on the bottom. Dreamweaver displays the Z-order of each layer in the Layers palette, and automatically adjusts Z-orders when you shuffle the stacking order.

From Here...

Many of the animation-based projects in the latter chapters of this book use layers to achieve their effects.

- To use layers to create a moving animation, see Chapter 21, "Creating Animations: Moving Objects."

- To use layers to create an animated-GIF-style animation, see Chapter 22, "Animations: Flashing Objects."

- To create a push-style animation (and dynamically load a Netscape <layer> while you're at it) see Chapter 23, "Animations: Creating Push Pages."

Adding Interactivity and Scripts

Adding Scripts to Pages

What Is a Script?

HTML is a markup language, not a programming language. Markup languages are designed for the labeling of page elements: this part of the page is a headline, this part is a block of body text, and so on. Programming languages are about making decisions: if this condition is true, perform procedure X; if the condition is not true, skip procedure X, and perhaps perform procedure Y or Z instead.

HTML's weak point is decision making: there's no mechanism within HTML for a Web page to decide what it wants to display. However, there are plenty of occasions when you'd like your HTML to be a little more flexible: you'd use the <h1> tag for headlines if you know the user has a 600×800 screen, but you'd use the <h2> tag if the user has a little 480×640 screen. Web page scripting languages, like Netscape's JavaScript and Microsoft's VBScript, give your Web pages decision-making ability. (In fact, scripting opens the door to plenty of possibilities, but decision making is really the core of scripting and programming.)

There's not enough room in this chapter (in fact, probably not enough room in this book) to teach you how to program in JavaScript or HTML. Rather, I'll focus on how you can use Dreamweaver to add finished scripts to your page.

If you're a seasoned scriptor, finding finished scripts to add to your page won't be a problem. If you're just getting started with scripting, I recommend the following titles:

- *Sams' Teach Yourself JavaScript in a Week* (Sams.net)
- *Dynamic HTML Unleashed* (Sams.net)

It's also possible to add scripting to your pages without knowing anything at all about what's going on inside a script, and, if this is your preference, you're using the right development tool. Dreamweaver writes plenty of its own scripts that you will never need or want to look at, and it makes it easy to use the cut-and-paste scripts commonly offered in books, magazines, and Web sites.

What Scripts Can and Can't Do

Scripts really open the doors of possibility for talented and imaginative developers. Some of the interesting things you can do with scripts include:

- *Create conditional HTML.* A script can write HTML on-the-fly as the page loads. This can be very simple—as simple as changing "Hello, Netscape Navigator user!" to "Hello, Microsoft Internet Explorer user!"—or very complex indeed. Depending on the version of the scripting language, scripts can test for such things as the user's browser, the user's operating system, the plug-ins installed on the browser, the size of the user's screen, and so on. (The latest version of MSIE allows changes to the HTML of the page after the page has been loaded.)

- *Inspect and change form contents.* Scripts can interact with the contents of forms—make sure that fields have been filled out, test whether check boxes are checked or unchecked, and so on. In fact, scripts can alter the value of form components as desired.

- *Create alert boxes.* Scripts can create standard operating system alert boxes to warn, cajole, or annoy users.

- *Replace images.* Scripts can swap in one image for another, even after the page has been loaded. (Nearly every "rollover" button that flashes or changes when the mouse passes over the button uses scripting to achieve the rollover effect.)

- *Perform calculations.* Scripts can do basic mathematical calculations and do some basic character-string wrangling. (Usually, calculations are used in a dog-and-pony show to demonstrate that scripts can perform calculations, but there are probably a few real-world applications out there.)

- *Communicate with Java applets.* Java is quite a bit more complicated than JavaScript and VBScript, and most amateur programmers just don't have the time to develop full-blown Java applications. Some Java applets can serve as "engines" that do powerful things—like access databases—and scripts can serve as throttle and steering wheel for such Java engines.

Why you should learn to script

I think that it's a good idea to spend just a little time learning about JavaScript and VBScript, even if you never plan to write your own scripts. If you have an inkling of how a ready-made script works, you'll find it easier to figure out what's going wrong when the script doesn't work, or behaves in a bizarre fashion. And, even though HTML isn't a programming language—it's really not even close—learning to program will probably sharpen your understanding of how HTML, browsers, and the Web work.

- *Redirect the browser to new locations.* A script can cause the browser to load a new page. Often, this technique is used when a page contains special content that older or plug-in-poor browsers can't read—the script redirects such browsers to friendlier pages.

- *Store information on the user's machine.* For security reasons, scripts can't read and write files on the user's machine, but scripts can store small bundles of information, called cookies, on the user's machine. Cookies are useful for tracking visitor movement through your site, storing passwords and other information for return visitors, and stirring up political turmoil in Internet newsgroups.

Scripts can't do everything, however. There are some limitations on the power of scripts; some are based on practical issues, and some limitations address security issues:

- *Change page items once the page is loaded.* With one important exception, scripts cannot change a page's HTML once the page has been displayed. (Replacing images, mentioned previously, isn't really changing the page's HTML.) What's the exception? MSIE 4 allows scripts to edit the HTML of a Web page after the page has loaded.

- *Access operating system information.* Certain information is off limits to scripts: the user's password, for instance, the user's email address, and other personal and private information. (Because scripts can freely submit form data, an evil script could send off any private information that it found to any address on the Net.)

- *Access the user's hard drive or other documents.* To prevent scripts from making virus-like attacks on the user's hard drive, scripts cannot write to the user's hard drive. To prevent scripts from pilfering private information (say, electronic tax files, old love letters, or copyrighted software), scripts cannot read files on the user's disk.

Choosing JavaScript or VBScript

In early 1998, there are two scripting languages available to Web developers: JavaScript (nee LiveScript), developed by Netscape; and VBScript, developed by Microsoft. Dreamweaver supports both languages.

Despite its name, JavaScript has very little to do with the famous Java programming language developed by Sun Microsystems. JavaScript was developed by Netscape primarily for Web page scripting, and JavaScript has few applications outside the world of Web page development.

VBScript was developed by Microsoft as part of Microsoft's Visual Basic technology family. As a result, VBScript will be very familiar to many Windows developers, and seem a little bizarre to UNIX and Macintosh developers.

There are actually three different implementations of JavaScript: versions 1.0, 1.1, and 1.2. The major browsers support scripting languages as follows:

NN 1.0, 1.1	no scripting support
MSIE 1.0	no scripting support
NN 2.0	JavaScript 1.0
MSIE 2.0	no scripting support
NN 3.0	JavaScript 1.0, 1.1
MSIE 3.0 for Windows	JavaScript 1.1, VBScript
MSIE 3.0 for Mac	JavaScript 1.1
NS 4.0	JavaScript 1.0, 1.1, 1.2
MSIE 4.0	JavaScript 1.1, VBScript

Microsoft's Windows 98

In late 1997, Microsoft announced that its Windows 98 operating system software would provide support for JavaScript as a systems scripting language. Essentially, developers will be able to replace those clunky old DOS batch files with more sophisticated JavaScript (and VBScript) scripts.

Creating the Script

First, you'll need a script to add to your page.

I've written a tiny script for use in this example. The script looks at the time of day, and adjusts the background color of the page accordingly: if the time is between sunrise and sunset, the page background turns light blue; if the time is before sunrise or after sundown, the page background turns dark blue.

Here's the script, which is written in JavaScript.

```
sunrise = 7;
sunset = 18;

today = new Date();
if ((today.getHours() >= sunrise) && (today.getHours() <=
sunset)) {
    document.bgColor = "#99ccff";
} else {
    document.bgColor = "#666699";
}
```

You're going to use this code several times, so it's a good idea to store it in its own file.

Storing the JavaScript in a text file

1. Launch your favorite text editor (such as Notepad on the PC, or SimpleText or BBEdit on the Macintosh).

2. Create a new text document with the text editor. Every text editor is different, but for almost all menu-driven editors select **File** and choose **New**.

3. Type in the code above exactly as it appears. Case is very important; for instance, be sure to type `bgColor`, rather than bgcolor or BGColor.

4. Save the text file. Give it the name day-night.js, and store the file in the directory that contains the HTML file for the Web page you want to enhance with the script.

Use the .js extension

When you create your own script files, use the .js extension so that browsers, servers, and non-Macintosh operating systems can identify the file as a script.

It can be hard to type out a whole script without making subtle mistakes that can be hard to see. Even small mistakes can make the script fail. If you're having script error problems, or you don't feel like typing out the script, you can cut and paste the script from the example page on this book's Web site.

Downloading the script

1. Use your Web browser to load the Chapter 19 page on the book's Web site at www.mcp.com/info, or the mirror page http://www.orbis-tertius/dreamweaver/ch19step.htm.

2. Use your browser's **View Source** command to look at the page's HTML. (If you're using a Netscape browser, select **View** and then choose **Page Source**. If you're using MSIE, select **View** and choose **Source**. If you're using another browser, consult your browser's documentation.)

3. Find the script that's written out earlier in this chapter; it's surrounded by a <script></script> tag pair, and is the only script on the page.

4. Select the script in the browser's source window. (Your browser may launch a helper application, rather than open-ing a special source window; that's perfectly OK.) Be sure that the section contains everything from the first line of the script, sunrise = 7, to the last line, which consists of a single right curly bracket on a line by itself. It's your choice whether or not to copy the two comment lines (marked with # at the beginning of each line), but don't select the <script> or the </script> tag!

5. Select the browser's (or helper application's, if launched by the browser) **Edit** command and then choose **Copy**.

6. Launch your favorite text editor (such as Notepad on the PC, or SimpleText or BBEdit on the Macintosh).

7. Create a new text document with the text editor. Every text editor is different, but for almost all menu-driven editors select **File** and choose **New**.

8. Select **Edit** and then choose **Paste** to paste the script into the new text document.

9. Save the text file. Give it the name day-night.js, and store the file in the directory that contains the HTML file for the Web page you want to enhance with the script.

Adding Scripts with the Insert Script Tool

Dreamweaver provides basic support for scripting. To be honest, script development isn't Dreamweaver's strongest area: there is

Typing can be a learning experience

If you're a novice programmer who's serious about learning how to script, I suggest you try to type out the script by hand, rather than cutting and pasting it. You can learn a lot by re-typing other people's scripts. Really. Think of it as paying your dues.

no way to test or debug scripts within Dreamweaver itself, and you may need to use Dreamweaver's HTML editor to hand-edit the `<script>` tag that Dreamweaver creates. (For the record, Dreamweaver's WYSIWYG competitors aren't really better at handling scripts.)

Adding a Local Script

Adding a local script to your page

1. Use your preferred text editor to open the day-night.js file you created in the previous section.
2. Select and copy all of the script. (Text editors vary, but to accomplish this in most you will select **Edit** and then choose **Copy**.)
3. In Dreamweaver, click **Mode** button at the top of the Objects palette (see Figure 19.1) and select **Invisibles** from the pop-up menu.
4. Click the **Insert Script** button.

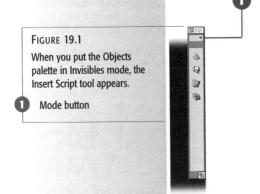

FIGURE 19.1

When you put the Objects palette in Invisibles mode, the Insert Script tool appears.

1 Mode button

5. Dreamweaver presents the Insert Script dialog box. Click to position the insertion point in the dialog box's Script window. (See Figure 19.2.)

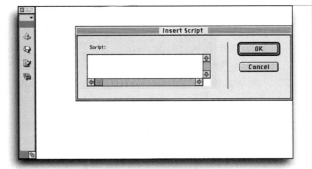

FIGURE 19.2
Use the Insert Script dialog box to paste scripts into your page.

6. Select **Edit** and then choose **Paste** to paste the script you copied in step 2 into the Insert Script dialog box's Script window.

7. Click **OK** button to close the dialog box. (Pressing **Enter** or **Return** on your keyboard will add a blank line to the script, rather than closing the dialog box.)

8. Dreamweaver adds a script marker to the layout, as shown in Figure 19.3. (The marker is for editing purposes only; it won't show up when the page is displayed by a Web browser.) Make sure that the script marker is selected. If the script marker isn't selected, click it with the mouse to select it.

FIGURE 19.3
Dreamweaver adds a script marker as an editing convenience. The marker won't appear when the page is displayed by a browser.

9. Select **JavaScript** from the Language pop-up menu in the Properties palette.

To see the script in action, load the page in a JavaScript-enabled Web browser. To do this you can press **F12**, or select a browser from the **File** menu and choose **Preview**. Remember, if you're testing the script in the daytime, the page will have an azure background. If you're testing the script at night, the page will have a dark blue background.

Adding a Linked Script

Creating a link to an external file is even easier than adding a local script. If you've followed the previous instructions to add a local script to your page, be sure to remove the old script by deleting the script marker in the Dreamweaver layout. (Adding two identical scripts won't hurt anything, but it looks dumb to other developers who are snooping through your source code.)

Adding a linked script

1. Make sure you created the day-night.js text file, as described in the "Creating the Script" section, earlier in this chapter.

2. In Dreamweaver, click the **Mode** button at the top of the Objects palette and select **Invisibles** from the pop-up menu.

3. Click the **Insert Script** button.

4. Dreamweaver presents the Insert Script dialog box. You don't need to enter anything into the dialog box; simply close it by clicking **OK**. (Pressing **Return** or **Enter** on the keyboard will add empty lines to the script, rather than closing the dialog box.)

5. Dreamweaver puts a script marker in the layout. The marker is an editing convenience, and won't show up when the page is displayed by a Web browser. Make sure that the marker is selected; if it's not, click it to select it.

6. In the Properties palette, click the folder-shaped button to the right of the Source field.

7. Dreamweaver presents the Select Script dialog box. Use the top portion of the box (which looks like a conventional file dialog box) to navigate to the day-night.js text file.

Storing your scripts

If you understand how relative URLs work, you can put the script wherever you like. For instance, it might make sense to create a scripts directory at the root level of your site. You know best what organization scheme you prefer.

8. Make sure that the URL field at the bottom of the Select Script dialog box reads simply day-night.js.

9. Make sure that the Relative To pop-up menu is set to **Document**.

10. Click **Open** to dismiss the dialog box.

Adding Scripts with the HTML Editor

Sometimes, the Insert Script tool is inadequate. If you're a serious script developer, you'll find that there are occasions when you will need to use Dreamweaver's HTML editor to add your scripts to your pages.

Here's the main problem: When you add a script to a page with the Insert Script tool, Dreamweaver places the script between the <body> and </body> tags. Many kinds of scripts work just fine in the <body> of the document, but Netscape recommends that certain kinds of scripts—namely, functions that are called by event handlers—be placed in the <head> portion of the document. (In fact, that's where Dreamweaver adds the scripts that it writes itself; it just won't add your scripts to the <head>.)

Let's say that you've written a custom script for a magazine's Web site. The site contains a subscription form like the one shown in Figure 19.4. When the user clicks the **Subscribe** button, his or her credit card is billed $50 for a U.S. Mail subscription to the magazine. Your custom script is simply a gentle reminder to the user that his or her credit card is about to be billed; in other words, the script acts as an event handler for the **Subscribe** button.

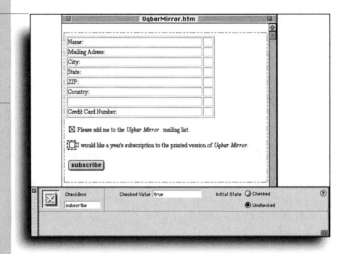

Create a script that acts like an event handler

1. First, you'll download a copy of the page that contains the sample form. Point your Web browser to `www.mcp.com/info`, or to the mirror page at `http://www.orbis-tertius.com/dreamweaver/ch19steps2.htm`.

2. If you're using MSIE or Netscape Navigator as your Web browser, select **File** and then choose **Save As**. (If you're using a different browser, consult your browser's documentation about how to save HTML files to disk, and skip to step 4.)

3. The Web browser, whether MSIE or Netscape, presents a file dialog box. Make sure that the Save As Type pop-up menu is set to HTML file, and save the page to disk.

4. In Dreamweaver, select **File** and choose **Open**. Use the resulting file dialog box to navigate to the HTML file you saved in step 3.

5. Select **Windows** and choose **HTML**, or simply press **F10**.

6. Locate the document's `<head>` tag.

7. Add the following script, including the `<script></script>`

tags, exactly as it is shown. Capitalization and punctuation are very important. Place the script directly after the `<meta http-equiv="Content-Type" content="text/html; charset=iso-8859-1">` tag.

```
<script language = "JavaScript">
function testForm() {
    if (document.Forms[0].subscribe.value == "true") {
        alert("Remember, your credit card will be
➥charged
        US$50 for your subscription. Thank you!");
    }
}
<script>
```

8. Find the tag `<input type="radio" name="subscribe" value="true">`. Add the parameter `onClick = "testForm()"` to the tag. The whole tag should read `<input type="radio" name="subscribe" value="true" onClick = "testForm()">`.

9. Close the HTML editor window by pressing **F10**.

The page is now ready for you to test in your browser.

From Here...

Dreamweaver offers a variety of ready-made scripts you can add to your page.

- Learn how to add a moving-animation script in Chapter 21, "Creating Animations: Moving Objects."

- For information about creating a push-style animation, see Chapter 23, "Animations: Creating Push Pages."

- For information about creating a layers-based animation, see Chapter 24, "Creating Rollovers."

Dreamweaver's script is similar, but...

Dreamweaver offers a ready-made behavior that's very similar to our custom script. (However, the canned script also reminds users that they'll need to pay when they uncheck the box. Very annoying.)

Validating Forms

How to set up form validation services

How to make a form element mandatory

How to check the formatting of form data

How to "hack" Dreamweaver into doing an element-level check

What Is Validation/Why Validate?

Forms are a great tool for getting feedback from the user. If you're a merchant trying to establish a presence on the Web, forms are also a great way to drum up business.

Unfortunately, forms can also serve as a great source of aggravation. If a visitor to your site fills out a form incompletely, you won't have the information you need from the user. You'll need to contact the user (if they have provided you with contact information) and ask for the rest of the data. This is a waste of your time, a waste of the user's time, and will very often spook the very user you're trying to attract.

In the Bad Old Days, one solution to this problem was to verify the form on the server-side. In fact, sever-side solutions are still widely deployed today. In such a system, when the user submits the form, the CGI that handles the form data checks to make sure that all of the important form fields have been filled out. If the form is incomplete, the CGI creates an error page that notifies the user that information is missing from the form. Simple error pages merely ask the reader to fill out the whole form again; sophisticated error pages may ask the user for the missing data in a little custom form right on the error page.

Server-side solutions work very well, but like all server-side technology, may place an unnecessary burden on the server machine. After all, the user's machine (the one that's running the Web browser) is a perfectly good computer in its own right, and it makes sense to offload the simple task of checking the finished form from the server machine to the client machine. A CGI on a high traffic site may be handling dozens or hundreds of form submissions simultaneously; the browser machine is (ordinarily) doing little or nothing immediately after the user clicks the submit button.

Browser-based scripting languages such as JavaScript and VBScript make it easy to check form content before the form is sent to the server. When the browser checks the form, everybody's happy:

- The user is happy, because they get immediate feedback, rather than waiting for the form to travel over the network to the server, waiting for the server to process the form, and waiting for the sever to send an error page back to the user.

- The server administrator is happy, because the server machine isn't wasting CPU cycles handling unfinished forms. The server can devote its resources to its proper task—routing data from finished forms to the data's final destination.

- You (or whoever deals with the form data) are happy, because you don't need to spend a lot of time emailing questions to people about their form submissions.

In this chapter, we'll imagine that you're building a Web site for a silent auction of vinyl jazz LP's. Visitors to the site can participate in the auction by filling out a form that specifies the visitors' bid for each title that interests them. The auction manager will compare all of the submitted bids after the close of the auction, and contact the winners by telephone to make payment and shipping arrangements. (Figure 20.1 shows what the auction bid form looks like.)

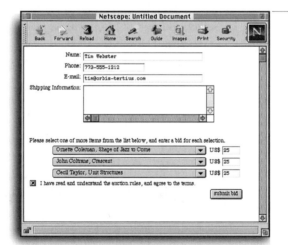

FIGURE 20.1

You'll use Dreamweaver to add client-side validation to this form.

Dreamweaver makes client-side form validation very easy. Using ready-made validation forms that are included with Dreamweaver, you can validate the following:

- That the user has filled out the name field
- That the email field has been filled out and contains a valid e-mail address
- That at least one bid has been filled out, and that it contains a bid for more than $20 (or whatever minimum bid you chose)

Build the Form

First, you'll need a form. I won't take you through the process of building the example form step-by-step; rather, you can download it from the book's Web site with Netscape Navigator or Microsoft Internet Explorer.

Download the sample form

1. Point your Web browser at the Chapter 20 page on the book's Web site at www.mcp.com/info, or the mirror page at http://www.orbis-tertius.com/dreamweaver/ch20-raw.htm.

2. Select **File** and choose **Save As**. The Web browser presents a standard dialog box.

3. Make sure that the dialog box's Save As Type pop-up menu is set to HTML. (In some versions of Navigator, the proper option is called "source," rather than "HTML").

4. Save the file to disk.

5. Open the file with Dreamweaver.

Where will the data go?

The sample form is set up to submit form data to NCSA's test server at http://hoohoo.ncsa.uiuc.edu/cgi-bin/query. If you want the test the form using your own server software, be sure to change the form's Action field in the Properties palette.

Set Up a Behavior for the Submit Button

Client-side form validation is carried out by a Web page script. Dreamweaver graciously writes the validation script for you; you just need to give Dreamweaver a little direction about what you want.

First, obviously, you must notify Dreamweaver that you need form validation services. To do so, you set up a behavior for the form's submit button. In Dreamweaver nomenclature, a behavior is an action (such as the running of a validation script) associated with an event (such as a mouse click). Events are tied to particular objects (such as the submit button). In other words, clicking the submit button is a different event than clicking a hypertext link.

Although the form consists of many different elements (the name field, the email field, and so on), you only need to concern yourself with the behavior of a single element of the form—the submit button.

Opening the Validate Form dialog box

1. Click with the mouse on the form's submit button to select the button.

2. Activate the Behaviors palette. If it isn't already visible, press **F8**, or select **Windows** and choose **Behaviors**. Figure 20.2 shows what the Behaviors palette looks like.

FIGURE 20.2

Use the Behaviors palette to assign the form validation script to the submit button.

1 Browsers and Versions pop-up

3. Select 3.0 + 4.0 browsers from the Browsers and Versions pop-up menu in the Events (left) column of the Behaviors palette.

4. Click the **+** button in the Events column. Dreamweaver presents a list of events that the selected browsers recognize for the currently selected object. The only option in the list that pops up for the select button is **onClick**; select it.

5. Click the **+** button in the Actions (right) column of the Behaviors palette. Dreamweaver presents a pop-up list of possible actions.

6. Chose **Validate form** from the pop-up list. Dreamweaver presents the Validate Form dialog box, shown in Figure 20.3. Here's where you'll enter the specific validation requests, discussed later in this chapter. For now, simply leave the dialog box open and read on.

FIGURE 20.3

Use the Validate Form dialog box to request all form validation services from Dreamweaver.

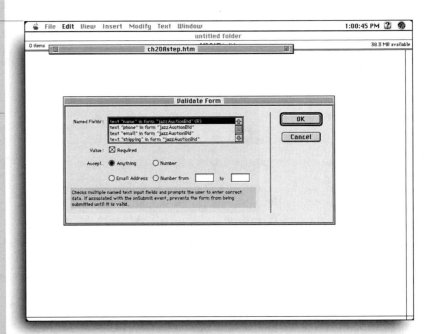

You can set up all of the form validation services you need with one visit to the Validate Form dialog box. However, you'll need to handle each form element individually within the dialog box, so I'll break out each element in its own section.

Verify User Name

Clearly, it's important that we get a name from each auction bidder.

Setting up the form's name field as a required element on the form

1. Choose Text Name in form jazzAuctionBid from the Named Fields list.

2. Click the Required checkbox next to the Value label. Now, if the name field is empty when the user submits the form, the Web browser will generate an error message like the one shown in Figure 20.4. More significantly, the form will not be submitted to the server.

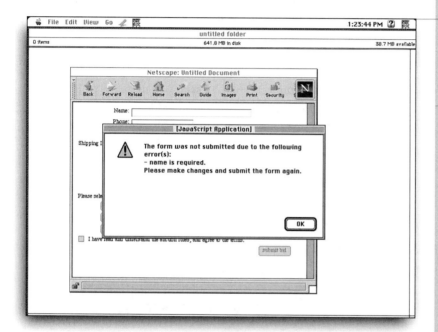

Click the **Anything** radio button near the Accept label. (The bidder's name will almost certainly not be a number or an email address, right?) Don't dismiss the Validate Form dialog box yet—keep it open for the next section.

Verify Email Address

The bidder's name doesn't do you a lot of good if you don't have a way to reach him or her. The phone number, email, and mailing address fields all provide information about contacting the bidder. Because we're Web developers, our preferred mode of communication is naturally email. Let's continue our work in the Validate Forms dialog box.

Reopening the Validate Form dialog box

If you do close the Validate Form dialog box prematurely, or you decide you want to change the way that you validate your form, you can reopen the dialog box. Select the **onClick** handler in the Events column of the Behaviors palette, and double click the **Validate Forms** entry in the Events column. Dreamweaver opens the dialog box, preserving all of the settings you may have configured in previous sessions with the dialog box.

Setting up email validation

1. Choose Text Email in form jazzAuctionBid from the Named Fields list.

2. Click the **Required** checkbox next to the Value label.

3. Click the **Email Address** radio button near the Accept label. When this option is selected, the validation script tests the contents of the email field when the form is submitted. The test is pretty simple: it simply checks for a **@** character somewhere in the middle of the contents of the field. (The script can't connect to a mail server to make sure that the email account really exists.) If the bidder submits a bad address in the email field, the Web browser generates an error message like the one shown in Figure 20.5.

FIGURE 20.5

When a user submits a form with a required field that is empty, the browser generates an error message.

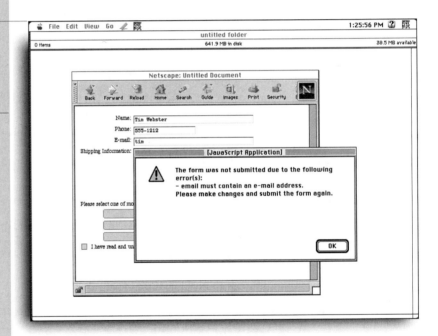

4. Don't close the Validate Form dialog box yet.

Verify Bid #1

Next, we'll verify that the bidder has sent in at least one bid for an item. (After all, if they haven't entered a bid, why are they filling out a bid form?) Let us say, for the sake of argument, that you have set the minimum bid at U.S. $20. (I don't know how much an original copy of *Shape of Jazz to Come* goes for nowadays.)

Verifying the first bid

1. Choose Text Bid1 in form jazzAuctionBid from the Named Fields list.
2. Click the **Required** checkbox next to the Value label.
3. Click the **Number From** radio button near the Accept label.
4. Enter 20 in the first Number From field.
5. Enter 1000 (or whatever you think is a sensible limit) in the second Number From field. Now, if the bidder leaves the first bid field blank, the browser will generate a standard error message. If the bidder enters anything other than a number between 20 and 1000 (inclusive) in the bid field, the browser generates the error message shown in Figure 20.6.

> **Be sure to set an upper bound!**
>
> You must enter a number in the second field in step 5. If you don't, Dreamweaver will discard the lower boundary that you set in step 4.

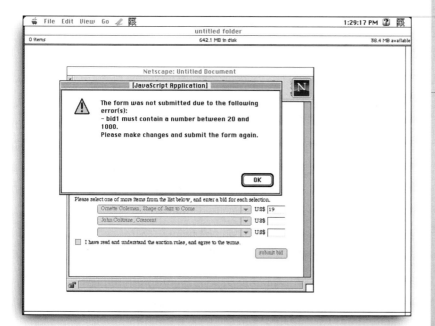

FIGURE 20.6

The browser generates an error message if the bid isn't in the correct range.

Verify Bids #2 and #3

Next, you'll set up verification for bids #2 and #3. We really shouldn't make these field mandatory—some visitors to the page may wish to bid on only one item—but it's helpful to make sure that any bid entered in this field exceeds the minimum bid.

Verifying bids #2 and #3

1. Make sure that you're still working in the Validate Forms dialog box.

2. Choose Text Bid2 in form jazzAuctionBid from the Named Fields list.

3. Make sure that the Required checkbox next to the Value label is not checked.

4. Click the **Number From** radio button near the Accept label.

5. Enter 20 in the first Number From field.

6. Enter 1000 (or whatever you think is a sensible limit) in the second Number From field.

7. Repeat steps 2-6 to set up validation for the Bid3 field.

8. Now, at long last, close the Validate Forms dialog box by clicking **OK**.

Now is a good time to test the form with your Web browser. Try filling out the form a few different ways, and, if possible, from a few different browsers and even a few different machines.

Mark Required Elements on Form Labels

After you're satisfied with the Form validation you set up, it's a good idea to mark the form's required fields for the user. Marking the required forms isn't necessary for validation, and it isn't necessary to make the form work; it's merely a courtesy to the bidder.

How shall you mark the required fields? That's really a design question, rather than a technical one. You can mark the required field in any way you like, including:

- Setting the label for the required field in a different color, such as red

- Adding an asterisk (*) at the end of the required field's label

- Setting the type for the required field's label in italic or bold

- Using a sans-serif font for required field labels

Implementing an Alternate Strategy

Our approach in this chapter has been to run the validation script when the user clicks on the submit button. Handling all of the validation tasks with a single behavior attached to a single submit button is probably the most efficient strategy, but it's not the only way to handle validation.

If you prefer, you can set up behaviors for individual fields of the form, so when the user changes the field—say, by typing something into it—the field is immediately validated.

For instance, you might want to check the validity of the user's bid as soon as the bid is entered, so the user doesn't waste time entering three illegal bids. (I'm not sure how much time would actually be wasted; setting item-level validation probably addresses the developer's anxiety more than it serves the user's needs.)

Setting up instant validation for the bid1 field

1. Click the Bid1 field to select it.

2. Make sure that the Behaviors palette is still visible. If not, press **F8** or select Windows and choose **Behaviors**.

3. Make sure that the Browsers and Versions pop-up menu in the Events (left) column of the Behaviors palette is set to 3.0 + 4.0 Browsers.

4. Click the **+** button in the Actions column. Dreamweaver displays a pop-up list of events that the selected browsers recognize for the bid1 field.

5. Choose **onChange** from the pop-up list. The onChange handler will activate the script after the user has changed and exited the bid1 field.

6. Click the **+** button in the Action (right) column of the Behaviors palette. Dreamweaver displays a pop-up list of available actions.

7. Choose **Validate Form** from the pop-up list. Dreamweaver presents the Validate Form dialog box.

8. Choose Text Bid1 in form jazzAuctionBid from the Named Fields list.

9. Don't click the required checkbox. (If the user has changed the field, they've already entered something in it, right?)

10. Click the **Number From** radio button.

11. Enter 20 in the first Number From field.

12. Enter 1000 (or a reasonable upper bound) in the second Number From field.

13. Click **OK** to exit the Validate Form dialog box.

That's it! Go ahead and test the field-level validation with your Web browser.

From Here...

- For information about adding custom scripts to your pages, including a custom validation script for checkboxes, see Chapter 19, "Adding Scripts to Pages."

Validation script message

Unfortunately, the validation script always starts with the same message `The form was not submitted to the server...`, even if the validation takes place before the user tries to submit the form.

Creating Animations: Moving Objects

How to create a layer for DHTML animation content

How to add material to the Dreamweaver Timeline

How to set the length of animations

How to set the beginning and ending points of an animation

How to add extra keyframes to an animation

How to fine-tune an animation

How to add a kill switch to a looping animation

How to add interactive layer-dragging

Not all browsers will see your animations

The effects you create in this chapter can only be seen by users with Netscape Navigator 4.0 or MSIE 4.0. Users of older browsers won't see the animation effect, and other side effects may occur. To create the animation, you'll need to put the page's content into a set of absolute-positioned layers, and a non-layer-friendly browser will simply display the layer content in the order it appears in the HTML file, without regard for the layer's proper position.

There's more than one way to deal with this problem. I'll provide one solution—a script that sends downlevel browsers to a new page—in the chapter, but you may wish to investigate other possibilities, such as server-side solutions that create downlevel pages for downlevel users.

How Does Animation Work?

There are lots of different kinds of animation that can take place on a Web page. Animated GIFs are one very common form of animation; for instance, an animated GIF is a GIF that contains a series of frames that are displayed in quick sequence. The result creates the illusion of motion. Chapter 7, "Adding and Changing Images," contains more information about adding animated GIFs and other basic images to your Web page.

Many of the Java applets that Sun distributes with the Java Development Kit are animations. Java animation works in pretty much the same way as an animated GIF; the applet flashes a series of images as quickly as it possibly can.

There are plenty of browser plug-ins that provide animation and animation-like features: Macromedia, the creator of Dreamweaver, offers both Shockwave and Flash.

Another approach commonly used in the early days of the Web was the "client pull" strategy. Under such systems, such as Netscape's late, great Fishcam, a simple GIF image is replaced by a new simple GIF image every few seconds. (A simple extension to the <img> tag causes the browser to continually request new images from the browser.) Client pull images are rare nowadays; they have been largely supplanted by animated GIFs and other strategies. For a version of client pull updated for the Dynamic HTML era, see Chapter 23, "Animations: Creating Push Pages," which shows how to simulate "push" pages with a DHTML-based implementation of client pull.

Here is the basic idea behind DHTML animation:

1. Put a Web page object—a picture, text, a Java applet, or whatever you like—inside a layer, so that you can position the layer and its contents at any arbitrary point upon the page.

2. Move the layer a short distance. Ordinarily, the movement is no more than five or ten pixels.

3. Repeat step 2 several dozen or several hundred times, or repeat it indefinitely. Depending on the script and the CPU power or the user's computer, 15 or more tiny movements can take place every second.

Don't worry too much about the specifics of how Web page animations are implemented. Dreamweaver will write the necessary code for you, and figure out all the hard stuff. You are free to concentrate on the look and feel of the animation.

Choosing Items to Animate

Dreamweaver's built-in animation tools animate layers, rather than individual page components such as images or text blocks. Because you can put any kind of page element you like into a layer, you can animate any kind of page element with Dreamweaver's tools.

Figure 21.1 shows the page that you'll be working with in this chapter. I've broken down the page into three pieces: the little cartoon character at the left side of the masthead (which is a small image file), the type in the masthead (which is simply a <h1> head), and the body text of the page (which is a composite of whole bunch of different kinds of things).

> **How does the layer move?**
>
> OK, you're saying to yourself, but how do I move the layer in step 2? Layers are represented as objects in Web page scripting languages, and the position of a layer is a property of the layer that a Web page script can access. Thus, it's a script that moves around the layer, and, more importantly, a script that repeats the same simple operation fifteen times a second.

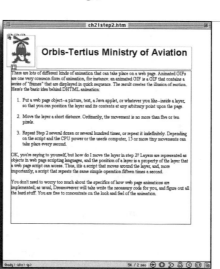

FIGURE 21.1

The sample page for this example is broken out into three separate layers.

Since this is a page about flying and animation, it makes sense to have the page elements fly into place after the page loads. (It makes sense to me, anyway.) I'll animate the cartoon character and the headline—I think it's overkill to make the body text swoop into place, too.

If you like, you can create your own image and content for the page. You can download project supplies from www.mcp.com/info or the mirror page at http://www.orbis-tertius.com/ dreamweaver/ch21step.htm.

Downloading project supplies

1. Load the page with your Web browser.

2. If you're using a PC, right-click the image. If you're using a Macintosh, Control-click. Your Web browser presents a contextual menu.

3. Choose **Save Image** from the contextual menu. The Web browser presents a standard file dialog box.

4. Use the file dialog box to save the image to disk. I'll use the default name, flyer.gif, to refer to this image in this chapter.

5. Choose **File** and select **Save As**. The Web browser presents a file dialog box.

6. Make sure the dialog box's format pop-up menu is set to **Source**.

7. Save the file to disk. I'll use the file's default name, ch24step.htm, to refer to the file in this chapter.

Put Animated Items in Layers

Once you've downloaded the files for the project, you can start construction of the page. In this section you'll create the three layers that make up the page, and add content to each layer.

Creating/drawing layers

1. Make sure that the Layers Palette is visible. If it's not, select **Windows** and choose **Layers** to display it.

2. Click the **Insert Marquee Layer** tool in the Objects Palette. Dreamweaver turns the arrow cursor into a crosshair cursor.

3. Draw a frame with the crosshairs cursor: Click and hold with the crosshairs at the point where you'd like the top-left corner of the box to appear in the layout, and drag down and to the right until the frame has the size and shape you

want. Don't worry if it's not exactly right; you can fix it later. Figure 21.2 shows what this first frame looks like after you draw it.

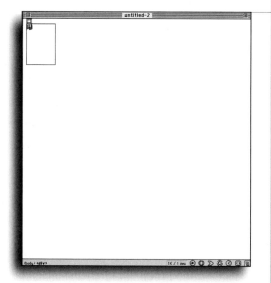

4. Repeat steps 1 and 2 to draw a long horizontal frame to the right of the first frame.

5. Repeat steps 1 and 2 to draw a large frame for the page content. After you've drawn the second and third frames, your page should look like Figure 21.3.

Next, we'll add stuff inside each layer. Adding content to layers is just as easy as adding content to ordinary pages.

Adding content to layers

1. Click inside the top-left layer. Dreamweaver highlights the layer: the layer border becomes black, rather than gray, and a handle appears at the top-left corner of the layer's border.

2. Click the **Insert Image** tool in the Objects Palette. Dreamweaver presents the Insert Image dialog box.

3. Click the **Browse** button in the Insert Image dialog box. Dreamweaver presents a standard file dialog box.

Want to be creative?

If you'd like to create your own content for each of the frames on the page, go ahead. There's nothing magical about any of the content. Remember, you can animate anything you like.

Collapsing layers

In Netscape browsers, some layers tend to collapse. You can prevent this by adding a transparent, single-pixel GIF to the layer.

4. Use the file dialog box to navigate to the flyer.gif image you downloaded in the previous section.

5. Select **File** and choose **Open**. Dreamweaver presents a standard file dialog box.

6. Use the file dialog to navigate to the ch21step.htm file you saved to disk previously.

7. Select the headline in top-right layer of ch21step.htm, and copy it with ⌘+**C**. (If you're using a PC, use **Ctrl+C**.)

8. Click with the mouse in the top-right frame of your layout. Dreamweaver highlights the border of the frame.

9. Paste the headline into your layout with ⌘+**V**. (On a PC, use **Ctrl+V**.)

10. Repeat steps 7 through 9 to cut and paste the contents of the body layer of ch21step.htm to the body layer of your layout.

FIGURE 21.3
You'll need to draw three frames.

After you've added the content to your page, your layout should look pretty much like Figure 21.1.

After the content is in place, you might want to make some small adjustments to the positioning of the layers.

Fine-tuning layer positioning

1. Click the layer to select it.
2. Click and hold the layer's handle (the little knob at the top).
3. Drag the handle to reposition the layer.

Add Objects to the Timelines

The basic tool for creating and controlling animations with Dreamweaver is the Timelines palette. (Somehow, "Timelines palette" seems a little too wordy, so henceforth I shall call it "the Timeline.") Figure 21.4 shows what the Timeline looks like.

Want to be more precise?

If you love precision, you can type position values for each layer directly in the Properties palette. Since text blocks aren't justified on Web pages, this kind of super-precise alignment isn't usually as important as it would be on a printed pages, but some folks just like to make sure that the numbers are exactly right. You know who you are.

Arrow keys work too

You can nudge a selected layer with any of the keyboard's arrow keys. Each press on the key moves the layer one pixel in that arrow's direction.

FIGURE 21.4
Use the Timeline to create animations with Dreamweaver.

Each row in the Timeline represents an object in the Web page; each column represents a tiny amount of time, usually a fraction of a second. (You'll see exactly how this works as we add elements to the Timeline.)

Dreamweaver supports a convenient drag-and-drop system that makes it easy to add objects to the Timeline.

Adding objects to the Timeline

1. Make sure that the Timeline is visible; press **F9**, or choose **Window** and select **Timelines**.
2. Click the cartoon character layer to select it.
3. Click and hold the layer handle.

4. Drag the layer by its handle onto the Timeline. When the layer is over the first row of the Timeline, the layer will turn into a thick blue animation bar like the one shown in Figure 21.5.

5. Repeat steps 2 through 4 to add the layer containing the headline (Layer2) into the Timeline. Place the animation bar for the second frame in row two of the Timeline, directly below the first animation bar.

FIGURE 21.5

The Timeline uses a thick blue line to represent objects on the page.

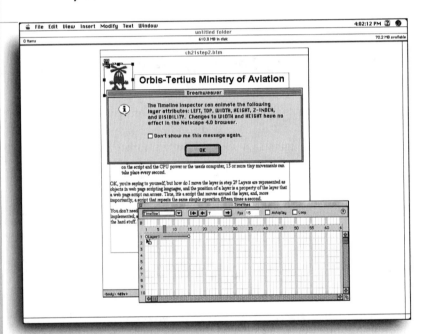

Choosing the Length of Animation in Seconds

OK, time to make an aesthetic decision. How long would you like your animation to last?

There certainly isn't a right answer here. Personally, I think that animations should be mercifully brief, so the user spends time reading the page, rather than looking at the animation. However, there really aren't any practical considerations: you can make the animation as short or as long as you like.

I think somewhere between three and five seconds is just about right for this animation. Four is right between three and five, so I'll use that as the length of the animation.

Setting Frame Rate

Now it's time to make another aesthetic decision. What frame rate do you want? "Frame" in this context doesn't refer to HTML `<frame>` tag; rather, it's a metaphor borrowed from the world of real-world movies, which consist of a series of frames on the filmstrip.

By default, Dreamweaver uses a frame rate of 15 frames per-second. This is a pretty respectable frame rate, and will yield fairly smooth animation. Higher frame rates will yield smoother animations, if the browser has the CPU power to support such a frame rate. In my experience, 100 to 133MHz PowerPC Macintoshes and Pentium-based PCs with modest memory can't really do much better than 15 frames/second. (There are plenty of factors that affect performance, such as the number of pro-grams running concurrently with the browser.)

Again, you don't need to make a final decision now. You'll have a chance to adjust the frame rather later, if you like.

Adjusting Animation Length

Dreamweaver reckons the length of animations in frames, rather than in seconds. In other words, an animation isn't really 4 sec-onds long or 10 seconds long; it's 60 frames long, 150 frames long, or whatever you choose.

Every column in the Dreamweaver Timeline represents a frame. Thus, an animation bar that is 30 columns wide lasts for exactly 30 frames. The duration in seconds depends upon the frame rate: the 30-frame animation takes 3 seconds to play at 10 frames/second, 2 seconds at 15 frames/second, and so on.

Once you have decided on the length of the animation in seconds and the frame rate of the animation, you're ready to

Animation length can be changed

You don't need to make a final decision now; you can change the length of the animation later, if you like.

calculate the length of the animation in frames. It's an easy calculation:

length in frames = length in seconds×frame rate

Let's plug in the numbers for this animation:

length in frames = 4 seconds×15 fps = 60 frames

Once you know the length of the animation in frames, you're ready to adjust the length of the object's timeline entry.

Setting animation length

1. Click and hold on the white circle at the right endpoint of the Layer1 object's entry in the timeline. Dreamweaver highlights the endpoint's box in the Timeline.

2. Drag the circle to the right until the circle is in the column labeled 60.

3. Repeat steps 1 and 2 to widen the Layer2 entry. When you're done, the Timelines Palette should look like Figure 21.6.

FIGURE 21.6

Widen each Timeline entry to a width of 60 frames.

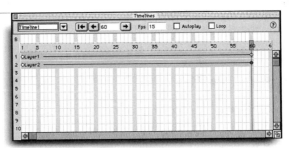

Specifying the Object's Path

A four-second animation where the objects stay in the same position throughout the animation isn't very interesting. In this section we'll set up a path for each of the objects to follow.

Those white circles at the ends of the animation bars are called *keyframes*. A keyframe is a special kind of frame in the life of an animation; it's a snippet of time when the position of the animated object is precisely defined.

In order to create an animation, we set the different positions for the starting and ending keyframes of the animation bar. When the Web browser plays Dreamweaver's ready-made animation script, it moves the animated object between the positions specified in the two keyframes. If we want to make a non-linear keyframe, we can add more keyframes to the animation bar. These new keyframes specify different positions the animated object must pass through as it moves from the beginning to end. (If this seems a little abstract right now, don't worry; it will become clearer as you work through the following steps.)

Setting the Starting Point

First, you'll specify a starting point for each animated element. We'd like to have the components fly in from outside the browser window and fall into their places in the layout.

Specifying the starting position of the animated elements

1. Click the left keyframe of the Layer1 animation bar in the Timeline. (Remember, keyframes are represented by white circles.) Dreamweaver highlights the frame box that contains the keyframe marker, and positions the red playback head in the first column of the timeline. (See Figure 21.7.)

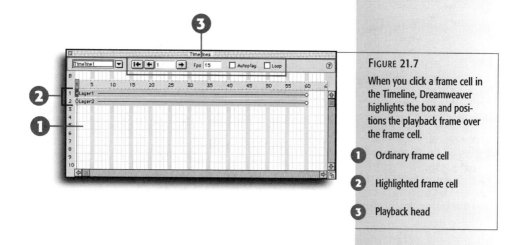

FIGURE 21.7

When you click a frame cell in the Timeline, Dreamweaver highlights the box and positions the playback frame over the frame cell.

1 Ordinary frame cell

2 Highlighted frame cell

3 Playback head

2. Click and hold on the handle of the layer that contains the cartoon character.

3. Drag the layer to its starting point. You can put it anywhere you want; I dragged mine a healthy distance down and to the right, so the layer will be outside all but the very biggest browser windows when the page loads. Dreamweaver draws a line in the display between the layer's original position and it's new position. (See Figure 21.8 to see what my line looks like.)

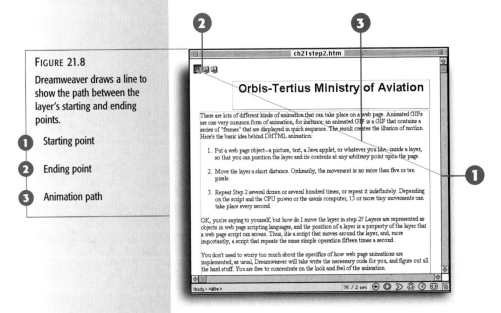

FIGURE 21.8

Dreamweaver draws a line to show the path between the layer's starting and ending points.

1. Starting point

2. Ending point

3. Animation path

4. Repeat steps 1 through 3 to set the starting position for the headline layer. (The layer's animation bar is labeled Layer2 in the Timeline.)

Setting the Ending Point

Congratulations, gentle reader: you have already set the ending point of your animation. You'd like the moving layers to come to a rest in the positions you gave them when you set up the page

Don't like your starting position—keep dragging

If you decide you don't like the new starting position, you can drag the layer somewhere else. It's the position of the layer at the keyframes, not the act of dragging, that defines the animation's path.

in the second section of this chapter. You haven't changed the right keyframe—at least you haven't if you've followed the step-by-steps— so the ending point is already in its proper place.

Skeptical? Curious? Confused? To make sure that each layer finishes its animation in the proper place, click the right keyframe in the Layer1 animation bar. Dreamweaver highlights the keyframe's cell and moves the playback head to the keyframe's column in the Timeline. More significantly, Dreamweaver moves Layer1 to its ending point at the top-left corner of the layout window. (See Figure 21.9.)

You can type starting point values

If you want to put the starting point crazy-far from the ending point so the layer really swoops in like a bat out of hell, you can position the layer by typing numbers into the L (for Left) and T (for Top) fields of the Properties palette, rather than dragging the layer by hand. In fact, I set up my Layer1 by typing 900 into the L field and 400 into the T field.

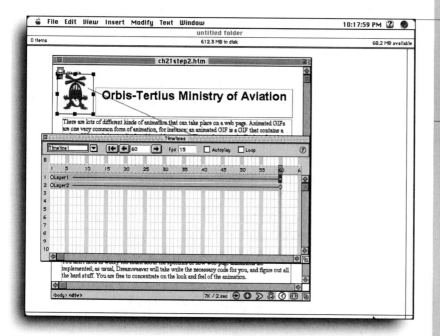

FIGURE 21.9

When you click a new keyframe in the Timeline, Dreamweaver displays the new position of the animated object.

Here's where Dreamweaver gets really, really cool. If you drag the playback head from the starting point of the Timeline to the ending point, Dreamweaver previews the animation as you drag. If you pause, the preview pauses; if you move the playback head backwards (for example, from right to left), the animation runs backwards. You can also step through the animation preview frame-by-frame by using the arrow buttons at the top of the Timelines Palette window.

Adding Keyframes

Let's say you don't want the moving layer to proceed in a straight line between the starting and ending points. You can specify an elegant Bézier curve for your animation's path by adding keyframes in the middle of the animation bar. When the browser plays the animation, the moving layer passes through any positions specified in the intermediary keyframes.

Adding intermediary keyframes to an object's route

1. Click the middle of Layer's animation bar in the Timeline. (Any frame near column 30 is fine.) Dreamweaver highlights the cell and moves the playback head to the cell's column.

2. If you're using a Macintosh, Control+click the highlighted cell. If you're using a PC, right-click. Dreamweaver presents a contextual menu.

3. Select **Add Keyframe** from the contextual menu. Dreamweaver adds a round keyframe marker to the selected frame.

4. While the new keyframe is still selected, move Layer1 to a new position by clicking and dragging on its handle. (If you can't see Layer1 on screen, think about changing your animation's starting point!) When you release the mouse button, Dreamweaver re-draws the animation's path as a curved line. You can see my curve in Figure 21.10.

5. Repeat steps 1 through 4 to add more keyframes to the animation bar, as desired. Figure 21.11 shows the demented flight pattern I've created for the flying cartoon.

6. If you like, repeat steps 1 through 5 to curve the path of the headline layer (Layer2) animation. I've opted to use a simple curve for Layer2.

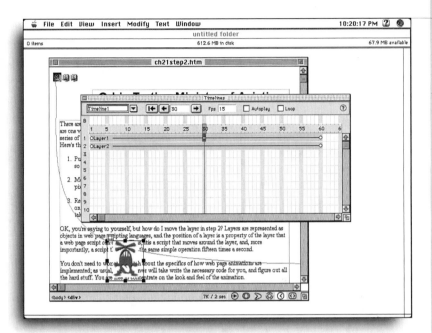

FIGURE 21.10
Add more keyframes to the animation bar to make the animation's path curve.

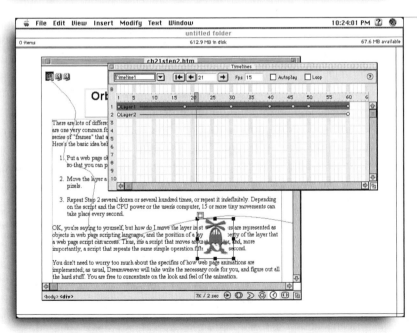

FIGURE 21.11
You can add as many keyframes as you like, allowing for very complex paths.

Finalizing the Animation

You're almost there. There are just a few finishing touches to add.

Finishing the animation

1. Click the Autoplay checkbox at the top of the Timelines so that the animation launches itself when the page loads.

2. If you want the animation to loop repeatedly, click the loop checkbox at the top of the Timeline. Personally, I think most looping animation looks very corny indeed; and this particular animation would be very distracting as a loop. (But it's your Web page, not mine—do whatever you like.)

Adding a Kill Switch for Looping Animations

If you've created a looping animation, it's nice to allow visitors to stop the animation. If you didn't create a looping animation, skip ahead to the next section of this chapter.

Adding a "kill switch"

1. Use the pop-up menu at the top of the Objects Palette to change the palette to **Forms** mode.

2. Use the **Insert Button** tool to add a button to your layout. You can add the button inside a moving layer if you must, but it's hard for users to click a moving button.

3. In the Properties Palette, set the button's action to **None**.

4. Type a descriptive label for the button in the Properties Palette's Label field. Stop the Animation, Stop the Insanity, and Please Kill Me are all good label candidates.

5. Make sure the new button is still selected. Bring up the Dreamweaver Behaviors Palette by pressing **F8** or choosing **Window** and selecting **Behaviors**.

6. Click and hold the **+** button in the left column of the Behaviors Palette.

7. Select **OnClick** from the pop-up menu.

8. Click and hold the **+** button in the right column of the Behaviors palette. Dreamweaver presents another pop-up menu.

9. Select **Timeline** and choose **Stop Timeline** from the pop-up menu. Dreamweaver presents the Stop Timeline dialog box. This dialog box contains a pop-up menu with a list of all of the timelines in the current page; the dialog box may need a few seconds to search for timelines and update the pop-up menu.

10. Wait for the pop-up menu to change from `****no timelines found****` to `**ALL TIMELINES**`. After the pop-up has updated itself, click **OK**.

Preview and Fine-Tune the Animation

Now, at long last, it's time to test the animation. Remember, the animation techniques described in this chapter require Netscape Navigator or MSIE 4.0 or later to play; I assume you haven't come this far if you don't have at least one of these browsers available.

If possible, it's a good idea to watch the animation run on a few different machines. If you're running Dreamweaver, you probably already have a pretty fast machine. Script-based animations can run fairly slowly, and it's a good idea to try your animation on the oldest, slowest dog of a computer that can still run a 4.0 browser.

Once you've seen the script in action in the real world, you may wish to make adjustments to the animation.

- *If the animation is jumpy*—It may be that the layers move too far with each frame. Either reduce the distance between the animation's starting and ending points by re-positioning the layers at the keyframes, or decrease the length of the animation by shortening the animation bar.

- *If the animation runs too slowly*—Try increasing the frame rate. (Remember, slower machines may not be able to manage the frame rate you specify, in which case the browser will play the animation at the fasted possible frame rate.)

■ *If the animation is jerky*—It may be too complex. If you have several components moving at once, or you're moving huge images or complex applets or plug-in content, you may need to simplify your animation—move fewer layers or put simpler content in your moving layers.

Letting the User Rearrange Your Page

The last animation effect we'll cover in this chapter lets the user drag and drop layers around your page. Why would you want to do such a thing?

There's a few. The first is for the fun of it. Take a look at `http://www.microsoft.com/gallery/files/html/alienhead.htm`. This is a page in the spirit of "Mister Potato Head" that lets you start with a blank face outline, then add various vegetables and other bits to create a rather imaginative new look. Nonsense, yes—but *entertaining* nonsense.

Other more practical uses include putting menus within the layer where they can be moved out of the way when not needed or letting the user drag a form next to information on filling out a specific element.

The caveat to all of this is that dragging layers only currently works with Internet Explorer 4 for Windows. Macintosh and Netscape users are out in the cold until Microsoft and Netscape extend this capability to more platforms.

The first step in setting up a layer-dragging effect is to create the layer—easy enough, but if you need a refresher, look back to the section "Put Animated Items in Layers" earlier in this chapter.

You'll also want to set the z-index attribute of the layer to the highest available on the page. Otherwise, it can get dropped when passing over other elements sensitive to mouse clicking, such as hyperlinks and other layers with dragging enabled.

With that preliminary out of the way, it's time for the actual work. You'll need the Behaviors palette (Press **F8**, or **Window**, **Behaviors**).

Other click-and-drag objects

This effect will also work with anchors and images outside of a layer. As a general style convention, though, I like to put each element that will move inside a layer. It just seems to make for a cleaner page and easier tracking of effects for later revision.

Dragging a layer

1. Select the layer to drag by clicking on its handle.

2. For the event platform, select **IE 4.0**.

3. Select **onMouseDown** as the event to look for. This event detects when the user has clicked the mouse button, but not released it yet.

4. For the behavior, select **Drag Layer**. This displays the Drag Layer dialog (see Figure 21.12).

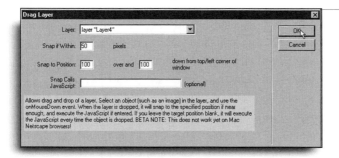

5. There are three areas to be concerned with in the Drag Layer dialog box: **Snap to Position**, **Snap if Within**, and **Snap Calls JavaScript**.

   - **Snap to Position**: You can define a place on the screen, in pixels measured from the top left corner of the browser window (or frame, if this page is framed), to lock in the layer. This is good for predefined docking locations for menus.

   - **Snap if Within**: This sets how close the user needs to be to the Snap to Position in order for it to take effect. The smaller the number, the more precise the user will need to be.

   - **Snap Calls JavaScript**: You can define a script to run after the layer snaps into place. Obvious choices for a script include changing the appearance of the layer (such as removing/adding a border), hiding the layer, or other visual-effect based options.

6. Click on OK to finalize your choices.

Dragging a different layer

The option at the top of the dialog box, **Layer**, lets you drag a layer other than the one the user has clicked on. It's a pretty peculiar feeling to click-and-drag one layer, only to have a different one move. Use this with caution and empathy for your user.

When the user clicks and drags on the layer, he or she is able to drag it virtually anywhere within the Internet Explorer 4 window, as long as he or she is using Windows. OK, that limits the effect quite a bit, but it's still pretty neat for the few folks who actually get to experience it. Obviously, it's not something that should be a crucial feature on your site.

From Here...

- To see about animation based on stacked layers, see Chapter 22, "Animations: Flashing Objects."
- To see a push-style animation, see Chapter 23, "Animations: Creating Push Pages."

Animations: Flashing Objects

How to create layers to hold content

How to stack layers on top of each other

How to add layers to the Timeline

How to set animation duration

How to set the visibility of a layer at a keyframe

Stacked layers won't work with all browsers

The techniques described in this chapter are complete anathema to the HTML purist. You'll be stacking layers on top of each other, and the resulting page will not work at all with browsers that are not CSS-P- and Dynamic HTML-compatible. Be sure to provide an alternate version of this page for users of downlevel browsers, and make sure to lead such users to the alternate pages.

What's Possible?

Dynamic HTML technology is very handy for controlling the visibility of elements on a Web page. Remember, any kind of basic page element—text, graphics, forms, tables, whatever—can go inside a DHTML layer, and layers can be hidden or displayed by a Web page script at any point in the page's life.

Everybody hates the <flash> tag, and with good reason. <flash> offers no control over the rate of blinking, which approximates that of an automobile's right turn signal. Furthermore, there's no mechanism to make <flash>ing content stop flashing, once it has attracted the reader's attention.

Thanks to Dynamic HTML, you can implement subtler forms of flashing. Figures 22.1 through 22.3 show the flashing logo we'll implement in this chapter: each part of the logo pops into view after a short delay. I'll show you how to build the phase-in logo, and then show how you can use the same basic technique to make any of the individual components of the animation flash at any rate and as many times as you like.

FIGURE 22.1

The first stage of our DHTML animation sequence.

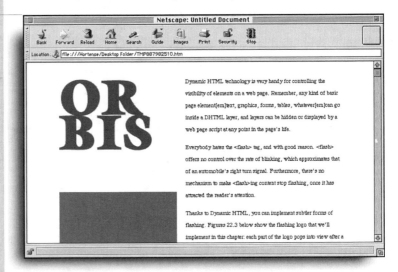

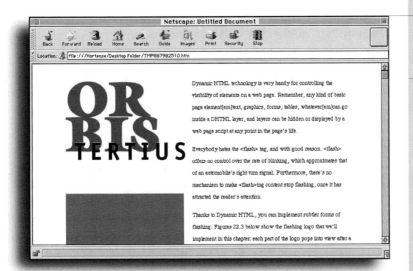

FIGURE 22.2

The second stage of our
DHTML animation sequence.

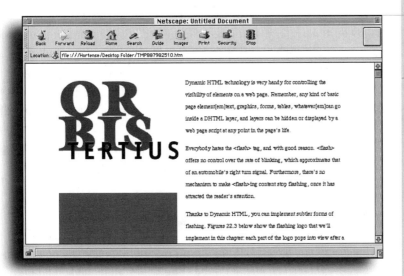

FIGURE 22.3

The third stage of our DHTML
animation sequence.

DHTML animation versus animated GIFs

"Hey," some of you are saying to yourselves, "couldn't I do the same thing with an animated GIF?"

Yes, you could. However, there are significant advantages of using DHTML to create the animation effect.

- An animated GIF supports a limited palette of colors. This particular set of images doesn't really approach that limit, but if you want to use a sequence of photographs with very different color schemes, you'll would probably need to make some quality compromises.

- The frames of an animated GIF are simply GIF images. The frames of a DHTML animation can be anything: GIFs, JPEGs, HTML text, Java applets, or whatever you like. (You could even use an animated GIF as a frame of the DHTML animation.)

- Animated GIFs are a pain to develop. In my opinion, Dreamweaver's Timeline tool allows far more sophisticated control over multiple animation frames than any of the animated GIF tools on the market.

Create your own content

Of course, feel free to create your own content for the layers. You don't need to feel limited to using GIF files: you can add JPEG or PNG images, plain old HTML text to the layer, plug-in-based content, or whatever you like.

Creating a Layered Image

Our animation is based on a stack of transparent images that are layered on top of each other to form a single composite image. You'll need a stack of images to work with. I've created a set of images that you can download from this chapter's page on the book's Web site or from the mirror site at `http://www.orbis-tertius.com/dreamweaver/ch22step.htm`.

Download the images with Netscape Navigator or MSIE.

1. Load the page with your Web browser.

2. If you're using a Macintosh, Control-click the image on the left. (The one that says "Orbis".) If you're using a PC, right-click the image. The Web browser presents a contextual menu.

3. Choose **Save Image As** from the contextual menu. The Web browser presents a standard file dialog box.

4. Use the file dialog box to save the image to disk. I'll use the default name orbis-stack.gif, to refer to the file throughout this chapter.

5. Repeat steps 1 through 4 to download the middle image (Tertius) to disk. I'll call this file by its default name, tertius-stack.gif.

6. Repeat teps 1 through 4 to download the image on the right to disk. I'll call this image online-stack.gif.

Adding Layers to a Page

It's always best to start with a basic idea of what the page will look like before you start putting down page elements. Figures 22.1 through 22.3 showed the basic design of the sample page: the animated logo is in the top-left corner of the page; there's a solid bar beneath the flashing logo—probably where we would add navigation links or a "What's New" section—and a body section on the right side of the page. For basic information on layers, see Chapter 18, "Working with Layers."

Because there are so many layers, and several of the layers are on top of each other, it's a good idea to name each layer as we put it down. You'll also find that the Layers palette is an invaluable tool for making sure the layers are stacked in the correct order.

Drawing the layers

1. Make sure that the Layers palette is visible. If it's not, press **F11** or select **Windows** and choose **Layers**.

2. Click the **Marquee Layer** tool in the objects palette. Dreamweaver's arrow cursor turns into a crosshairs cursor.

3. Use the crosshairs to draw a good-sized layer in the top-left corner of the layout. To draw, click and hold with the mouse where you'd like the top-left corner of the layer to appear, and drag the mouse down and to the left. Dreamweaver creates a border for the layer, and a layer marker box, as shown in Figure 22.4.

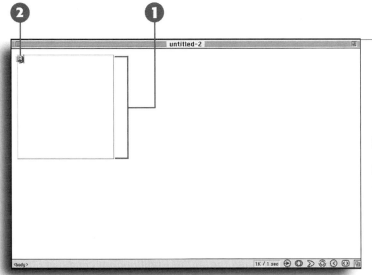

4. Click the layer marker to select it. When the marker is selected, Dreamweaver highlights the layer marker, and draws the layer's border in black, rather than gray.

Photoshop

I used Photoshop to create the images in this chapter, because the way that Photoshop layers stack on top of each other is pretty much the same as the way that DHTML layers do. Chapter 24, "Creating Rollovers," contains a detailed explanation of using Photoshop's layer tools.

Editing borders and markers

The layer border and layer marker are editing conveniences only; neither one will appear when the page is loaded by a Web browser.

FIGURE 22.4

Dreamweaver shows the border of the layer you created, and a marker to show where the layer's HTML is positioned on the page.

① Layer border

② Layer marker box

5. In the Layers palette, double-click the name Layer1. After a very short delay, the name will become highlighted, indicating that you may edit the name. Change it to Orbis.

6. Copy the current label. Select **Edit** and choose **Copy**, or press **Ctrl+C** (if you're a PC user) or ⌘**+C** (if you're a Macintosh user).

7. Click with the mouse an inch or so to the right of the frame border. Dreamweaver will de-select the Orbis layer, and position the position point directly after the layer marker.

8. Choose **Edit** and select **Paste**. (Macintosh users can press ⌘**+V**, and PC users can press **Ctrl+V**.) Dreamweaver pastes in a new layer. You won't see the new layer border—it's directly over the first layer, and exactly the same size—but you will see a new layer marker beside the first one. (See Figure 22.5.)

FIGURE 22.5

Dreamweaver pastes the copied layer directly over the first layer.

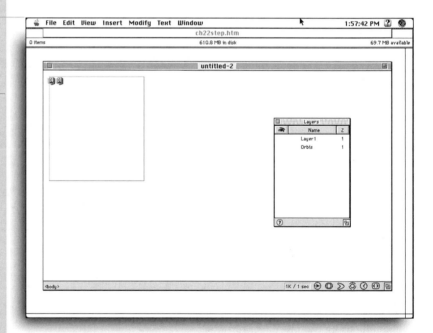

9. Check the Layer palette for the new layer. It should appear with the name Layer1 directly above the Orbis layer. Double-click the new layer's name, and change it to Tertius.

10. Again, select **Edit** and choose **Paste** (⌘+**V** for the Mactintosh or **Ctr+V** for PCs) to add a third copy of the layer directly over the first two.

11. Double-click the new layer's name in the Layers palette. (Once again, it will be called Layer1, because that was its name when we copied it.) Rename this layer `Online`.

12. Click the **Marquee Layer** tool in the Objects palette. The arrow cursor turns into a crosshairs cursor.

13. Use the crosshairs to draw a column underneath the first set of layers. (Refer to Figures 22.1 through 21.3 to see what my column looks like.)

14. Double-click the new layer's name in the Layers palette, and name it `sidebar`.

15. Repeat steps 12 though 14 to draw the frame for the body text on the right side of the layout. Name this layer `bodyText`.

At this point, your layout should look like Figure 22.6, and your Layers palette should look like Figure 22.7.

Can't find your layer marker?

If your layer's border is over the second layer marker (as it is in Figure 22.5), you may find it difficult to select the layer marker. You can always select a layer by clicking its name in the Layers palette.

Don't use hyphens!

When you're making up your own names for layers, be sure to use one-word names. Don't use hyphens in layer names! Underscores (body_text my_layer) are okay. Hyphenated layer names will really screw up Dreamweaver's built-in scripts.

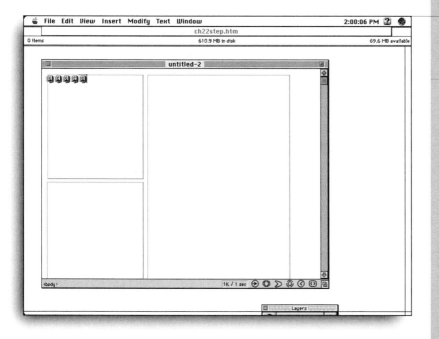

FIGURE 22.6

Use a set of layers to hold the page's content.

FIGURE 22.7

The layers palette allows you to control the way frames are used on the page.

Adding Content to Layers

Once the layers are in place, you can add stuff inside the them.

Adding content to layers

1. Click (don't double-click) on the Orbis layer's name in the Layers palette. Dreamweaver highlights the layer's entry in the Layer table and selects the layer border in the main Dreamweaver window.

2. Click inside the Orbis layer's border to position the insertion point inside the layer.

3. Click the **Insert Image** tool in the Objects palette. Dreamweaver presents a standard file dialog box.

4. Use the file dialog box to navigate to the orbis-stack.gif image you downloaded in the first section of this chapter. Dreamweaver adds the image to the layer.

5. Click on the Tertius layer's name in the Layers dialog box. Dreamweaver highlights the Tertius layer's border.

6. Click inside the layer's border to position the insertion point inside the layer.

7. Click the **Insert Image** tool in the Objects palette. Dreamweaver presents a standard file dialog box.

8. Use the file dialog box to navigate to the tertius-stack.gif image you downloaded previously. Dreamweaver adds the image to the layer on top of the orbis-stack.gif image. (See Figure 22.8.)

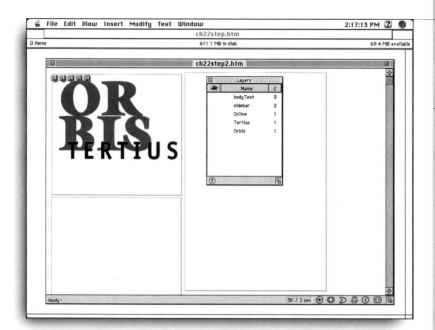

FIGURE 22.8
Because the layers are stacked on top of each other, so are the images that the layers contain.

9. Repeat teps 1 through 4 to add the online-stack.gif to the layer named online.
10. Click the sidebar layer's name in the Layer palette.
11. Click and hold on the bgColor swatch in the Properties palette. Dreamweaver displays a pop-up swatchbook.
12. Select a color from the swatchbook. (I've used **#6666FF**, but you can use whatever color you like.)
13. Click the bodyText layer's name in the Layers palette.
14. Click inside the bodyText layer to position the insertion point inside the layer.
15. Add some content to the body layer: type in your own content, cut and paste some stuff from another page or an old word processor file, or cut and paste the text from the bodyText layer of the Web site.

At this point, your layout should look like Figure 22.9.

Make your images transparent

The images I created for this are transparent GIFs, so you can see the orbis-stack.gif image under the tertius-stack.gif image. If you create your own content for the stacked layers, remember to make the top images transparent, make them smaller, or offset their positions to show the bottom images.

FIGURE 22.9

We've added content to each of the layers in the layout.

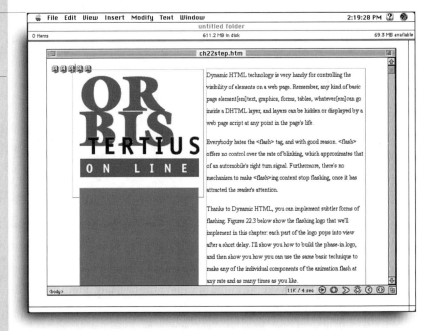

Adding Layers to Timeline

Now that the layers have content, let's make them interesting. You'll use the same Timelines palette that was introduced in Chapter 21, "Creating Animations: Moving Objects." When you created a moving animation in Chapter 21, you used the Timeline to change the position of objects over a stretch of time; this time, you'll use the Timeline to change the visibility of objects over time.

Adding layers to Timeline

1. Bring up the Timeline if it's not already on screen. Press **F9**, or select **Windows** and choose **Timelines**.

2. Click the Orbis layer's name in the Layers palette. Dreamweaver highlights the layer's border.

3. Click and hold the layer's handle. (The handle is the little # at the top of the layer; see Figure 22.10.)

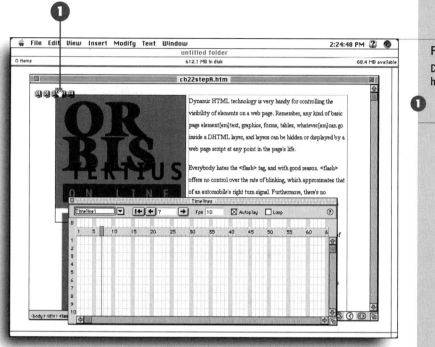

FIGURE 22.10

Drag the layer by clicking and holding its handle.

1 Layer handle

4. Drag the layer by its handle onto the Timeline. When the cursor is over the first row of the Timeline, the layer will turn into an animation bar. Make sure that the left endpoint of the animation bar is in the first column of the Timeline, as shown in Figure 22.11, and release the mouse.

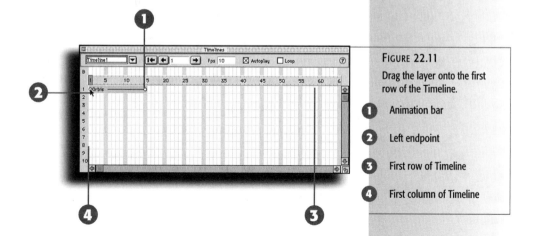

FIGURE 22.11

Drag the layer onto the first row of the Timeline.

1 Animation bar

2 Left endpoint

3 First row of Timeline

4 First column of Timeline

5. Repeat steps 1 through 4 to drag the Tertius layer onto the second row of the Timeline.

6. Repeat steps 1 through 4 to drag the Online layer onto the third row of the Timeline.

When you're done, the Timeline should look like Figure 22.12.

FIGURE 22.12

Add all three of the stacked layers to the Timeline.

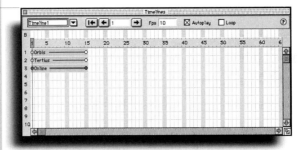

Setting Animation Bar Lengths

OK, time for an aesthetic decision: how long do you want the fade-in animation to last? Really, it's entirely up to you. Personally, I think that long, drawn-out animations are kinda dopey, but my taste isn't perfect: I still have a copy of *Tales From Topographical Oceans*. This chapter's animated logo isn't quite as distracting as the flying cartoon in Chapter 21, so I'm willing to let it ride a little longer—say five seconds or so.

Dreamweaver doesn't reckon animation duration in seconds; rather, it figures the duration of the animation in frames, and allows you to set a frames-per-second rate that the computer displaying the animation may or may not be able to keep up with.

This chapter's animation doesn't move at all, so we don't need to worry too much about kicking up the frame rate to keep the animation smooth. I'm going to set the frame rate at 10 frames per second, so that there are plenty of frames to play with if you want to do some fancy (or spasmodic) flashing later.

To calculate the length of an animation bar, we use the following simple formula:

length of animation in frames = length of animation in seconds×frame rate

I've decided on the length of the animation (5 seconds) and the frame rate (10 frames/second), so we can plug them into the formula:

length of animation in frames = 5×10 = 50

Thus, we'll set the length of the longest animation bar to a width of 50 frames. We don't want all of the layers to appear at the same time, so we'll make the other bars a little shorter—say, 20 and 35 frames long respectively.

Setting animation length

1. Enter the value 10 in the Fps field at the top of the Timeline window, replacing the default value of 15.

2. Click and hold the little white circle at the right endpoint of the Orbis animation bar. Dreamweaver highlights the circle and the frame cell that contains it.

3. Drag the endpoint to Column 20 of the timeline.

4. Repeat steps 1 through 3 to drag the endpoint of the Tertius animation bar to Column 35 of the timeline.

5. Repeat steps 1 through 3 to drag the endpoint of the Online animation bar to Column 50 of the timeline.

When you're done, your Timeline should look like Figure 22.13.

These settings aren't carved in stone

You're not cutting diamonds here: you don't need to set the animation bars to the exact lengths I've suggested. In fact, you can use any length that you like. If you want to make the Tertius line longer than the Orbis line, go for it.

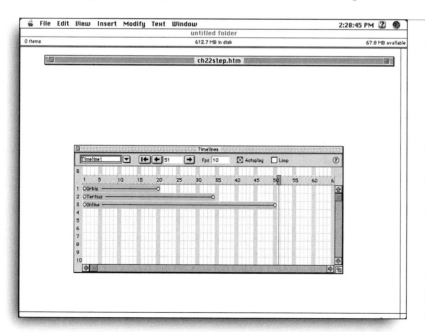

FIGURE 22.13

Resize each animation bar to set the duration of each layer's animation.

Setting Visibility Properties of Keyframes

Now things get interesting.

Keyframes, as you learned in Chapter 21, are special frames of an animation bar; during a keyframe, the characteristics of an animated object can be changed.

Keyframes are marked on the animation bar with little white circles, and, as you can see, each animation bar has two built-in keyframes: one at the beginning of the animation, and one at the end. In this animation, we'll be changing the visibility attributes of each of the stacked layers: we'll make each layer invisible in its initial keyframe, and visible in its final keyframe.

Setting visibility of layers

1. In the Timeline, click the Orbis animation bar's left keyframe. Dreamweaver highlights the cell that contains the keyframe.

2. In the Properties palette, select **hidden** from the Vis pop-up menu. (Vis is short for visibility, by the way.) Dreamweaver hides the Orbis layer.

3. Back in the Timeline, click the Orbis animation bar's right keyframe. Dreamweaver highlights the keyframe's cell.

4. In the Properties palette, make sure that **visible** is selected in the Vis pop-up menu.

5. Repeat steps 1 through 4 to set up the Tertius animation bar. Set the left keyframe to **hidden** and the right keyframe to **visible**, just as you did with the Orbis bar.

6. Repeat steps 1 through 4 to set up the Online bar. Again, set the left keyframe to **hidden** and the right keyframe to **visible**.

7. Click inside the bodyText layer in the main window, so that all of the stacked windows are deselected.

8. Click the Timeline palette on the "1" label just above the first column of the timeline. Dreamweaver will position the red playback head in the first column. (See Figure 22.14.) Note that all of the stacked frames are invisible at this point.

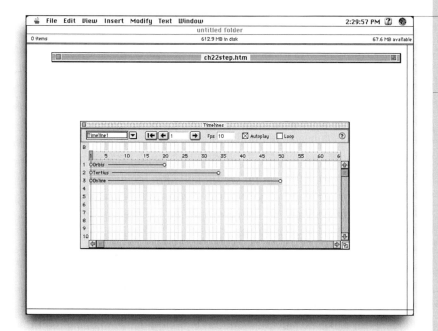

FIGURE 22.14
Click above the first column to position the playback head above the column.

9. Click repeatedly on the right-arrow button at the top of the Timeline's window to advance the playback head. Each button-click moves the playback a single frame. Notice that the Orbis frame appears when the playback head reaches the right keyframe of the Orbis animation bar.

Go ahead and preview the page with a DHTML-compatible browser. If you like, you can adjust the speed of the animation by changing the animation's frame rate, or adjust the speed at which individual layers appear by changing the length of the layer's animation bar.

Adding Additional Keyframes

If the animation isn't quite flashy enough for you, you can add additional keyframes to any of the stacked layers' animation bars. For instance, you could set up the Orbis bar so that the Orbis layer flashes on and off three times in the interval before the Online layer appears. It's your Web page; do what you want.

Move the playback head by dragging

You can also move the playback head by dragging it with the mouse.

Let's add another pair of keyframes to the Orbis bar, so the Orbis frame appears and disappears twice before the animation is finished.

Adding extra keyframes

1. In the Timeline, click the Orbis animation bar in column seven or eight or so. Dreamweaver highlights the bar with dark blue, and positions the playback head in the column where you clicked.

2. If you're a Macintosh user, control-click on the Orbis bar. If you're a PC user, right-click. Dreamweaver presents a contextual menu.

3. Choose **Add keyframe** from the contextual menu. Dreamweaver adds an additional keyframe marker (a small circle) in the frame that contains the playback head.

4. In the Properties palette, set the Vis pop-up menu to **visible**.

5. Repeat steps 1 through 3 to add a keyframe to the Orbis animation bar on or around frame 14.

6. While the new keyframe is still selected, set the Vis pop-up menu in the Properties palette to **hidden**.

Adding Jump Script

In the introduction to this chapter, I warned you that stacked layers only work in DHTML browsers like Netscape Navigator 4.0 and MSIE, and that this page will fall apart completely—explode!—when it is viewed by a downlevel browser.

There are many different ways to handle this problem: for instance, you could divide your site into DHTML-enhanced pages and compatibility-enhanced pages, and provide an entrance to each "track" at the site's front door. A similar approach has been used for years to divide sites into high-bandwidth and low-bandwidth tracks.

If, however, you wish to put this page in a place where downlevel visitors can find it, or you're afraid that downlevel users will enter the page via a link from a search engine, you can add a jump script to your page to redirect downlevel users to an alternate page.

From Here...

- To build an animation that moves across your page, see Chapter 21, "Creating Animations: Moving Objects."
- To create a push-style animation, see Chapter 23, "Animations: Creating Push Pages."

Animation: Creating Push Pages

How to add page-level behaviors to the Timeline

How to load *<frame>* content dynamically with the Go To URL behavior

How to load *<layer>* content dynamically with the Change Property action

What Is Push?

One of the Web developer's flavor-of-the-month topics in 1997 was "push" technology. In a push system, information—Web pages, A/V streams, files, or whatever—moves from a server to a client machine automatically, without any user intervention.

Push is a lot like television and radio. You don't need to repeatedly press a reload button on your television set to get each frame of the television broadcast; you tune your television to the appropriate channel, and the broadcast information comes without further action on your part, freeing you up to eat potato chips.

In this chapter, I'll show you how to make two different kinds of push-based pages. In both cases, the page will update itself automatically every five minutes, incorporating changes based on your edits to an HTML file called headlines.htm. The first push system incorporates the new information into a separate frame on the page; the second push system adds the new information to a floating layer on the push page.

Push systems make the most sense on a Web site where there's lots of new content being published constantly—say, a newspaper site, or a stockbroker's site. If you edit your headlines.htm file constantly (at least a few times an hour during the day), a push system makes sense. If your new material arrives every other week, pushing updates every five minutes doesn't make any sense.

Frames Version

Figure 23.1 shows my model for the frames version of the news-pushing page. The page contains two frames: a masthead frame on the left, which contains a simple logo and a set of navigation links, and a headlines window on the right, which displays a list of up-to-the-minute headlines. Every five minutes, the headlines frame of the page hits the server to reload the contents of the headline frame.

This isn't "strict" push technology

The techniques that I describe in this chapter aren't push technology in the strictest sense of the word. From the user's point of view, the pages update themselves automatically without any user activity. Even though the user isn't repeatedly requesting information from the server, the browser program is making such requests on the client's behalf. (Technically, this system is called "client pull.") In a completely kosher push system, all transfers are initiated by the server, not the browser.

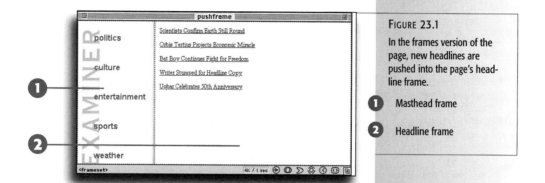

FIGURE 23.1

In the frames version of the page, new headlines are pushed into the page's headline frame.

1 Masthead frame

2 Headline frame

Creating Frameset Contents

Start by creating content for each of the page's frames. If you like, you can download the component pages for our eaxmple Web site, or you can create your own stuff to put inside the frames.

Downloading the page components

1. First, grab the HTML for the masthead frame. Point your browser at this chapter's page on the book's Web site (www.mcp.com/info) or the mirror page at http://www.orbis-tertius.com/dreamweaver/raw-masthead.htm.

2. Select **File** and choose **Save As**. The browser presents a standard file dialog box.

3. Make sure that the file dialog's Save as Type pop-up menu is set to **HTML**. (Some versions of the major browsers use Source, rather than HTML in the pop-up menu.)

4. Save the file to disk. I'll refer to this file as masthead.htm throughout this chapter.

5. Repeat steps 1 through 3 to download the background image for the masthead page from the book's Web site (see step 1) or http://www.orbis-tertius.com/dreamweaver/raw-masthead.gif. (Save the file as a GIF, rather than as an HTML file, of course).

URLs in these files are empty anchors

The links in the sample headlines.htm and masthead.htm files on the Web site don't hook up to real (or imagined) addresses—they're essential empty anchors that don't do anything. I'm assuming that you're not going to use my fanciful headlines on your own live page, and you (or your editor or whoever) will come up with headlines and URLs for your own stories after the stories are written.

Where to save the frameset

It's easiest to save the frameset in the directory that contains the HTML files you downloaded in the first section of this chapter, but you can save it anywhere you like.

6. Repeat steps 1 through 3 to download the HTML for the headlines frame from the book's Web site or `http://www.orbis-tertius.com/dreamweaver/raw-headline.htm`. I'll refer to this file as headline.htm in this chapter.

Adding Content to a Frameset

Next, you'll create a frames-based page to hold the content.

Adding content to a frameset

1. Create a new document in Dreamweaver by selecting **File** and choosing **New**.

2. Split the document into two frames by selecting **Modify**, choosing **Frameset**, and then choosing **Split Frame Left**.

3. Select **File** and choose **Save Frameset** to save the new document.

4. Bring up the Frames palette by selecting **Windows** and choosing **Frames**.

5 The Frames window shows a thumbnail view of the page's frames structure. Click the left frame (labeled (no name)) in the Frames palette.

6. In the Properties palette, type the name masthead in the unlabeled box at the left of the palette.

7. Type masthead.htm in the Src field. Dreamweaver displays the masthead page you downloaded earlier in the new page's left frame.

8. In the Frames palette, click the right frame.

9. In the Properties palette, type headlines in the unlabeled field at the left of the palette.

10. Type headlines.htm in the Src field. At this point, your layout should look line the finished page shown back in Figure 23.1, and your Frames palette should look like Figure 23.2.

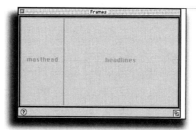

FIGURE 23.2

The frames palette shows a thumbnail of the page's frame structure.

If you like, you can test your page in the browser to make sure the frames work properly. Once you're satisfied with the way the frames work, we'll add the push behavior.

Adding Reload Behavior to Timeline

We'll rely on our old friend the Timeline to handle push behavior. However, you'll use the Timeline in a slightly different fashion than you did in Chapter 21, "Creating Animations: Moving Objects," and Chapter 22, "Animations: Flashing Objects." Rather than using the Timeline to alter the properties of particular page's elements, you'll use the Timeline to trigger scripts that aren't really associated with any particular page's objects.

The Timeline supports as many as 300 frames of animation, and frames can be played as slowly as one frame per second. Thus, we can set up an event to be repeated once every 300 seconds— once every five minutes. That seems about right for a site that delivers several new dispatches every hour.

Adding push behavior to the page

1. Bring up the Timeline if it isn't visible already. (Press **F9**, or select **Windows** and choose **Timelines**.)

2. Enter 300 in the unlabeled field between the left-arrow button and right-arrow button at the top of the Timeline window. Dreamweaver positions the red playback head over column 300 of the Timeline, and scrolls the Timeline in its window so that the playback head is visible.

3. Enter 10 in the Fps field at the top of the Timeline window. (This value will cause the page to reload every thirty seconds; you'll adjust the value so that the page reloads every five minutes after you've tested the page.)

4. Click the Autoplay checkbox. (Dreamweaver may show you an alert box notifying you that it's changing your HTML; ignore the message and close the alert box by clicking **OK**.)

5. Click the Loop checkbox at the top of the Timeline window. (Dreamweaver may present another alert box; ignore it.)

6. If you're using a Macintosh, Ctrl-click in column 300 of the B row in the Timeline. If you're using a PC, right-click. Dreamweaver presents a contextual menu.

7. Choose **Add Behavior** from the Contextual menu. Dreamweaver brings up the Behaviors palette, with the action on Frame300 added to the Actions column. (See Figure 23.3.)

FIGURE 23.3

When you add a behavior to the Timeline, Dreamweaver adds a special class of event to the Behaviors palette.

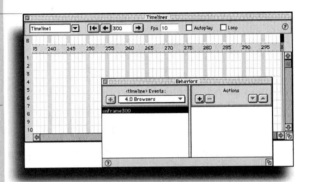

8. Click the + button in the Actions column of the Behaviors palette. Dreamweaver presents a pop-up list of available actions.

9. Choose **Go to URL** from the pop-up list. Dreamweaver presents the Go To URL dialog box shown in Figure 23.4.

FIGURE 23.4

Use the Go To URL dialog box to specify the headlines.htm page.

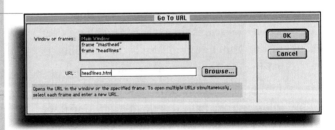

10. Give the dialog box a few seconds to update itself with a list of available targets. When the `***Loading Menu...******` message disappears, you're ready to roll.

11. Choose **frame headlines** from the menu in the Windows or frames field.

12. Enter `headlines.htm` in the URL field.

13. Click **OK** to dismiss the dialog box.

Editing the Headlines File

At this point, your page will autonomously update the headlines frame every thirty seconds. Let's test the system to see how it works.

Creating the headlines file

1. Preview the page with your Web browser. Press **F12**, or select **File**, choose **Preview**, and choose a browser from the menu that appears.

2. While the page is still loaded in your browser, open headlines.htm with Dreamweaver.

3. Make some changes to the headlines in the headlines.htm file, using the standard Dreamweaver text-editing tools. Add some new headlines "Uqbar Examiner adds Push Technology to Web Site," delete some, add a picture to the page, or do whatever you like.

4. Save the changes by selecting **File** and choosing **Save** (⌘**+S** for Macintosh users, and **Ctrl+S** for PC users.)

5. Click your Web browser's title bar to activate the browser window. (If necessary, un-hide the browser application, or restore it, or do whatever you need to do to get a good look at the browser window.) Do not click on the browser's refresh button.

6. If the headlines frame of the Web pages doesn't already reflect the edits you made in step 3, wait. In less than 30 seconds, the page will update to show your changes.

Adjusting Reload Time

Thirty seconds is just too brief a delay between reloads. Constant re-loading will annoy the user, affect your server's performance, and waste bandwidths. A five minute update interval is much more appropriate.

To change the reload rate to a more reasonable speed, simply enter a value of 1 in the Fps field at the top of the Timelines window.

<layer> Version

The layers created by Netscape's `<layer>` tag behave very much like `<frame>`s that are free to take any size or position on the page. Like the contents of `<frame>`s, the contents of `<layer>`s can by dynamically updated, and the contents of the `<layer>` can be read from an HTML source file or any other legal URL. For a basic introduction to layers, see Chapter 18, "Working with Layers."

Because `<layer>`s are similar to `<frame>`s, you can construct a `<layer>`-based push page using techniques that are very similar to the ones used to create our first push page. The page will load the contents of headline.htm into a `<layer>`, and, using the Timeline as a stopwatch, update the layer with information from headline.htm every five minutes.

Creating a Base Page

I've decided to create the `<layer>` page with a slightly sleeker profile than that of the `<frame>`-based page. After all, it's our fantasy that users will keep the page open on screen while they're working on other things, and such users will appreciate a page that doesn't use up a lot of screen real estate.

Figure 23.5 shows what I have in mind: the page contains only a very short, wide masthead and an elegant little row of text links, with the headline stuff sandwiched between.

Only Netscape 4.0 supports the `<layer>` tag

The only browser that supports the `<layer>` tag is Netscape Navigator 4.0. Older versions of Navigator and all other browsers will not see updates to the page. However, the layout of the page holds up pretty well when displayed by downlevel browsers.

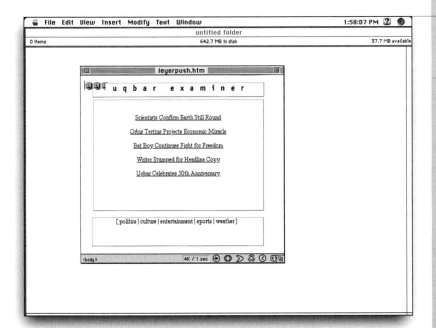

FIGURE 23.5
Here's what the *<layer>*-based
push page looks like.

Because the layers are drawn in order from the top to the bottom of the page, without stacking or side-by-side layers, even browsers that ignore the <layer> tag—every browser in the world other than Netscape Navigator—will display the content in a way that's similar to the frames layout.

Drawing the layers that structure the page

1. Create a fresh Dreamweaver layout by selecting **File** and choosing **New**.

2. Click the **Marquee Layer** tool in the Objects palette. The arrow cursor turns into a crosshairs cursor.

3. Draw a horizontal layer at the top of the layout. Click and hold with the crosshairs where you'd like the top-left corner of the layer to appear, and drag down and right with the mouse.

4. Click the layer's handle (the little **#** nubby at the top-left corner) to select it.

5. In the Properties palette, name the layer masthead. Type the name in the unlabeled field on the left side of the palette.

6. In the Properties palette, select **LAYER** from the Tag menu.

7. Use the Marquee layer tool to draw a square layer under the first one.

8. Click the second layer's handle to select it.

9. In the Properties palette, name this layer headlines.

10. Select **LAYER** from the Tag pop-up menu.

11. Use the Marquee Layers tool to draw a third, horizontal layer beneath the second layer.

12. Click the third layer's handle to select the layer.

13 In the Properties palette, name the layer links.

14. Choose **LAYER** from the Tag pop-up menu.

At this point you have a basic shell for the page; your layout should look pretty much like Figure 23.6. In the next section, we'll add some substance to each of the layers.

Adding Content

You can make up your own content for the layer push page, or copy the content from the sample page on this book's Web site.

Downloading the page content

1. Point your browser at this chapter's Web page on the book's site, or at http://www.orbis-tertius.com/dreamweaver/ue.gif.

2. Select File and choose **Save As**. I'll refer to this image as ue.gif.

3. Use your browser to load the page from this book's Web site or from http://www.orbis-tertius.com/dreamweaver/ch23stepB.htm.

4. Select **File** and choose **Save As**. The browser presents a file dialog box.

5. Make sure that the Save as Type pop-up menu is set to **HTML**. (If HTML isn't one of the options on the menu, as is the case with some versions of Netscape Navigator, choose **Source**.)

6. Save the file to disk as ch23stepB.htm.

7. In Dreamweaver, click with the mouse inside the top frame you created earlier.

8. In the Properties palette, click the **Align Center** button.

9. Click the Object palette's **Insert Image** tool. Dreamweaver presents a standard file dialog box.

10. Use the file dialog to navigate to the ue.gif image you saved to disk in step 2.

11. Use Dreamweaver to open the ch23stepB.htm file you saved to disk in step 6.

12. Select all of the text in the middle layer of ch23stepB.htm.

13. Select **Edit** and choose **Copy**, or press **[cmd]+C** (for the Macintosh) or **Ctrl+C** (for PCs).

14. In your layout, click with the mouse to position the insertion point inside the middle frame.

15. In the Properties palette, click the **Align Center** button.

16. Select **Edit** and choose **Paste**, or press **[cmd]+V** (for the Macintosh) or **Ctrl+V** (for PCs).

17. Repeat steps 11 through 16 to cut the contents of the links layer in ch23stepB and paste them into the links layer of your layout. (For extra credit, say "the text of the instruction" three times fast out loud.)

At this point, you can take a look at the page in the browser to make sure that all of the layers work. (Don't expect the push feature to work yet; we'll add that in the next section.)

Adding Reload Behavior to Timeline

We're going to follow the same basic strategy used in the `<frame>`-based push page: use the Timeline to schedule a page-level behavior to be executed every five minutes. However, this time, we'll use a slightly different kind of behavior.

Adding reload behavior

1. If the Timelines palette isn't visible, bring it up by pressing **F9** or selecting **Windows** and choosing **Timelines**.

2. Enter 300 in the unlabeled text field between the left-arrow button and the right-arrow button. Dreamweaver scrolls to the right edge of the Timeline, and positions the red play-back head over column 300 of the timeline.

3. Enter 10 in the Fps field at the top of the timeline. (This value will make the layer reload every 30 seconds; you'll adjust it to a smaller value after you've tested the page.)

4. Click the Autoplay checkbox at the top of Timeline window. (If Dreamweaver presents an alert box, ignore it.)

5. Click the Loop checkbox at the top of the Timeline. Again, ignore any alert boxes.

6. If you're using a PC, right-click in the B row of the Timetable, right above column 300. If you're using a Macintosh, control-click. Dreamweaver displays a contextual menu.

7. Choose **Add Behavior** from the contextual menu. Dreamweaver brings up the Behaviors palette (if it wasn't up already) and adds a special event, onFrame300, to the Event column of the Behaviors palette.

8. Click the **+** button in the Action (right) column of the Behaviors palette. Dreamweaver presents a pop-up list of legal actions.

9. Choose **Change Property** from the pop-up list. (Notice that this is a different choice than you made when you were creating the <frame>-based page.) Dreamweaver presents the Change Property dialog box.

10. In the Change Property dialog box, choose **LAYER** from the Type of Object pop-up menu.

11. Choose layer **Layer2** from the Named Object pop-up menu.

12. Click the **Enter** radio button below and to the right of the Property label.

13. Type src in the Enter field.

14. Type headlines.htm in the New Value dialog box.

15. Click **OK** to close the Change Property dialog box.

At this point, you can test the page in Netscape Navigator 4. (You can test it in any browser any browser, but remember that the push effect will only appear in Navigator 4.)

Testing the page

1. If Netscape Navigator 4.0 is your primary browser, press **F12**; otherwise, select **File**, choose **Preview**, and choose Navigator 4 from the submenu.

2. While Navigator is still running, use Dreamweaver to edit the headlines.htm file. Add a few heads of your own (such as "Orang-Utan Attack Feared"), delete some of the example heads, or just bang away at the keyboard to get some new characters in there.

3. Save your changes to headline.htm.

4. Bring back Netscape Navigator from wherever you put it while you were working in Dreamweaver. Are your changes from step 2 visible? If not, don't hit the reload button—wait, and in about 30 seconds they'll appear.

After you've tested the page, you can reconfigure the period that the browser waits between reloads from 30 seconds to 5 minutes. Simply change the Fps setting at the top of the Timelines window from 15 to 1.

From Here...

- To learn how to create an animation that moves across the Web page, see Chapter 21, "Creating Animations: Moving Objects."

- To create a GIF-style animation using Dynamic HTML, see Chapter 23, Animations: Fladhing Objects."

Keep waiting...

Maybe I'm just impatient, but the reload process seems to take more than 30 seconds during testing of the `<layer>`-based push page. It works. Really.

Creating Rollovers

What rollovers are

How to create a basic set of rollover images

How to swap in a new image when the mouse passes over the base image

How to restore the original image when the mouse exits the rollover

What are Rollovers?

A rollover is an image that changes as a visitor to a Web page interacts with the page. Ordinarily, rollovers take the form of buttons: when the user moves the mouse over the button, the button's appearance changes to show the user that the button responds to the mouse. The nature of the change in the button's appearance can be very creative: I've seen buttons that flash, dogs that turn into cats, even an image of a human eye that opens and closes. (That eyeball one is pretty darn creepy! I'd show it to you, but it was created by the developers of Dreamweaver's competition.)

Figures 24.1 and 24.2 show a typical rollover image from the real-world. This example is from the upcoming episodes page of X-Files Web site, which you can find at `http://www.thex-files.com/upepis.htm`. (I strongly recommend that you load this page; the best way to appreciate a rollover is to try it out.) Figure 24.1 shows the base state of the rollover: the X in the middle of the image is a light gray, and the circle around it is dark red. When the mouse passes over the image, as in Figure 24.2, the colors reverse. By the way, the little circles in the navigation bar on the left side of the page are rollovers, too.

FIGURE 24.1

This rollover image will change.

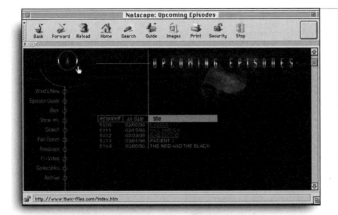

FIGURE 24.2

When the user positions the mouse over the image, the image changes.

Create the Button Images

First, you'll need to create a pair of images for use in the Rollover. Figure 24.3 shows the two images that I've created for this example.

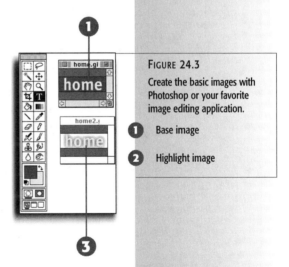

FIGURE 24.3

Create the basic images with Photoshop or your favorite image editing application.

1 Base image

2 Highlight image

I'm going to use the image with the solid background (the one on the top) as the image that's displayed when the browser loads; I'll call it the base image in the following steps. The image with the neon effect will replace the base image when the mouse passes over the button; I'll call this replacement image the highlight image.

There are a few basic ideas to keep in mind when you're cooking up rollover components:

- *Make both buttons the same size.* Technically, you can use different sizes for the base image and the highlight image, but aesthetically, it's important to make sure the image sizes match. When the browser performs the rollover swap, it will resize the hightlight image to the size of the base image. At best, resizing will pixelate your image; at worst, resizing will completely squash it, as shown in Figure 24.4.

FIGURE 24.4

Be sure your base image and highlight image are the same size, or your highlight image may be squashed or distorted when it's displayed by the browser.

- *Make the buttons small, or pre-load images.* The rollover effect loses much of its smoothness when the highlight image takes more than a second or two to load. Try to keep rollover file sizes under 5K. (If you absolutely must use a large rollover, load the highlight images into an invisible layer when you load the page, so that the browser can cache the images. Once the highlight images are cached, the browser can swap them into the rollover in a snap.)

- *Synchronize button content.* If the base image and highlight image share identical content (such as the word "home" in Figure 24.3), position the repeated content in *exactly* the same place in both images. Otherwise, the repeated content will "jump" when the highlight image swaps in, making the rollover seem less smooth.

Adobe Photoshop is a great tool for creating rollover sequences. Photoshop's layer model makes it easy to create a master image that contains all of the components of the base and highlight images. Using a single master image ensures that the base and highlight images are the same size, and that elements that are repeated in both images are positioned correctly.

Figure 24.5 shows the master image as it appears in Adobe Photoshop. Pay special attention to the Layers palette. The type is in its own layer; we'll use this layer in both images. Two layers contain solid backgrounds; there's a solid purple background in Layer 1, and a solid white background in the background layer. Finally, the purple neon effect (which I created with some purple type and selecting **Filter**, choosing **Blur**, and then choosing **Gaussian Blur**) is broken out into its own layer.

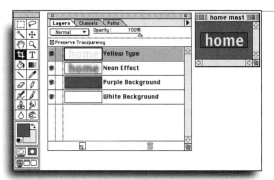

FIGURE 24.5
Photoshop's layer model makes it easy to create a sequence of images for a rollover.

If you're a Photoshop user (and you should be!) you can download the master image file from www.mcp.com/info, or from the mirror site at ftp://ftp.orbis-tertius.com/homeButton.psd. If you're not a Photoshop user, or you don't care to mess around in Photoshop, swipe the finished component images from www.mcp.com/info or http://www.orbis-tertius.com/dreamweaver/ch24step.htm, and skip to the "Adding the Base Image to the Page" section, later in this chapter.

Creating the Base Image

Creating basic button images in Photoshop

1. Open the master image, homeButton.psd, with Photoshop.

2. Select **File** and choose **Save As**. Adobe Photoshop presents a file dialog box. Use the dialog box to save the image to disk as home.gif. You won't be able to save the image as a GIF at this point; don't worry about it.

Photoshop LE won't work

You'll need to use Photoshop 3.0 or better to open the sample file that I've posted. Photoshop LE, the limited edition software that's bundled with a lot of scanners, doesn't support layers, and won't do the trick. Buy yourself a copy of the real thing—it's worth every penny.

3. Make sure that the Photoshop Layers palette is visible. Select **Windows** and choose **Layers** if necessary to bring up the palette.

4. Working in the Layers palette, drag the layer labeled Neon Effect onto the trash can icon on the right side of the bottom of the Layers palette.

5. Drag the layer labeled White Background onto the Layer palette's trash can.

6. If you're using Photoshop 3.0, select **Mode** and choose **Indexed Color**. If you're using version 4.0, select **Image**, choose **Mode**, and then choose **Indexed Color**.

7. Photoshop presents an alert box that asks if you want to flatten the image. Click **OK**.

8. In the Indexed Color dialog box, set the Palette to **Adaptive**, Dither to **None**, and the number of colors to **8**.

9. Select **File** and choose **Save As**. If you're using Photoshop 3, set the Format pop-up menu to Compuserve GIF; if you're using version 4.0, set the format to GIF89a.

Creating the highlight image with Photoshop

1. Open the master image, homeButton.psd, with Photoshop.

2. Select **File** and choose **Save As**. Adobe Photoshop presents a file dialog box. Use the dialog box to save the image to disk as home2.gif. You won't be able to save the image as a GIF at this point; don't worry about it.

3. Working in the Layers palette, drag the layer labeled Purple Background onto the trash can icon on the right side of the bottom of the Layers palette.

4. If you're using Photoshop 3.0, chose Mode, Indexed Color. If you're using version 4.0, chose Image, Mode, Indexed Color.

5. Photoshop presents an alert box that asks if you want to flatten the image. Click **OK**.

6. In the Indexed Color dialog box, set the Palette to **Adaptive**, Dither to **None**, and the number of colors to **64**. (Note that the number of colors is higher in the highlight image than in the base image, because the highlight image contains a gradient that will really fall apart if rendered with eight colors.)

7. Select **File** and choose **Save As**. If you're using Photoshop 3, set the Format pop-up menu to Compuserve GIF; if you're using version 4.0, set the format to GIF89a.

Adding the Base Image to the Page

Now, add the base image to your page. This is really the easy part; you'll add the base image in the same way that you'd add any other image to the layout.

Adding the base image to the page

1. In Dreamweaver, click the **Insert Image** tool in the Objects palette.

2. Dreamweaver presents a file dialog box. Use it to navigate to the base image, home.gif, that you either created or down-loaded in the last section.

3. Click the new image to select it. In the Properties palette, give the image a name by typing homeButton in the unlabeled field at the left side of the Properties palette. (See Figure 24.6.) Even if you don't normally name your images, be sure to name this one, or you won't be able to turn the image into a rollover.

FIGURE 24.6

Be sure to name your rollover image.

1 Add a name your image here

Adding a MouseOver Behavior to the Image

Don't use hyphens in your name

Don't use any hyphens in the name of your rollover image—Dreamweaver's canned rollover JavaScript thinks that the hyphen is an operator, rather than part of a name, and the script won't work when you preview the rollover in the browser.

Wrap your image in an anchor

Technically speaking, not every kind of object can accept an event-handler script. Specifically, images don't take event handlers. Sure, you could add an event handler parameter to the image's `<img>` tag, but the browser would simply ignore it. You'll need to wrap up the image in an anchor, because anchors can take event handlers. Actually, you don't really need to worry about it, because Dreamweaver automatically offers to add the anchor.

Once you've added the image, it's time to add behaviors to the image. A behavior is simply a script tied to the object with a special parameter in the object's HTML tag. This parameter specifies a certain kind of event—like a mouse click, or mouse movement— as a "trigger" for the script. When the Web browser detects the triggering event in the object's territory, the browser automatically executes the scripts. Web Script developers call these attached scripts event handlers.

If this sounds complicated, it is. What makes event handlers even more frustrating is that different browsers recognize different kinds of events; even within a particular browser program, different versions of the software recognize different sets of events.

In the particular case of this example, the object that interests us is the rollover's base image, and the event that interests us is the incursion of the user's mouse into the base image's airspace.

Fortunately, event handler management is one of Dreamweaver's strongest features. Dreamweaver makes it easy to attach useful, ready-made scripts to objects, and it's even fairly easy to sort out platform and version issues when you're adding event handlers.

Adding *onMouseover* behavior

1. Make sure that the home.gif image you added in the previous section of this chapter is selected. If it's not, click it to select it.

2. Press **F8** to bring up the Behaviors palette. (See Figure 24.7 to see what the Behaviors palette looks like.) If your keyboard doesn't have function keys, select **Windows** and choose **Behaviors**.

3. First, specify the browser brands and versions you'd want to be able to handle. Chose 3.0 + 4.0 browsers from the browser and version pop-up menu.

FIGURE 24.7

The Behaviors palette makes it easy to attach event handlers to objects.

4. Click and hold on the **Event** button to see a pop-up menu of the events that are supported by the browser or browsers currently selected in the Browser and Version pop-up menu you set in step 3. Select (OnMouseOver) from the menu.

5. Dreamweaver presents an alert box like the one shown in Figure 24.8. This is just a friendly reminder from Dreamweaver; you don't need to do anything special to add the anchor. (It's up to you whether or not you want to cancel future displays of the warning box.)

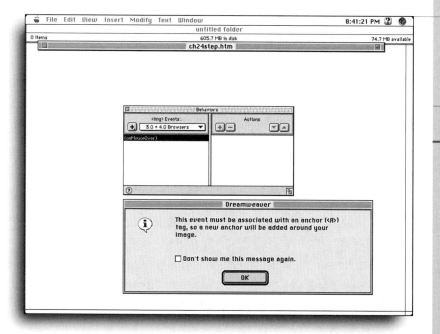

FIGURE 24.8

Dreamweaver provides a friendly reminder that it is adding an anchor to your page.

Making compatibility choices

The choices in the browser and version pop-up menu reflect the limitations of the browsers as they are. Choosing a particular browser or version from the menu doesn't necessarily mean that your rollover won't work with a different browser or version. For instance, if you set the browser and version pop-up to IE3, any onMouseover handler you set up will work with IE4, as well as Netscape Navigator 3.0 and 4.0

6. Click on the **+** button in the Action column of the Behaviors palette. Dreamweaver presents a pop-up menu of ready-made behaviors you can attach to this particular object. Choose **Swap Image**.

7. Dreamweaver presents the Swap Image dialog box shown in Figure 24.9. Select the image named homeButton from the Named Images list. (You named the button in step 3 earlier in this chapter.)

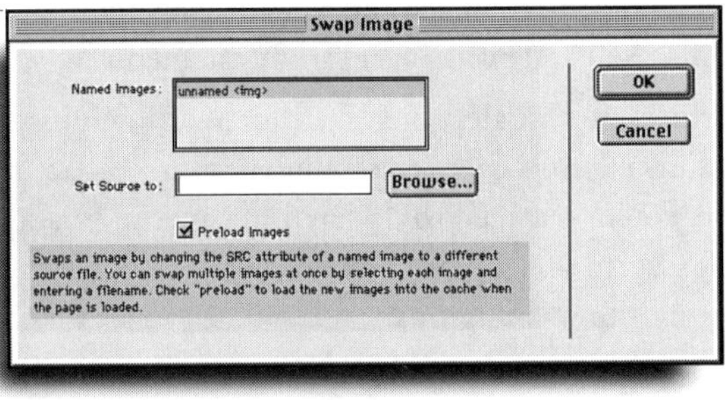

FIGURE 24.9

Use the Swap Image dialog box to specify the base image and the highlight image.

Swap Image

Named Images: unnamed <img>

Set Source to:

Browse...

OK

Cancel

☑ Preload Images

Swaps an image by changing the SRC attribute of a named image to a different source file. You can swap multiple images at once by selecting each image and entering a filename. Check "preload" to load the new images into the cache when the page is loaded.

Parentheses indicate anchors

Dreamweaver lumps events into two categories; events that Dreamweaver can attach directly to the selected object, and events that Dreamweaver can attach to an anchor that it wraps around the object. Dreamweaver puts parentheses around this latter category. Remember, image's can't take event handlers directly, so onMouseOver and every other item in the menu in step 4 is wrapped in parentheses. If you try to add an event to a plain text link, you'll see that there are no parentheses around the event names.

8. Click the **Browse** button to the left of the Set Source to: field. Dreamweaver presents a standard file dialog box; use this dialog box to navigate to the home2.gif button you created (or downloaded) in the second section of this chapter. The Preload Image option is selected to load the image into the browser cache before it is needed.

9. Click **OK** to close the Swap Image dialog box, and press **F8** to hide the Behaviors palette.

10. Make sure that the image is still selected. Adjust the URL in the link field of the Properties palette as desired—use the folder-shaped browse button to link the image to your home page, type in the URL of any other page you like, or simply leave it as it is.

Once you've set up the Swap Image behavior, you can test the rollover in your browser. Press **F12**, or select **File**, choose **Preview**, and then pick a browser from the submenu that appears. You will not be able to preview the rollover effect in the Dreamweaver window.

Adding a MouseOut Behavior to the Image

At this point, the highlight image will smoothly replace the base image when you move the cursor over the image in the browser window. However, if you move the cursor out of the rollover's territory, the highlight image remains. Traditionally, rollovers revert to the base image after the mouse passes out of the image's territory.

To finish the rollover, we'll add a second behavior. (You probably spotted the second behavior's name when you added the first behavior: it's called Swap Image Restore.)

Add *onMouseOut* behavior

1. In Dreamweaver, make sure that the base image is still selected. If it's not, click it with the cursor to select it.

2. Bring back the Behavior palette, if necessary, by pressing **F8**.

3. Choose 4.0 Browsers from the Browsers and Versions pop-up in the Events column of the Properties window.

4. Click the **+** button in the Events column, and pick (**OnMouseOut**) from the pop-up menu.

5. Click the **+** button in the Actions column of the Behaviors palette. Dreamweaver presents a pop-up menu of canned behaviors; choose **Swap Image Restore**.

6. Dreamweaver presents an alert box that explains what Swap Image Restore does. You don't need to take any action within the alert box. Take a moment to think kindly thoughts about the Dreamweaver development team, and then click **OK** to dismiss the dialog.

That's it—your basic rollover is done. To see it in action, you'll need to look at the page in the browser window: Press **F12**, or select **File**, choose **Preview**, and then pick a browser from the submenu that appears.

Cat and OnMouseOver

You probably noticed that we switched from 3.0 and 4.0 browsers when we added the OnMouseOver handler to 4.0 browsers when we added OnMouseOut. That's because Dreamweaver doesn't seem to think that OnMouseOut works with Internet Explorer 3.0; however, last time I checked, the Dreamweaver code worked just fine with MSIE 3.

From Here...

- For information about adding basic images to your page, see Chapter 7, "Adding and Changing Images."
- For another interesting behavior-based effect, see the collapsible outline project in Chapter 25, "Creating a Collapsible Outline."

Creating a Collapsible Outline

How to manually mark up your document with *<span>* tags

How to set up *onClick* and *onDoubleClick* handlers for objects

How to hide page elements dynamically

How to modify event handlers once you've put them on the page

How to set up your page so that page elements are hidden when the page loads

How to create a two-level collapsible outline

What Is a Collapsible Outline?

Microsoft's implementation of Dynamic HTML is just pretty darn incredible. Developers aren't limited to shuffling around the content of page elements inside <div> layers; you can change any page element after the page has been displayed. If that's not cool enough for you, ponder the notion that Microsoft Internet Explorer 4.0 automatically re-formats the page to reflect any changes you've made.

In this chapter, we'll take advantage of this snazzy Microsoft feature to create a Web page that features a collapsible outline. A collapsible outline allows the user to hide and restore paragraphs by clicking the outline's heads. (Collapsible outlines are all over Microsoft software: they're used in Windows Explorer, Microsoft Word's Outline mode, and dozens of other products.)

Figures 25.1 and 25.2 illustrate how the basic collapsible outline mechanism work. In Figure 25.1, the paragraphs below the first headline ("Uqbar to begin new era of mathematics") are displayed normally. When the user double-clicks the headline, the paragraphs below the head disappear, and the next headline ("Tlön residents remember El Niño") closes the gap to appear directly under the first head.

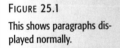

FIGURE 25.1

This shows paragraphs displayed normally.

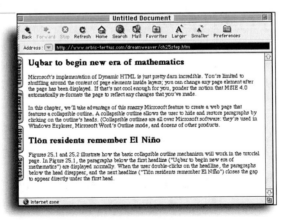

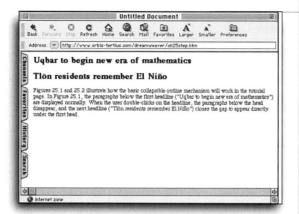

FIGURE 25.2

When the user double-clicks on the 1st headline, the paragraph beneath the head disappears. Double-clicking on the headline restores the hidden paragraph.

Creating Page Content

First, you'll need to create some content for your page.

You can certainly create your own content for this exercise. Really, all you need is two headlines, and two paragraphs to go under each head. (If you've got content for a page you've been dying to lay out, go ahead and use it.)

If you like, you can cut and paste the content from the sample page for this chapter on the book's Web site.

Downloading the raw materials for the page

1. Point your Web browser at www.mcp.com/info or the mirror page at http://www.orbis-tertius.com/ dreamweaver/ch25step.htm.

2. Use the mouse to select the text in the step 1 section of the page.

3. Select **Edit**, and choose **Copy**. (If you're using a bizarre non-standard browser, there's an astronomically small chance that your browser doesn't support cut and paste—if so, use another browser for this procedure.)

4. In Dreamweaver, paste the text into your layout by choosing **Edit** and choosing **Paste**.

5. Break the text into separate blocks for each headline and paragraph: position the insertion point at the start of each block, and press **Enter** (for PCs) or **Return** (for the Macintosh).

Collapsing outlines on work in Internet Explorer 4.0

The collapsing outline effect described in this chapter only works when the page is displayed by Microsoft Internet Explorer 4.0. That's the bad news; the good news is that the page displays just fine as a noncollapsing outline in every other Web browser, including the ultimate yardstick of backwards compatibility, Lynx.

6. Stylize each headline as an <h2> head: click anywhere inside the headline and, in the Properties palette, choose **Heading 2** from the Format pop-up menu.

Adding *<span>* Tags

Next, we'll add <span> tags to mark the sections we want to collapse. Each paragraph or group of paragraphs will be surrounded with its own pair of <span> and </span> tags; each span will be assigned a unique ID property.

In theory, Dreamweaver can add <span> tags automatically via the Marquee Layers tool. In practice, this is a lot of extra work, and not really worth the trouble. It's much easier to simply add the tag by hand with Dreamweaver's HTML editor. (Dreamweaver will redeem itself later by writing a nice little script for you.)

Here's the model for the opening span tag:

```
<span ID = "graf1">
```

Remember, each span will have its own unique ID, so you'll substitute graf2, graf3, and so on in the subsequent sections of your page.

Adding the *<span>* tags

1. Press **F10** to open the HTML editor, or select **Windows** and choose **HTML**.

Where's the source code?

If you have trouble finding the headline in the source code, highlight the head in the main Dreamweaver window before you open the HTML editor. Dreamweaver will highlight the HTML that generates the head in the source code.

2. Locate the first headline in the page's source listing. If you used the text from the sample page, the head with HTML should look like the following:

```
<h2>Uqbar to begin new era of mathematics</h2>
```

3. Add <span ID = "graf1"> after the head's closing </h2> tag, and before the subsequent opening <p> tag. The results should look like the following:

```
<h2>Uqbar to begin new era of mathematics</h2>
<span ID = "graf1">
<p>Microsoft's implementation of Dynamic HTML is just
pretty darn incredible. [example text continues.]
```

4. Locate the next head. If you used the sample text from the Web page, it will look like the following:

```
<h2>Tlön residents remember El Niño</h2>
```

5. Insert the closing `</span>` tag after the previous paragraph's closing `</p>` tag and before the headline's opening `<h2>` tag. If you're using the sample text from the Web page, it should look like the following:

```
[more body text] and dozens of other products. </p>
</span>
<h2>Tlön residents remember El Niño</h2>
```

Using your editor's search function

If you're using an external editor, like BBEdit or Homesite, you can use your editor's search function to find the next `<h2>` tag. For more information about these editors, see Appendix A, "BBEdit Quick Reference," and Appendix B, "HomeSite Quick Reference."

6. Insert the tag `<span ID = "graf2">` after the second head's closing `</h2>` tag. Note the subtle difference between the tag in step 3: the new tag has an ID value of graf2, rather than graf1. If you're using the sample text, your HTML should look like the following:

```
</span>
<h2>Tlön residents remember El Niño</h2>
<span ID = "graf2">
```

7. Locate the closing `</p>` tag of the paragraph(s) under the second head. If you're using the text from the sample page, you should find the `</p>` tag right above the document's closing `</body>` tag.

8. Insert the closing `</span>` tag directly after the closing `</p>` tag. If you're using the sample text, here's what your HTML should look like:

```
[more body text] under the first head. </p>
</span>
</body>
```

9. If you're using your own text, wrap up any subsequent body text with `<span></span>` pairs, following the basic pattern used in steps 1 through 8.

10. Close the HTML editor window by pressing **F10** or clicking on its close box.

At this point, you shouldn't be able to see your work in the main Dreamweaver window. (If you see any yellow HTML-error markers in the layout, double check to make sure that you have paired up your `<span>` and `</span>` tags correctly.

Adding *onClick* Handlers

Next, you'll add event handlers for each of the headlines on the page. An event handler is a script associated with an object that is run automatically when a designated event, such as a mouse click, is detected in the object's territory. Dreamweaver will provide the event handler script and take care of attaching it to the headline objects.

The event that we're interested in here is a single mouse click. When the user clicks a headline, we want the script to rewrite the `display` property of the paragraph under the headline.

Adding event handlers

1. Click anywhere on the first headline to position the insertion point inside the headline.

2. If the Behaviors palette isn't visible, bring it up by pressing **F8**, or selecting **Windows** and choosing **Behaviors**.

3. In the Events (left) column of the Behaviors palette, choose **Internet Explorer 4** from the browsers and versions pop-up menu. (See Figure 25.3.)

4. In the Events column of the Behaviors palette, click and hold the **+** button. Dreamweaver presents a list of IE4-legal events. Choose `onClick` from this list. At this point, your Behaviors palette should look like 25.3.

5. Click and hold the **+** button in the Actions (right) column of the Behavior palette. Dreamweaver presents a pop-up list of possible actions.

6. Select **Change Property** from the pop-up action list. Dreamweaver presents the Change Property dialog box, shown in Figure 25.4.

Each headline needs its own event handler

You'll need to set up separate event handlers for each headline in the outline. There isn't an easy way to create a generalized script that hides everything between heads; after all, you don't really know how many paragraphs, if any, are between the headlines, and what else may be mixed in with the text paragraphs.

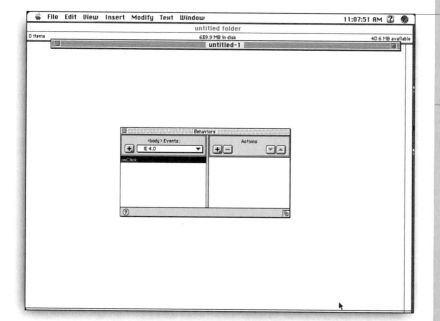

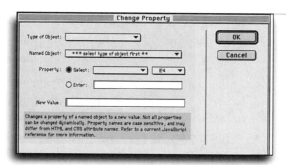

All IDs must be unique

Sometimes Dreamweaver gets a little nuts here, and lists the `<span>` as `span"all ['graf1'][0]"`, a sequence of such names, or something similarly bizarro. This happens when more than one object in the page has the same ID—according to the CSS specifications, all IDs in a page should be unique.

7. Select **SPAN** from the Type of Object pop-up menu.

8. Select **graf1** from the Named Object pop-up menu. (That's the ID we gave the `<span>` of text below the head, right?)

9. Click the **Enter** radio button.

10. Enter `style.display` in the Enter field. The property name is case sensitive; type it exactly as it appears here.

11. Enter `none` in the New Value field. Be sure to type it exactly as shown.

FIGURE 25.5

If you change the *<span>*'s *visibility* property, rather than its *display* property, the outline will not collapse.

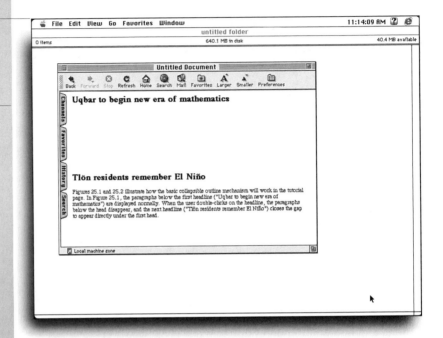

display **versus** visibility

If you've worked through Chapter 22, "Animations: Flashing Objects," you may be wondering about the difference between an object's `style.display` property and its `style.visibility` property.

The `visibility` property affects whether or not the object is visible—well, duh!—but it does not affect how much screen real estate the object uses. If you were to set the <span> of text's `visibility` to `hidden`, the text would vanish, but the second head would not collapse to a position directly under the first head. See Figure 25.5 to see what this state of affairs looks like on screen.

12. Repeat steps 1 through 11 to add an event handler to the second headline. Be sure to pick **graf2** rather than graf1 in step 8.

At this point, you can preview the page in Microsoft Internet Explorer 4. If MSIE 4 is set to your primary browser, press **F12** to look at the page. If you use another browser brand or version as your default preview browser in Dreamweaver select **File**, and choose **Preview**, and choose MSIE from the submenu.

At this point, when you click either headline in MSIE, you'll find that the paragraph(s) below the head disappear in a very satisfactory manner. Unfortunately, there's no way to bring the paragraphs back once they're gone. You'll remedy this problem in the next section.

Adding the *onDblClick* Handler

To allow the user to bring text back once it has been hidden, we'll set up an event handler for the onDoubleClick event.

Adding an `onDoubleClick` handler is pretty much the same as adding the `onClick` handler. This time, the event handler script will set the `style.display` property to `block`, which will cause MSIE to restore the hidden paragraphs.

Adding the double-click handler

1. Click anywhere on the first headline to position the insertion point inside the headline.

2. In the Events (left) column of the Behaviors palette, make sure that IE4 is still selected from the browsers and versions pop-up menu.

3. In the Events column of the Behaviors palette, click and hold the **+** button. Dreamweaver presents a list of IE4-legal events. Choose **onDoubleClick** from this list.

4. Click and hold the **+** button in the Actions (right) column of the Behavior palette. Dreamweaver presents a pop-up list of possible actions.

5. Select **Change Property** from the pop-up action list. Dreamweaver presents the Change Property dialog box.

6. In the Change Property dialog box, select **SPAN** from the Type of Object pop-up menu.

7. Select **graf1** from the Named Object pop-up menu.

8. Click the **Enter** radio button.

9. Enter `style.display` in the Enter field. The property name is case sensitive; type it exactly as it appears here.

10. Enter `block` in the New Value field. Be sure to type it exactly as shown.

11. Repeat steps 1 through 10 to add an `onDoubleClick` event handler to the second headline. Be sure to pick **graf2** rather than graf1 in step 7.

That's it, friends. Your collapsible outline is ready to wow the MSIE 4-using public.

Explore Variations

I have a few ideas about how you might want to personalize the collapsing outline you built in this chapter. You can apply an combination of these variations to your pages with excellent results.

Change the Event Handlers

I'm not sure exactly why I set up the page so that a click collapses an outline section and a double click restores the section. If you like, you can swap the handlers so that double-clicks collapse sections and single clicks restore them.

Swapping event handlers

1. Click the **onClick** event's name in the Events column of the Behaviors palette.

2. Double-click the **Change Property action's name** in the Actions column. Dreamweaver presents the Change Property dialog box, in exactly the same state that you left it in when you first used it.

3. Enter `block` in the New Value field. Click **OK** to close the dialog box.

4. Click the **onDoubleClick** event's name in the Events column of the Behaviors palette.

5. Double-click the **Change Property action's name** in the Actions column. Dreamweaver presents the Change Property dialog box, in exactly the same state that you left it in when you first used it.

6. Enter `none` the New Value field. Click **OK** to close the dialog box.

That's it. Test the new configuration in MSIE4.

"Pre-Collapse" the Outline

Perhaps it makes more sense to you to load the page with the text blocks hidden and allow the reader to expand sections of the outline as desired, rather than loading the outline fully expanded.

Actually, it makes more sense to me to start with a collapsed outline. There is a significant disadvantage to this approach: Netscape Navigator 4.0 users will see a collapsed outline, but will not be able to expand the outline. (Older browsers of all brands will see the expanded outline when the page loads.) If you don't care about Navigator 4 users (and you know who you are), or you're willing to take measures to route Navigator 4 users to a new page, you can certainly "pre-collapse" the outline.

To hide the paragraphs when the page loads, you'll need to make a small adjustment to the <span> tag you added in the second section of this chapter. Simply add the parameter

```
style = "display:none"
```

to each of the span tags, that is, change

```
<span ID = "graf1">
```

to

```
<span style = "display:none" ID = "graf1">
```

and so on for each of the <span> tags. You don't need to make any changes to any of the closing </span> tags.

Adding a Second Tier of Headline

There's no reason why you can't add a second level of headlines, and make the second level of headlines collapsible too. (I'm not counting "I'd like to see my family" or "I haven't been outside since Netscape 3.0 was released" as reasons.)

I'm not going to write out a complete step-by-step for this approach—it's just too long—but I'll give you a push in the right direction.

Here's what a skeleton of the document's HTML would look like:

```
<head>
<!--head stuff-->
</head>

<body>
```

External HTML editors

If you're using an external HTML editor, like HomeSite or BBEdit, use your editor's search and replace function to replace `<span ID` with `<span style = "display:none" ID`.

```
<h1>Headline A</h1>
<span ID = graf1>
    <p><!--paragraph(s) of text--></p>
    <h2>Subhead 1</h2>
        <span ID = subGraf1>
        <p><!--paragraph(s) of text--></p>
        </span> <!-- closes subGraf1 -->
<h2>Subhead 2</h2>
        <span ID = subGraf2>
        <p><!--paragraph(s) of text--></p>
        </span> <!-- closes subGraf2 -->
</span><!-- closes graf1 -->


<h1>Headline B</h1>
<span ID = graf2>
    <p><!--paragraph(s) of text--></p>
    <h2>Subhead 3</h2>
        <span ID = subGraf3>
        <p><!--paragraph(s) of text--></p>
        </span> <!-- closes subGraf3 -->
<h2>Subhead 4</h2>
        <span ID = subGraf4>
        <p><!--paragraph(s) of text--></p>
        </span> <!-- closes subGraf4 -->
</span><!-- closes graf2 -->


<!-- and so on... -->


</body>
```

In this kind of page, you would set up event handlers between
the <h1> heads and graf family of <span> tags. For instance,
you'd set up an onClick handler for Headline A to hide graf1,
and and onClick handler for Headline B to hide graf2.

Similarly, you would set up event handlers between the <h2>
heads and the subGraf family of <span>s. Subhead 1 would show
and hide the contents of subGraf1, Subhead 2 would show and
hid subGraf2, and so on.

From Here...

- To learn how to apply styles to text, see Chapter 6, "Formatting Text with Style Sheets."
- To learn how to add your own custom script, see Chapter 19, "Adding Scripts to Pages."

Site Management and Troubleshooting

Making Your Site Work

Determine the best way to implement style sheets

Set up Library Objects for repeating site elements to make global changes to multiple pages

Use the built-in FTP capabilities in Dreamweaver to gain full control over updating and maintaining your site

Learn strategies for setting up server files and folders

Learn strategies for archiving current and obsolete pages and graphics

Designing a Manageable Site

In the long run, it's not enough to create a cool graphic or a nice looking Web page. Real success in designing and managing a Web site comes in creating a site that looks great, AND is easy to manage. A manageable site is one that is easy to update and change, competently archived, and flexible enough to port to any server or OS environment. Remember to keep these ideals in view as you create a site, otherwise you may find yourself doing a lot of extra work on the back end once the site is designed.

In order to create a manageable site, a little planning and forethought are required at the start. You should determine that you are building a SITE, and not just a random group of pages. To this end, it is important to build in consistency in the graphics, placement, and navigational approach for each page. That doesn't mean that each page is a carbon copy of the one before it, but the pages should all resemble each other in style. Once you see a site's home page, you should be able to identify a related page due to common elements, colors, or layouts.

The reason I'm going into some detail on design and layout is that a well designed site is almost always easy to manage. The common elements and design choices all lend themselves to using Libraries, Cascading Style Sheets, and formatting options such as frames and tables. This chapter looks at how these and other features deliver a site that is easy to modify and care for. At the same time, you will probably make it a bit nicer to look at and navigate.

Setting Up for Mass Production

Creating Web pages one at a time and fussing over each unique and individual graphic is OK when you are building a ten page site. Conversely, when you are assigned a 100 page site that's due in two weeks, you find yourself looking for ways to speed things up without sacrificing navigation or aesthetics. The two easiest and time saving options are to use library images and Style Sheets.

Style Sheets

A style sheet is a list of parameters that define what a page is going to look like. They have been used in page layout programs for years, and are a natural weapon in the arsenal of any Web page designer. Style sheet parameters are loaded in the <head> </head> tags, and determine how the browser displays fonts, background colors, images, and a host of other options.

To be specific, Dreamweaver allows you to set-up parameters that control type formats, backgrounds, block (paragraph formatting), box (table cell), borders, lists, text and object positioning, and extensions (see Figure 26.1). Virtually any attribute that can be specified on a page, such as a margin, text color, or background object, can be entered into a style sheet. For basic details on setting up style sheets, see Chapter 6, "Formatting Text with Style Sheets."

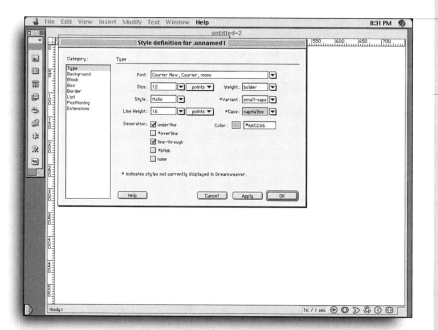

FIGURE 26.1

Style sheets allow you to control a wide range of parameters.

Style sheets are more powerful than individual attributes because they group attributes together, allowing you to apply the entire set with just one command. This not only saves time, but it also ensures consistency, making sure that the exact same settings are applied every time.

This raises the question of how and when you apply the style sheet. Like an attribute, you can apply a style sheet on an inline level to a single tag. You can also apply multiple style sheets to different sections of a page, as well as applying them to the entire document. Rather than having them reside in the <head></head> section of the document, it is also possible to define style sheets in a separate file that resides outside of the HTML document. This allows the same style sheet file to control the look of multiple documents, even an entire site.

There are three different kinds of style sheets supported by Dreamweaver: Custom Styles, Redefine HTML tags, and Cascading Style Sheets. When you create a new style in Dreamweaver, it launches a dialog box that lets you select from these three options (see Figure 26.2).

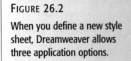

FIGURE 26.2
When you define a new style sheet, Dreamweaver allows three application options.

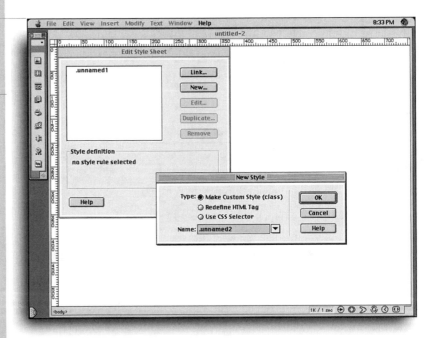

Custom Styles

These are commonly known as Style classes. These styles allow you to create multiple sets of styles that can be used in a single document, or externally throughout your site. A common use for this style type is if you want to format parts of your page differently. Perhaps you want the introductory paragraph larger, flush left, and with red type, while the second section needs a different font and italics. You would simply create class styles that reflect these parameters, select the text areas, and apply the styles. Dreamweaver works behind the scenes adding the class attributes to each selection.

Redefine HTML Tags

This option allows you to select a specific HTML tag and apply additional attributes mentioned. This approach can work very well if you manage the changes closely.

Use CSS Selector

This option allows you to define styles and apply them to sections based on a CSS selector attribute.

Using Style Sheets

If used intelligently, external style sheets are the most flexible option for creating a manageable Web site. External style sheets are not a part of any one document, rather they exist in a separate file in the site folder. Dreamweaver refers to these external sheets without including them in the local document. By setting up a separate document and referring to it as needed, you can update and change those parameters across your entire site by tweaking the one external style sheet file. Again, if you have a 100 page site, this is a good option.

Keep style files small

Remember that external style sheets need to be loaded along with any pages they are associated with, which can slow downloads. Keep the size of the style file as small as possible.

In doing this, you still need to think ahead and isolate the parameters that are likely to be common across the board. Things like font selection, margins, background color, and alignment options are all likely suspects for inclusion.

Libraries

In the same way that style sheets streamline the creation of page formatting, libraries streamline the creation of images and imagemaps. In the same way that style sheets reference a single object across multiple pages, libraries place common elements and objects in a central location, allowing site-wide access. Things like your logo, product images, and navigation buttons and bars are obvious examples. Libraries allow you to store all of these items in the same place, placing them on each individual page as they are needed.

The great thing about libraries is that although you place an item on a page, it actually resides in a library folder that is stored at the root level of your site. The page actually contains a dynamic reference to them in the folder. This approach is similar to the way page layout programs work, in that even though you place an image on a page or in a box, the actual image file must still be included with the layout. This centralized approach allows you to edit the library item only once, having it automatically update each page. Again, if you have 100 pages, you're going to love this feature.

Library items can be images, graphics, text, scripts, or imagemaps. Someone who is casually looking at the library function is liable to say. "Hey, this is no different from placing a shared images folder within my site." He or she would of course be wrong, or I wouldn't have listed this as an example, and Macromedia wouldn't have included it in the feature set.

The power is in understanding that anything can be a library item. Repeated text can be an item, which means that the copyright information at the bottom of your page can be stored in your library. Change the text or the date as often as you want, and it updates across all your pages. Let's consider things further.

You may use a navigation bar that is an imagemap. While you may have the actual image stored in that shared images folder, you can't store the related imagemap coordinates and link information. This means that the imagemap information must be re-entered manually for each page. I've done this for a large site, and I promise you it's not fun. Libraries allow the entire imagemap, links and all, to be stored. Change a link and it's updated across the board. Broaden your definition of what can go in a library, and think about text, scripts, and other objects. For complete details on using libraries, see Chapter 8, "Reusable Parts for Web Pages."

How Library Images Work

The approach for adding an object to a library couldn't be easier. It's as simple as selecting an item and clicking the **Create** button in the Library window.

Adding an object to a library

1. Select the item to be added to the library.

2. Select **Window** and choose **Library** to open the Library window.

3. Click the **Create** button to add the object to the list.

Once an image is part of the library, you have 3 options:

- You can drag the item to the page, or select the **Add To Page** button.

- You can double click or select the **Edit** button to open the item in a separate window for editing.

- You can delete the item from the list by selecting the **Delete** button.

If you should modify a library item, you can apply the changes to library items on the current page you're working on, or across the entire site. Select **Modify**, choose **Library**, and choose **Update Current Page** to make local changes, or select **Modify**, choose **Library**, and then choose **Update Entire Site** to make global changes.

Editing Library Items

Once an item is on the page, you can choose to edit it further by highlighting the item and selecting the **Make Editable** button from the Properties inspector. Clicking **Make Editable** breaks the connection to the source file in the library, and makes the object unique. After editing, it is also possible to place the item back in the library by selecting the **Recreate** button, which overwrites the library item with the current selection.

Strategies for Using Libraries

You can have a different library group for each site you create, as listed in the Edit Sites dialog box. When you select **File** and choose **New**, a library attaches itself to that new page based on the site root folder. Initially, the site root folder is determined by which site has the Default Site Root checkbox selected in the Site Information dialog box (see Figure 26.3). If you change site root folders, the existing library items for that page will be replaced by broken image icons.

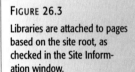

FIGURE 26.3

Libraries are attached to pages based on the site root, as checked in the Site Information window.

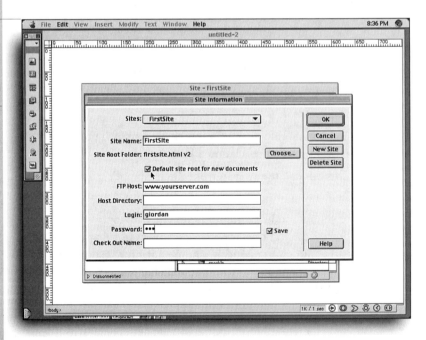

The most requested feature for this version of Dreamweaver is to segment libraries in some way so that logos are in one set, text is in another, scripts in another, and so on, and they are all separated from each other. This may be coming in the next release, but, in the meantime, there are a few things you can do to make things easier. One simple approach is to add a one letter or number prefix to each library file name. Preceding each logo with an "l", or each script with the number "3" will group each of these items together in the library window.

Another dilemma is how to move library items from one site to another. The ability to import and export library items would be a most welcome addition to upcoming releases. One way to handle this now is to change the root structure for each library item from document- or site-relative, to absolute, so Dreamweaver knows where to look for the file. Given the work involved, you may opt to simply place the images in the page all over again, assigning them as new library items for the site as you go.

Other Options for Easy Updates

Whether you are swapping a dozen image files on a catalog page, or swapping text blocks as part of an update, your goal is to make the changes without disturbing the placement of other objects on the page. When things move, text and images reflow, and redesign often follows. A simple image swap can turn into a time consuming headache if you're not careful.

You can minimize these problems by setting your pages up in tables, frames, or layers (keeping in mind that layers only display properly in 4.0 browsers). If you have a page that you know is going to be updated often, take the time to build a modular page grid using one or more of these options. Set up a separate cell, row, or frame for each section that is likely to change. This will not only make updates easier, but it will also impose a grid that will help to organize your page.

Use Frames for Navigation

The most common site update requirement has got to be navigation changes. Each time a page or department is added to a site, a new link or navigation button also has to be added. These navigation items tend to spread out, occupying more space and challenging your organizational skills.

Rather than recreate the same navigational images, links, or imagemaps on each page, it can be effective to create a frameset to hold your navigation page in one frame. Subsequent pages are loaded into a primary frame, while the navigation stays the same. This functions similar to a library item, allowing you to make one change that becomes global for your entire site. See Chapter 16, "Working with Frames," and Chapter 17, "Creating a Frame-Based Navigation System," for complete details on setting up and working with frames.

File Management

Uploading files to a remote server

1. Make sure that your PPP setup is in synch with your server or Web host, and reflects the necessary settings.

2. Activate the autoconnect feature, which will automatically connect to the remote server each time you launch Dreamweaver or your Web browser.

3. Make sure that your server follows the standard UNIX directory structure, rather than a DOS format.

4. Make sure you use the same directory and folders each time you Put images to the server. When images cannot be found on the server, it is almost always because they were dragged or Put in the wrong place, probably in a folder that can't be read.

5. Select **View**, choose **Site Window**, and then choose **Select Newer Local**, and drag the selected files to the remote directory. This selects only the newer files, leaving the unchanged files as they are.

6. Scour your site on a regular basis to weed out orphaned files that don't correspond to a particular page.

For complete details on how to use Dreamweaver's FTP feature, check out Chapter 2, "Working with Files."

Options for Setting Up Folders

As you prepare to upload files, the question arises of how to structure your files and folders on the server. One option is to create a single image folder and to place all of the HTML files in the root folder. The other is to create a separate image folder for each corresponding HTML page. This is assuming you are using a library for shared images, which must also be on the remote server.

Your main goal in setting up the remote server should be to quickly search and find files as you need them. Therefore, the separate folder-per-page approach works well when you have a lot of images. If you use fewer images, you may find that a single image folder gives faster access.

Archival Options

Everyone who owns a computer knows that it's important to archive things. The nature of Web site management places specific requirements on how we store and access files that go beyond a simple backup. The reason is that a Web site accumulates different types of information that need to be accessed in different ways.

Working Data

You start with a group of files on your local drive that you shape into a Website. This local working site will probably contain random images and pages that were present as source material, but didn't make it into the final designs. This area might contain images and text intended for the next round of pages you have planned, or maybe you just ran out of time or room for them. This is all natural and acceptable, as long as this area does not become your only storage place for site files.

Uploading the Final Site

Once you carve out your site locally, you should upload the files to the remote server, and test it rigorously. You should already have tested for browser compatibility, so now is the time to test all of the links to make sure the paths are intact. Click each link and navigation element, and open each page to make sure all of the images and related files load. With an acceptable site on the remote server, create a new location on your local hard drive that will be your site archive. Name a folder with the site name and date, and move all files to that folder.

You now have a working site at the remote server, a backup of that site on your local drive, and a second backup of that site in the local working site on your hard drive. As you continue to develop pages, make sure you use the working site only, testing and uploading to the server from there. Archive each addition or change to the site, storing the changes in a separate dated folder.

A last, and strongly recommended precaution is to make another backup onto removable media such as optical or floppy disk, and store it in a remote site. This gives you a clean backup that is safe from fire, flood, or other acts of God. It also protects you in case your system is stolen or crashes.

Keep in mind that Web design is an ongoing project, just like the other marketing tasks an organization undertakes. A company would be foolish to run one ad and then stop advertising, or to do one mailing and stop. It's a continual process that gets honed and refined over time, as the technology enables us to do more and more. A modular site and an organized file structure will optimize your efforts as your Web involvement grows.

From Here...

- For more information on using Dreamweaver's FTP options, see Chapter 2, "Working with Files."

- For more information on making your site compatible with the major web browsers, see Chapter 28, "Targeting Your Page for Internet Explorer or Navigator."

- For more information on making your site downward compatible for all users, see Chapter 29, "Targeting Your Page for Everyone."

- For more information on setting up CSS parameters, see Appendix D, "CSS Quick Reference."

Troubleshooting Dreamweaver

Solving Basic Problems

The difficulty in troubleshooting Web page issues is that there are a number of things that can create problems as you work with Dreamweaver, and only a few of them are directly tied into Dreamweaver itself. Issues like HTML protocols, FTP connectivity, browser nuances, and faulty Java and ActiveX scripts lie in wait to derail an unsuspecting page.

While this one chapter can't deliver the answers to all of these issues, it does try to cover the basics in a number of different areas. It is divided into three sections: Starting with the right expectations, HTML troubleshooting, and Dreamweaver specifics. Taking this approach will give you a head start in determining where the basic problem lies and how to go about solving it.

Great Expectations

You've just created an awesome site that you're pretty happy with. It looks great in Netscape 4.0, but you happen to launch it in MS Internet Explorer and discover that it looks bad. The text formatting is now garbled, and the images are all off center. Welcome to the wonderful world of Web design.

If you haven't figured it out by now, please understand that HTML browsers interpret HTML pages differently. That includes moving from version to version as well as from Netscape to Microsoft. Each browser has its own way of looking at things, and there is nothing you can do about that. You should also understand that HTML text flows to fill its current window, and that it will reflow when the window is resized. This means that two people looking at a page with the same browser but different size browser windows will see something different. And to make things more complex, people can custom configure their browsers to show larger text sizes or to omit images completely.

The point is that you will never create a design that is so bullet-proof that users can't make it look messy if they try hard enough. There is always some variable you can't account for. As an example, I had one client call me and ask me why my Web page had large gaping holes in the middle of the text blocks. I double- and triple-checked everything and found no evidence of these holes. I ultimately paid him a visit and discovered that his system used a 4-bit video card that could only show 16 colors. The links I created were blending in with the background because the video card couldn't distinguish between the colors. I know this sounds extreme, but it really happened.

Working Within the Limitations

The first question to ask is whether it matters to you that people with 4-bit video cards can't see your links. If you are designing for an upscale or creative audience, you may decide that it doesn't. If it does matter, there are three areas you need to accommodate: text alignment, font selection, and color selection. A possible fourth would be slower modems, which could restrain the size of your images. But this would only make things run sluggishly, it wouldn't change the look of your page or cause any trouble.

Text Alignment

Generally speaking, set up your text to align flush left. Don't set any hard returns because they will generate unwanted line breaks when the text is reflowed in a different size window. Don't expect specific lines or words to line up exactly with an image or specific spot on the page, and build in some latitude for variance with the text placement. If more precise text placement is needed, create tables to contain the text, which will impose rigid margins.

Check and fix download times

Download statistics in Dreamweaver do not account for slow downs and fluctuations in the physical networks and server environments of the real world. If a projected download time is on the edge, take the time to fix it.

Font Selection

Don't agonize too long over a particular font selection, because the best-case scenario says that only about half of your audience is going to see it. The only way to specify fonts viewers can see on their systems is to use style sheets or TrueDoc technology, both of which are limited to 4.0 browsers. This means that anyone with a 3.0 or earlier browser is left out in the cold.

This simple fact has forced most designers to use standard Times and Helvetica fonts for most pages. Since this is a sacrilegious act for most designers, more work has been done to give Web designers their fonts back than just about any other development effort. The current best option, short of transforming the text into an image file, is to use style sheets. The most common form are Cascading Style Sheets, which allow you to specify font, color, size, and a host of other parameters. TrueDoc actually creates a profile of the font information, which is downloaded along with the page itself. Unfortunately, TrueDoc only works with Netscape 4.0, making it even more limited as an option.

The following summarizes your options:

- If a text component absolutely has to look the same in all instances, bring it into Photoshop and convert it to an image.

- Remember to make your page look good with a basic serif or sans serif font, for all the 3.0 people out there.

- Use style sheets for more control, making sure to set a serif or sans serif font as an option.

Color Selection

For a number of reasons too detailed to explore here, browsers are only capable of displaying 256 different colors. These colors cover a wide spectrum, so chances are you will be able to choose something you like. When a color is specified that a browser cannot render, it approximates the closest option. This usually is not a problem, but you should be cautious if an exact match is required.

One workaround for backgrounds and images is to approximate a specific color by using a dither pattern. These dither options combine two browser-safe colors into a wide variety of options. The market is full of plug-ins and applets that do this kind of work for you, and they are a very good option for those who require more specificity.

HTML Troubleshooting

Please understand that this section is not intended to teach you about HTML. It's just a list of points to remember and check on if a page isn't loading properly. The basic areas that can cause problems are the document structure, text commands, and link commands.

Document and Tag Structure

The basic structure of a document, using the `<html>`, `<head>`, and `<body>` tags, is very important. Remember that the visible portion of the HTML document must fall between the `<body>` tags, and that the document must begin and end with the `<HTML>` tag. You should also check for closing tags, which always show a / before the title of the tag, as in `</HTML>`.

The following are points to check:

- Make sure that the `<HTML>`, `<head>`, and `<body>` tags are all present, and that there is a corresponding closing tag for each.

- Make sure that all scripts, style sheets, meta tags and other objects are completely enclosed in the `<head>` `</head>` tag set.

- Enclose all of the visible elements of a page within the `<body></body>` tags.

- Make sure all tag attributes are enclosed within their respective brackets.

- Always check for closing tags (`</>`).

Know your syntax!

Make sure you are fully versed in tag and attribute syntax because keyboard errors and misplaced characters can be the most time-consuming to spot.

- When nesting tags, remember that the closing order should be to close the most recent tag first, working out to the older ones. The last tag should be the one you started with.

- Check that your comments are enclosed within the <!-- --> tag set.

Text Commands

This area deals with text formatting. Questions like "Why is there so much space between my lines?" and "Why does this heading look bold?" are all text-related. If text elements are not looking the way you expect them to, start by reviewing these basics.

There are three options for line spaces, make sure you are using them correctly: a division (<div>), paragraph (<p>), and line-break (<br>). The division tag divides the document into distinct sections, while the paragraph tag signals the start of a new paragraph. The line-break tag simply forces a carriage return, and inserts less vertical space than a <p> tag.

The following are things to check:

- Make sure that no carriage returns have been inserted for line breaks.

- Remember that if you do not have an end tag set for various formatting tags, the effect carries on throughout the document.

- Check for alignment attributes within text tags. Commands such as =center will instruct the browser to change things like text alignment and the style of the text.

Link Commands

So what do you do when you click a link expecting to go somewhere and nothing happens? Better yet, what happens when you end up going to a blank window that says something like Error 404, URL not found, or just gives you an ugly gray icon. If it's someone else's site, you're annoyed, if it's your site, you're embarrassed. You can avoid these occurrences with thorough testing and a little common sense.

As mentioned previously in this chapter, please make sure you are previewing your pages in Netscape Navigator and Communicator, as well as Internet Explorer 3.0 and 4.0. As you load pages in these browsers, click all links and check that all images load correctly. If an image doesn't load, you need to check the image tag (`<img>`) to see if it's looking in the right place as it references the file. In most cases, you have entered the image location incorrectly, or you have not set up the tag properly. Double-check the location of the file on your remote server, and check the HTML source data to make sure they match. For details on the proper HTML tags and when to use them, check out Appendix C, "HTML 4 Quick Reference."

As far as links are concerned, check that the URL address is entered correctly, and make sure the file is in the right place on the server. Most of the time it really is that simple; the browser is looking in a specific place for the file, and it isn't there. Remember to check for simple things like a comma used instead of a period, forgetting www, and getting the suffix wrong (don't always assume .com).

> **Keep your HTML window open**
>
> When placing anchor and line-break tags, keep the HTML window open as well as the main window, so you can drag these elements into position while tracking them within the HTML source.

Application Problems

While HTML errors can create a wide range of problems, there comes a time when you need to look at Dreamweaver itself and determine if the application is to blame. The remainder of this chapter will look at specific questions and known problems in working with Dreamweaver.

Dreamweaver seems unstable when I launch; it freezes, hangs, or takes forever to load.

Especially for Macintosh users, Dreamweaver has been known to conflict with various system extensions, which is the first thing you should check. Since Dreamweaver needs some extensions to load, you need to load only those extensions required to launch the program. Follow these steps to reboot with the minimum extension set:

1. Open Extensions Manager and turn off all extensions by deselecting the checkbox next to the extensions folder icon.

2. Check the Microsoft OLE Automation version 2.06, Microsoft OLE Extension version 2.06, Microsoft OLE Library version 2.06, and Winsock Lib. extensions to reactivate them.

3. Restart your computer and launch Dreamweaver to check for the problem.

If problems persist, try the following, restarting and checking the results after each step.

1. Allocate as much memory as possible to the application and turn off Virtual Memory.

2. Disable RAM Doubler, DiskDoubler, and any other applications that manipulate memory or disk space.

3. Remove ATM, ATM Deluxe, Suitcase, and/or Type Reunion from the System folder and reboot.

4. Defragment and optimize your hard drive.

5. Reinstall Dreamweaver from the original system disks, making sure that you disable all extensions and inits before the installation takes place.

6. Remove all fonts from the fonts folder except the base set that the system comes with. (If this solves the problem, you have a corrupt font and must load a few fonts at a time, rebooting as you do until you find the culprit.)

Why does Dreamweaver autoconnect to my ISP when I launch the application?

This is because you have enabled the autoconnect setting in your PPP control panel. You can either disable it in the PPP dialog box, or you can click Cancel when it tries to connect. Given that this same setting controls the autoconnect when your browser launches, you may want to just hit Cancel and leave things as they are.

Site and FTP Problems

When I upload files to the remote server, why do my loaded files become read-only and won't save?

This is due to the Check-in/Check-out feature that requires that files be checked in and out via Dreamweaver's Site window each time they are opened. You can easily disable this by selecting **Preferences**, choosing **Site FTP**, and deselecting the Enable File Check in/Check out and check out files when opening features in the Site FTP preferences dialog box.

When I create a new page it attaches itself to the wrong site.

Check the Edit Sites dialog box by selecting **File**, choosing **Open Sites**, and selecting **Edit Sites**. Select the site desired as the default site, and make sure the Default site root for new documents check box is checked. All new pages will default to the site that has this checkbox active.

I FTP my files to my remote server, but when I look for them they're gone.

This is always a problem with the target directory on your remote server. Before you upload files, double-check to see that they are going to the proper nested folder. Dreamweaver's drag-and-drop copy feature is convenient, but it also makes it very easy to make mistakes.

How can I update my remote site with the local files that have changed, ignoring unchanged files?

This is easily accomplished by selecting **View**, choosing **Site Window**, and selecting **Select Newer Local**. Dreamweaver runs a check of the local and remote directories and automatically selects the new files on your local site. You can then drag them to the remote site, leaving the older files untouched. There is also a **Select Newer Remote** command for those wanting to go the other way.

Page Problems

When I paste text, it comes in as one long string. How can I avoid this?

This is because Dreamweaver looks at text the same way that a browser looks at text, ignoring any line breaks that are not directed by tags. To circumvent this, select **Paste As Text** rather than the Paste command, which inserts line breaks at each carriage return.

Why is my text spaced so far apart in the browser?

Try using a line-break (<br>) tag instead of a paragraph (<p>) tag by selecting **Shift+Enter** instead of Enter. Paragraph tags insert more space between lines than line breaks, because they are meant to start new paragraphs, not just break a line.

Can I set different spacing beyond *
* and *<p>* tags?

Another option is to specify a leading value in a style sheet, which will give you more spacing control in the 4.0 browsers. Follow these steps to set up a style sheet for exact line spacing:

1. Select **Text**, choose **Custom Style**, choose **Edit Style Sheet**, and then select the **New** or **Edit** button.
2. Select the class, HTML, or CSS Style type. This brings you to the Style Definition dialog box.
3. Enter a value in the Line Height field, keeping it in relation to the value in the Size field.

How do I insert spaces between characters in a line of text?

Add a non-breaking space ( ) to lines of text and images by pressing Spacebar-Shift-Control on Windows or Spacebar-Shift-Option on the Macintosh.

Why don't my objects align properly?

Since the nature of HTML is to flow text and images into the space presented, it is an ongoing challenge to get objects to align themselves across a range of browsers and monitors. Try creating tables to get things to line up, and remember to use the cell alignment controls and check for extra spaces in the cells. For your 4.0 browser audience, place objects in layers for exact positioning.

My background images appear garbled when the screen redraws them.

This is a known Dreamweaver bug on the Macintosh. You must allocate more memory to Dreamweaver when using large background images, otherwise the screen renderings corrupt, and things slow down or stop. Please note that the problem is only with screen redraw, and your pages will display fine in the browser.

My linked image has a blue/colored box around it— how do I lose it?

In the property inspector, set the border value to 0.

When drawing an imagemap, why can't I close the Polygon Shape tool?

Double click the tool to close the shape.

How do I get rid of the border on my table?

Select the table, and set the border value to 0 in the Attributes Inspector.

Why don't my tables align properly?

It can be difficult to resize table columns and rows when they are populated with objects. Try dragging the table gridlines first and then add the objects. Also remember that a table cell expands to hold the object within it. A last suggestion is to check the Vertical/Horizontal align option in each cell to make sure everything is set the same.

Why can't I specify the height of a table row?

Although you can drag to intuitively set the row height, the only way to numerically set it is in the HTML Source window. Modify the `<td>` tag by adding a `height=xx` attributes value, inserting the height pixel value for the *xx*.

My tables look different in different monitors.

This is caused by setting an absolute pixel value for your table parameters. Since monitors use different resolutions, the size of a 100 pixel box will be much smaller on a 1200×1600 display than it will on a 1024×768 display. It's the same situation when you change monitor resolutions and all the windows on your screen get larger or smaller. To fix this problem, set your table dimensions to percentages, which will divide the table consistently across a range of monitors and resolutions.

I try to click in a table cell and nothing happens, it won't let me enter data.

You have an invalid table. When a table is created, Dreamweaver inserts an ` ` placeholder within the `<td></td>` tags to keep the space open and active. You can either retype the ` ` value in the table tags, or simply delete the table and drag out a new one.

How do I insert a link that creates an email message?

Type `mailto:yourname@yourserver.xxx` in the URL section of the `<href>` tag.

Frame Problems

Why do I get a white space between frames I'm trying to align?

Make sure the images are background images only. You cannot seamlessly align other types of objects between frames.

How do I change the relative or constant formatting options for my frames?

Change this in the Frames window by following these steps:

1. Select **Window**, choose **Frames**, and make sure all frames are defined.

2. In the Frames window, click the outside border to select the entire framset. The Properties Inspector will change to show value and unit information for rows and columns.

3. In the frameset thumbnail, click the bar that corresponds to each row or column in your frameset, and set the values as desired. Select Pixels, Percent, or Relative formats for each row or column, mixing and matching as required.

Why do my borderless frames have borders when viewed in Internet Explorer 3.0?

Be sure to enter a value of 0 for your framespacing, frameborder, and border.

Why do my borderless frames show a black frame on mouseclick when viewed in Netscape 3.0?

This is a Netscape 3.0 bug, and there is no way to avoid this. Thankfully, version 4.0 fixes the problem.

I'm having problems getting my page to load into frames.

Check the HTML file names and make sure the required .htm or .html extensions are present. Also, save each internal frame document before preview because Dreamweaver can't generate a TMP file for frame information.

From Here...

Additional troubleshooting support is available from any one of the excellent HTML reference books on the market, as well as the appendixes in this book. You should also familiarize yourself with the Dreamweaver newsgroups and the Macromedia Dreamweaver Web site, which contains a wealth of tech notes, FAQs, and access to the Macromedia support team.

Targeting Your Page for Internet Explorer or Navigator

Configuring preview browsers

Checking a page against a specific browser

HTML traps on Netscape Navigator

HTML traps on Microsoft Internet Explorer

Best Viewed On...

Dreamweaver offers an important capability in this world of competing and often incompatible browsers—the ability to make sure your pages are compatible with a specific version of a browser. By the same token, you can also work to make sure your pages work exclusively with one browser, making the pages prone to break down or display incorrectly on other browsers.

With that last statement, let it be known that this chapter leads you into potentially hostile territory. Targeting your pages to either of the "Big Two" browsers at the expense of any other could lead to some rather harsh email in your in-box.

Dreamweaver includes a utility to check your Web pages against a specific browser to see if any tags or attributes are unsupported by that browser. This check only generates a report of inconsistencies—it doesn't fix anything or change any part of your page—so you can use it without fear of ruining your pages.

However, before this feature works you'll need to configure Dreamweaver with one or more preview browsers. A preview browser is typically installed automatically during Dreamweaver installation. For more information about the installation, see Appendix F, "Installing Dreamweaver and Accessories."

If a preview browser wasn't configured, you can still add a browser now.

Configuring a preview browser

1. Select **Edit** and choose **Preferences**, or press **Ctrl+U** (in Windows) or **Command+U** (for the Macintosh).

2. Select **Preview in Browser** from the Category list (see Figure 28.1).

3. If there are no browsers on the list, click the **Add** button (see Figure 28.2). Find the browser program on your computer, edit the name as necessary, and select whether or not it's primary or secondary. Click **OK** when you're done.

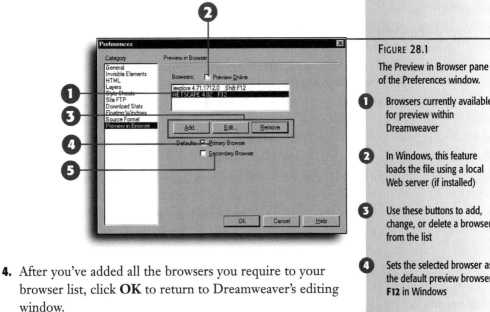

FIGURE 28.1

The Preview in Browser pane of the Preferences window.

❶ Browsers currently available for preview within Dreamweaver

❷ In Windows, this feature loads the file using a local Web server (if installed)

❸ Use these buttons to add, change, or delete a browser from the list

❹ Sets the selected browser as the default preview browser, **F12** in Windows

❺ Sets the selected browser as the secondary preview browser, **Shift+F12** in Windows

4. After you've added all the browsers you require to your browser list, click **OK** to return to Dreamweaver's editing window.

With at least one preview browser in place, you're ready to check your page against a target browser. This feature relies on a set of text files, each of which contains a profile on a specific browser. The text file includes all of the HTML tags supported by that browser. As part of its installation, Dreamweaver includes predefined profiles for Netscape Navigator 2.0 through 4.0, and Microsoft Internet Explorer 2.0 through 4.0.

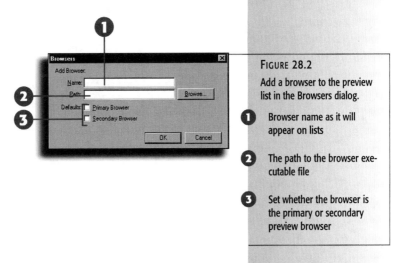

FIGURE 28.2

Add a browser to the preview list in the Browsers dialog.

❶ Browser name as it will appear on lists

❷ The path to the browser executable file

❸ Set whether the browser is the primary or secondary preview browser

SEE ALSO

➤ *Creating a browser profile, page 430*

Checking a page against a target browser

1. Load a Web page into the Dreamweaver editing window (Select **File** and choose **Open**, or **Ctrl+O**), or save the changes (select **File** and choose **Save**, or **Ctrl+S**) to your current file. Dreamweaver will not automatically save changes before beginning this process, relying on the last saved version.

2. Select **File** and choose **Check Target Browser** (see Figure 28.3). If you haven't selected a primary browser, Dreamweaver prompts you to do so (see the preceding step-by-step for more information).

FIGURE 28.3

Select one or more browsers from the target browsers list.

3. Select one or more browsers from the list. A browser is included in this list if Dreamweaver finds a browser profile for it. To select more than one browser, hold down the **Ctrl** (in Windows) or **Shift** (for the Macintosh) while selecting browsers.

4. Click the **Do Check** button. Dreamweaver performs the check and launches the primary preview browser to view the results (see Figure 28.4).

5. Print a copy of the report to have it handy while revising the Web page. Or, you can show the report to your boss to prove you know what you're doing.

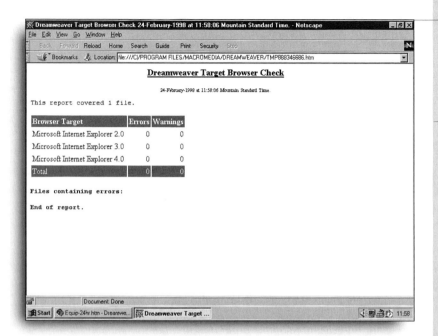

FIGURE 28.4

A report is generated for the page, listing any possible errors or incompatibilities of the current file with any of the selected browsers.

If the thought of checking one file at a time on a site that contains more than one page just turns your stomach, you're not alone. Lucky for both of us, Dreamweaver includes the capability to check a directory or an entire site for compatibility issues.

Checking a directory or site against a target browser

1. To run the check on a directory or site, open the Site window (select **Window** and choose **Site**) and open one of your sites. Then, select a folder from the Local directory (this doesn't work on Remote directories). To check the entire site, select the top (root) directory of the site. The browser check is performed on all the Web pages in the selected directory plus any subdirectories.

2. Select **File** and choose **Check Target Browsers** from the Site window (see Figure 28.5). Click a browser version to select it for checking, or select more than one by using **Ctrl+Click** (in Windows) or **Shift+Click** (for the Macintosh).

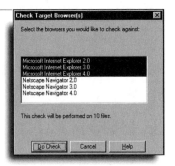

3. Click **Do Check** to start the browser checking process.

4. The report is generated into the preview browser, listing errors and warnings on a file-by-file basis. If you checked a lot of files, this could be a very big page.

Now that we've had a chance to check some files against the most common two browsers on the Web, it's time to take a look at some of the problems you might encounter when checking either browser.

Stuff That Doesn't Work

As browsers progress, there's a continuing issue of backward-compatibility. Pages that worked on a previous version of the browser will probably still work on a newer version, but the reverse isn't necessarily so. This is because new tags and attributes are added in the newer browser that the older browser knows nothing about.

Luckily, the vast majority of browsers handle this rather gracefully. They ignore the stuff they don't understand. In most cases, this doesn't create any problems, but you'll want to check just to be sure.

In the following two sections, I'll talk about the more common elements that aren't supported by the newest versions of these browsers, including proprietary elements, and items to avoid if your audience is primarily using older versions of these programs. I'll try to give you an idea of what to worry about, and what you can safely ignore under most situations.

Stuff That Doesn't Work on Navigator

Netscape Navigator is an interesting beast. In previous editions, it has developed a reputation as a very innovative product that dramatically pushed the envelope of expectations on the Web. With Navigator 4.0, that innovation has slowed dramatically, and now it finds itself incompatible, or at least inoperable, with several important developments in HTML.

The first problem you'll run into with Navigator 4.0 is the <OBJECT> tag. The <OBJECT> tag was invented by Microsoft to insert ActiveX controls, and was recently adopted by the World Wide Web Consortium to insert all manner of content, including Netscape plug-ins, Java applets, and even images. Since the tag was originally used to insert Microsoft-proprietary content, Netscape opted not to include support for it. Now that it's part of the standard, you can probably expect Netscape to include it as part of the browser.

For the time being, you'll still need to use the <EMBED> tag to include plug-ins and <APPLET> to include Java applets, and any <OBJECT> tags will be ignored by Navigator. The <EMBED> and <APPLET> tags are supported by all versions of Navigator beginning with 2.0. Including multimedia content with the <OBJECT>, <EMBED>, and <APPLET> tags is explained in Chapter 9, "Working with Multimedia Content."

Earlier in this book, there was a chapter about layers, and the various incompatibilites involved in implementing them on the two leading browsers. Navigator recognizes and can implement positioning with <LAYER> or <DIV> tags. The kicker comes when you try to implement layers and scripting. Navigator 4.0 has dynamic control over the <LAYER> tag, but not the <DIV> tag. Internet Explorer has dynamic control over the <DIV> tag, but doesn't even recognize the <LAYER> tag.

So, if you want to work dynamically with layers on your Web page, you'll need to integrate support for both layer models. None of the layer tags are supported by versions of Navigator earlier than 4.0.

Learn a lot more about layers in Chapter 18, "Working with Layers," including the differences between the various types of layers and page divisions.

Another important partially supported feature you'll bump up against with Navigator is event handling. Netscape has expanded slightly the tags that can recognize the user is doing something to them, such as placing the mouse pointer over them, clicking, or other similar types of actions. But, unlike Internet Explorer, this functionality is limited to tags that are traditionally manipulated by the user. Part IV, "Adding Interactivity and Scripts," includes information on events and scripting, and how to implement them on your Web pages.

Navigator 4.0 only recognizes events associated with these tags: `<BODY>`, `<A>`, `<LAYER>`, `<FRAMESET>`, `<IFRAME>`, `<IMG>`, `<AREA>`, `<FORM>`, `<INPUT>`, `<SELECT>`, and `<TEXTAREA>`. Navigator 3.0 and 2.0 is limited even further: `<BODY>`, `<A>`, `<FRAMESET>`, `<FORM>`, `<INPUT>`, `<SELECT>`, and `<TEXTAREA>`.

Navigator 4.0 is the earliest version that supports style sheets—Cascading Style Sheets (CSS) or JavaScript Style Sheets (JSSS). If you use Dreamweaver or HomeSite to create your Web pages, this shouldn't be an issue since they only support styles through CSS. Appendix D, "CSS Quick Reference," is a handy reference for the various settings and attributes possible within a style sheet.

SEE ALSO
➤ *For more information on creating style sheets with Dreamweaver, page 94*

Stuff That Doesn't Work on Microsoft

For being a latecomer, Microsoft has done an admirable job of developing its browser into a serious contender and trendsetter. The latest version, Internet Explorer 4.0, reliably incorporates the HTML 4.0 standard for the World Wide Web Consortium (W3C), in addition to meeting the preliminary requirements of Dynamic HTML and eXtensible Markup Language (XML). Internet Explorer still doesn't meet all the standards to the letter, however, which results in some incompatibilities with Netscape Navigator.

The first problem you'll run into with Internet Explorer 4.0 is the <EMBED> tag. The <EMBED> tag was invented by Netscape to insert plug-ins, and has never been supported by Microsoft. Microsoft favored its own version, <OBJECT>, which was originally used exclusively for ActiveX content and eventually incorporated by the W3C as part of the official HTML standard for including anything—from Java to ActiveX to plug-ins to pictures. If your multimedia content only comes as a plug-in, you're out of luck. Otherwise, Dreamweaver allows you to nest an <EMBED> within an <OBJECT> so that you're covered either way.

You'll still need to use an <APPLET> tag with Internet Explorer to add Java and <IMG> for images, as the Microsoft product doesn't support the multi-use version of <OBJECT>. Including multimedia content with <OBJECT>, <EMBED>, and <APPLET> tags is explained in Chapter 9.

Navigator was the first browser to debut with layers capability using the <LAYER> tag. Unfortunately, the W3C had its own ideas, and favored the <DIV> tag over <LAYER> for creating layers. Microsoft actually got ahead of the game by releasing its most recent version of Internet Explorer a little later, with support exclusively for <DIV>. Netscape included support for <DIV> at the last minute so it could be in step with the W3C, but Microsoft didn't reciprocate. As a result, any attempt to implement animations or positioning using a <LAYER> tag in Internet Explorer won't work.

The <DIV> tag and its cousin <SPAN> are not supported by versions of Internet Explorer earlier than 4.0. Learn a lot more about layers in Chapter 18, including the differences between the various tupes of layers and page divisions.

A real fun part of Internet Explorer 4.0 is its scripting capability, especially when it comes to recognizing events. Using events and scripting, you can detect virtually any event for any tag, from mouse-clicks on paragraphs to mouseovers on block quotes.

While Internet Explorer 4.0 supports a comprehensive event handling capability, Internet Explorer 3.0 recognizes events for a limited set of tags: <BODY>, <A>, <FRAMESET>, <FORM>, <INPUT>,

<SELECT>, and <TEXTAREA>. Internet Explorer 2.0 doesn't recognize any events.

Cascading Style Sheets (CSS) are supported by Internet Explorer 3.0 and 4.0. However, Netscape's JavaScript Style Sheets (JSSS) are not. Since Dreamweaver doesn't support JSSS creation, this shouldn't be an issue.

From Here...

- While you're fine-tuning pages, you'll also want to make sure your site is organized and functional. Tips and advice are found in Chapter 26, "Making Your Site Work"

- Since everyone's bound to make mistakes in checking browsers and creating interactive sites, you'll want to read Chapter 27, "Troubleshooting Dreamweaver."

- More help on checking your pages against other browsers is found in Chapter 29, "Targeting Your Page for Everyone."

Targeting Your Page for Everyone

Converting files for advanced and legacy

Creating a new browser profile

JavaScript in non-JavaScript browsers

Working around proprietary tags

Creating Content for All Users

Dreamweaver comes bundled with timely releases of the latest browsers from Netscape and Microsoft. These are without a doubt the most powerful browsers on the market today. But not everyone runs out to get a copy of the latest and greatest browser when it's released.

As a matter of fact, there are people still using old copies of Netscape 1.0 and 2.0, many others who use version 2.0 or 3.0 of Mosaic, and still others that use the text-only Lynx Web browser. None of these other browsers support dynamic HTML—all of that neat content that employs animation and rollovers will be lost on these folks.

That's ok. They don't have to see everything, as long as they get to see the substance of your page. That's where targeting for other browsers comes into play. One of the purposes of using dynamic HTML is to create pages that sing and dance on the best and brightest browsers, while gracefully degrading to an acceptable appearance on other browsers. This chapter explains how to create browser profiles to check your pages against other browsers to see if your page is going to have problems when it faces the reality of the real world.

Dreamweaver Page Conversions

Dreamweaver also offers you the opportunity to create duplicate sets of pages for different types of browsers. This feature is targeted towards browsers that use layers and Cascading Style Sheets for layout, and those that rely on tables and the <FONT> tag.

For example, begin with a page that uses the latest and greatest features of Internet Explorer 4 and Navigator 4, and follows the strict W3C HTML 4 recommendation. This page will most likely take advantage of layers (with <DIV>) for layout and positioning, and CSS to control appearance. This page will also never appear the way you intended on older browsers. To get around this, you can create a new page from the current page that converts all the 4.0 elements into elements readable by most earlier browsers. We'll start with the HTML page in Listing 29.1.

LISTING 29.1.   **A basic cover page designed with layers and CSS.**

```html
<html>
<head>
<title>Welcome!</title>
<meta http-equiv="Content-Type" content="text/html;
      charset=iso-8859-1">
<style type="text/css">
<!--
.title {
   font-family: Arial, Helvetica, sans-serif; font-style: italic;
   color: RED; text-align: right
}
.copyright {
   font-family: Arial, Helvetica, sans-serif; font-size: small;
   font-style: italic
}
--></style></head>

<body bgcolor="#FFFFFF">
<div id="Layer1" style="position:absolute; left:11px; top:12px;
     width:114px; height:171px; z-index:1">
  <img src="images/umc-logo.gif" width="108" height="168">
</div>
<div id="Layer2" style="position:absolute; left:131px; top:35px;
     width:228px; height:117px; z-index:2">
  <h1>Yellowstone<br>
    Annual<br>
    Conference</h1>
</div>
<div id="Layer3" style="position:absolute; left:131px; top:167px;
     width:262px; height:42px; z-index:3">
  <h1 class="title">ConnectiOnLine</h1>
</div>
<div id="Layer4" style="position:absolute; left:473px; top:348px;
     width:300px; height:106px; z-index:4">
  <p><em>Produced and maintained by the <strong>Conference
  Committee on Communications</strong>. Comments and hot dishes
  accepted and encouraged.</em></p>
  <p class="copyright"><em>(c)MCMXCVIII Yellowstone Annual
  Conference United Methodist Church</em></p></div>
      </body>
</html>
```

Step by Step: Converting 4.0 Pages to 3.0 Pages

1. Complete a Web page with Cascading Style Sheets and layers, or open an existing page that takes advantage of 4.0-level features (see Figure 29.1).

FIGURE 29.1

The page as it exists currently uses layers for positioning and layout.

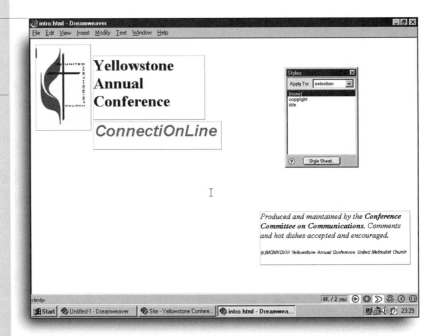

2. Start the conversion utility:
   - Press Ctrl+F6 (Windows) or Option+F6 (Macintosh).
   - Select File, Convert, 3.0 Browser Compatible.
3. The Convert dialog box gives a choice of converting layers to tables, CSS to font tags, or both.
4. Dreamweaver opens a new editing window, and performs the conversion (see Figure 29.2). The resulting code is a bit convoluted, but it does work. See Listing 29.2.

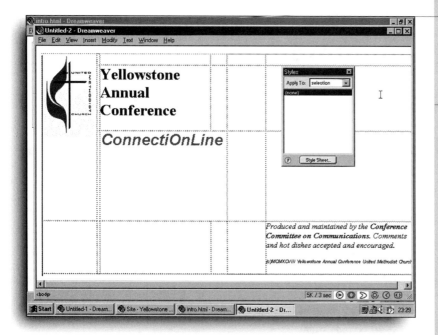

FIGURE 29.2

The page as it was converted for use by 3.0 compatible browsers. It's not exact, but it's really close.

LISTING 29.2 **The same page as Listing 29.1, only now rendered with tables and font tags.**

```
<html>
<head>
<title>Welcome!</title>
<meta http-equiv="Content-Type" content="text/html;
      charset=iso-8859-1">
</head>

<body bgcolor="#FFFFFF">
<table cellspacing="0" cellpadding="0" border="0">
  <tr>
    <td width="114" height="336" rowspan="3" valign="top">
      <img src="images/umc-logo.gif" width="108" height="168"></td>
    <td width="6" height="23" valign="top"></td>
    <td width="228" height="23" valign="top"></td>
```

continues…

LISTING 29.2 **Continued**

```
    <td width="34" height="23" valign="top"></td>
    <td width="80" height="23" valign="top"></td>
    <td width="307" height="23" valign="top"></td>
  </tr>
  <tr>
    <td width="6" height="132" valign="top"></td>
    <td width="228" height="132" valign="top">
  <h1>Yellowstone<br>
    Annual<br>
    Conference </h1>
</td>
    <td width="34" height="132" valign="top"></td>
    <td width="80" height="132" valign="top"></td>
    <td width="307" height="132" valign="top"></td>
  </tr>
  <tr>
    <td width="6" height="181" valign="top"></td>
    <td width="262" height="181" colspan="2" valign="top">
      <h1 align="right"><i>
      <font face="Arial, Helvetica, sans-serif" color="RED">
        ConnectiOnLine</font></i></h1>
</td>
    <td width="80" height="181" valign="top"></td>
    <td width="307" height="181" valign="top"></td>
  </tr>
  <tr>
    <td width="114" height="106" valign="top"></td>
    <td width="6" height="106" valign="top"></td>
    <td width="228" height="106" valign="top"></td>
    <td width="34" height="106" valign="top"></td>
    <td width="80" height="106" valign="top"></td>
    <td width="307" height="106" valign="top">
      <p><em>Produced and maintained by the <strong>Conference
      Committee on Communications</strong>. Comments and hot dishes
      accepted and encouraged.</em></p>
      <p><i><font face="Arial, Helvetica, sans-serif" size="1">
      <em>(c)MCMXCVIII Yellowstone Annual Conference United
```

```
        Methodist Church</em></font></i></p>
  </td>
  </tr>
  <tr>
    <td width="114" height="1" valign="top">
      <img width="114" height="1" src="transparent.gif"></td>
    <td width="6" height="1" valign="top">
      <img width="6" height="1" src="transparent.gif"></td>
    <td width="228" height="1" valign="top">
      <img width="228" height="1" src="transparent.gif"></td>
    <td width="34" height="1" valign="top">
      <img width="34" height="1" src="transparent.gif"></td>
    <td width="80" height="1" valign="top">
      <img width="80" height="1" src="transparent.gif"></td>
    <td width="307" height="1" valign="top">
      <img width="307" height="1" src="transparent.gif"></td>
  </tr>
</table>
</body>
</html>
```

The opposite is also true—you can convert a page which includes a layout with tables into a 4.0-level page with layers. Unfortunately, you'll still need to convert the font tags by hand. What's the advantage to just turning tables into layers? As far as managing and tweaking layouts goes, it's easier to drag a layer to the right location than reorganizing a stack of table cells. To reverse the conversion, begin with your legacy page in the Dreamweaver editing window, then begin conversion with one of these methods:

- Select Ctrl+Shift+F6 (Windows) or Option+Shift+F6 (Macintosh).
- Select File, Convert, Tables to Layers.

  The process is quick, as Dreamweaver opens a new editing window and writes the converted code. Again, the results (see Listing 29.3 and Figure 29.3) are very accurate and true to the spirit of our original page.

FIGURE 29.3

This page had its complex table structure (see Listing 29.2) removed and replaced with layers, very similar to Listing 29.1.

LISTING 29.3   **The same page as Listing 29.2, only now rendered again with layers through Dreamweaver's conversion utility. Note the font tags are not affected.**

```html
<html>
<head>
<title>Welcome!</title>
<meta http-equiv="Content-Type" content="text/html;
      charset=iso-8859-1">
</head>


<body bgcolor="#FFFFFF">
<div id="Layer1" style="position: absolute; left: 11px; top: 15px;
     width: 108px; height: 168px; z-index: 1">
  <img src="images/umc-logo.gif" width="108" height="168"></div>
<div id="Layer2" style="position: absolute; left: 131px; top: 38px;
     width: 228px; height: 108px; z-index: 2">
  <h1>Yellowstone<br>
    Annual<br>
    Conference </h1></div>
<div id="Layer3" style="position: absolute; left: 131px; top: 170px;
     width: 262px; height: 36px; z-index: 3"><h1 align="right">
```

```
<i><font face="Arial, Helvetica, sans-serif" color="RED">
ConnectiOnLine</font></i></h1></div>
<div id="Layer4" style="position: absolute; left: 473px; top: 351px;
    width: 307px; height: 87px; z-index: 4"><p><em>Produced and
maintained by the <strong>Conference Committee on
Communications</strong>. Comments and hot dishes accepted and
encouraged.</em></p>
<p><i><font face="Arial, Helvetica, sans-serif" size="1">
<em>(c)MCMXCVIII Yellowstone Annual Conference United Methodist
Church</em></font></i></p></div>
</body>
</html>
```

Of course, now the issue is making sure the right browser gets the right page. This is accomplished with the Check Browser behavior. You'll need the Behavior palette for this (F8, or Window, Behaviors).

Step by Step: Browser-Specific Page Routing

1. The simplest way to make sure the right browser gets the right page is to begin with a hyperlink to your 3.0-compatible page.

2. With the hyperlink still selected, select **3.0 + 4.0 Browsers** as the category of events.

3. Click on the plus (+) button to add a new event, and select **onClick** from the drop-down list.

4. On the Actions side of the palette, click on the plus (+) button to view the list. Select **Check Browser**, and the Check Browser dialog is displayed (see Figure 29.4).

5. Since we're working with pages for 4.0 browsers, and tables for all others, I can leave the version numbers alone. As a practical limit, the earliest versions detected are Navigator 2.0 and Internet Explorer 3.0 (the first two with scripting support).

6. For each type of browser there are three choices for a URL—stay where you are, use the main URL or select an alternate URL. Since Dreamweaver was created for 4.0 browsers, it defaults to the 4.0 destination as the main destination, and less-capable browsers as the alternate destination.

Opposites attract

This is opposite of what was entered into the URL for the hyperlink tag. This is because non-scripting browsers have no way to run the script. Essentially, the **href** attribute becomes the alternate URL of last resort. This could even be a third and completely separate page from the other two for browsers that don't support any scripting.

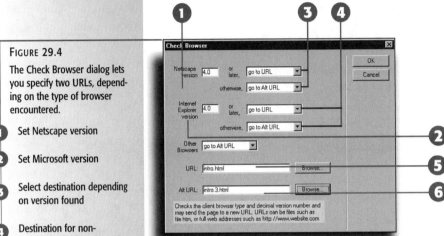

FIGURE 29.4

The Check Browser dialog lets you specify two URLs, depending on the type of browser encountered.

1 Set Netscape version

2 Set Microsoft version

3 Select destination depending on version found

4 Destination for non-Netscape or Microsoft browsers

5 Main URL for a successful match

6 Alternate URL for older browsers

7. Enter the URL of your 4.0-level browser in the **URL** field, and the URL for browsers below 4.0 in the **Alt URL** field.

8. Click on OK to close the dialog.

If a user has a 4.0-level browser, the URL in the hyperlink is trumped with a new URL by the script, and the advanced page is loaded. If a non-4.0 browser is used, the script returns the alternate URL, and the legacy page is loaded. If a non-scripting browser is loaded (including 4.0 browsers with scripting disabled), the contents of the hyperlink URL is used.

Creating a Browser Profile for Other Browsers

In the previous chapter, I talked a bit about browser profiles. These are the files that include information about which HTML tags and attributes are supported by a specific browser. They are very similar to a special document called a Document Type Definition (DTD) that defines the official rules for a specific standard or version of HTML.

Dreamweaver comes equipped with browser profiles for the last three versions of both Netscape Navigator (2.0 through 4.0) and Microsoft Internet Explorer (2.0 through 4.0). However, that doesn't limit you to checking your pages only against these products. You can also create your own browser profile for your favorite browser, or a profile that represents a specific version of HTML, such as the current HTML 4.0 specification. You can read more about HTML specifications and standards at the World Wide Web Consortium's Web site, http://www.w3.org.

You can create a browser profile in two ways. First, you can start with one of the existing browser profiles and modify it to suit your needs. Or, you can start from scratch and create a profile from the ground up. The first option is a bit easier to take care of, but I'll cover some tips for the harder method later in this section.

Creating a new user profile from an existing one

1. Using a text editor, open the profile that is the closest match to the browser for which you're writing. The older or simpler the browser you're creating the profile for, the earlier version of Navigator or Internet Explorer you can use.

   The browser profiles are found in /Dreamweaver/Configuration/BrowserProfiles folder.

2. At the top of the file is a line that identifies the specific version of the browser. Change this line to reflect the new browser for which you're working. For example, if you're modifying a profile to support Internet Explorer 5.0, the first line would look like the following:
   ```
   Microsoft Internet Explorer 5.0
   ```

   The next line is
   ```
   PROFILE_TYPE=BROWSER_PROFILE
   ```

   It doesn't change under any circumstance, or the profile won't work.

3. Save the profile as a new name using the name of the new browser or standard, such as Mosaic_3.0.txt or HTML_4.0.txt.

4. Remove any tags that aren't supported by the browser. If you're creating a profile that updates a previous profile version, this step should be easy. The two biggest browsers rarely stop supporting old tags, even when most of the Web community has stopped using them.

5. Add any new tags and attributes that are now supported by the browser.

The basic format for a tag is

```
<!ELEMENT tag>
```

Where *tag* is how the element is used within a document. For example, let's say Microsoft creates a new tag called `<IMP>` to mark Important Material. The minimum syntax to add this to a browser profile would be

```
<!ELEMENT IMP>
```

Attributes are added in a similar manner. If the new `<IMP>` tag can accept `name`, `id` and `class` as attributes, the syntax to add these would be

```
<!ATTLIST IMP
    name
    id
    class
>
```

6. Save the profile and exit the text editor.

Creating a browser profile from scratch is a little more involved because you must type each tag and its attributes by hand. For older browsers, this may not be so bad. But for new browsers that include many legacy items for previous versions, it can be a daunting task—you're probably better off starting with an existing profile.

Creating a browser profile from an existing one

1. Open a new file with a text editor such as Windows NotePad or Macintosh SimpleText.

2. The first line of the file is the name for the profile, such as `Lynx 1.0`.

3. After a carriage return, the second line must be

```
PROFILE_TYPE=BROWSER_PROFILE
```

Dreamweaver depends on this line to know that your file is a browser profile, and not a letter to the editor or some other type of file.

4. If you'd like to include a comment, such as a copyright notice, or an explanation of what your profile is for, type two hyphens (- -) at the beginning of the line. Dreamweaver ignores all lines beginning with two hyphens.

5. The complete entry for a tag includes two parts—one for the tag name and another for the list of attributes. The syntax is

```
<!ELEMENT tag Name="Tag description">
<!ATTLIST tag
attribute1 ( value1 ¦ value2 ¦ valueN )
attribute2
badAttribute1 !Error !msg="Message"
badAttribute2 !Error !htmlmsg="HTML-encoded message"
>
```

Don't worry, it only looks complicated. The first line, `<!ELE-MENT>`, is used to define a valid tag, such as the paragraph tag `<P>` and a long version of its name.

```
<!ELEMENT P Name="Paragraph">
```

If a tag isn't found in the profile, it's assumed that it won't work in the browser.

The second part of the definition lists all of the possible attributes for a tag, including an optional list of values. Let's look at two attributes for `<P>`—the `ID` and `align` attributes.

```
<!ATTLIST P
ID
Align ( left ¦ center ¦ right )
>
```

This definition says that the tag `<P>` can include an attribute called `ID` with any value, and the attribute `Align` with a value of `left`, `center` or `right` only. As this definition exists, any other attribute for `<P>` would generate an error.

Going one step further, let's say we're creating a browser profile that encourages use of HTML 4.0 and style sheets instead of old attributes such as Align. Our new attribute list could now look like this, with a warning not to use the Align attribute:

```
<!ATTLIST P
ID
Class
Style
Align !Warning !msg="Align is deprecated. Use a style
sheet instead."
>
```

Now, when this profile is used for browser targeting and a <P> tag is found with the Align attribute, Dreamweaver generates an error message that alerts the user not to use the attribute. You can also include formatting within the message:

```
... !htmlmsg="<EM>Align</EM> is deprecated. Use a style
sheet instead."
```

6. Repeat step 5 for each tag and set of attributes until you've included everything the browser supports. Anything not found in your browser profile is assumed to be incompatible with the browser and will generate an error during target browser checking.

7. Save the file with the name of the browser, such as Lynx_1.0.txt.

Your browser profile is now included in the Check Target Browser list, and you can see how your page will fare when it's viewed on the new browser. Of course, the best option of all is to actually view the page on the selected browser. There's no substitute for the real thing.

Using JavaScript in Non-JavaScript Browsers

One of the cornerstones of dynamic HTML is JavaScript. So, if you're going to include interactive behavior in your Web page, you're going to have to use JavaScript. The problem is that there are only two major browsers that support JavaScript (Internet Explorer and Navigator), plus two other lesser-known applications that support JavaScript to a lesser degree (Opera and HotJava).

If your readers happen to be using Mosaic, Lynx, or an older version of Internet Explorer (2.0 or earlier), there are some features of your pages they won't be able to experience. That's easy enough to take care of with alternate content. The real problem is hiding all the code so it doesn't gum up the page.

The first step is where you place the scripts. Functions should be placed in the head of the page, where they're loaded, ready, and out of sight from the rest of the page. Scripts that must be placed within the page, such as scripts that generate HTML as the page is loaded, need hiding, or they'll display their guts right in the middle of your beautiful layout (see Figure 29.5).

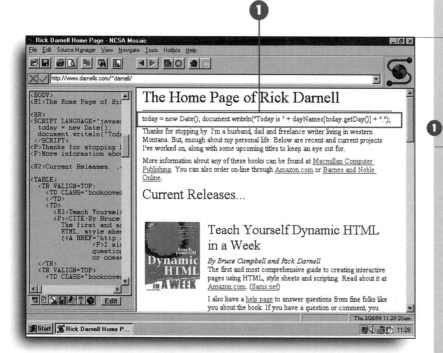

FIGURE 29.5

Without some method to hide scripts, incompatible browsers assume their contents are just more text to display.

1 Script hanging out in Mosaic

The way around this is by enclosing the script in comment tags. This task is handled automatically by some editors, Dreamweaver and HomeSite not included. The way these editors insert scripts is

```
<SCRIPT language="Javascript">
...script stuff here...
</SCRIPT>
```

To hide the script stuff from incompatible browsers, add two lines within the script tags, but outside of the actual script:

```
<SCRIPT language="Javascript">
<!--
...script stuff here...
-->
</SCRIPT>
```

When this technique is used with an incompatible browser, it's ignored and blocked from display (see Figure 29.6).

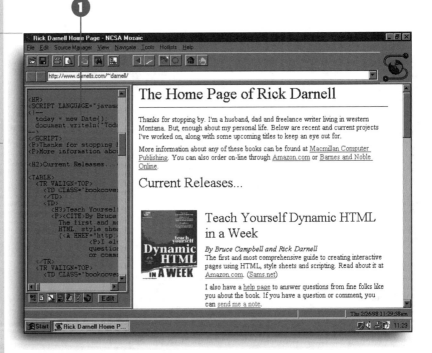

FIGURE 29.6

Now the script is blocked from view, which keeps the page clutter-free.

1 Script is still here, but now it's hidden

If your page specifically refers to features that depend on
JavaScript, you'll need to include a hyperlink to alternate content, or some sort of disclaimer that tells the user what sort of
software is required. One of the ways to handle this situation is
to use a non-JavaScript page as the destination of a hyperlink,
and then use a script in the head of that page to refer JavaScript
browsers to the feature-rich page. The hyperlink typically looks
like the following:

```
Check out our new <A href="catalog.html">catalog</a>.
```

While a short script within the <HEAD> of the destination does the
work:

```
<HEAD>
  <TITLE>Catalog</TITLE>
  <SCRIPT type="text/javascript">
    document.location="catalog-js.html"
  </SCRIPT>
</HEAD>
```

Browsers without JavaScript capability will load the target
defined in href, and render the entire page because the incompatible browser will ignore the script tags in the head.
JavaScript-capable browsers will start working with the script
right away and load the JavaScript-powered page into the browser. The user may see a quick flash of the generic page, but this
should be fleeting.

Working Around Proprietary HTML

Proprietary tags are one of the biggest problems you'll
encounter as you design pages for the latest and greatest from
the big two. Microsoft and Netscape have been known for their
ability to dream up tags which, although they might serve some
useful purpose, become a white elephant in the world of HTML.
Examples of these types of tags include <CENTER>, <MARQUEE>,
<BLINK> and more recently, <LAYER>.

So what's a designer to do? The best option is to avoid their use
altogether. With the advent of an official HTML 4.0 standard,
much of the functionality envisioned by these proprietary tags
has been implemented in a cleaner fashion. For example, instead

of <CENTER>, you can use align="center", or better yet, a style sheet.

The same is also true of the <BLINK> tag. For the most part, <BLINK> is panned by the Web design community. There's nothing to it other than a bit of blinking text, and it only works on Internet Explorer and Navigator. Really, that's all. If you still feel the need to put blinking text in your page, you can include it with a style sheet, such as the following:

```
.blinkText { text-decoration: blink }
```

Other features are a little trickier. Take <MARQUEE> for example. With this tag, Microsoft introduced a quick and easy way to scroll a piece of text across the screen. The problem is, Microsoft browsers are the only pieces of software that take advantage of this feature. There are two solutions to people who feel they absolutely must have scrolling text on their site.

The first is the ActiveX control for a marquee. This is a little different from the tag in that it can use entire text files instead of one line of text. The downside is that Microsoft browsers are still the only ones that support ActiveX, but we can hope that perhaps Netscape and Opera will also eventually support this type of content.

The other option, with a bit wider acceptance, is to use one of the many Java applets that have been designed for this purpose. Using applets, your marquee will be visible to users of Internet Explorer, Navigator, and HotJava. Opera is probably not far behind in their support of Java, either. A large selection of applets for this purpose can be found through the Gamelan Web site (http://www.gamelan.com).

Both the ActiveX and Java options are not nearly as easy or clean-cut as the <MARQUEE> tag, but they do offer the possibility of a wider audience for your special content.

One of the last major proprietary items that you've probably heard a lot about is Netscape's <LAYER> tag. This tag was Netscape's guess at how the World Wide Web Consortium (W3C) was going to implement positioning for Web pages, and

Netscape missed. The W3C went with the <DIV> tag, which
Netscape also supports. The problem is that if you want to do
dynamic things with layers, such as animations and rollovers,
Navigator can only interact with the <LAYER> tag, whereas
Internet Explorer only uses the <DIV> tag. In this case, you'll
need to include both types of tags, with the <DIV> tag nested
within the <LAYER>, plus a special gatekeeper script to make sure
the right set of code is invoked.

The following is an example of a gatekeeper script:

```
<SCRIPT type="text/javascript">
function layerGatekeeper( where-to ) {
    if (document.all) {
        useIEScript ( where-to );
    } else {
        useNavScript ( where-to );
    }
}
</SCRIPT>
```

The gatekeeper function accepts one argument, called where-to,
that tells the next function what needs to be done (such as hide a
layer, move a layer, and so on). The script then checks for the
all object of the document object. The all object is currently
only supported by Internet Explorer, so the script is routed to
the Internet Explorer script handler. Otherwise, it's passed to the
Navigator script handler.

As each of the browser developers adds new tags that are not
part of the HTML standard, you'll need to evaluate each one in
turn to see what it's purpose is, and what other methods are
available to accomplish the end result. Your options will depend
on your specific situation and needs. If you're working with an
intranet where everyone uses the same browser brand and version, you can use proprietary tags with impunity. But if you're
developing pages for the World Wide Web, you'll need to balance your desire to use the latest and greatest capabilities with
the cost of excluding some readers from the fun. Nobody ever
said this stuff was going to be easy.

From Here...

- Learn a lot more about scripting beginning in Part IV, "Adding Interactivity and Scripts."

- Creating style sheets to customize Web pages is explained in Chapter 6, "Formatting Text with Style Sheets."

- The overs-and-unders of layers are made clear in Chapter 18, "Working with Layers."

BBEdit Quick Reference

What is BBEdit?

At first glance it might seem redundant, if not downright silly for Macromedia to include a copy of BBEdit along with each Macintosh version of Dreamweaver. Why would they include an established, competing product such as BBEdit at no extra charge? While it may seem like bad business on the surface, it is actually a very perceptive decision on the part of Macromedia, in that it makes Dreamweaver even more powerful and flexible to an even wider range of users.

BBEdit, from Barebones software, is a text editing application with special formatting features for programmers and HTML designers. While BBEdit supports a wide range of programming languages, this appendix will focus on how it facilitates HTML-based documents. Specifically, we will consider how BBEdit compliments and differs from Dreamweaver as an HTML editing tool.

An Overview of the BBEdit Environment

When you open a new BBEdit file, you see some additional features built right into the document window itself, organized into two areas called the Status bar and the Split bar.

The Split Bar exists as a small black bar icon in the upper right of the document window. A simple click and drag of the Split Bar separates the window into two sections with separate scroll bars. This feature allows you to view two sections of an active document at the same time, helping you manage long documents where you may need to cross reference information. Double clicking the Split Bar instantly splits the active window into two equal halves, or returns a split window to a singular state (see Figure A.1).

FIGURE A.1

The BBEdit document window.

1 Status bar

2 Split bar

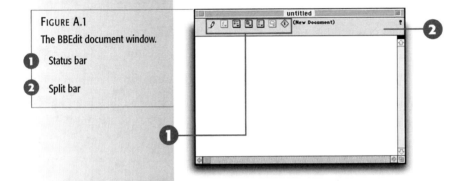

Status Bar

The status bar consists of 8 icons running across the top of the window, along with a status line. The Status bar can be revealed or hidden using the toggle switch in the upper-right corner of the window. A description of each icon follows:

- The Diamond icon is either missing, solid black, or hollow. A solid diamond indicates that actual file data has been modified since the current file was last saved. A hollow diamond indicates that no data has been modified, although cosmetic changes such as scrolling or changing preferences have occurred since the last save. A missing diamond indicates that no changes of any kind have taken place since the last save.

- The Write Protect icon shows either a normal pencil, or a pencil with a line through it. A normal pencil indicates that the current file is not write protected and can be modified. A pencil with a slash through it indicates that the file is write protected or that the disk is locked.

- The Function pop-up menu allows access to the language functions and routines that BBEdit can parse. This option is grayed out if the active document is not a source file. Contents will vary depending on the file type opened.

- The Window Options pop-up menu controls how text is displayed in the window. Its commands allow you to activate soft text wrap, invisibles, line numbers, and other formatting options. A very useful feature for source files is the Syntax Coloring command, which color codes the tags, text, and image references for easy navigation.

- The File pop-up allows various file saving options, including formatting options for target platforms.

- The Insert pop-up allows you to insert entire files, folders, lists, or page breaks into the active document.

- The Path pop-up menu displays the directory string for the active document, showing all folders for the entire path. Any of these folders can be opened from this pop-up menu.

- The Info button displays information on the active document, including running totals of lines, characters, words, and pages.

- The Document Icon button acts like a Finder Alias for the active document, showing the current path and date and time it was last saved. Clicking the icon launches the Finder window containing the actual file. If the document has not been saved, the icon does not appear, and the text reads (New Document).

The Text Menu

In addition to standard text commands found in most word processors, BBEdit also includes commands especially suited to working with HTML documents (see Figure A.2). Table A.1 lists the menu options and their functions.

FIGURE A.2

The BBEdit text menu.

TABLE A.1   **BBEdit menu choices.**

Option	Description
Balance (Command-B)	This command checks the accuracy of brackets and parentheses based on cursor position. Click the cursor within a bracketed tag or command, select **Text** and choose **Balance**. The bracket components are unbalanced; BBEdit beeps a warning.
Twiddle (Command-`)	Twiddle transposes characters or works, based on the insertion point in the document. A blinking insertion transposes the characters on either side. Holding down the Option key with this command transposes entire words instead of characters. If a block of text is selected, Twiddle transposes the characters on the ends of the selection.
Change Case...	Converts from upper to lower case. Especially useful when moving existing files to a UNIX server, where case sensitivity could be an issue.
Shift Left and Shift Right (Command [and Command])	Moves the selected text left or right by one tab stop. Combining it with the Shift key changes the movement from one tab stop to one space.
Insert Line Breaks and Remove Line Breaks	Inserts or removes a hard line break at the end of each line, as long as the Soft Wrap feature is selected.
Hard Wrap... (Command-\)	Wraps long lines of text with hard line breaks.
Zap Gremlins...	This command set removes unwanted characters and commands from the active file. This can help in creating formatting text and character specs for different platforms.

Option	Description
Entab... and Detab...	Converts sequences of spaces into tabs and vice versa, based on the settings in the Font and Tab dialog boxes.
Check Spelling (Command-Y)	Checks the spelling in the active document.

The HTML Tools Palette

The heart of BBEdit for the HTML author is the HTML Tools palette (see Figure A.3). This floating palette allows you to insert a wide array of HTML commands into your active document without typing the tag information directly. The default configuration of BBEdit launches the palette each time the application is opened. You can enable or disable this function through the Startup Preferences section in the Preferences palette, accessed by choosing **Edit** and selecting **Preferences**.

The Tools palette commands are also accessible through the Tools Menu, and the Tools List window, which is launched from the Tools Menu. The Tools Menu also contains programming and compiling options that do not relate to HTML. These options which will not be covered in this appendix.

You can expand or contract the palette by clicking the toggle switch in the upper-left corner of the palette. The pop-up command in the upper-right of the palette allows you to select thick or thin tile formats, as well as to configure which commands appear in the palette.

Each tile applies its command in one of three ways: directly, through a dialog box, or through a pop-up menu. The direct tiles have no dots following the command name, and apply their commands globally or at the active cursor insertion point, whichever is appropriate. The dialog box commands have three dots following the command name, and launch a dialog box when clicked, allowing you to make further choices. The pop-up commands are identified by an arrow at the left side of the tile. Click and hold the arrow to see the command options.

Some tiles have double hash marks on their right side, indicating drag-and-drop support. These commands can be dragged into the active window and placed anywhere in the document. Some pop-up menu tiles also have hash marks, which launch a dialog box once the mouse is released after dragging. It is also possible to select portions of text and drag it onto certain tiles. A portion of text can be selected and dragged onto the styles tile for example, which launches the Style Options dialog box.

FIGURE A.3

The BBEdit HTML tools palette.

Table A.2 lists the tile options in the BBEdit HTML tools palette and their functionality.

TABLE A.2   **BBEdit HTML tools palette options.**

Option	Function
New Document...	Launches a dialog box to create a new document. Includes control over HTML, Head, and Body tags, SGML Prolog, and BBEdit credits. Document title, Meta, and Link info is also customizable, along with template selection, and the ability to designate a new window for the document.
Update...	Updates the Current Document of the entire site, filling in any Placeholder data as available.
Document Color...	Launches the color selection palette, allowing text, link and background color changes via a nine-color swatch palette. Double click each swatch to open a color picker for other color selections. A background image can also be placed via the Image... button.
Frames	This pop-up menu allows the insertion of a Frameset tag, frame-targeting parameters, and the No Frames tag.
Script	This pop-up menu allows you to determine which scripting language to use via the Options command. The Script command inserts a script tag set based on the scripting language selected, and the No Script command inserts a NoScript tag set.
Stylesheets	This pop-up menu allows you to determine which style sheet format to use via the options menu. Selecting **Styles** applies the current style.
Divisions...	Launches a dialog box to insert a logical division tag, and allows the text within it to be aligned to the left, center, right, or justified.
Anchor...	This command can be accessed by clicking it, dragging it into the document, or dragging selected text onto the tile. Once activated, it will first prompt you to save your file if you have not done so. It will not create an anchor if the file is not saved. Once saved, it launches a dialog box that allows you to specify the file accessed, Full, Root, or Relative addressing, tags, file names, and target information. There is also a preferences area giving control over image file visibility and warning options.

continues...

TABLE A.2   Continued

Option	Function
Image...	This command can be accessed by clicking it, dragging it into the document, or dragging selected text onto the tile. This command launches a dialog box that inserts an Image Source tag at the active insertion point of the document. File and addressing controls are presented, along with Image and Alt Image paths. Although size attribute options are presented, they are handled automatically for GIF, JPEG, and PNG files.
Heading	This pop-up menu allows you to insert an open heading command at the active insertion point. Relative size levels ranging from 1 to 6 are presented, along with an Options dialog box that allows text alignment to be specified for each level.
Font	Inserts a Font tag at the insertion point or applies it to the selected text. Available tags include 1-7 size tags, Big, Small, Font Color, and Small Caps. The **Options** command allows the application of all tags expect Color and Small Caps, from one dialog box.
Font Color	This tile opens the font color dialog box, which allows a choice from nine different color swatches. Double click a swatch to change its color via the color picker. This is the same command that appears as Font Color in the Font tile pop-up menu.
Style	This pop-up menu tile applies text style tags to selected text, or inserts an open set of tags at a blinking insertion point. Available text style tags are: Bold, Underline, Italic, Blinking, Strike, Subscript, Superscript, Centered, Typewriter, and Preformatted. Information, or contextual tags are: Emphasis, Sample, Citation, Keyboard, Strong, Code, Variable, Block Quote, Definition, and Address. These options are available individually through the pop-up menu, or in a dialog box via the Options command.
Paragraph	Inserts a paragraph tag set. You can also click and drag this tile into the document, which will insert the tags at the point where the mouse is released. Drag selected text to this tile to isolate it in a separate paragraph.

Option	Function
Line Break	Click this command to insert a Line Break tag. You can also click and drag this tile into the document, which will insert the line break at the point where the mouse is released. Drag selected text to this tile to insert a break tag immediately following the selection.
Horizontal Rule	Inserts a horizontal rule tag. You can also click and drag this tile into the document, which will insert the tag at the point where the mouse is released.
Lists	This pop-up menu creates a list tag set at the current insertion point, or converts selected text to the list type specified. List types are: Unordered, Ordered, Definition, Directory, and Menu. The **New Item** command inserts a new list item into an existing list, based on the insertion point.
Table	This pop-up menu inserts various table related tags into the document, based on the current selection point. It is also possible to drag this tile into the document to place the desired information. When the mouse is released a dialog box will prompt you to designate the desired table component. (See Table A.3 for table command options.)
Table Builder	Launches the Table Builder application, which allows interactive table creation via a drag-and-drop interface.
Form	Launches a dialog box that allows the creation of a form field. The dialog allows the URL specification, as well as a choice between Get and Post options.
Applet	This tile inserts an Applet tag at the active insertion point. Applet Parameter and Textflow tags are also accessible from this tile.
Custom	Inserts an HTML macro at the current insertion point. Macros can be defined by choosing **Tools**, selecting **HTML Custom Markup**, and choosing **Custom Markup**.
Check HTML	Checks the entire document for HTML syntax errors. These will be reported in a separate window for correction.
Check Links	Checks the entire document for link accuracy. BBEdit looks at all images and link information, and reports any errors in a separate window for correction.

continues...

TABLE A.2   Continued

Option	Function
Check Site Links	Checks the entire site for link accuracy. BBEdit looks at all images and link information, and reports any errors in a separate window for correction.
Check Link Options	Launches a dialog box that configures how BBEdit check link accuracy. Options are for how to show warnings, remote link checking, folder aliases, and naming and case accuracy.
Balance Tags	Looks at the tag set containing the insertion point or selection, and ensures that the tags and/or brackets are balanced properly.
Format	Formats the text flow within the document. Options are: Hierarchical, Gentle Hierarchical, Plain, Compact, and Document Skeleton. These options effect the readability of the document only, and do not change the way the file is displayed in the browser.
Document Size	Launches a dialog box that shows the collective byte size of text and images in the document.
Index Site	Creates an Unordered List tag set within a site or folder.
Entities	Allows the placement of special characters and symbols within the current document. Clicking the tile launches a dialog box displaying all available symbols, which can be modified or inserted using the character name or its associated code.
Utilities	This tile includes four utility options, accessible via a pop-up menu. See Table A.4 for the Utilities options.
Preview	This pop-up menu previews the active document in a Web browser, as text, or within another application of your choosing. Browser options correspond to those currently loaded on your system.

TABLE A.3   Table command options in BBEdit HTML tools palette.

Option	Function
Table	Creates a basic table tag set you can type data into, or encloses selected text within the tag set.

Option	Function
Row	Creates a basic table row tag set you can type data into, or encloses selected text within the tag set.
Cell Header	Creates a basic table header tag set you can type data into, or encloses selected text within the tag set.
Caption	Creates a basic table row tag set you can type data into, or encloses selected text within the tag set.
Convert	Opens table dialog box to convert any selected text into a table format. Text must be selected to access this option.
Options	Launches a dialog box for controlling table cell parameters: border, spacing, and width options, and the basic table type.

TABLE A.4   Utilities command options in BBEdit HTML tools palette.

Option	Function
Remove Tags	Removes all tags from the selected area, or from the entire document if nothing is selected.
Comment	Inserts HTML comment tag set at the current insertion point, or converts a text selection into an HTML comment.
Uncomment	Removes HTML comment tag information from a current selection, converting the comment data into part of the viewable document. Comment text must be selected in order for this command to have an effect.
Insert Hotlist	Inserts a hotlist, (aka bookmark list) at the current active insertion point. The list may be inserted as plain text, or as an active set of links.

The Utilities submenu in the Tools Menu contains four additional utilities, not found in the Tools Palette. They are Entities, Pagemill Cleaner, Translate, and Web Color Palette, and are described in Table A.5.

TABLE A.5   **Utilities submenu choices.**

Command	Function
Entities	Allows the placement of special characters and symbols within the current document. This option launches a dialog box displaying all available symbols, which can be modified or inserted using the character name or its associated code.
PageMill Cleaner	Corrects some of the known programming problems present in documents created or edited in Adobe PageMill. The corrections are made to the entire document, or, if a selection is present, it will correct that section only.
Translate	Offers a range of text translation options via a detailed dialog box. Options available are Text to HTML, HTML to text, ISO Latin-1 to Mac character sets, replace 8 Bit & Gremlins with ASCII equivalents, Remove Tags when converting to text, convert special characters to their HTML Entities, and add or remove Paragraph tags.
Web Color Palette	Launches a swatch palette of Web-safe colors. Dragging the color swatch into the document inserts the corresponding hexadecimal code.

Templates and Placeholders

BBEdit allows you to create template files that serve as starting points for HTML documents or can be inserted into existing documents. You can use this to set up files that include header and footer information, formatting, or unique image files.

It is also possible to insert a placeholder command into any document or template. A placeholder creates a space for specific data points, such as server URLs or document names, which may not be available until later. Once a placeholder is inserted, the actual data can be reflowed by using the **Update** command from the Tools palette. Placeholders always appear as two number symbols surrounding the placeholder name: #placeholder-name#. Placeholders and templates streamline the document creation process, and should be implemented in any HTML production environment.

The following details how to open an HTML Template in BBEdit.

1. Select **File**, choose **New**, and select **HTML Document** to open the New file dialog box.

2. Click and hold the Templates pop-up menu, which displays the current template options, available in BBEdit templates folder.

3. Click **OK** to create a new untitled document based on the selected template. The original template document is left untouched.

To create a new Template for BBEdit, perform the following steps.

1. Create a new BBEdit document by selecting **File**, choosing **New**, selecting **HTML Document**, and clicking **OK**.

2. Create the desired information in the document and select **File** and choose **Save**. Within the Save dialog box, name the file as desired, adding a .tmpl suffix at the end of the file name.

3. Target the templates folder of the BBEdit application folder as the save destination, and click **OK**. The template will now appear in the Templates pop-up menu as described in the previous example of how to open an HTML Template.

Placeholder Reference

The available placeholder commands for BBEdit are as follows:

- #TITLE#   Looks for the title of the current document, as entered in the New Document dialog box.

- #LINK#   Looks for the Link information for the current document, as entered in the Link section of the New Document dialog box.

- #BASE#   Looks for the Base tag information for the current document, as entered in the Base section of the New Document dialog box.

- #META#   Looks for Meta tag information for the current document, as listed in the Meta section of the New Document dialog box.

- #USERNAME#   Looks for the user name information, as found in the File Sharing or Sharing Setup control panel on the current machine.

- #MACHINE#   Looks for the machine name, as found in the File Sharing or Sharing Setup control panel on the current machine.

- #IC_EMAIL#   Looks for the email value as found in the Internet Config preferences dialog box.

- #CREATIONDATE#   Looks for the creation date of the current file, as listed by the Date & Time control panel.

- #CREATIONTIME#   Looks for the creation time of the current file, as listed by the Date & Time control panel.

- #MODIFIEDDATE#   The modified date of the file at the moment a template using this tag is launched.

- #MODIFIEDTIME#   The modified time of the file at the moment a template using this tag is launched.

- #MONTHDAYNUM#   The numeric value of the day of the month, as listed in the Date & Time control panel.

- #WEEKNUM#   The numeric value of the current week, as listed in the Date & Time control panel.

- #MONTHNUM#   The numeric value of the current month, as listed in the Date & Time control panel.

- #YEARNUM#   The numeric value of the current year, as listed in the Date & Time Control panel.

HomeSite Quick Reference

B

HomeSite makes an ideal companion to Dreamweaver. While Dreamweaver is very strong on implementing Dynamic HTML and giving a visual representation of your pages, it's really pretty weak when it comes to fine-tuning a page, or working directly with source code. HomeSite is one of the very best HTML editors available for Windows. It allows you to get into the nitty gritty of a page and tweak each of the details so that it looks and acts just right. Thanks to Macromedia for bundling a full-release version of HomeSite with their Dreamweaver package.

This appendix gives a quick overview of some of the more basic tasks in HomeSite. It's not meant as a comprehensive manual—just a list of common jobs and how to accomplish them. Although Dreamweaver doesn't include a printed copy of the HomeSite User Guide, an electronic version is available within HomeSite's help menu.

The HomeSite Workspace

There are four basic parts to the HomeSite window (see Figure B.1), which is tailored to make creating and editing Web pages as efficient as possible.

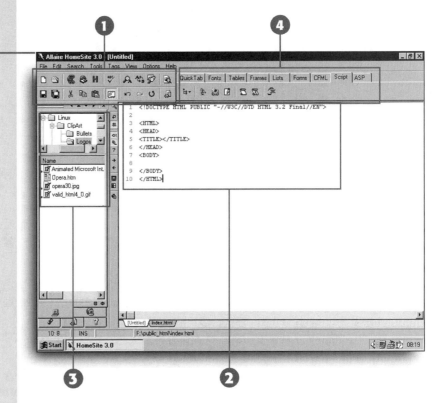

FIGURE B.1

The Allaire workspace includes a variety of windows and toolbars to make creating Web pages a pick-and-choose process.

1 General file and editing options, including open and save files, link checking, HTML validation, and page preview

2 Also works as a browser view when configured with Internet Explorer

3 General resources on a page and site-level. Includes remote file access project management, on-line help, and reusable sections of HTML

4 A set of tabbed toolbars that organize the most popular tags by their use, including tags for tables, frames, forms, and JavaScript

Here is a quick overview of the basic tools available from each section:

- *Toolbar.* The toolbar is divided into two parts. The first is a horizontal collection at the top of the window. It includes buttons to create and save a page, check links, validate the code, spell check, search and replace, and insert code snippets.

  The vertical portion of the toolbar includes buttons to switch the editing window to an internal browser, launch Dreamweaver, and set the indenting of your code. It also includes toggles for line-wrap, line numbers, full-screen editing, color palettes, and tag completion helps.

- *Tag toolset.* A set of tabbed toolbars that organize the most popular tags by their use, including tags for tables, frames, forms, and JavaScript.

- *Editing Window*. The editing window is essentially a text editor that uses the Web page editing features provided by HomeSite. Clicking the Toggle browser button at the top of the vertical toolbar turns the editing window into a browser using Internet Explorer.

- *Resources*. There are five resources that HomeSite provides. The first two are directory views of pages on your Local computer and for any Remote servers. Double-clicking a file in the Local or Remote resource tabs will open the file for editing.

  The Project resource allows you to organize your files by project or site, including file upload and download as needed for editing.

  The Tag Snippet resource is a collection of bits of HTML you can save for reuse. Position the cursor on your page and then double-click a snippet to insert it. This is an easy way to save and use items such as copyright notices, contact information, and often-used images.

  The last resource is a collection of helps, including an online version of the HomeSite documentation, plus additional documents for HTML and style sheets.

Look under Customizing the Environment, in the Help Resource, for more information on using and adjusting the HomeSite workspace to your needs.

Configuring HomeSite with Browsers

Currently, the only browser that will work with HomeSite internally is Internet Explorer, version 3.01 or later (Dreamweaver ships with Internet Explorer 4.0), and the following steps assume you've already installed it.

Configuring HomeSite with Internet Explorer

1. Select **Options** and choose **Settings**, or press F8.
2. Select the **Internal Browser** tab (see Figure B.2).

Why only Internet Explorer?

Microsoft built their browser in several chunks. The most important chunk contains the "basic browser," including all the code needed to read, interpret, and display a Web page. It created an interface into this special section so that it could be used by other applications, such as other members of the Microsoft Office suite or outside applications such as HomeSite.

Currently, Microsoft is the only vendor to supply their browser in this configuration. If other browser vendors restructure their programs to provide a core browser module that can stand alone, you'll have more than one choice for this feature.

FIGURE B.2

The Internal Browser tab controls whether Internet Explorer is used, and if so, how.

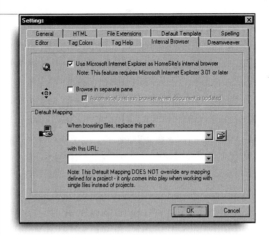

3. The first choice selects Internet Explorer as the internal browser. Select the checkbox to enable this feature.

4. By default, the browser will take the place of the editing window. If **Browse in Separate Plane** is selected, a new pane is created at the bottom of the HomeSite window. This can create a very crowded workspace if you're using a screen resolution smaller than 1024 by 768 pixels.

   In addition, as you edit and update the current page, HomeSite can automatically prod the browser to update its display.

5. Click **OK** to save the changes.

 To view your page with Internet Explorer within HomeSite, click the **Toggle Browser** button or press **F12**.

Of course, you're not limited to Internet Explorer if you want to view your page in another browser. HomeSite can also launch virtually any browser, if you tell HomeSite where to find it.

Configuring HomeSite with an external browser

1. Select **Options** and choose **External Browsers** to view the External Browser dialog box (see Figure B.3).

2. Select a choice for what should happen to the file when the browser is launched. The default is to create and load a temporary copy of the page. This is good for a quick preview of current changes without having to save the current document, but won't reflect subsequent changes without starting a new instance of the browser.

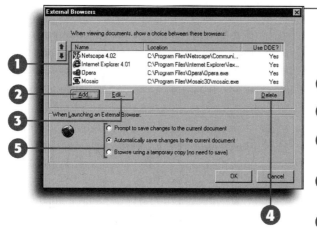

Two other choices are for you to decide every time whether or not to save changes to the current document (**Prompt to save**), or to automatically save the changes and load the current document. In both cases, the most recently saved version is loaded into the browser.

3. The current default browser is shown as the only browser in the list. To add a new browser, click **Add** (see Figure B.4).

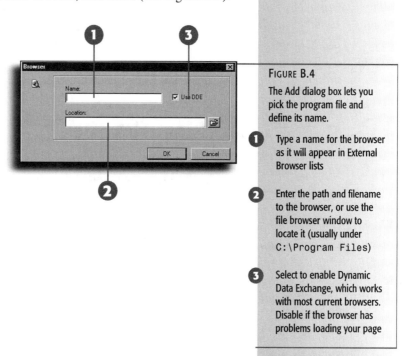

4. Fill out the fields of the Add dialog box in reverse order. Begin by selecting the program. In most Windows environments, the program is located in C:\Program Files, although your situation may be different. You can use the Browse button to navigate through the computer to find what you need.

5. After the program file is selected, a default title is entered in the Name field. Edit this name to give a more accurate description of the browser. In this case, I'll call it Mosaic 3.01.

6. You can leave the DDE selection alone for now. If your browser has problems starting from HomeSite, open this dialog box again and deselect DDE.

7. Click **OK** for the Add dialog box, and your browser and its associated icon appears in the External Browsers list.

8. If you want the new browser to be the default external browser, use the arrow keys to the left of the list to move the new entry to the top of the list.

9. Click **OK** again to save your selections.

To view a page with the external browser, click the **External Browser** button on the toolbar, which displays a list of the currently configured browsers. Select the desired one from the list, and you can preview your page as it will appear to your readers. Or, press **F11** to launch the first external browser on the list.

Working with Files

Using the Local and Remote resource tabs gives access to Web pages on your computer and on FTP servers to which you have access. To open a file from your computer, you can use any of the following techniques:

- Click the **File Open** button from the toolbar.
- Select **File** and choose **Open (Ctrl+O)**.
- Double-click a file in the file list (see Figure B.5).

FIGURE B.5

Double-clicking a file in the
file-list opens it for editing. A
red dot denotes a read-only
file that cannot be edited.

1 Local computer drives and
folders File list

You can use similar techniques to open files directly from the
Internet or your corporate intranet. The first step is configuring
HomeSite for a specific FTP server.

Configuring an FTP server

1. Open the **Remote resource** tab (see Figure B.6).

2. Right-click within the list, and select **Add FTP Server**.

3. The Configure FTP Server dialog box opens (see Figure
   B.7). Add a Description (displayed in the server list), Host
   Name (the server name), and User Name (a login name).

4. You can also add additional information as needed, including
   a starting directory and password.

5. Click **OK** when you're finished.

After the FTP server is configured, you can double-click it in the
file list, or select it from the drop-down list, to connect to it.
From there, you can browse the list the same as if it were a
Local computer. Double-click a file to download it and open it
into the editor.

FIGURE B.6

The Remote resource lists any
currently configured FTP
servers and their directories
and files (when connected).

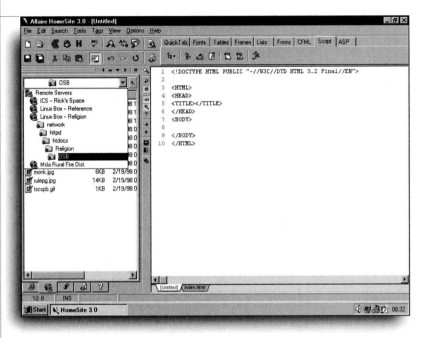

In addition, you can also open files from the Web, even if you
don't have FTP access. Select **File** choose **Open From Web**,
and enter the URL of the page. You can also select an address
from Internet Explorer's list of favorites or Netscape's bookmark
list.

Adding Content

The first step to adding content is creating the base page. There
are two ways to accomplish this:

- Click the **New document** icon. This loads a default shell,
  including <!DOCTYPE> tag, head, and body.
- Select **File** choose **New**, and select a pre-defined template
  or wizard. There are wizards to create frames and style
  sheets, synchronize multimedia, and open browser windows.
  Templates are available for blank documents, glossaries, and
  a table of contents.

- If you use the blank document template, select a version of HTML to use from the **Quick start** button on the **Quick Tab**. This loads a wizard that allows you to set the version of HTML, document title, keywords, and background and text colors. When the wizard is finished, the document shell is in place with all of the basic elements.

With a document shell in place, you can begin to add content between the `<BODY>` tags:

- Type text directly into the document.
- Select **File** and choose **Insert** to insert the contents of a Web page, text file, style sheet, or Cold Fusion page.
- For extended and special characters, select **View** and choose **Special Characters (Ctrl+Shift+X)**. Double-click a character to insert it.
- Cut and paste from other documents in open windows, including text from word processors.

To add formatting to the text, highlight the text and select the appropriate tag from the **Tag Toolset** tabs at the top of the page. You can also add tags directly into the document as you type.

Some tags, such as headings and hyperlinks, are completed automatically as they're typed. If you begin by typing `<H1>`, HomeSite completes the tag by adding `</H1>` and places cursor in between the two tags. You can type the heading and then move the cursor out of the tags to begin the next line. This only occurs on tags that require a closing tag.

Once a tag is added, you can edit its attributes in one of several ways. If you're familiar with HTML, you can type the attributes and corresponding values directly into the tag; or you can use the tag editing windows provided by HomeSite (see Figure B.7):

- Press **F4**.
- Right click the tag, and select **Edit Tag** from the pop-up menu.
- Position the cursor over the tag, select **Tags**, and then choose **Edit Current Tag**.

FIGURE B.7

HomeSite tag editing windows are customized to edit the attributes for each tag.

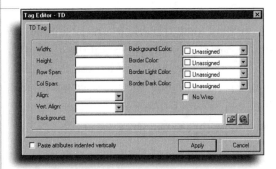

Each tag editing dialog box is customized to a specific tag. The hyperlink tag editing window includes only the attributes available for hyperlinks, the body tag editing window includes only attributes available for the body, and so on.

Adding a Hyperlink

Depending on where you're linking to, there are two methods to add a hyperlink to your page. One of the simplest methods creates a hyperlink to a page within your current site. Highlight the text that will become the hyperlink, and then select the destination from the Resource pane on the left side of the screen. Drag the page on to your text and release it. A hyperlink anchor tag now encases the text with a relative URL to the page.

If you need a little more flexibility in where your link jumps to, you can

- Select the **Anchor** button from the **Quick Tab**.
- Select **Tools** and then choose **Quick Anchor**.
- Press **Shift+Ctrl+A**.

Any of these methods displays the Anchor tag editor (see Figure B.8). Enter a URL in the HREF field in one of five ways:

- Type the URL directly if you know it.
- Select a URL from the current editing session from the drop-down list.
- Select a file from the current site by clicking the **Browse** button.

- Select a page from the Windows Favorites list by clicking the **Internet Explorer** button.

- Select a page from Navigator's bookmark list by clicking the **Navigator** button.

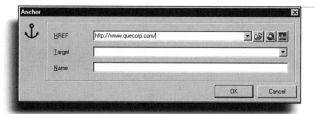

FIGURE B.8

The Anchor tag editing window lets you set the link URL and the text the user clicks.

When you've selected a destination, move down to the Description field and type the text the user will click. When you press **OK**, the completed hyperlink is added to the page, ready for action.

Adding Images and Other Items

HomeSite supports including any image, including bitmaps (BMP), graphics interchange (GIF), J-peg (JPG), and portable network graphics (PNG).

To limit the file display to images only, right click in the file resource tab and select **Filter** and choose **Web Images**. Click the thumbnail button below the file list to display a miniature representation of each file.

Adding an image to the page is very similar to adding a hyperlink:

- Drag a file from the file list to your document.
- Click the **Image** button from the **Quick Tab**.
- Select **Tools** and choose **Quick Image**.
- Select **Shift+Ctrl+I**.

In the dialog box that appears, enter the name of the image file or browse to it using the same techniques as creating a hyperlink.

Which picture to use

GIF and JPG files are the most common on the Web, and are still the best to use on your Web pages. GIFs offer several unique capabilities such as animation and transparency, when created with compatible image software. JPGs offer a small file size with superior resolution when speed matters.

BMP files tend to be much larger files compared to GIFs or JPGs, and are not widely used for this reason. Wherever possible, you should use imaging software to convert a BMP to one of the other two formats.

The PNG format is a new addition to the Web, and is still not widely supported, although this is expected to change. It offers increased efficiency in size and resolution over JPG, and is expected to be easier to implement across platforms.

You can also add ActiveX content or Java applets by clicking the appropriate button from the **Script** tab in the HomeSite window. Both of these buttons load dialog screens that contain fields for each of the attributes that control this type of content.

Finishing Touches

There are several utilities offered by HomeSite to help finish off your page. First is checking the spelling of the current document:

- Click the spelling button from the toolbar.
- Select **Tools** and choose **Spell Check** (**Spell Check All** for all open documents).
- Press **F7** (**Shift+F7** for all open documents).

What you may discover is that the spell checker stops at all of your HTML tags. This unnecessarily consumes a lot of time because you have to manually bypass each one. You can avoid checking the tags from the Settings dialog box. Select **Options**, choose **Settings** (**F8**), select the **Spelling** tab, and click **Skip tags when checking spelling** option.

Finding HTML tags with the spell checker brings up another issue—validating your HTML against what's legal to use on a page. HomeSite is integrated with Alsoft's CSE 3310 HTML Validator to look for HTML syntax errors.

- Click the **Validate** button on the toolbar.
- Select **Tools** and choose **Validate HTML**.
- Press **F6**.

After running the validator, any offending lines are highlighted and a box appears at the bottom of the page listing any errors (see Figure B.9).

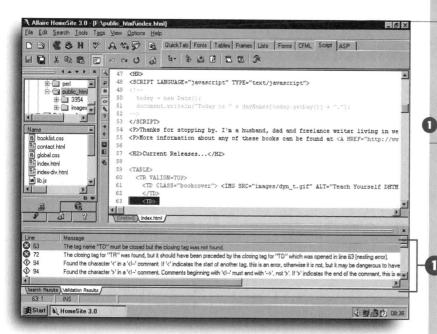

FIGURE B.9

An extra window appears at the bottom of the screen with a report of errors. Select **View** and choose **Results** to hide the window when you're done.

1 HTML errors are listed here

One of the common problems for a Web page that is not caught by the validator is verifying the destination for hyperlinks. This is a good task to perform on a regular basis, given the fact that Web pages are often changing. You'll need to make sure you have a connection to the Internet before beginning this process:

- Click the **Verify Links** button on the toolbar.
- Select **Tools** and choose **Verify Links**.

HomeSite will open the Link Checker window (see Figure B.10). It lists any source documents that are targeted for checking, and all the links within those documents.

The bottom window displays the results of checking as the process continues. Click the plus (+) or minus (-) button to add or remove additional pages for checking. To check relative URLs, add a Root URL to the field at the top of the screen. When you're ready to begin the checking, click the single link button to check the currently selected document, or the double-link to check all of the documents.

FIGURE B.10

The Link Checker window allows you to verify the destinations of all links and external contact within one or more pages.

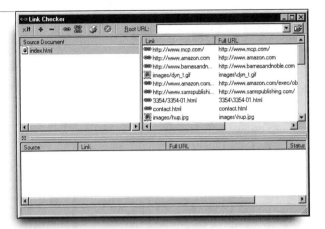

Another feature of HomeSite that can help you make your pages friendlier for everyone is the document weight utility. Document weight is the time it takes for a page to completely load on the user's browser, depending on the type of connection he or she has to the Internet. It depends on the size of the page and the size of all the content within, including images and multimedia items. Open a page in HomeSite, and then

- Click the **Document Weight** button on the toolbar.
- Select **Tools** and choose **Document Weight**.

The current document is evaluated and the results are displayed in a special dialog box (see Figure B.11).

Each piece of dependent (external) content is listed, along with its size. At the bottom of the screen, the document size is displayed, along with the total of each piece of dependent content and the total of both. Then, there is a list of times for three different modem speeds (14.4, 28.8, 56.6). Understand that these numbers are not set in stone, and also depend on the quality of the user's connection and choice of browser, traffic on the Internet, and current connections to the affected Web servers.

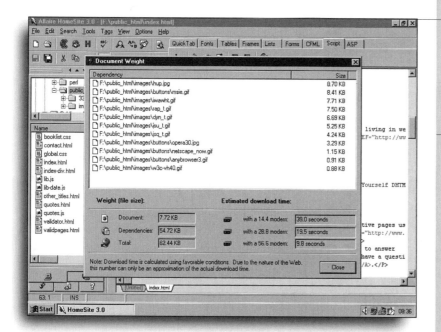

FIGURE B.11

The Document Weight dialog box shows the various files your page depends on, and how long it will take your page to load with all of these files given different modem speeds.

HTML 4 Quick Reference

HTML 4 is an ambitious attempt to meet the needs of Web developers worldwide, both casual and professional. This appendix provides a quick reference to all the elements and attributes of the language.

In order to make the information readily accessible, this appendix organizes HTML elements by their function in the following order:

- Structure
- Text phrases and paragraphs
- Text font elements
- Lists
- Links
- Tables
- Frames
- Embedded content
- Style
- Forms
- Scripts

More information

This appendix is based on the information provided in the *HTML 4 Specification W3C Recommendation* 18-Dec-1997. The latest version of this document can be found at `http://www.w3.org/TR/REC-html40/`.

What does deprecated mean?

Several elements and attributes have been deprecated, which means they have been outdated by the current HTML version, and you should avoid using them. The same or similar functionality is provided using new features.

New attributes are noted

HTML 4 introduces several new attributes that apply to a significant number of elements. These are referred to within each element listing as `core`, `i18n`, and `events`.

Within each section the elements are listed alphabetically and the following information is presented:

- *Usage.* A general description of the element
- *Start/End Tag.* Indicates whether these tags are required, optional, or illegal
- *Attributes.* Lists the attributes of the element with a short description of their effect
- *Empty.* Indicates whether the element can be empty
- *Notes.* Relates any special considerations when using the element and indicates whether the element is new, deprecated, or obsolete

Following this, the common attributes and intrinsic events are summarized.

Structure

HTML relies upon several elements to provide structure to a document (as opposed to structuring the text within), as well as provides information that is used by the browser or search engines.

<BDO>...</BDO>

Usage	The bidirectional algorithm element is used to selectively turn off the default text direction.
Start/End Tag	Required/Required.
Attributes	core
	`lang="..."` The language of the document.
	`dir="..."` The text direction (`ltr`, `rtl`).
Empty	No.
Notes	This element is new to HTML 4. The `dir` attribute is mandatory.

<BODY>...</BODY>

Usage
: Contains the content of the document.

Start/End Tag
: Optional/Optional.

Attributes
: `core, i18n, events`

: `background="..."` Deprecated. URL for the background image.

: `bgcolor="..."` Deprecated. Sets background color.

: `text="..."` Deprecated. Text color.

: `link="..."` Deprecated. Link color.

: `vlink="..."` Deprecated. Visited link color.

: `alink="..."` Deprecated. Active link color.

: `onload="..."` Intrinsic event triggered when the document loads.

: `onunload="..."` Intrinsic event triggered when document unloads.

Empty
: No.

Notes
: There can be only one BODY and it must follow the HEAD. The BODY element can be replaced by a FRAMESET element. The presentational attributes are deprecated in favor of setting these values with style sheets.

Comments <!-- ... -->

Usage	Used to insert notes or scripts that are not displayed by the browser.
Start/End Tag	Required/Required.
Attributes	None.
Empty	Yes.
Notes	Comments are not restricted to one line and can be any length. The end tag is not required to be on the same line as the start tag.

<DIV>...</DIV>

Usage	The division element is used to add structure to a block of text.
Start/End Tag	Required/Required.
Attributes	`core, i18n, events`
	`align="..."` Deprecated. Controls alignment (`left, center, right, justify`).
Empty	No.
Notes	Cannot be used within a P element. The `align` attribute is deprecated in favor of controlling alignment through style sheets.

Use style sheets rather than deprecated attributes

You will notice that the oft-used `align` attribute has been deprecated. This affects a large number of elements whose rendered position was controlled by setting the alignment to a suitable value such as `right` or `center`. Also deprecated is the `<CENTER>` element. The W3C strongly encourages users to begin using Style Sheets to modify the visual formatting of an HTML document.

<!DOCTYPE...>

Usage	Version information appears on the first line of an HTML document and is a Standard Generalized Markup Language (SGML) declaration rather than an element.

<H1>...</H1> through <H6>...</H6>

Usage	The six headings (H1 is the uppermost, or most important) are used in the BODY to structure information in a hierarchical fashion.
Start/End Tag	Required/Required.
Attributes	core, i18n, events
	align="..." Deprecated. Controls alignment (left, center, right, justify).
Empty	No.
Notes	Visual browsers will display the size of the headings in relation to their importance, with H1 being the largest and H6 the smallest. The align attribute is deprecated in favor of controlling alignment through style sheets.

<HEAD>...</HEAD>

Usage	This is the document header and contains other elements that provide information to users and search engines.
Start/End Tag	Optional/Optional.
Attributes	i18n
	profile="..." URL specifying the location of META data.
Empty	No.
Notes	There can be only one HEAD per document. It must follow the opening HTML tag and precede the BODY.

<HR>

Usage	Horizontal rules are used to separate sections of a Web page.

Start/End Tag	Required/Illegal.
Attributes	`core`, `events`
	`align="..."` Deprecated. Controls alignment (`left`, `center`, `right`, `justify`).
	`noshade="..."` Displays the rule as a solid color.
	`size="..."` Deprecated. The size of the rule.
	`width="..."` Deprecated. The width of the rule.
Empty	Yes.

<HTML>...</HTML>

Usage	This `HTML` element contains the entire document.
Start/End Tag	Optional/Optional.
Attributes	`i18n`
	`version="..."` URL of the document type definition specifying the HTML version used to create the document.
Empty	No.
Notes	The version information is duplicated in the `<!DOCTYPE...>` declaration and is therefore not essential.

<META>

Usage	Provides information about the document.
Start/End Tag	Required/Illegal.
Attributes	`i18n`
	`http-equiv="..."` HTTP response header name.

	`name="..."` Name of the meta information.
	`content="..."` Content of the meta information.
	`scheme="..."` Assigns a scheme to interpret the meta data.
Empty	Yes

\<SPAN\>...\</SPAN\>

Usage	Organizes the document by defining a span of text.
Start/End Tag	Required/Required.
Attributes	`core`, `i18n`, `events`
Empty	No.
Notes	This element is new to HTML 4.

\<TITLE\>...\</TITLE\>

Usage	This is the name you give your Web page. The `TITLE` element is located in the `HEAD` element and is displayed in the browser window title bar.
Start/End Tag	Required/Required.
Attributes	`i18n`
Empty	No.
Notes	Only one title allowed per document.

Text Phrases and Paragraphs

Text phrases (or blocks) can be structured to suit a specific purpose, such as creating a paragraph. This should not be confused with modifying the formatting of the text.

<ABBR>...</ABBR>

Usage	Used to define abbreviations.
Start/End Tag	Required/Required.
Attributes	core, i18n, events
Empty	No.
Notes	This element is new to HTML 4. The material enclosed by the tag is the abbreviated form, whereas the long form is defined by attributes within the tag.

<ACRONYM>...</ACRONYM>

Usage	Used to define acronyms.
Start/End Tag	Required/Required.
Attributes	core, i18n, events
Empty	No.
Notes	This element is new to HTML 4.

<ADDRESS>...</ADDRESS>

Usage	Provides a special format for author or contact information.
Start/End Tag	Required/Required.
Attributes	core, i18n, events
Empty	No.
Notes	The BR element is commonly used inside the ADDRESS element to break the lines of an address.

<BLOCKQUOTE>...</BLOCKQUOTE>

Usage	Used to display long quotations.
Start/End Tag	Required/Required.
Attributes	core, i18n, events
	cite="..." The URL of the quoted text.
Empty	No.

*
*

Usage	Forces a line break.
Start/End Tag	Required/Illegal.
Attributes	`core`, `i18n`, `events`
	`clear="..."` Sets the location where next line begins after a floating object (`none`, `left`, `right`, `all`).
Empty	Yes.

<CITE>...</CITE>

Usage	Cites a reference.
Start/End Tag	Required/Required.
Attributes	`core`, `i18n`, `events`
Empty	No.

<CODE>...</CODE>

Usage	Identifies a code fragement for display.
Start/End Tag	Required/Required.
Attributes	`core`, `i18n`, `events`
Empty	No.

<DEL>...</DEL>

Usage	Shows text as having been deleted from the document since the last change.
Start/End Tag	Required/Required.
Attributes	`core`, `i18n`, `events`
	`cite="..."` The URL of the source document.
	`datetime="..."` Indicates the date and time of the change.
Empty	No.
Notes	This element is new to HTML 4.

<DFN>...</DFN>

Usage	Defines an enclosed term.
Start/End Tag	Required/Required.
Attributes	core, i18n, events
Empty	No.

<EM>...</EM>

Usage	Emphasized text.
Start/End Tag	Required/Required.
Attributes	core, i18n, events
Empty	No.

<INS>...</INS>

Usage	Shows text as having been inserted in the document since the last change.
Start/End Tag	Required/Required.
Attributes	core, i18n, events
	cite="..." The URL of the source document.
	datetime="..." Indicates the date and time of the change.
Empty	No.
Notes	This element is new to HTML 4.

<KBD>...</KBD>

Usage	Indicates text a user would type.
Start/End Tag	Required/Required.
Attributes	core, i18n, events
Empty	No.

<P>...</P>

Usage	Defines a paragraph.
Start/End Tag	Required/Optional.
Attributes	core, i18n, events
	align="..." Deprecated. Controls alignment (left, center, right, justify).
Empty	No.

<PRE>...</PRE>

Usage	Displays preformatted text.
Start/End Tag	Required/Required.
Attributes	core, i18n, events
	width="..." The width of the formatted text.
Empty	No.

<Q>...</Q>

Usage	Used to display short quotations that do not require paragraph breaks.
Start/End Tag	Required/Required.
Attributes	core, i18n, events
	cite="..." The URL of the quoted text.
Empty	No.
Notes	This element is new to HTML 4.

<SAMP>...</SAMP>

Usage	Identifies sample output.
Start/End Tag	Required/Required.
Attributes	core, i18n, events
Empty	No.

<STRONG>...</STRONG>

Usage	Stronger emphasis.
Start/End Tag	Required/Required.
Attributes	core, i18n, events
Empty	No.

_{...}

Usage	Creates subscript.
Start/End Tag	Required/Required.
Attributes	core, i18n, events
Empty	No.

^{...}

Usage	Creates superscript.
Start/End Tag	Required/Required.
Attributes	core, i18n, events
Empty	No.

<VAR>...</VAR>

Usage	A variable.
Start/End Tag	Required/Required.
Attributes	core, i18n, events
Empty	No.

Text Formatting Elements

Text characteristics such as the size, weight, and style can be modified using these elements, but the HTML 4.0 specification encourages you to use style instead.

<B>...</B>

Usage	Bold text.
Start/End Tag	Required/Required.
Attributes	`core, i18n, events`
Empty	No.

<BASEFONT>

Usage	Sets the base font size.
Start/End Tag	Required/Illegal.
Attributes	`size="..."` The font size (1 through 7 or relative, that is +3).
	`color="..."` The font color.
	`face="..."` The font type.
Empty	Yes.
Notes	Deprecated in favor of style sheets.

<BIG>...</BIG>

Usage	Large text.
Start/End Tag	Required/Required.
Attributes	`core, i18n, events`
Empty	No.

<FONT>...</FONT>

Usage	Changes the font size and color.
Start/End Tag	Required/Required.
Attributes	`size="..."` The font size (1 through 7 or relative, that is, +3).
	`color="..."` The font color.
	`face="..."` The font type.
Empty	No.
Notes	Deprecated in favor of style sheets.

<I>...</I>

Usage	Italicized text.
Start/End Tag	Required/Required.
Attributes	core, i18n, events
Empty	No.

<S>...</S>

Usage	Strikethrough text.
Start/End Tag	Required/Required.
Attributes	core, i18n, events
Empty	No.
Notes	Deprecated.

<SMALL>...</SMALL>

Usage	Small text.
Start/End Tag	Required/Required.
Attributes	core, i18n, events
Empty	No.

<STRIKE>...</STRIKE>

Usage	Strikethrough text.
Start/End Tag	Required/Required.
Attributes	core, i18n, events
Empty	No.
Notes	Deprecated.

<TT>...</TT>

Usage	Teletype (or monospaced) text.
Start/End Tag	Required/Required.
Attributes	core, i18n, events
Empty	No.

<U>...</U>

Usage	Underlined text.
Start/End Tag	Required/Required.
Attributes	`core, i18n, events`
Empty	No.
Notes	Deprecated.

Lists

You can organize text into a more structured outline by creating lists. Lists can be nested.

<DD>...</DD>

Usage	The definition description used in a `DL` (definition list) element.
Start/End Tag	Required/Optional.
Attributes	`core, i18n, events`
Empty	No.
Notes	Can contain block-level content, such as the `<P>` element.

<DIR>...</DIR>

Usage	Creates a multi-column directory list.
Start/End Tag	Required/Required.
Attributes	`core, i18n, events`
	`compact` Deprecated. Compacts the displayed list.
Empty	No.
Notes	Must contain at least one list item. This element is deprecated in favor of the `UL` (unordered list) element.

<DL>...</DL>

Usage	Creates a definition list.
Start/End Tag	Required/Required.
Attributes	`core`, `i18n`, `events`
	`compact` Deprecated. Compacts the displayed list.
Empty	No.
Notes	Must contain at least one `<DT>` or `<DD>` element in any order.

<DT>...</DT>

Usage	The definition term (or label) used within a `DL` (definition list) element.
Start/End Tag	Required/Optional.
Attributes	`core`, `i18n`, `events`
Empty	No.
Notes	Must contained text (which can be modified by text markup elements).

<LI>...</LI>

Usage	Defines a list item within a list.
Start/End Tag	Required/Optional.
Attributes	`core`, `i18n`, `events`
	`type="..."` Changes the numbering style (`1`, `a`, `A`, `i`, `I`), ordered lists, or bullet style (`disc`, `square`, `circle`) in unordered lists.
	`value="..."` Sets the numbering to the given integer beginning with the current list item.
Empty	No.

<MENU>...</MENU>

Usage	Creates a single-column menu list.
Start/End Tag	Required/Required.
Attributes	`core`, `i18n`, `events`
	`compact` Deprecated. Compacts the displayed list.
Empty	No.
Notes	Must contain at least one list item. This element is deprecated in favor of the `UL` (unordered list) element.

<OL>...</OL>

Usage	Creates an ordered list.
Start/End Tag	Required/Required.
Attributes	`core`, `i18n`, `events`
	`type="..."` Sets the numbering style (`1`, `a`, `A`, `i`, `I`).
	`compact` Deprecated. Compacts the displayed list.
	`start="..."` Sets the starting number to the chosen integer.
Empty	No.
Notes	Must contain at least one list item.

<UL>...</UL>

Usage	Creates an unordered list.
Start/End Tag	Required/Required.
Attributes	`core`, `i18n`, `events`
	`type="..."` Sets the bullet style (`disc`, `square`, `circle`).
	`compact` Deprecated. Compacts the displayed list.
Empty	No.
Notes	Must contain at least one list item.

Links

Hyperlinking is fundamental to HTML. These elements enable you to link to other documents.

<A>...</A>

Usage	Used to define links and anchors.
Start/End Tag	Required/Required.
Attributes	core, i18n, events

charset="..." Character encoding of the resource.

name="..." Defines an anchor.

href="..." The URL of the linked resource.

target="..." Determines where the resource will be displayed (user-defined name, _blank, _parent, _self, _top).

rel="..." Forward link types.

rev="..." Reverse link types.

accesskey="..." Assigns a hotkey to this element.

shape="..." Enables you to define client-side imagemaps using defined shapes (default, rect, circle, poly).

coords="..." Sets the size of the shape using pixel or percentage lengths.

tabindex="..." Sets the tabbing order between elements with a defined tabindex.

Empty	No.

<BASE>

Usage	All other URLs in the document are resolved against this location.
Start/End Tag	Required/Illegal.

Attributes	`href="..."` The URL of the linked resource.
	`target="..."` Determines where the resource will be displayed (user-defined name, _blank, _parent, _self, _top).
Empty	Yes.
Notes	Located in the document HEAD.

<LINK>

Usage	Defines the relationship between a link and a resource.
Start/End Tag	Required/Illegal.
Attributes	core, i18n, events
	`href="..."` The URL of the resource.
	`rel="..."` The forward link types.
	`rev="..."` The reverse link types.
	`type="..."` The Internet content type.
	`media="..."` Defines the destination medium (screen, print, projection, braille, speech, all).
	`target="..."` Determines where the resource will be displayed (user-defined name, _blank, _parent, _self, _top).
Empty	Yes.
Notes	Located in the document HEAD.

Tables

Tables are meant to display data in a tabular format. Before the introduction of HTML 4.0, tables were widely used for page layout purposes, but with the advent of style sheets this is being discouraged by the W3C.

<CAPTION>...</CAPTION>

Usage	Displays a table caption.
Start/End Tag	Required/Required.
Attributes	core, i18n, events
	align="..." Deprecated. Controls alignment (left, center, right, justify).
Empty	No.
Notes	Optional.

<COL>

Usage	Groups columns within column groups in order to share attribute values.
Start/End Tag	Required/Illegal.
Attributes	core, i18n, events
	span="..." The number of columns the group contains.
	width="..." The column width as a percentage, pixel value, or minimum value.
	align="..." Horizontally aligns the contents of cells (left, center, right, justify, char).
	char="..." Sets a character on which the column aligns.
	charoff="..." Offset to the first alignment character on a line.
	valign="..." Vertically aligns the contents of a cell (top, middle, bottom, baseline).
Empty	Yes.

<COLGROUP>...</COLGROUP>

Usage	Defines a column group.
Start/End Tag	Required/Optional.

Attributes   `core`, `i18n`, `events`

`span="..."` The number of columns in a group.

`width="..."` The width of the columns.

`align="..."` Horizontally aligns the contents of cells (`left`, `center`, `right`, `justify`, `char`).

`char="..."` Sets a character on which the column aligns.

`charoff="..."` Offset to the first alignment character on a line.

`valign="..."` Vertically aligns the contents of a cell (`top`, `middle`, `bottom`, `baseline`).

Empty   No.

Notes   This element is new to HTML 4.

<TABLE>...</TABLE>

Usage   Creates a table.

Start/End Tag   Required/Required.

Attributes   `core`, `i18n`, `events`

`align="..."` Deprecated. Controls alignment (`left`, `center`, `right`, `justify`).

`bgcolor="..."` Deprecated. Sets the background color.

`width="..."` Table width.

`cols="..."` The number of columns.

`border="..."` The width in pixels of a border around the table.

`frame="..."` Sets the visible sides of a table (`void`, `above`, `below`, `hsides`, `lhs`, `rhs`, `vsides`, `box`, `border`).

`rules="..."`   Sets the visible rules within a table (none, groups, rows, cols, all).

`cellspacing="..."`   Spacing between cells.

`cellpadding="..."`   Spacing in cells.

Empty   No.

<TBODY>...</TBODY>

Usage	Defines the table body.
Start/End Tag	Optional/Optional.
Attributes	core, i18n, events

`align="..."`   Horizontally aligns the contents of cells (left, center, right, justify, char).

`char="..."`   Sets a character on which the column aligns.

`charoff="..."`   Offset to the first alignment character on a line.

`valign="..."`   Vertically aligns the contents of cells (top, middle, bottom, baseline).

Empty	No.
Notes	This element is new to HTML 4.

<TD>...</TD>

Usage	Defines a cell's contents.
Start/End Tag	Required/Optional.
Attributes	core, i18n, events

`axis="..."`   Abbreviated name.

`axes="..."`   axis names listing row and column headers pertaining to the cell.

`nowrap="..."`   Deprecated. Turns off text wrapping in a cell.

`bgcolor="..."` Deprecated. Sets the background color.

`rowspan="..."` The number of rows spanned by a cell.

`colspan="..."` The number of columns spanned by a cell.

`align="..."` Horizontally aligns the contents of cells (`left`, `center`, `right`, `justify`, `char`).

`char="..."` Sets a character on which the column aligns.

`charoff="..."` Offset to the first alignment character on a line.

`valign="..."` Vertically aligns the contents of cells (`top`, `middle`, `bottom`, `baseline`).

Empty   No.

`<TFOOT>...</TFOOT>`

Usage   Defines the table footer.

Start/End Tag   Required/Optional.

Attributes   `core`, `i18n`, `events`

`align="..."` Horizontally aligns the contents of cells (`left`, `center`, `right`, `justify`, `char`).

`char="..."` Sets a character on which the column aligns.

`charoff="..."` Offset to the first alignment character on a line.

`valign="..."` Vertically aligns the contents of cells (`top`, `middle`, `bottom`, `baseline`).

Empty   No.

Notes   This element is new to HTML 4.

<TH>...</TH>

Usage	Defines the cell contents of the table header.
Start/End Tag	Required/Optional.
Attributes	`core, i18n, events`

`axis="..."`   Abbreviated name.

`axes="..."`   `axis` names listing row and column headers pertaining to the cell.

`nowrap="..."`   Deprecated. Turns off text wrapping in a cell.

`bgcolor="..."`   Deprecated. Sets the background color.

`rowspan="..."`   The number of rows spanned by a cell.

`colspan="..."`   The number of columns spanned by a cell.

`align="..."`   Horizontally aligns the contents of cells (`left`, `center`, `right`, `justify`, `char`).

`char="..."`   Sets a character on which the column aligns.

`charoff="..."`   Offset to the first alignment character on a line.

`valign="..."`   Vertically aligns the contents of cells (`top`, `middle`, `bottom`, `baseline`).

Empty	No.

<THEAD>...</THEAD>

Usage	Defines the table header.
Start/End Tag	Required/Optional.
Attributes	`core, i18n, events`

`align="..."`   Horizontally aligns the contents of cells (`left`, `center`, `right`, `justify`, `char`).

char="..." Sets a character on which the column aligns.

charoff="..." Offset to the first alignment character on a line.

valign="..." Vertically aligns the contents of cells (top, middle, bottom, baseline).   .

Empty   No.

Notes   This element is new to HTML 4.

<TR>...</TR>

Usage   Defines a row of table cells.

Start/End Tag   Required/Optional.

Attributes   core, i18n, events

align="..." Horizontally aligns the contents of cells (left, center, right, justify, char).

char="..." Sets a character on which the column aligns.

charoff="..." Offset to the first alignment character on a line.

valign="..." Vertically aligns the contents of cells (top, middle, bottom, baseline).

bgcolor="..." Deprecated. Sets the background color.

Empty   No.

Frames

Frames create new "panels" in the Web browser window that are used to display content from different source documents.

\<FRAME\>

Usage	Defines a FRAME.
Start/End Tag	Required/Illegal.
Attributes	name="..." The name of a frame.
	src="..." The source to be displayed in a frame.
	frameborder="..." Toggles the border between frames (0, 1).
	marginwidth="..." Sets the space between the frame border and content.
	marginheight="..." Sets the space between the frame border and content.
	noresize Disables sizing.
	scrolling="..." Determines scrollbar presence (auto, yes, no).
Empty	Yes.
Notes	This element is new to HTML 4.

\<FRAMESET\>...\</FRAMESET\>

Usage	Defines the layout of FRAMES within a window.
Start/End Tag	Required/Required.
Attributes	rows="..." The number of rows.
	cols="..." The number of columns.
	onload="..." The intrinsic event triggered when the document loads.
	onunload="..." The intrinsic event triggered when the document unloads.
Empty	No.
Notes	This element is new to HTML 4. FRAMESETs can be nested.

<IFRAME>...</IFRAME>

Usage	Creates an inline frame.
Start/End Tag	Required/Required.
Attributes	`name="..."` The name of the frame.
	`src="..."` The source to be displayed in a frame.
	`frameborder="..."` Toggles the border between frames (`0`, `1`).
	`marginwidth="..."` Sets the space between the frame border and content.
	`marginheight="..."` Sets the space between the frame border and content.
	`scrolling="..."` Determines scrollbar presence (`auto`, `yes`, `no`).
	`align="..."` Deprecated. Controls alignment (`left`, `center`, `right`, `justify`).
	`height="..."` Height.
	`width="..."` Width.
Empty	No.
Notes	This element is new to HTML 4.

<NOFRAMES>...</NOFRAMES>

Usage	Alternative content when frames are not supported.
Start/End Tag	Required/Required.
Attributes	None.
Empty	No.
Notes	This element is new to HTML 4.

Embedded Content

Also called inclusions, embedded content applies to Java applets, imagemaps, and other multimedia or programattical content that is placed in a Web page to provide addional functionality.

<APPLET>...</APPLET>

Usage	Includes a Java applet.
Start/End Tag	Required/Required.
Attributes	`codebase="..."` The URL base for the applet.
	`archive="..."` Identifies the resources to be preloaded.
	`code="..."` The applet class file.
	`object="..."` The serialized applet file.
	`alt="..."` Displays text while loading.
	`name="..."` The name of the applet.
	`width="..."` The height of the displayed applet.
	`height="..."` The width of the displayed applet.
	`align="..."` Deprecated. Controls alignment (`left`, `center`, `right`, `justify`).
	`hspace="..."` The horizontal space separating the image from other content.
	`vspace="..."` The vertical space separating the image from other content.
Empty	No.
Notes	Applet is deprecated in favor of the `OBJECT` element.

<AREA>

Usage	The `AREA` element is used to define links and anchors.
Start/End Tag	Required/Illegal.
Attributes	`shape="..."` Enables you to define client-side imagemaps using defined shapes (`default`, `rect`, `circle`, `poly`).
	`coords="..."` Sets the size of the shape using pixel or percentage lengths.

`href="..."`   The URL of the linked resource.

`target="..."`   Determines where the resource will be displayed (user-defined name, _blank, _parent, _self, _top).

`nohref="..."`   Indicates that the region has no action.

`alt="..."`   Displays alternative text.

`tabindex="..."`   Sets the tabbing order between elements with a defined `tabindex`.

Empty   Yes.

<IMG>

Usage   Includes an image in the document.

Start/End Tag   Required/Illegal.

Attributes   `core, i18n, events`

`src="..."`   The URL of the image.

`alt="..."`   Alternative text to display.

`align="..."`   Deprecated. Controls alignment (`left`, `center`, `right`, `justify`).

`height="..."`   The height of the image.

`width="..."`   The width of the image.

`border="..."`   Border width.

`hspace="..."`   The horizontal space separating the image from other content.

`vspace="..."`   The vertical space separating the image from other content.

`usemap="..."`   The URL to a client-side imagemap.

`ismap`   Identifies a server-side imagemap.

Empty   Yes.

`<MAP>...</MAP>`

Usage	When used with the AREA element, creates a client-side imagemap.
Start/End Tag	Required/Required.
Attributes	core
	`name="..."` The name of the imagemap to be created.
Empty	No.

`<OBJECT>...</OBJECT>`

Usage	Includes an object.
Start/End Tag	Required/Required.
Attributes	core, i18n, events
	`declare` A flag that declares but doesn't create an object.
	`classid="..."` The URL of the object's location.
	`codebase="..."` The URL for resolving URLs specified by other attributes.
	`data="..."` The URL to the object's data.
	`type="..."` The Internet content type for data.
	`codetype="..."` The Internet content type for the code.
	`standby="..."` Show message while loading.
	`align="..."` Deprecated. Controls alignment (`left`, `center`, `right`, `justify`).
	`height="..."` The height of the object.
	`width="..."` The width of the object.
	`border="..."` Displays the border around an object.

hspace="..."   The space between the sides of the object and other page content.

vspace="..."   The space between the top and bottom of the object and other page content.

usemap="..."   The URL to an imagemap.

shapes=   Enables you to define areas to search for hyperlinks if the object is an image.

name="..."   The URL to submit as part of a form.

tabindex="..."   Sets the tabbing order between elements with a defined tabindex.

Empty	No.
Notes	This element is new to HTML 4.

<PARAM>

Usage	Initializes an object.
Start/End Tag	Required/Illegal.
Attributes	name="..." Defines the parameter name.

value="..."   The value of the object parameter.

valuetype="..."   Defines the value type (data, ref, object).

type="..."   The Internet media type.

Empty	Yes.
Notes	This element is new to HTML 4.

Style

Style sheets (both inline and external) are incorporated into an HTML document through the use of the STYLE element.

<STYLE>...</STYLE>

Usage	Creates an internal style sheet.
Start/End Tag	Required/Required.
Attributes	i18n
	type="..." The Internet content type.
	media="..." Defines the destination medium (screen, print, projection, braille, speech, all).
	title="..." The title of the style.
Empty	No.
Notes	Located in the HEAD element.

Forms

Forms create an interface for the user to select options and submit data back to the Web server.

<BUTTON>...</BUTTON>

Usage	Creates a button.
Start/End Tag	Required/Required.
Attributes	core, i18n, events
	name="..." The button name.
	value="..." The value of the button.
	type="..." The button type (button, submit, reset).
	disabled="..." Sets the button state to disabled.

tabindex="..."   Sets the tabbing order between elements with a defined tabindex.

onfocus="..."   The event that occurs when the element receives focus.

onblur="..."   The event that occurs when the element loses focus.

Empty   No.

Notes   This element is new to HTML 4.

\<FIELDSET>...\</FIELDSET>

Usage   Groups related controls.

Start/End Tag   Required/Required.

Attributes   core, i18n, events

Empty   No.

Notes   This element is new to HTML 4.

\<FORM>...\</FORM>

Usage   Creates a form that holds controls for user input.

Start/End Tag   Required/Required.

Attributes   core, i18n, events

action="..."   The URL for the server action.

method="..."   The HTTP method (get, post). get is deprecated.

enctype="..."   Specifies the MIME (Internet media type).

onsubmit="..."   The intrinsic event that occurs when the form is submitted.

onreset="..."   The intrinsic event that occurs when the form is reset.

target="..."   Determines where the resource will be displayed (user-defined name, _blank, _parent, _self, _top).

accept-charset="..."   The list of character encodings.

Empty   No.

<INPUT>

Usage   Defines controls used in forms.

Start/End Tag   Required/Illegal.

Attributes   core, i18n, events

type="..."   The type of input control (text, password, checkbox, radio, submit, reset, file, hidden, image, button).

name="..."   The name of the control (required except for submit and reset).

value="..."   The initial value of the control (required for radio and check-boxes).

checked="..."   Sets the radio buttons to a checked state.

disabled="..."   Disables the control.

readonly="..."   For text password types.

size="..."   The width of the control in pixels except for text and password controls, which are specified in number of characters.

maxlength="..."   The maximum number of characters that can be entered.

src="..."   The URL to an image control type.

alt="..."   An alternative text description.

usemap="..."   The URL to a client-side imagemap.

align="..."   Deprecated. Controls alignment (left, center, right, justify).

tabindex="..."   Sets the tabbing order between elements with a defined tabindex.

onfocus="..."   The event that occurs when the element receives focus.

onblur="..."   The event that occurs when the element loses focus.

onselect="..."   Intrinsic event that occurs when the control is selected.

onchange="..."   Intrinsic event that occurs when the control is changed.

accept="..."   File types allowed for upload.

Empty   Yes.

<ISINDEX>

Usage   Prompts the user for unput.

Start/End Tag   Required/Illegal.

Attributes   core, i18n

prompt="..."   Provides a prompt string for the input field.

Empty   Yes.

Notes   Deprecated.

<LABEL>...</LABEL>

Usage   Labels a control.

Start/End Tag   Required/Required.

Attributes   core, i18n, events

	`for="..."` Associates a label with an identified control.
	`disabled="..."` Disables a control.
	`accesskey="..."` Assigns a hotkey to this element.
	`onfocus="..."` The event that occurs when the element receives focus.
	`onblur="..."` The event that occurs when the element loses focus.
Empty	No.
Notes	This element is new to HTML 4.

<LEGEND>...</LEGEND>

Usage	Assigns a caption to a `FIELDSET`.
Start/End Tag	Required/Required.
Attributes	`core, i18n, events`
	`align="..."` Deprecated. Controls alignment (`left, center, right, justify`).
	`accesskey="..."` Assigns a hotkey to this element.
Empty	No.
Notes	This element is new to HTML 4.

<OPTGROUP>...</OPTGROUP>

Usage	Used to group form elements within a `SELECT` element.
Start/End Tag	Required/Required.
Attributes	`core, i18n, events`
	`disabled` Not used
	`label="..."` Defines a group label
Empty	No.
Notes	This element is new to HTML 4.

<OPTION>...</OPTION>

Usage	Specifies choices in a SELECT element.
Start/End Tag	Required/Optional.
Attributes	core, i18n, events

selected="..."   Specifies whether the option is selected.

disabled="..."   Disables control.

value="..."   The value submitted if a control is submitted.

Empty	No.

<SELECT>...</SELECT>

Usage	Creates choices for the user to select.
Start/End Tag	Required/Required.
Attributes	core, i18n, events

name="..."   The name of the element.

size="..."   The width in number of rows.

multiple   Allows multiple selections.

disabled="..."   Disables the control.

tabindex="..."   Sets the tabbing order between elements with a defined tabindex.

onfocus="..."   The event that occurs when the element receives focus.

onblur="..."   The event that occurs when the element loses focus.

onselect="..."   Intrinsic event that occurs when the control is selected.

onchange="..."   Intrinsic event that occurs when the control is changed.

Empty	No.

<TEXTAREA>...</TEXTAREA>

Usage	Creates an area for user input with multiple lines.
Start/End Tag	Required/Required.
Attributes	`core, i18n, events`

`name="..."`   The name of the control.

`rows="..."`   The width in number of rows.

`cols="..."`   The height in number of columns.

`disabled="..."`   Disables the control.

`readonly="..."`   Sets the displayed text to read-only status.

`tabindex="..."`   Sets the tabbing order between elements with a defined `tabindex`.

`onfocus="..."`   The event that occurs when the element receives focus.

`onblur="..."`   The event that occurs when the element loses focus.

`onselect="..."`   Intrinsic event that occurs when the control is selected.

`onchange="..."`   Intrinsic event that occurs when the control is changed.

Empty	No.
Notes	Text to be displayed is placed within the start and end tags.

Scripts

Scripting language is made available to process data and perform other dynamic events through the `SCRIPT` element.

<SCRIPT>...</SCRIPT>

Usage	The SCRIPT element contains client-side scripts that are executed by the browser.
Start/End Tag	Required/Required.
Attributes	type="..." Script language Internet content type.
	language="..." Deprecated. The scripting language, deprecated in favor of the type attribute.
	src="..." The URL for the external script.
Empty	No.
Notes	You can set the default scripting language in the META element.

<NOSCRIPT>...</NOSCRIPT>

Usage	The NOSCRIPT element provides alternative content for browsers unable to execute a script.
Start/End Tag	Required/Required.
Attributes	None.
Empty	No.
Notes	This element is new to HTML 4.

Common Attributes and Events

Four attributes are abbreviated as core in the preceding sections. They are:

- id="..."   A global identifier
- class="..."   A list of classes separated by spaces
- style="..."   Style information
- title="..."   Provides more information for a specific element, as opposed to the TITLE element, which entitles the entire Web page

Two attributes for internationalization (i18n) are abbreviated
as i18n:

- lang="..."   The language identifier.
- dir="..."   The text direction (ltr, rtl).

The following intrinsic events are abbreviated events:

- onclick="..."   A pointing device (such as a mouse) was
  single-clicked.
- ondblclick="..."   A pointing device (such as a mouse)
  was double-clicked.
- onmousedown="..."   A mouse button was clicked and held
  down.
- onmouseup="..."   A mouse button that was clicked and
  held down was released.
- onmouseover="..."   A mouse moved the cursor over an
  object.
- onmousemove="..."   The mouse was moved.
- onmouseout="..."   A mouse moved the cursor off an
  object.
- onkeypress="..."   A key was pressed and released.
- onkeydown="..."   A key was pressed and held down.
- onkeyup="..."   A key that was pressed has been released.

CSS Quick Reference

This appendix provides an overview of the attributes with which you can control the appearance of your HTML documents through style sheets. The World Wide Web Consortium (W3C) set the current standard for style sheets as Cascading Style Sheets 1 (CSS1). W3C's complete recommendation for CSS is located at the W3C Web site at http://www.w3.org/pub/WWW/TR/REC-CSS1.

Basic Syntax

All styles within a style sheet definition follow the same basic syntax. You'll notice that there are a lot of opportunities to add other attributes or members of a group:

```
SELECTOR[.class] [,SELECTOR2[.class2]] ...
{ attribute1: value1  [;
  attribute2: value2] [;
  ... ]               [;
  attributen: valuen] }
```

The SELECTOR is how the style is referenced within the rest of the HTML page. It uses one of the existing HTML tags, such as <CODE> or <P>, along with an optional class to create additional sub-styles. A class is a subset of a selector, allowing the same element to have a variety of styles. For example, you could color code block quotes to identify sources or speakers.

In addition to the standard HTML tags, you can use two other values for a selector: `first-line` and `first-letter`. The `first-line` value sets the style for the first line of text in a document or several passages within a document, such as paragraph or block quote. The `first-letter` value creates drop caps and other special effects on the first letter in a document or passage.

Groups of selectors and their classes are separated by commas. Any member of the group receives the same style as any other member in the group. For example, if you wanted all headings to be displayed in red, you could list H1 through H6 with the attributes to set the color to red. All other tag attributes, such as size, would remain unaffected.

Another option is contextual selectors, which tell the browser what to do with a certain tag when found nested within the parent tag.

```
OUTER_SELECTOR INNER_SELECTOR {attribute;value}
```

This means that when `INNER_SELECTOR` is used within the `OUTER_SELECTOR`, the style is used. Otherwise, other occurrences of `INNER_SELECTOR` are handled according to browser default.

After making all of the selector and group definitions, use a curly bracket along with a series of attributes and their values. Mate each attribute with its value by using a colon and separate each pair from the next pair by a semicolon. The values within a definition, such as the name of a typeface or a color value, are not case-sensitive. For example, for `font-family`, you can have Garamond, garamond, or GARAMOND, and it will all work out the same in the browser.

As with all good syntax, you can place style definitions in three ways within a document: with an embedded style sheet, a linked style sheet, and an inline style sheet.

Embedded Style Sheet

The `<STYLE>` tags contain an embedded style sheet. As a matter of structure, the format of an HTML page with an embedded style sheet is as follows:

```
<HTML>
<HEAD>...</HEAD>
<STYLE>...</STYLE>
```

```
<BODY>...</BODY>
</HTML>
```

The `<STYLE>` tags contain the list of selectors and styles.

Linked Style Sheet

The linked style sheet is a `.css` file that contains nothing but a set of `<STYLE>` tags and their contents. Identify the style file within an HTML document using the `<LINK>` tag in the head:

```
<HEAD>
<LINK rel=stylesheet href="filename.css" type="text/css">
</HEAD>
```

At runtime, the browser will load the style in the `.css` file and use it to format the document. If the HTML page also includes an embedded style sheet that conflicts with the linked style sheet, the embedded version also takes precedence.

Inline Style Sheet

The last option, inline style sheets, uses style sheet syntax, although it's technically not a style sheet implementation. This option uses the style sheet nomenclature to customize single incidents of tags within the document:

```
<TAG style="attribute1:value1; ...">
```

Essentially, this is a way to customize HTML tags on a case-by-case basis. When you use all three forms of syntax, they occur in a cascading form of precedence. The highest priority is inline, followed by embedded, and then linked.

Style Attributes

Several classes of attributes are used within the definition for a selector. The following sections cover each of the attributes within a class.

There is a predictable way the rules are applied when faced with conflicts between styles on a page. To determine how an element will appear on the page, follow these rules, in order:

1. First, find all of the declarations that apply to the element in question. Style declarations apply if the selector matches the element in question. If no declarations apply, the element's style is inherited from its parent, or if no parent applies with any unspecified values handled according to browser defaults.

2. For multiple declarations, any styles marked !important carry more weight than unmarked declarations.

3. Next, comes origin priority. The author's style sheets override the reader's style sheet which override the browser's default values. Linked styles are considered the same origin as the author.

4. Next comes specificity. A more specific selector overrides less specific selectors. For example, if you set BODY as black text on a white background, and then set BLOCKQUOTE as red text on a white background, a block quote within the body will be red, because BLOCKQUOTE is more specific than BODY.

5. Sort by the order in which the styles are specified. If two rules have the same weight, the last definition wins. So, a linked style sheet at the beginning of the document sets the first style. Any discrepancies between the linked style and an embedded style default to the embedded style. If for some reason the embedded style includes two definitions for the same element, such as two sets of properties for BLOCKQUOTE, the last BLOCKQUOTE wins.

Using these rules, you can accurately predict how your style sheet will be applied when interpreted by a browser.

Fonts

There are no current standards for typefaces and their use on different user machines, so you'll need to choose carefully and include several options to achieve the desired effect for the user.

The *font-family* Attribute

The font-family attribute lists font families in order of preference, separated by commas. Two types of variables are used: family name and generic family.

```
BODY {font-family: Garamond, Palatino, Serif}
```

A family name is the name of a specific typeface such as Helvetica, Garamond, Palatino, or Optima. Enclose font names with spaces in quotes, such as "Gil Sans". The generic family is one of five choices that classifies the typeface by its style and is recommended as the last option in a font-family list:

- *Serif.* Fonts with accents at the tips of the lines (for example, Times)
- *Sans-serif.* Fonts without finishing accents (for example, Helvetica)
- *Cursive.* Scripts that more closely resemble hand-drawn calligraphy (for example, Zapf Chancery)
- *Fancy.* Special-use decorative fonts (for example, Comic Book Sans)
- *Monospace.* Fonts that maintain uniform spacing despite letter width (for example, Courier)

The *font-style* Attribute

This attribute specifies the type of treatment a font receives and is represented by the values normal, italic, or oblique. The normal value is also referred to as Roman in some typeface references. The oblique value is similar to italic except that is usually slanted manually by the system rather than by a separate style of the font, like italic.

```
BODY {font-style: italic}
```

The *font-variant* Attribute

Similar to font-style, this attribute sets small caps. Its two values are normal and small-caps.

```
BODY {font-variant: small-caps}
```

If there is no true small caps version of the typeface, the system will attempt to scale the capital letters to a smaller size for lowercase letters. As a last resort, the text will appear in all capitals.

The *font-weight* Attribute

A number of values for this attribute set the darkness or lightness of a typeface. The primary values are normal and bold. You can substitute these values with one of a list of values from 100 to 900. If a typeface includes a "medium" weight, it will correspond to 500. Bold is represented by 700.

```
BODY {font-weight: bold}
```

Two additional values are bolder and lighter, which increase the weight from the current parent weight by one level, such as 200 to 300 for bolder or 700 to 600 for lighter.

The *font-size* Attribute

Four methods can define the size of a font in a style—absolute size, relative size, length, or percentage.

- *Absolute size.* This method is represented in several ways. The first is with a value that represents its size relative to other sizes within the family (xx-small, x-small, small, medium, large, x-large, xx-large). You can also use a numerical value, such as 12pt (12 points).

    ```
    BODY {font-size: 18pt}
    ```

- *Relative size.* This method sets the size relative to the parent style. It can be one of two values, smaller or larger, and it adjusts the size up or down the scale of sizes. If a font doesn't include a mapping to size names, a scaling of 1.5 is recommended between sizes. For example, a 10pt font would be scaled larger to 15pt or smaller to 7pt.

    ```
    P {font-size: smaller}
    ```

- *Length.* This method is another form of relative size that sets the size by the scale factor of the width of an em, such as 1.5em.

    ```
    P {font-size: 2em}
    ```

- *Percentage*. This method is also a relative specification that multiplies the size of the parent font by the percentage value to achieve the new size, such as 150%.

```
H3 {font-size: 300%}
```

The *font* Attribute

This attribute provides a shorthand way to set all of the previous attributes under one umbrella. The order of the attributes should be font-style, font-variant, font-weight, font-size, line-height, font-family. Place no commas between each of the attribute values, except for listed font families:

```
BODY {font: small-caps bold 14pt garamond, palatino, serif}
```

Color and Background

These elements set the color values for the text (foreground) and the area behind the text (background). In addition to setting a background color, you can also define a background image. All color values are defined using the same methods as the color attribute.

The *color* Attribute

This attribute defines the color of the text element and is specified using one of the color keywords (such as red). You can also define the color using a hexadecimal triplet, denoting the mix of red, green, and blue (such as rgb(255,0,0)).

```
BLOCKQUOTE {color: rgb(0,255,255)}
```

The *background-color* Attribute

This attribute sets the background color for a style. You can set this attribute independently of a background color for the document to enable you to highlight text in a different manner.

```
BLOCKQUOTE {background-color: blue}
```

The *background-image* Attribute

This attribute specifies a background image for a style element. Use it in conjunction with background-color to ensure a substitute effect if the image becomes unavailable. If the image is available, it will display on top of the background color.

```
BLOCKQUOTE {background-image: url(logo.gif)}
```

The *background-repeat* Attribute

If the background image should be repeated (tiled), use this attribute to define how. Its values include repeat, repeat-x, and repeat-y. The repeat value indicates that the image should be tiled normally. The repeat-x value repeats the image in a single horizontal line, and the repeat-y value repeats the image in a vertical line.

```
BLOCKQUOTE {background-image: url(logo.gif);
            background-repeat: repeat-x}
```

The *background-attachment* Attribute

This attribute, an extended feature of background images not seen in HTML before, sets whether the background image is attached to the foreground text (scroll) or anchored to the back-ground (fixed). This feature is apparent only when the user scrolls across a selection of text.

```
BLOCKQUOTE {background-image: url(logo.gif);
            background-attachment: repeat-x}
```

The *background-position* Attribute

When you use a background image through normal HTML, the starting point is always the top left of the screen. With a style sheet, you can specify a starting point anywhere within the box that contains the style content.

You can specify the image's starting position in three ways. The first way is with key word locations. For horizontal placement, your choices are left, center, or right. For vertical placement, your choices are top, center, or bottom. Alternatively, you can represent the position as a percentage of the available area, with 0% 0% being the top left (default) and 100% 100% being the bottom right. The last option is to specify an actual measurement in centimeters or inches.

If only one value for the placement is given, it's used as the horizontal position. If both values are given, the first is evaluated as horizontal and the second as vertical.

```
BLOCKQUOTE {background-image: url(logo.gif);
            Background-repeat: repeat-y;
            background-position: right top; }
```

The *background* Attribute

This shorthand attribute, similar to font, enables you to define a set of values for the background in one stop. The order is background-color, background-image, background-repeat, background-attachment, background-position.

```
P { background: black url(logo.gif) repeat-y fixed right top
}
```

Text

This set of style attributes covers the values that can affect the appearance of text, but not by directly changing the typeface. This includes values for spacing, underlining, blinking, and strike-through. It also supports some of the positioning attributes, including left and right justification and indents.

The *word-spacing* Attribute

This attribute indicates an addition to the default amount of space between individual words and is specified in ems. An *em* is the space occupied by the letter "m" and is the baseline for determining widths within a font. To return the value to its default, use 0em or normal.

```
BODY { word-spacing: 1em }
```

The *letter-spacing* Attribute

The letter-spacing attribute is similar to word-spacing, except that letter-spacing adds an extra bit of spacing between individual letters. In addition to the default method the browser uses to determine spacing, additional letter spacing is also affected by text alignment.

```
BODY { letter-spacing: 0.2em }
```

The *text-decoration* Attribute

This attribute is more closely related to its cousins in the font family. It specifies extra text flourishes, such as underline, strike-through, and blinking. The four values are none, underline, over-line, line-through, and blink.

```
STR.blink { text-decoration: underline blink }
```

The *vertical-align* Attribute

This attribute sets the vertical position of the text either to an absolute reference or in relation to the parent element. It supports a range of values and keywords:

- Baseline Aligns the baseline of the style with the baseline of the parent element

- Sub Assigns the style to a subscript relative to the parent element

- Super   Assigns the style to a superscript relative to the parent element

- Text-top Aligns the top of the text with the top of the parent's text

- Text-bottom Aligns the bottom of the text with the bottom of the parent's text

- Middle Aligns the vertical halfway point of the element with the baseline of the parent plus half of the x-height of the parent (x-height is the height of the lowercase x of the font)

- Top Aligns the top of the element with the tallest element on the current line

- Bottom Aligns the bottom of the element with the lowest element on the current line

- (Percentage) Using a positive or negative percentage value, raises or lowers the element beyond the baseline of the parent

  ```
  SUB { vertical-align: -10% }
  ```

The *text-transform* Attribute

This attribute sets the capitalization of the affected text to one of four choices: capitalize (first letter of every word), uppercase (all letters in capitals), lowercase (all letters in lowercase), and none.

```
STR.caps { text-transform: uppercase }
```

The *text-align* Attribute

This attribute moves beyond the standard HTML left-right-center alignment to provide full justification (justify left and right). If a browser doesn't support justify, it will typically substitute left.

```
BLOCKQUOTE { text-align: justify }
```

The *text-indent* Attribute

The text-indent attribute, specified in an absolute value measured in ems or inches, defines the amount of space that is added before the first line.

```
P { text-indent: 5em }
```

The *line-height* Attribute

This attribute sets the distance between adjacent baselines using a length (in ems), multiplication factor, or percentage. Factors are indicated without any units, such as 1.5. When you use this method, the child inherits the factor, not the resulting value.

```
DIV { line-height: 1.5; font-size: 12pt }
```

In this instance, the line height becomes 18 points and the font size remains at 12 points.

Margins, Padding, and Borders

Each element created in a style sheet is presented in its own "box." All of the styles from the element inside the box are applied, although the box itself can have its own properties that define how it relates to adjoining elements on the page. Length is specified in inches (in), centimeters (cm), ems (em), points (pt), or pixels (px).

Box properties are divided into three basic categories. Margin properties set the border around the outside of the box, padding properties determine how much space to insert between the border and the content, and border properties define graphical lines around an element.

Additional properties of the box include its width, height, and physical position.

The *margin-top, margin-bottom, margin-right,* and *margin-left* Attributes

These four attributes set the amount of space between the element and adjoining elements, whether defined by length or percentage of parent text width or handled automatically.

```
BLOCKQUOTE { margin-top: 4em;
             Margin-bottom: auto }
```

The *margin* Attribute

The margin attribute provides a shorthand method for setting the four margin values.

When you specify the four values, they are applied, in order, to the top, right, bottom, and left. If you provide only one value, it applies to all sides. If you use two or three values, the missing values are copied from the opposite sides.

```
BLOCKQUOTE {margin: 4em 2em}
```

The *padding-top, padding-bottom, padding-right,* and *padding-left* Attributes

These attributes set the distance between the boundaries of the box and the elements inside the box. It can use any of the physical measurements or a percentage of the parent's width.

```
BLOCKQUOTE {padding-top: 110%; padding-bottom: 115%}
```

The *padding* Attribute

The padding attribute provides a shorthand method for setting the four padding values.

When you specify the four values, they are applied, in order, to the top, right, bottom, and left. If you provide only one value, it applies to all sides. If you use two or three values, the missing values are copied from the opposite sides.

```
BLOCKQUOTE {padding: 10pt 12pt}
```

The *border-top, border-bottom, border-right,* and *border-left* Attributes

These four attributes set the style and color of each border around an element. Specify styles with one of the border style keywords: none, dotted, dashed, solid, double, groove, ridge, inset, and outset. For more information on these, see the information on border-style later in this appendix.

Specify colors using a color keyword. For more information, see the border-color later in this appendix.

```
BLOCKQUOTE {border-left: solid red}
```

The *border-top-width, border-bottom-width, border-right-width,* and *border-left-width* Attributes

These attributes define a physical border around the box, similar to the border used for HTML tables. In addition to defining a specific width in ems, you can also use the keywords thin, medium, and thick. Using a measurement in ems results in a border whose width changes in relation to the size of the current font.

```
STR {border-right-width: 2pt;
     border-left-width: 2pt }
```

The *border-width* Attribute

The border-width attribute provides a shorthand method for setting the width of the four borders.

When you specify the four values, they are applied, in order, to the top, right, bottom, and left. If you provide only one value, it applies to all sides. If you use two or three values, the missing values are copied from the opposite sides.

```
BLOCKQUOTE {border-width: medium 0pt 0pt thick}
```

The *border-color* Attribute

This attribute sets the color of all four borders and uses one color keyword as its value. You cannot set the color of each side independently.

```
BLOCKQUOTE {border-color: yellow}
```

The *border-style* Attribute

The border's appearance can take on several different settings, represented by none, dotted, dashed, solid, double, groove, ridge, inset, and outset. The last four values are represented in 3D, if the browser supports it. Alternatively, the browser also can present all of the variations as a solid line, except none.

Like border-color, the style is applied uniformly to all four sides.

```
BLOCKQUOTE {border-style: groove}
```

The *border* Attribute

The border attribute provides a shorthand method for setting all of the border variables, including width, style, and color. It sets the values for all four sides at the same time, overriding any individual settings that may have been set previously for the same element.

```
BLOCKQUOTE {border: 1.5pt double black}
```

The *height* Attribute

This attribute sets the overall height of the bounding box that contains either the text or image element. If the content is text, scrollbars are added as needed so that all of the material is still available to the user. If the content is an image, it's scaled to fit inside the area. You can set a physical value or use auto to let the browser allocate space as needed.

```
BLOCKQUOTE {height: 100px}
```

The *width* Attribute

Similar to height, the width attribute sets the overall width of the bounding box that contains the element. If the content is text, scrollbars are added as needed so that all of the material is still available for the user. If both elements are used with an image and the value of one element is auto, the aspect ratio for the image is maintained.

```
BLOCKQUOTE {width: auto}
```

The *float* Attribute

This attribute sets a value similar to the align attribute used in HTML. The three possible values are left, right, and none. The none value allows the element to fall where it may, and the other two values force the element to the left or right of the screen with text wrapping around the opposite side.

```
BLOCKQUOTE {float: right}
```

The *clear* Attribute

This attribute mimics the clear attribute used with the HTML <BR> tag and uses the same keywords as float. If you use it with right or left, elements will move below any floating element on that respective side. If you set it to none, floating elements are allowed on both sides.

```
BLOCKQUOTE {clear: left right}
```

Classification

These attributes control the general behavior of other elements more than actually specifying an appearance. In addition, classification includes the attributes for list items, identified in HTML with the <LI> tag.

The *display* Attribute

This attribute identifies when and if a style element should be used. Four keywords determine its behavior:

- Inline A new box is created within the same line as adjoining text items and is formatted according to the size and amount of content within its borders, such as an image (IMG) or text (STR).

- Block   A new box is created relative to the surrounding elements. This is common with elements such as H1 and P.

- List-item   Similar to block, only list item markers, which behave more like inline content, are added.

- None   Turns off the display of the element in any situation, including for children of the element.

```
IMG {display: inline}
BLOCKQUOTE {display: block}
```

The *white-space* Attribute

The name of this attribute is a bit misleading because it relates to how spaces and line breaks are handled. The choices are normal (in which extra spaces are ignored), pre (as in preformatted HTML text), and nowrap (in which lines are broken only with <BR>).

```
BLOCKQUOTE {white-space: pre}
```

The *list-style-type* Attribute

This element sets the type of markers used for a list. Your choices are disc, circle, square, decimal, lower-roman, upper-roman, lower-alpha, upper-alpha, and none.

```
LI.outline1 {list-style-type: upper-roman}
LI.outline2 {list-style-type: upper-alpha}
LI.outline3 {list-style-type: decimal}
```

The *list-style-image* Attribute

In lieu of a text marker for the list item, you can also specify the URL of an image to use. If the image is unavailable, the text marker is used as default.

```
LI.general {list-style-image: url(bullet.jpg)}
```

The *list-style-position* Attribute

The two values for this attribute, inside and outside, determine the formatting of text following the list item marker. The outside value, the default value, lines up the additional lines of text beyond the first line with the first character in the first line. If you use the `inside` value, the second and following lines are justified with the list item marker.

```
LI {list-style-position: inside}
```

The *list-style* Attribute

This attribute is a shorthand element for the `list-style-type`, `list-style-image`, and `list-style-position` attributes.

```
OL {list-style: lower-alpha outside}
UL {list-style: square url(bullet.jpg) inside}
```

JavaScript Quick Reference

The first part of this reference is organized by object, with properties and methods listed by the object to which they apply. The second part covers independent functions in JavaScript not connected with a particular object, as well as operators in JavaScript.

A Note About JavaScript 1.2

JavaScript 1.2 is designed to interface seamlessly with Netscape Navigator 4.0. New features have been introduced in various areas of the language model, including but not limited to

- Events
- Objects
- Properties
- Methods

Netscape Navigator 4.0 has been coded to support these new features, but earlier versions of Navigator have not. Backward compatibility is therefore an issue.

In this appendix, techniques that work only in Netscape Navigator 4.0 and above are clearly marked. At each heading, the words "Navigator 4.0 Only" will appear.

Finally, note that in development, you should now clearly identify which version of JavaScript you are using. If you fail to do so, your scripts might not work. You do this by using the LANGUAGE attribute within the <SCRIPT> tag. The following are some examples:

```
<Script Language = "JavaScript"> - Compatible with 2.0 and
above
```
```
<Script Language = "JavaScript 1.1"> - Compatible with 3.0
and above
```
```
<Script Language = "JavaScript 1.2"> - Compatible with 4.0
and above
```

The following codes are used to indicate where objects, methods, properties, and event handlers are implemented:

- C—Client JavaScript (Server JavaScript is not covered in this appendix)
- 2—Netscape Navigator 2
- 3—Netscape Navigator 3
- 4—Netscape Navigator 4 only (this is not to say Navigator 4 will work with these items only, Navigator 4 will handle all implementations)
- I—Microsoft Internet Explorer 3

The *anchor* Object [C|2|3|4|I]

The anchor object reflects an HTML anchor.

Properties

- name   A string value indicating the name of the anchor. [Not 2|3]

The *applet* Object [C|3]

The applet object reflects a Java applet included in a Web page with the APPLET tag.

Properties

- name   A string reflecting the NAME attribute of the APPLET tag.

The *area* Object [C|3]

The area object reflects a clickable area defined in an imagemap. area objects appear as entries in the links array of the document object.

Properties

- hash   A string value indicating an anchor name from the URL.

- host   A string value reflecting the host and domain name portion of the URL.

- hostname   A string value indicating the host, domain name, and port number from the URL.

- href   A string value reflecting the entire URL.

- pathname   A string value reflecting the path portion of the URL (excluding the host, domain name, port number, and protocol).

- port   A string value indicating the port number from the URL.

- protocol   A string value indicating the protocol portion of the URL, including the trailing colon.

- search   A string value specifying the query portion of the URL (after the question mark).

- target   A string value reflecting the TARGET attribute of the AREA tag.

Methods

- getSelection   Gets the current selection and returns this value as a string.

Event Handlers

- onDblClick   Specifies JavaScript code to execute when the user double-clicks the area. (Not implemented on Macintosh) Netscape Navigator 4.0 only.

■ onMouseOut   Specifies JavaScript code to execute when the mouse moves outside the area specified in the AREA tag.

New Properties with JavaScript 1.2

type	Indicates a MouseOut event.
target	Indicates the object to which the event was sent.
layer[n]	Where [n] represents X or Y, used (in conjunction with page[n] and screen[n]) to describe the cursor location when the MouseOut event occurred.
page[n]	Where [n] represents X or Y, used (in conjunction with layer[n] and screen[n]) to describe the cursor location when the MouseOut event occurred.
screen[n]	Where [n] represents X or Y, used (in conjunction with layer[n] and page[n]) to describe the cursor location when the MouseOut event occurred.

■ onMouseOver   Specifies JavaScript code to execute when the mouse enters the area specified in the <AREA> tag.

New Properties with JavaScript 1.2

type	Indicates a MouseOver event.
target	Indicates the object to which the event was sent.
layer[n]	Where [n] represents X or Y, used (in conjunction with page[n] and screen[n]) to describe the cursor location when the MouseOver event occurred.
page[n]	Where [n] represents X or Y, used (in conjunction with layer[n] and screen[n]) to describe the cursor location when the MouseOver event occurred.
screen[n]	Where [n] represents X or Y, used (in conjunction with layer[n] and page[n]) to describe the cursor location when the MouseOver event occurred.

The *Array* Object [C|3|I]

The Array object provides a mechanism for creating arrays and working with them. New arrays are created with *arrayName* = new Array() or *arrayName* = new Array(*arrayLength*).

Properties

- length   An integer value reflecting the number of elements in an array.
- prototype   Provides a mechanism to add properties to an Array object.

Methods

- concat(*arrayname*)   Combines elements of two arrays and returns a third, one level deep, without altering either of the derivative arrays. Netscape Navigator 4.0 only.
- join(*string*)   Returns a string containing each element of the array separated by *string*. (Not I)
- reverse()   Reverses the order of an array. (Not I)
- slice(arrayName, beginSlice, endSlice)   Extracts a portion of some array and derives a new array from it. The beginSlice and endSlice parameters specify the target elements at which to begin and end the slice. (Netscape Navigator 4.0 only.)
- sort(*function*)   Sorts an array based on function which indicates a *function* defining the sort order. *function* can be omitted in which case the sort defaults to dictionary order. Note: sort now works on all platforms.

The *button* Object [C|2|3|I]

The button object reflects a pushbutton from an HTML form in JavaScript.

Properties

- enabled   A Boolean value indicating whether the button is enabled. (Not 2|3)
- form   A reference to the form object containing the button. (Not 2|3)
- name   A string value containing the name of the button element.
- type   A string value reflecting the TYPE attribute of the INPUT tag. (Not 2|I)
- value   A string value containing the value of the button element.

Methods

- click()   Emulates the action of clicking the button.
- focus()   Gives focus to the button. (Not 2|3)

Event Handlers

- onMouseDown   Specifies JavaScript code to execute when a user presses a mouse button.
- onMouseUp   Specifies JavaScript code to execute when the user releases a mouse button.
- onClick   Specifies JavaScript code to execute when the button is clicked.
- onFocus   Specifies JavaScript code to execute when the button receives focus. (Not 2|3)

The *checkbox* Object [c|2|3|I]

The checkbox object makes a checkbox in an HTML form available in JavaScript.

Properties

- checked   A Boolean value indicating whether the checkbox element is checked.

- defaultChecked   A Boolean value indicating whether the checkbox element was checked by default (that is, it reflects the CHECKED attribute).

- enabled   A Boolean value indicating whether the checkbox is enabled. (Not 2|3)

- form   A reference to the form object containing the checkbox. (Not 2|3)

- name   A string value containing the name of the checkbox element.

- type   A string value reflecting the TYPE attribute of the INPUT tag. (Not 2|I)

- value   A string value containing the value of the checkbox element.

Methods

- click()   Emulates the action of clicking the checkbox.
- focus()   Gives focus to the checkbox. (Not 2|3)

Event Handlers

- onClick   Specifies JavaScript code to execute when the checkbox is clicked.

- onFocus   Specifies JavaScript code to execute when the checkbox receives focus. (Not 2|3)

The *combo* Object [C|I]

The combo object reflects a combo field in JavaScript.

Properties

- `enabled`   A Boolean value indicating whether the combo box is enabled. (Not 2|3)
- `form`   A reference to the `form` object containing the combo box. (Not 2|3)
- `listCount`   An integer reflecting the number of elements in the list.
- `listIndex`   An integer reflecting the index of the selected element in the list.
- `multiSelect`   A Boolean value indicating whether the combo field is in multiselect mode.
- `name`   A string value reflecting the name of the combo field.
- `value`   A string containing the value of the combo field.

Methods

- `addItem(index)`   Adds an item to the combo field before the item at *index*.
- `click()`   Simulates a click on the combo field.
- `clear()`   Clears the contents of the combo field.
- `focus()`   Gives focus to the combo field.
- `removeItem(index)`   Removes the item at *index* from the combo field.

Event Handlers

- `onClick`   Specifies JavaScript code to execute when the mouse clicks the combo field.
- `onFocus`   Specifies JavaScript code to execute when the combo field receives focus.

The *Date* Object [C|2|3|I]

The `Date` object provides mechanisms for working with dates and times in JavaScript. Instances of the object can be created with the following syntax:

```
newObjectName = new Date(dateInfo)
```

Where *dateInfo* is an optional specification of a particular date and can be one of the following:

`"month day, year hours;minutes;seconds"`

`year, month, day`

`year, month, day, hours, minutes, seconds`

where the later two options represent integer values.

If no *dateInfo* is specified, the new object will represent the current date and time.

Properties

- `prototype`   Provides a mechanism for adding properties to a `Date` object. (Not 2)

Methods

- `getDate()`   Returns the day of the month for the current `Date` object as an integer from 1 to 31.

- `getDay()`   Returns the day of the week for the current `Date` object as an integer from 0 to 6 (where 0 is Sunday, 1 is Monday, and so on).

- `getHours()`   Returns the hour from the time in the current `Date` object as an integer from 0 to 23.

- `getMinutes()`   Returns the minutes from the time in the current `Date` object as an integer from 0 to 59.

- `getMonth()`   Returns the month for the current `Date` object as an integer from 0 to 11 (where 0 is January, 1 is February, and so on).

- `getSeconds()`   Returns the seconds from the time in the current `Date` object as an integer from 0 to 59.

- `getTime()`   Returns the time of the current `Date` object as an integer representing the number of milliseconds since 1 January 1970 at 00:00:00.

- `getTimezoneOffset()`   Returns the difference between the local time and GMT as an integer representing the number of minutes.

- getYear() Returns the year for the current Date object as a two-digit integer representing the year less 1900.

- parse(*dateString*) Returns the number of milliseconds between January 1, 1970 at 00:00:00 and the date specified in *dateString*. *dateString* should take the following format: (Not I)

  Day, DD Mon YYYY HH;MM;SS TZN
  Mon DD, YYYY

- setDate(*dateValue*) Sets the day of the month for the current Date object. *dateValue* is an integer from 1 to 31.

- setHours(*hoursValue*) Sets the hours for the time for the current Date object. *hoursValue* is an integer from 0 to 23.

- setMinutes(*minutesValue*) Sets the minutes for the time for the current Date object. *minutesValue* is an integer from 0 to 59.

- setMonth(*monthValue*) Sets the month for the current Date object. *monthValue* is an integer from 0 to 11 (where 0 is January, 1 is February, and so on).

- setSeconds(*secondsValue*) Sets the seconds for the time for the current Date object. *secondsValue* is an integer from 0 to 59.

- setTime(*timeValue*) Sets the value for the current Date object. *timeValue* is an integer representing the number of milliseconds since January 1, 1970 at 00:00:00.

- setYear(*yearValue*) Sets the year for the current Date object. *yearValue* is an integer greater than 1900.

- toGMTString() Returns the value of the current Date object in GMT as a string using Internet conventions in the form

  Day, DD Mon YYYY HH;MM;SS GMT

- toLocaleString() Returns the value of the current Date object in the local time using local conventions.

- UTC(*yearValue, monthValue, dateValue, hoursValue, minutesValue, secondsValue*) Returns the number of milliseconds since January 1, 1970 at 00:00:00 GMT. *yearValue* is an integer greater than 1900. *monthValue* is an integer from 0 to 11. *dateValue* is an integer from 1 to 31. *hoursValue* is an integer from 0 to 23. *minutesValue* and *secondsValue* are integers from 0 to 59. *hoursValue*, *minutesValue*, and *secondsValue* are optional. (Not I)

The *document* Object [C|2|3|I]

The document object reflects attributes of an HTML document in JavaScript.

Properties

- alinkColor   The color of active links as a string or a hexa-decimal triplet.

- anchors   Array of anchor objects in the order they appear in the HTML document. Use anchors.length to get the number of anchors in a document.

- applets   Array of applet objects in the order they appear in the HTML document. Use applets.length to get the number of applets in a document. (Not 2)

- bgColor   The color of the document's background.

- cookie   A string value containing cookie values for the current document.

- embeds   Array of plugin objects in the order they appear in the HTML document. Use embeds.length to get the number of plug-ins in a document. (Not 2|I)

- fgColor   The color of the document's foreground.

- forms   Array of form objects in the order the forms appear in the HTML file. Use forms.length to get the number of forms in a document.

- images   Array of image objects in the order they appear in the HTML document. Use images.length to get the number of images in a document. (Not 2|I)

- lastModified   String value containing the last date of modification of the document.

- `linkColor` The color of links as a string or a hexadecimal triplet.
- `links` Array of link objects in the order the hypertext links appear in the HTML document. Use `links.length` to get the number of links in a document.
- `location` A string containing the URL of the current document. Use `document.URL` instead of `document.location`. This property is expected to disappear in a future release.
- `referrer` A string value containing the URL of the calling document when the user follows a link.
- `title` A string containing the title of the current document.
- `URL` A string reflecting the URL of the current document. Use instead of `document.location`. (Not I)
- `vlinkColor` The color of followed links as a string or a hexadecimal triplet.

Event Handlers

- `onMouseDown` Specifies JavaScript code to execute when a user presses a mouse button.
- `onMouseUp` Specifies JavaScript code to execute when the user releases a mouse button.
- `onKeyUp` Specifies JavaScript code to execute when the user releases a specific key. (Netscape Navigator 4.0 only)
- `onKeyPress` Specifies JavaScript code to execute when the user holds down a specific key. (Netscape Navigator 4.0 only)
- `onKeyDown` Specifies JavaScript code to execute when the user presses a specific key. (Netscape Navigator 4.0 only)
- `onDblClick` Specifies JavaScript code to execute when the user double-clicks the area. (Not implemented on Macintosh) (Netscape Navigator 4.0 only)

Methods

- `captureEvents()`   Used in a window with frames (in conjunction with `enableExternalCapture`), this specifies that the window will capture all specified events. New in JavaScript 1.2.

- `clear()`   Clears the document window. (Not I)

- `close()`   Closes the current output stream.

- `open(mimeType)`   Opens a stream that allows `write()` and `writeln()` methods to write to the document window. *mimeType* is an optional string that specifies a document type supported by Navigator or a plug-in (for example, `text/html` or `image/gif`).

- `releaseEvents(eventType)`   Specifies that the current window must release events (as opposed to capture them) so that these events can be passed to other objects, perhaps further on in the event hierarchy. New in JavaScript 1.2.

- `routeEvent(event)`   Sends or routes an event through the normal event hierarchy.

- `write()`   Writes text and HTML to the specified document.

- `writeln()`   Writes text and HTML to the specified document followed by a newline character.

The *FileUpload* Object [C|3]

Reflects a file upload element in an HTML form.

Properties

- `name`   A string value reflecting the name of the file upload element.

- `value`   A string value reflecting the file upload element's field.

The *form* Object [C|2|3|I]

The form object reflects an HTML form in JavaScript. Each HTML form in a document is reflected by a distinct instance of the form object.

Properties

- action   A string value specifying the URL to which the form data is submitted.
- elements   Array of objects for each form element in the order in which they appear in the form.
- encoding   String containing the MIME encoding of the form as specified in the ENCTYPE attribute.
- method   A string value containing the method of submission of form data to the server.
- target   A string value containing the name of the window to which responses to form submissions are directed.

Methods

- reset()   Resets the form. (Not 2|I)
- submit()   Submits the form.

Event Handlers

- onReset   Specifies JavaScript code to execute when the form is reset. (Not 2|I)
- onSubmit   Specifies JavaScript code to execute when the form is submitted. The code should return a true value to enable the form to be submitted. A false value prevents the form from being submitted.

The *frame* Object [C|2|3|I]

The frame object reflects a frame window in JavaScript.

Properties

- frames   An array of objects for each frame in a window. Frames appear in the array in the order in which they appear in the HTML source code.

- onblur   A string reflecting the onBlur event handler for the frame. New values can be assigned to this property to change the event handler. (Not 2)

- onfocus   A string reflecting the onFocus event handler for the frame. New values can be assigned to this property to change the event handler. (Not 2)

- parent   A string indicating the name of the window containing the frameset.

- self   An alternative for the name of the current window.

- top   An alternative for the name of the top-most window.

- window   An alternative for the name of the current window.

Methods

- alert(*message*)   Displays *message* in a dialog box.

- blur()   Removes focus from the frame. (Not 2)

- clearInterval(*intervalID*)   Cancels time outs that are created with the setInterval method. New in JavaScript 1.2.

- close()   Closes the window.

- confirm(*message*)   Displays *message* in a dialog box with OK and Cancel buttons. Returns true or false based on the button clicked by the user.

- focus()   Gives focus to the frame. (Not 2)

- open(*url*,*name*,*features*)   Opens *url* in a window named *name*. If *name* doesn't exist, a new window is created with that name. *features* is an optional string argument containing a list of features for the new window. The feature list contains any of the following name-value pairs separated by commas and without additional spaces:

`toolbar=[yes,no,1,0]`	Indicates whether the window should have a toolbar
`location=[yes,no,1,0]`	Indicates whether the window should have a location field
`directories=[yes,no,1,0]`	Indicates whether the window should have directory buttons
`status=[yes,no,1,0]`	Indicates whether the window should have a status bar
`menubar=[yes,no,1,0]`	Indicates whether the window should have menus
`scrollbars=[yes,no,1,0]`	Indicates whether the window should have scrollbars
`resizable=[yes,no,1,0]`	Indicates whether the window should be resizable
`width=pixels`	Indicates the width of the window in pixels
`height=pixels`	Indicates the height of the window in pixels

- `print()`   Prints the contents of a frame or window. This is the equivalent of the user pressing the Print button in Netscape Navigator. New in JavaScript 1.2.

- `prompt(message,response)`   Displays *message* in a dialog box with a text entry field with the default value of *response*. The user's response in the text entry field is returned as a string.

- `setInterval(function, msec, [args])`   Repeatedly calls a function after the period specified by the *msec* parameter. New in JavaScript 1.2.

- `setInterval(expression, msec)`   Evaluates *expression* after the period specified by the *msec* parameter. New in JavaScript 1.2.

- setTimeout(*expression*,*time*)   Evaluates *expression* after *time* where *time* is a value in milliseconds. The time out can be named with the following structure:
  name = setTimeOut(*expression*,*time*)

- clearTimeout(*name*)   Cancels the time out with the name *name*.

Event Handlers

- onBlur   Specifies JavaScript code to execute when focus is removed from a frame. (Not 2)

- onFocus   Specifies JavaScript code to execute when focus is removed from a frame. (Not 2)

- onMove   Specifies JavaScript code to execute when the user moves a frame. (Netscape Navigator 4.0 Only)

- onResize   Specifies JavaScript code to execute when a user resizes the frame. (Netscape Navigator 4.0 Only)

The *Function* Object [C|3]

The Function object provides a mechanism for indicating JavaScript code to compile as a function. The syntax to use the Function object is:

```
functionName = new Function(arg1, arg2, arg3, ...,
functionCode)
```

This is similar to

```
function functionName(arg1, arg2, arg3, ...) {
    functionCode
}
```

except that in the former *functionName* is a variable with a reference to the function, and the function is evaluated each time it is used rather than being compiled once.

Properties

- arguments   An integer reflecting the number of arguments in a function.
- prototype   Provides a mechanism for adding properties to a Function object.

The *hidden* Object [C|2|3|I]

The hidden object reflects a hidden field from an HTML form in JavaScript.

Properties

- name   A string value containing the name of the hidden element.
- type   A string value reflecting the TYPE property of the INPUT tag. (Not 2 | I)
- value   A string value containing the value of the hidden text element.

The *history* Object [C|2|3|I]

The history object enables a script to work with the Navigator browser's history list in JavaScript. For security and privacy reasons, the actual content of the list is not reflected into JavaScript.

Properties

- length   An integer representing the number of items on the history list. (Not I)

Methods

- back()   Goes back to the previous document in the history list. (Not I)
- forward()   Goes forward to the next document in the history list. (Not I)

- go(*location*)   Goes to the document in the history list specified by *location*. *location* can be a string or integer value. If it is a string it represents all or part of a URL in the history list. If it is an integer, *location* represents the relative position of the document on the history list. As an integer, *location* can be positive or negative. (Not I)

The *Image* Object [C|3]

The Image object reflects an image included in an HTML document.

Properties

- border   An integer value reflecting the width of the image's border in pixels.

- complete   A Boolean value indicating whether the image has finished loading.

- height   An integer value reflecting the height of an image in pixels.

- hspace   An integer value reflecting the HSPACE attribute of the IMG tag.

- lowsrc   A string value containing the URL of the low-resolution version of the image to load.

- name   A string value indicating the name of the Image object.

- prototype   Provides a mechanism for adding properties as an Image object.

- src   A string value indicating the URL of the image.

- vspace   An integer value reflecting the VSPACE attribute of the IMG tag.

- width   An integer value indicating the width of an image in pixels.

Event Handlers

- onKeyUp   Specifies JavaScript code to execute when the user releases a specific key. (Netscape Navigator 4.0 only)

- onKeyPress   Specifies JavaScript code to execute when the user holds down a specific key. (Netscape Navigator 4.0 only)

- onKeyDown   Specifies JavaScript code to execute when the user presses a specific key. (Netscape Navigator 4.0 only)

- onAbort   Specifies JavaScript code to execute if the attempt to load the image is aborted. (Not 2)

- onError   Specifies JavaScript code to execute if there is an error while loading the image. Setting this event handler to null suppresses error messages if an error occurs while loading. (Not 2)

- onLoad   Specifies JavaScript code to execute when the image finishes loading. (Not 2)

The *Layer* Object [4] Netscape Navigator 4.0 Only

The Layer object is used to embed layers of content within a page. These can be hidden or not. Either type are accessible through JavaScript code. The most common use for layers is in the development of Dynamic or DHTML. Layers enable you to create animations or other dynamic content on a page by cycling through the layers you have defined.

Properties

- above   Places a layer on top of a newly created layer.
- background   Used to specify a tiled background image of the layer.
- below   Places a layer below a newly created layer.
- bgColor   Sets the background color of the layer.

- clip(*left, top, right, bottom*)   Specifies the visible boundaries of the layer.
- height   Specifies the height of the layer, expressed in pixels (integer) or by a percentage of the instant layer.
- ID   Previously called NAME. Used to name the layer so that it can be referred to by name and accessed by other JavaScript code.
- left   Specifies the horizontal positioning of the top-left corner of the layer. Used in conjunction with the Top property.
- page[*n*]   Where [*n*] is X or Y. Specifies the horizontal (X) or vertical (Y) positioning of the top-left corner of the layer, relative to the overall, enclosing document. (Note: this is different than the Left and Top properties.)
- parentLayer   Specifies the layer object that contains the present layer.
- SRC   Specifies HTML source to be displayed with the target layer. (This source can also include JavaScript within it.)
- siblingAbove   Specifies the layer object immediately above the present one.
- siblingBelow   Specifies the layer object immediately below the present one.
- top   Specifies the vertical positioning of the top-left corner of the layer. (Used in conjunction with the Left property.)
- visibility   Specifies the visibility of the layer. There are three choices: show (it is visible), hidden (it is not visible), and inherit (the layer inherits the properties of its parent.)
- width   Specifies the width of the layer. Used for wrapping procedures; that is, the width denotes the boundary after which the contents wrap inside the layer.
- z-index   Specifies the Z-order (or stacking order) of the layer. Used to set the layer's position within the overall rotational order of all layers. Expressed as an integer. (Used where there are many layers.)

Events

- `onBlur`   Specifies JavaScript code to execute when the layer loses focus.

- `onFocus`   Specifies JavaScript code to execute when the layer gains focus.

- `onLoad`   Specifies JavaScript code to execute when a layer is loaded.

- `onMouseOut`   Specifies JavaScript code to execute when the mouse cursor moves off the layer.

  ### New Properties

`type`	Indicates a `MouseOut` event.
`target`	Indicates the object to which the event was sent.
`layer[n]`	Where `[n]` represents X or Y, used (in conjunction with `page[n]` and `screen[n]`) to describe the cursor location when the `MouseOut` event occurred.
`page[n]`	Where `[n]` represents X or Y, used (in conjunction with `layer[n]` and `screen[n]`) to describe the cursor location when the `MouseOut` event occurred.
`screen[n]`	Where `[n]` represents X or Y, used (in conjunction with `layer[n]` and `page[n]`) to describe the cursor location when the `MouseOut` event occurred.

- `onMouseover`   Specifies the JavaScript code to execute when the mouse cursor enters the layer.

  ### New Properties with JavaScript 1.2

`type`	Indicates a `MouseOver` event.
`target`	Indicates the object to which the event was sent.
`layer[n]`	Where `[n]` represents X or Y, used (in conjunction with `page[n]` and `screen[n]`) to describe the cursor location when the `MouseOver` event occurred.

page[*n*]   Where [*n*] represents X or Y, used (in conjunction with layer[*n*] and screen[*n*]) to describe the cursor location when the MouseOver event occurred.

screen[*n*]   Where [*n*] represents X or Y, used (in conjunction with layer[*n*] and page[*n*]) to describe the cursor location when the MouseOver event occurred.

Methods

- captureEvents()   Used in a window with frames (in conjunction with enableExternalCapture), this specifies that the window shall capture all specified events. New in JavaScript 1.2.

- load(*source*, *width*)   Alters the source of the layer by replacing it with HTML (or JavaScript) from the file specified in *source*. Using this method, you can also pass a width value (in pixels) to accommodate the new content.

- moveAbove(*layer*)   Places the layer above *layer* in the stack.

- moveBelow(layer)   Places the layer below *layer* in the stack.

- moveBy(*x*,*y*)   Alter the position of the layer by the specified values, expressed in pixels.

- moveTo(*x*,*y*)   Alter the position of the layer (within the containing layer) to the specified coordinates, expressed in pixels.

- moveToAbsolute(*x*,*y*)   Alter the position of the layer (within the page) to the specified coordinates, expressed in pixels.

- releaseEvents(*eventType*)   Specifies that the current window should release events instead of capturing them so that these events can be passed to other objects, perhaps further on in the event hierarchy. New in JavaScript 1.2.

- resizeBy(*width*,*height*)   Resize the layer by the specified values, expressed in pixels.

- resizeTo(*width*,*height*)   Resize the layer to the specified height and size, expressed in pixels.

- routeEvent(event)   Sends or routes an event through the normal event hierarchy.

The *link* Object [C|2|3|I]

The link object reflects a hypertext link in the body of a document.

Properties

- hash   A string value containing the anchor name in the URL.

- host   A string value containing the host name and port number from the URL.

- hostname   A string value containing the domain name (or numerical IP address) from the URL.

- href   A string value containing the entire URL.

- pathname   A string value specifying the path portion of the URL.

- port   A string value containing the port number from the URL.

- protocol   A string value containing the protocol from the URL (including the colon, but not the slashes).

- search   A string value containing any information passed to a GET CGI-BIN call (such as any information after the question mark).

- target   A string value containing the name of the window or frame specified in the TARGET attribute.

Event Handlers

- onMouseDown   Specifies JavaScript code to execute when a user presses a mouse button. (JavaScript 1.2 and Netscape Navigator 4.0 only)

- onMouseOut   Specifies JavaScript code to execute when the user moves the mouse cursor out of an object. (JavaScript 1.2 and Netscape Navigator 4.0 only)

New Properties with JavaScript 1.2

type   Indicates a MouseOut event.

target   Indicates the object to which the event was sent.

layer[n]   Where [n] represents X or Y, used (in conjunction with page[n] and screen[n]) to describe the cursor location when the MouseOut event occurred.

page[n]   Where [n] represents X or Y, used (in conjunction with layer[n] and screen[n]) to describe the cursor location when the MouseOut event occurred.

screen[n]   Where [n] represents X or Y, used (in conjunction with layer[n] and page[n]) to describe the cursor location when the MouseOut event occurred.

- onMouseUp   Specifies the JavaScript code to execute when the user releases a mouse button.

- onKeyUp   Specifies the JavaScript code to execute when the user releases a specific key. (Netscape Navigator 4.0 only)

- onKeyPress   Specifies the JavaScript code to execute when the user holds down a specific key. (Netscape Navigator 4.0 only)

- onKeyDown   Specifies the JavaScript code to execute when the user presses a specific key. (Netscape Navigator 4.0 only)

- onDblClick   Specifies the JavaScript code to execute when the user double-clicks the area. (Not implemented on Macintosh) (Netscape Navigator 4.0 only)

- moveMouse   Specifies the JavaScript code to execute when the mouse pointer moves over the link. (Not 2|3)

- onClick   Specifies the JavaScript code to execute when the link is clicked.

- onMouseOver   Specifies the JavaScript code to execute when the mouse pointer moves over the hypertext link.

New Properties with JavaScript 1.2

type	Indicates a MouseOver event.
target	Indicates the object to which the event was sent.
layer[n]	Where [n] represents X or Y, used (in conjunction with page[n] and screen[n]) to describe the cursor location when the MouseOver event occurred.
page[n]	Where [n] represents X or Y, used (in conjunction with layer[n] and screen[n]) to describe the cursor location when the MouseOver event occurred.
screen[n]	Where [n] represents X or Y, used (in conjunction with layer[n] and page[n]) to describe the cursor location when the MouseOver event occurred.

The *location* Object [C|2|3|I]

The location object reflects information about the current URL.

Properties

- hash   A string value containing the anchor name in the URL.

- host   A string value containing the host name and port number from the URL.

- hostname   A string value containing the domain name (or numerical IP address) from the URL.

- href   A string value containing the entire URL.

- pathname   A string value specifying the path portion of the URL.

- port   A string value containing the port number from the URL.

- protocol   A string value containing the protocol from the URL (including the colon, but not the slashes).

- search   A string value containing any information passed to a GET CGI-BIN call (such as information after the question mark).

Methods

- reload()   Reloads the current document. (Not 2|I)

- replace(*url*)   Loads *url* over the current entry in the history list, making it impossible to navigate back to the previous URL with the back button. (Not 2|I)

The *Math* Object [C|2|3|I]

The Math object provides properties and methods for advanced mathematical calculations.

Properties

- E   The value of Euler's constant (roughly 2.718) used as the base for natural logarithms.

- LN10   The value of the natural logarithm of 10 (roughly 2.302).

- LN2   The value of the natural logarithm of 2 (roughly 0.693).

- LOG10E   The value of the base 10 logarithm of e (roughly 0.434).

- LOG2E   The value of the base 2 logarithm of e (roughly 1.442).

- PI   The value of PI; used to calculate the circumference and area of circles (roughly 3.1415).

- SQRT1_2   The value of the square root of one-half (roughly 0.707).

- SQRT2   The value of the square root of two (roughly 1.414).

Methods

- abs(number)   Returns the absolute value of *number*. The absolute value is the value of a number with its sign ignored so abs(4) and abs(-4) both return 4.

- acos(*number*)   Returns the arc cosine of *number* in radians.

- asin(*number*)   Returns the arc sine of *number* in radians.

- atan(*number*)   Returns the arc tangent of *number* in radians.

- atan2(*number1*,*number2*)   Returns the angle of the polar coordinate corresponding to the Cartesian coordinate (*number1*,*number2*). (Not I)

- ceil(*number*)   Returns the next integer greater than *number* in other words, rounds up to the next integer.

- cos(*number*)   Returns the cosine of *number*, where *number* represents an angle in radians.

- exp(*number*)   Returns the value of E to the power of *number*.

- floor(*number*)   Returns the next integer less than *number*— in other words, rounds down to the nearest integer.

- log(*number*)   Returns the natural logarithm of *number*.

- max(*number1*,*number2*)   Returns the greater of *number1* and *number2*.

- min(*number1*,*number2*)   Returns the smaller of *number1* and *number2*.

- pow(*number1*,*number2*)   Returns the value of *number1* to the power of *number2*.

- random()   Returns a random number between zero and 1 (at press time, this method was available only on UNIX versions of Navigator 2.0).

- round(*number*)   Returns the closest integer to *number*—in other words, rounds to the closest integer.

- sin(*number*)   Returns the sine of *number*, where *number* represents an angle in radians.

- sqrt(*number*)   Returns the square root of *number*.

- tan(*number*)   Returns the tangent of *number*, where *number* represents an angle in radians.

The *mimeType* Object [C|3]

The mimeType object reflects a MIME type supported by the client browser.

Properties

- type   A string value reflecting the MIME type.
- description   A string containing a description of the MIME type.
- enabledPlugin   A reference to plugin object for the plug-in supporting the MIME type.
- suffixes   A string containing a comma-separated list of file suffixes for the MIME type.

The *navigator* Object [C|2|3|I

The navigator object reflects information about the version of Navigator being used.

Properties

- appCodeName   A string value containing the code name of the client (for example, "Mozilla" for Netscape Navigator).
- appName   A string value containing the name of the client (for example, "Netscape" for Netscape Navigator).
- appVersion   A string value containing the version information for the client in the form
  versionNumber (platform; country)

  For example, Navigator 2.0, beta 6 for Windows 95 (international version), would have an appVersion property with the value "2.0b6 (Win32; I)".

- language   Specifies the translation of Navigator. (A read-only property.) New in JavaScript 1.2.
- mimeTypes   An array of mimeType objects reflecting the MIME types supported by the client browser. (Not 2 | I)

- platform   Specifies the platform for which Navigator was compiled. (For example, Win32, MacPPC, UNIX.) New in JavaScript 1.2.

- plugins   An array of plugin objects reflecting the plug-ins in a document in the order of their appearance in the HTML document. (Not 2|I)

- userAgent   A string containing the complete value of the user-agent header sent in the HTTP request. This contains all the information in appCodeName and appVersion:

  Mozilla/2.0b6 (Win32; I)

Methods

- javaEnabled()   Returns a Boolean value indicating whether Java is enabled in the browser. (Not 2|I)

- preference(*preference.Name*, setValue)   In signed scripts, this method enables the developer to set certain browser preferences. Preferences reachable with this method are:

general.always_load_images	true/false value that sets whether images are automatically loaded
security.enable_java	true/false value that sets whether Java is enabled
javascript.enabled	true/false value that sets whether JavaScript is enabled
browser.enable_style_sheets	true/false value that sets whether style sheets are enabled
autoupdate.enabled	true/false value that sets whether autoinstall is enabled
network.cookie. cookieBehavior(0,1,2)	Value that sets the man ner in which cookies are handled. There are three parameters. 0 accepts all

cookies; 1 accepts only those that are forwarded to the originating server; 2 denies all cookies.

`network.cookie.warnAboutCookies`

`true`/`false` value that sets whether the browser will warn on accepting cookies

The *Option* Object [C|3]

The `Option` object is used to create entries in a select list using the syntax

```
optionName = new Option(optionText, optionValue,
defaultSelected, selected)
```

and then

```
selectName.options[index] = optionName.
```

Properties

- `defaultSelected`   A Boolean value specifying whether the option is selected by default.

- `index`   An integer value specifying the option's index in the select list.

- `prototype`   Provides a mechanism to add properties to an `Option` object.

- `selected`   A Boolean value indicating whether the option is currently selected.

- `text`   A string value reflecting the text displayed for the option.

- `value`   A string value indicating the value submitted to the server when the form is submitted.

The *password* Object [C|2|3|I]

The password object reflects a password text field from an HTML form in JavaScript.

Properties

- defaultValue   A string value containing the default value of the password element (such as the value of the VALUE attribute).
- enabled   A Boolean value indicating whether the password field is enabled. (Not 2|3)
- form   A reference to the form object containing the password field. (Not 2|3)
- name   A string value containing the name of the password element.
- value   A string value containing the value of the password element.

Methods

- focus()   Emulates the action of focusing in the password field.
- blur()   Emulates the action of removing focus from the password field.
- select()   Emulates the action of selecting the text in the password field.

Event Handlers

- onBlur   Specifies JavaScript code to execute when the password field loses focus. (Not 2|3)
- onFocus   Specifies JavaScript code to execute when the password field receives focus. (Not 2|3)

The *plugin* Object

The plugin object reflects a plug-in supported by the browser.

Properties

- name   A string value reflecting the name of the plug-in.
- filename   A string value reflecting the filename of the plug-in on the system's disk.
- description   A string value containing the description supplied by the plug-in.

The *radio* Object [C|2|3|I]

The radio object reflects a set of radio buttons from an HTML form in JavaScript. To access individual radio buttons, use numeric indexes starting at zero. For example, individual buttons in a set of radio buttons named testRadio could be referenced by testRadio[0], testRadio[1], and so on.

Properties

- checked   A Boolean value indicating whether a specific button is checked. Can be used to select or deselect a button.
- defaultChecked   A Boolean value indicating whether a specific button was checked by default (that is, it reflects the CHECKED attribute). (Not I)
- enabled   A Boolean value indicating whether the radio button is enabled. (Not 2|3)
- form   A reference to the form object containing the radio button. (Not 2|3)
- length   An integer value indicating the number of radio buttons in the set. (Not I)
- name   A string value containing the name of the set of radio buttons.

- value   A string value containing the value of a specific radio button in a set (that is, it reflects the VALUE attribute).

Methods

- click()   Emulates the action of clicking a radio button.
- focus()   Gives focus to the radio button. (Not 2|3)

Event Handlers

- onClick   Specifies the JavaScript code to execute when a radio button is clicked.
- onFocus   Specifies the JavaScript code to execute when a radio button receives focus. (Not 2|3)

The *RegExp* Object

The RegExp object is relevant to searching for regular expressions. Its properties are set before or after a search is performed. These do not generally exercise control over the search itself, but instead articulate a series of values that can be accessed throughout the search.

Properties

- input   The string against which a regular expression is matched. New in JavaScript 1.2.
- multiline [true, false]   Sets whether the search continues beyond line breaks on multiple lines (true) or not (false). New in JavaScript 1.2.
- lastMatch   Property that indicates the characters last matched. New in JavaScript 1.2.
- lastParen   Property that indicates the last matched string that appeared in parentheses. New in JavaScript 1.2.
- leftContext   Property that indicates the string just before the most recently matched regular expression. New in JavaScript 1.2.

- `rightContext`   Property that indicates the remainder of the string, beyond the most recently matched regular expression. New in JavaScript 1.2.

- `$1,..$9`   Property that indicates the last nine substrings in a match, where those substrings are enclosed in parentheses. New in JavaScript 1.2.

The *Regular Expression* Object

The Regular Expression object contains the pattern of a regular expression.

Parameters

- `regexp`   Parameter that specifies the name of the regular expression object. New in JavaScript 1.2.

- `pattern`   Parameter that specifies the text of the regular expression. New in JavaScript 1.2.

Flags

- `i`   Option that specifies that during the regular expression search, case is ignored (that is, the search is not case sensitive).

- `g`   Option that specifies that during the regular expression search, the match (and search) should be global.

- `gi`   Option that specifies that during the regular expression search, case is ignored and during the regular expression search, the match (and search) should be global.

Properties

- `global [true,false]`   A property that sets the `g` flag value in code, for example, whether the search is global (`true`) or not (`false`). New in JavaScript 1.2.

- `ignoreCase [true,false]`   A property that sets the `i` flag value in code, for example, whether the search is case sensitive (`true`) or not (`false`). New in JavaScript 1.2.

- `lastIndex`   A property (integer value) that indicates the index position at which to start the next matching procedure (for example, `lastIndex == 2`). New in JavaScript 1.2.

- `source`   A property (read-only) that contains the pattern's text. New in JavaScript 1.2.

Methods

- `compile`   Compiles the regular expression. This method is usually invoked at script startup, when the regular expression is already known and will remain constant. New in JavaScript 1.2.

- `exec(str)`   Executes a search for a regular expression within the specified string (`str`). New in JavaScript 1.2. Note: this uses the same properties as the `RegExr` object.

- `test(str)`   Executes a search for a regular expression and a specified string (`str`). New in JavaScript 1.2. Note: this uses the same properties as the `RegExr` object.

The *reset* Object [C|2|3|I]

The `reset` object reflects a reset button from an HTML form in JavaScript.

Properties

- `enabled`   A Boolean value indicating whether the reset button is enabled. (Not 2|3)

- `form`   A reference to the `form` object containing the reset button. (Not 2|3)

- `name`   A string value containing the name of the reset element.

- `value`   A string value containing the value of the reset element.

Methods

- `click()` Emulates the action of clicking the reset button.
- `focus()` Specifies the JavaScript code to execute when the reset button receives focus. (Not 2|3)

Event Handlers

- `onClick` Specifies the JavaScript code to execute when the reset button is clicked.
- `onFocus` Specifies the JavaScript code to execute when the reset button receives focus. (Not 2|3)

The *Screen* Object (New in JavaScript 1.2)

The `Screen` object describes (or specifies) the characteristics of the current screen.

Properties

- `availHeight` Property that specifies the height of the screen in pixels. (Minus static display constraints set forth by the operating system.) New in JavaScript 1.2.
- `availWidth` Property that specifies the width of the current screen in pixels. (Minus static display constraints set forth by the operating system.) New in JavaScript 1.2.
- `height` Property that specifies the height of the current screen in pixels. New in JavaScript 1.2.
- `width` Property that specifies the width of the current screen in pixels. New in JavaScript 1.2.
- `pixelDepth` Property that specifies the number of bits (per pixel) in the current screen. New in JavaScript 1.2.
- `colorDepth` Property that specifies the number of possible colors to display in the current screen. New in JavaScript 1.2.

The *select* Object [C|2|3]

The select object reflects a selection list from an HTML form in JavaScript.

Properties

- length   An integer value containing the number of options in the selection list.
- name   A string value containing the name of the selection list.
- options   An array reflecting each of the options in the selection list in the order they appear. The options property has its own properties:

defaultSelected	A Boolean value indicating whether an option was selected by default (that is, it reflects the SELECTED attribute).
index	An integer value reflecting the index of an option.
length	An integer value reflecting the number of options in the selection list.
name	A string value containing the name of the selection list.
selected	A Boolean value indicating whether the option is selected. Can be used to select or deselect an option.
selectedIndex	An integer value containing the index of the currently selected option.
text	A string value containing the text displayed in the selection list for a particular option.
value	A string value indicating the value for the specified option (that is, reflects the VALUE attribute).

- `selectedIndex`   Reflects the index of the currently selected option in the selection list.

Methods

- `blur()`   Removes focus from the selection list. (Not 2|3)
- `focus()`   Gives focus to the selection list. (Not 2|3)

Event Handlers

- `onBlur`   Specifies the JavaScript code to execute when the selection list loses focus.
- `onFocus`   Specifies the JavaScript code to execute when focus is given to the selection list.
- `onChange`   Specifies the JavaScript code to execute when the selected option in the list changes.

The *String* Object [C|2|3|1]

The `String` object provides properties and methods for working with string literals and variables.

Properties

- `length`   An integer value containing the length of the string expressed as the number of characters in the string.
- `prototype`   Provides a mechanism for adding properties to a `String` object. (Not 2)

Methods

- `anchor(name)`   Returns a string containing the value of the string object surrounded by an A container tag with the NAME attribute set to *name*.
- `big()`   Returns a string containing the value of the string object surrounded by a BIG container tag.

- `blink()` Returns a string containing the value of the string object surrounded by a `BLINK` container tag.

- `bold()` Returns a string containing the value of the string object surrounded by a `B` container tag.

- `charAt(index)` Returns the character at the location specified by `index`.

- `charCodeAt(index)` Returns a number representing an ISO-Latin-1 codeset value at the instant `index`. (Netscape Navigator 4.0 and above only)

- `concat(string2)` Combines two strings and derives a third, new string. (Netscape Navigator 4.0 and above only)

- `fixed()` Returns a string containing the value of the string object surrounded by a `FIXED` container tag.

- `fontColor(color)` Returns a string containing the value of the string object surrounded by a `FONT` container tag with the `COLOR` attribute set to `color`, where `color` is a color name or an RGB triplet. (Not I)

- `fontSize(size)` Returns a string containing the value of the string object surrounded by a `FONTSIZE` container tag with the size set to `size`. (Not I)

- `fromCharCode(num1, num2, ...)` Returns a string constructed of ISO-Latin-1 characters. Those characters are specified by their codeset values, which are expressed as `num1`, `num2`, and so on.

- `indexOf(findString,startingIndex)` Returns the index of the first occurrence of `findString`, starting the search at `startingIndex`, where `startingIndex` is optional—if it is not provided, the search starts at the start of the string.

- `italics()` Returns a string containing the value of the string object surrounded by an `I` container tag.

- `lastIndexOf(findString,startingIndex)` Returns the index of the last occurrence of `findString`. This is done by searching backward from `startingIndex`. `startingIndex` is optional and is assumed to be the last character in the string if no value is provided.

The *String* Object [C|2|3|1]

- link(*href*)   Returns a string containing the value of the string object surrounded by an A container tag with the HREF attribute set to *href*.

- match(*regular_expression*)   Matches a regular expression to a string. The parameter *regular_expression* is the name of the regular expression, expressed either as a variable or a literal.

- replace(*regular_expression*, newSubStr)   Find and replace *regular_expression* with newSubStr.

- search(*regular_expression*)   Find *regular_expression* and match it to some string.

- slice(*beginSlice*, [*endSlice*])   Extract a portion of a given string and derive a new string from that excerpt. *beginSlice* and *endSlice* are both zero-based indexes that can be used to grab the first, second, and third character, and so on.

- small()   Returns a string containing the value of the string object surrounded by a SMALL container tag.

- split(*separator*)   Returns an array of strings created by splitting the string at every occurrence of *separator*. (Not 2|I) split has additional functionality in JavaScript 1.2 and for Navigator 4.0 and above. That new functionality includes the following elements:

Regex and fixed string splitting	One can now split the string string by both regular expression argument and fixed string.
Limit Count	One can now add a limit count to prevent the inclusion of empty elements within the string.
White Space Splitting	The capability to split on white space (including any white space, such as space, tab, newline, and so forth).

- `strike()`   Returns a string containing the value of the string object surrounded by a STRIKE container tag.

- `sub()`   Returns a string containing the value of the string object surrounded by a SUB container tag.

- `substr(start, [length])`   Used to extract a set number (length) of characters within a string. Use start to specify the location at which to begin this extraction process. New in JavaScript 1.2.

- `substring(firstIndex,lastIndex)`   Returns a string equivalent to the substring beginning at *firstIndex* and ending at the character before *lastIndex*. If *firstIndex* is greater than *lastIndex*, the string starts at *lastIndex* and ends at the character before *firstIndex*. Note: in JavaScript 1.2, x and y are no longer swapped. To obtain this result, you must specify JavaScript 1.2 with the language attribute within the <SCRIPT> tag.

- `sup()`   Returns a string containing the value of the string object surrounded by a SUP container tag.

- `toLowerCase()`   Returns a string containing the value of the string object with all characters converted to lowercase.

- `toUpperCase()`   Returns a string containing the value of the string object with all characters converted to uppercase.

The *submit* Object [C|2|3|I]

The submit object reflects a submit button from an HTML form in JavaScript.

Properties

- `enabled`   A Boolean value indicating whether the submit button is enabled. (Not 2|3)

- `form`   A reference to the form object containing the submit button. (Not 2|3)

- `name`   A string value containing the name of the submit button element.

- type   A string value reflecting the TYPE attribute of the INPUT tag. (Not 2|I)
- value   A string value containing the value of the submit button element.

Methods

- click()   Emulates the action of clicking the submit button.
- focus()   Gives focus to the submit button. (Not 2|3)

Event Handlers

- onClick   Specifies the JavaScript code to execute when the submit button is clicked.
- onFocus   Specifies the JavaScript code to execute when the submit button receives focus. (Not 2|3)

The *text* Object [C|2|3|I]

The text object reflects a text field from an HTML form in JavaScript.

Properties

- defaultValue   A string value containing the default value of the text element (that is, the value of the VALUE attribute).
- enabled   A Boolean value indicating whether the text field is enabled. (Not 2|3)
- form   A reference to the form object containing the text field. (Not 2|3)
- name   A string value containing the name of the text element.
- type   A string value reflecting the TYPE attribute of the INPUT tag. (Not 2|I)
- value   A string value containing the value of the text element.

Methods

- focus()   Emulates the action of focusing in the text field.
- blur()   Emulates the action of removing focus from the text field.
- select()   Emulates the action of selecting the text in the text field.

Event Handlers

- onBlur   Specifies the JavaScript code to execute when focus is removed from the field.
- onChange   Specifies the JavaScript code to execute when the content of the field is changed.
- onFocus   Specifies the JavaScript code to execute when focus is given to the field.
- onSelect   Specifies the JavaScript code to execute when the user selects some or all of the text in the field.

The *textarea* Object [C|2|3|I]

The textarea object reflects a multiline text field from an HTML form in JavaScript.

Properties

- defaultValue   A string value containing the default value of the textarea element (that is, the value of the VALUE attribute).
- enabled   A Boolean value indicating whether the textarea field is enabled. (Not 2|3)
- form   A reference to the form object containing the textarea field. (Not 2|3)
- name   A string value containing the name of the textarea element.
- type   A string value reflecting the type of the textarea object. (Not 2|I)

- `value`   A string value containing the value of the textarea element.

Methods

- `focus()`   Emulates the action of focusing in the textarea field.
- `blur()`   Emulates the action of removing focus from the textarea field.
- `select()`   Emulates the action of selecting the text in the textarea field.

Event Handlers

- `onKeyUp`   Specifies the JavaScript code to execute when the user releases a specific key. (Netscape Navigator 4.0 only)
- `onKeyPress`   Specifies the JavaScript code to execute when the user holds down a specific key. (Netscape Navigator 4.0 only)
- `onKeyDown`   Specifies the JavaScript code to execute when the user presses a specific key. (Netscape Navigator 4.0 only)
- `onBlur`   Specifies the JavaScript code to execute when focus is removed from the field.
- `onChange`   Specifies the JavaScript code to execute when the content of the field is changed.
- `onFocus`   Specifies the JavaScript code to execute when focus is given to the field.
- `onSelect`   Specifies the JavaScript code to execute when the user selects some or all of the text in the field.

The *window* Object [C|2|3|I]

The `window` object is the top-level object for each window or frame and is the parent object for the document, location, and history objects.

Properties

- `defaultStatus` A string value containing the default value displayed in the status bar.

- `frames` An array of objects for each frame in a window. Frames appear in the array in the order in which they appear in the HTML source code.

- `innerHeight()` Specifies the vertical size of the content area (in pixels). New in JavaScript 1.2.

- `innerWidth()` Specifies the horizontal size of the content area (in pixels). New in JavaScript 1.2.

- `length` An integer value indicating the number of frames in a parent window. (Not I)

- `name` A string value containing the name of the window or frame.

- `opener` A reference to the `window` object containing the `open()` method used to open the current window. (Not 2 I I)

- `pageXOffset` Specifies the current X position of the viewable window area (expressed in pixels). New in JavaScript 1.2.

- `pageYOffset` Specifies the current Y position of the viewable window area (expressed in pixels). New in JavaScript 1.2.

- `parent` A string indicating the name of the window containing the frameset.

- `personalbar [visible=true,false]` Represents the Directories bar in Netscape Navigator and whether it is visible. New in JavaScript 1.2.

- `scrollbars [visible=true,false]` Represents the scrollbars of the instant window and whether they are visible. New in JavaScript 1.2.

- `self` A alternative for the name of the current window.

- `status` Used to display a message in the status bar—this is done by assigning values to this property.

- `statusbar=[true,false,1,0]` Specifies whether the status bar of the target window is visible.

- `toolbar=[true,false,1,0]` Specifies whether the toolbar of the target window is visible.

- `top` An alternative for the name of the top-most window.

- `window` An alternative for the name of the current window.

Methods

- `alert(message)` Displays *message* in a dialog box.

- `back()` Sends the user back to the previous URL stored in the history list. (Simulates a click on the Back button in Navigator.) New in JavaScript 1.2.

- `blur()` Removes focus from the window. On many systems, this sends the window to the background. (Not 2|I)

- `captureEvents()` Used in a window with frames (in conjunction with `enableExternalCapture`), this specifies that the window will capture all specified events.

- `clearInterval(intervalID)` Cancels time outs that are created with the `setInterval` method. New in JavaScript 1.2.

- `close()` Closes the window. (Not I)

- `confirm(message)` Displays *message* in a dialog box with OK and Cancel buttons. Returns `true` or `false` based on the button clicked by the user.

- `disableExternalCapture()` Prevents the instant window with frames from capturing events occurring in pages loaded from a different location. New in JavaScript 1.2.

- `enableExternalCapture()` Enables the instant window (with frames) to capture events occurring in pages loaded from a different location. New in JavaScript 1.2.

- `find([string], [true, false], [true, false])` Finds `string` within the target window. There are two true/false parameters: the first specifies the Boolean state of case sensitivity in the search; the second specifies whether the search is performed backward. New in JavaScript 1.2.

- `focus()`   Gives focus to the window. On many systems, this brings the window to the front. (Not 2 | I)

- `forward()`   Sends the user to the next URL in the history list. (Simulates a user clicking the Forward button in Navigator.) New in JavaScript 1.2.

- `home()`   Sends the user to the user's Home Page URL. (Example: in a default configuration of Netscape Navigator, this will send the user to `http://home.netscape.com`.) New in JavaScript 1.2.

- `moveBy(horizontal, vertical)`   Moves the window according to the specified values `horizontal` and `vertical`. New in JavaScript 1.2.

- `moveTo(x, y)`   Moves the top-left corner of the window to the specified location, where *x* and *y* are screen coordinates. New in JavaScript 1.2.

- `navigator(url)`   Loads *url* in the window. (Not 2 | 3)

- `open(url,name,features)`   Opens *url* in a window named *name*. If *name* doesn't exist, a new window is created with that name. *features* is an optional string argument containing a list of features for the new window. The feature list contains any of the following name-value pairs separated by commas and without additional spaces: (Not I)

`toolbar=[yes,no,1,0]`	Indicates whether the window should have a toolbar.
`location=[yes,no,1,0]`	Indicates whether the window should have a location field.
`directories=[yes,no,1,0]`	Indicates whether the window should have directory buttons.
`status=[yes,no,1,0]`	Indicates whether the window should have a status bar.
`menubar=[yes,no,1,0]`	Indicates whether the window should have menus.

`scrollbars=[yes,no,1,0]`	Indicates whether the window should have scrollbars.
`resizable=[yes,no,1,0]`	Indicates whether the window should be resizable.
`width=pixels`	Indicates the width of the window in pixels.
`alwaysLowered=[yes,no,1,2]`	Indicates (if true) that the window should remain below all other windows. (This feature has varying results on varying window systems.) New in JavaScript 1.2. Note: the script must be signed to use this feature.
`alwaysRaised=[yes,no,1,2]`	Indicates (if true) that the window should always remain the top-level window. (This feature has varying results on varying window systems.) New in JavaScript 1.2. Note: the script must be signed to use this feature.
`dependent[yes,no,1,2]`	Indicates that the current child window will die (or close) when the parent window does. New in JavaScript 1.2.
`hotkeys=[yes,no,1,2]`	Indicates (if true) that most hotkeys are disabled within the instant window. New in JavaScript 1.2.
`innerWidth=pixels`	Indicates the width (in pixels) of the instant window's content area. New in JavaScript 1.2.

`innerHeight=pixels`	Indicates the height (in pixels) of the instant window's content area. New in JavaScript 1.2.
`outerWidth=pixels`	Indicates the instant window's horizontal outside width boundary. New in JavaScript 1.2.
`outerHeight=pixels`	Indicates the instant window's horizontal outside height boundary. New in JavaScript 1.2.
`screenX=pixels`	Indicates the distance that the new window is placed from the left side of the screen (horizontally). New in JavaScript 1.2.
`screenY=pixels`	Indicates the distance that the new window is placed from the top of the screen (vertically). New in JavaScript 1.2.
`z-lock=[yes,no,1,2]`	Indicates that the instant window does not move through the cycling of the Z-order; that is, it does not rise above other windows, even if activated. New in JavaScript 1.2. Note: the script must be signed for this feature to work.
`height=pixels`	Indicates the height of the window in pixels.

- `print()` Prints the contents of a frame or window. This is the equivalent of the user pressing the Print button in Netscape Navigator. New in JavaScript 1.2.

- `prompt(message,response)` Displays *message* in a dialog box with a text entry field with the default value of *response*. The user's response in the text entry field is returned as a string.

- `releaseEvents(eventType)` Specifies that the current window should release events instead of capturing them so that these events can be passed to other objects, perhaps further on in the event hierarchy. New in JavaScript 1.2.

- `resizeBy(horizontal, vertical)` Resizes the window, moving from the bottom-right corner. New in JavaScript 1.2.

- `resizeTo(outerWidth, outerHeight)` Resizes the window utilizing `outerWidth` and `outerHeight` properties. New in JavaScript 1.2.

- `routeEvent(event)` Sends or routes an event through the normal event hierarchy. New in JavaScript 1.2.

- `scrollBy(horizontal, vertical)` Scroll the viewing area of the current window by the specified amount. New in JavaScript 1.2.

- `scrollTo(x, y)` Scrolls the current window to the specified position, calculated in x and y coordinates, starting at the top-left corner of the window. New in JavaScript 1.2.

- `setInterval(function, msec, [args])` Repeatedly calls a function after the period specified by the `msec` parameter. New in JavaScript 1.2.

- `setInterval(expression, msec)` Evaluates *expression* after the period specified by the `msec` parameter. New in JavaScript 1.2.

- `setTimeout(expression,time)` Evaluates *expression* after *time*, where *time* is a value in milliseconds. The time out can be named with the structure

    `name = setTimeOut(expression,time)`

- `scrollTo(x,y)` Scrolls the window to the coordinate *x,y*. (Not 2|I)

- `stop()` Stops the current download. This is the equivalent of the user pressing the Stop button in Netscape Navigator.

- `clearTimeout(name)` Cancels the time out with the name *name*.

Event Handlers

- `onDragDrop` Specifies the JavaScript code to execute when the user drops an object onto the window. (Netscape Navigator 4.0 only)

- `onBlur` Specifies the JavaScript code to execute when focus is removed from a window. (Not 2|I)

- `onError` Specifies the JavaScript code to execute when a JavaScript error occurs while loading a document. This can be used to intercept JavaScript errors. Setting this event handler to `null` effectively prevents JavaScript errors from being displayed to the user. (Not 2|I)

- `onFocus` Specifies the JavaScript code to execute when the window receives focus. (Not 2|I)

- `onLoad` Specifies the JavaScript code to execute when the window or frame finishes loading.

- `onMove` Specifies the JavaScript code to execute when the user moves a window. (Netscape Navigator 4.0 only)

- `onResize` Specifies the JavaScript code to execute when a user resizes the window.

- `onUnload` Specifies the JavaScript code to execute when the document in the window or frame is exited.

Independent Functions, Operators, Variables, and Literals

Independent Functions

- `escape(character)` Returns a string containing the ASCII encoding of *character* in the form %xx, where xx is the numeric encoding of the character. (C|2|3|I)

- eval(*expression*)   Returns the result of evaluating *expression*, where *expression* is an arithmetic expression. (C|2|3|I)

- isNaN(*value*)   Evaluates *value* to see if it is NaN. Returns a Boolean value. (C|2|3|I) (On UNIX platforms, not 2)

- parseFloat(*string*)   Converts *string* to a floating point number and returns the value. It continues to convert until it hits a non-numeric character and then returns the result. If the first character cannot be converted to a number, the function returns NaN (zero on Windows platforms). (C|2|3|I)

- parseInt(*string*,*base*)   Converts *string* to an integer of base *base* and returns the value. It continues to convert until it hits a non-numeric character and then returns the result. If the first character cannot be converted to a number, the function returns NaN (zero on Windows platforms). (C|2|3|I)

- taint(*propertyName*)   Adds tainting to *propertyName*. (C|3)

- toString()   This is a method of all objects. It returns the object as a string or returns "[object *type*]" if no string representation exists for the object. (C|2|3) Note: in JavaScript 1.2, this will covert objects and strings to literals.

- unescape(*string*)   Returns a character based on the ASCII encoding contained in *string*. The ASCII encoding should take the form "%integer" or "hexadecimalValue". (C|2|3|I)

- untaint(*propertyName*)   Removes tainting from *propertyName*. (C|3)

Statements

- break   Terminates a while or for loop and passes program control to the first statement following the loop. (2|3|4) Note: in JavaScript 1.2, break has the added functionality of being able to break out of labeled statements.

- `comment`   Used to add a comment within the script. This comment is ignored by Navigator. Comments in JavaScript work similar to those in C. These are enclosed in a `/*` (start), `*/` (end) structure. (2|3|4)

- `continue`   Terminates execution of statements within a `while` or `for` loop and continues iteration of the loop. (2|3|4) Note: in JavaScript 1.2, `continue` has added functionality that enables you to continue within labeled statements.

- `do while`   Sets up a loop that continues to execute statements and code until the condition evaluates to `false`. New in JavaScript 1.2.

- `export`   Used in conjunction with the `import` statement. In secure, signed scripts, this enables the developer to export all properties, functions, and variables to another script. New in JavaScript 1.2.

- `for([initial-expression]; [condition]; [incremental-expression];))`   Specifies the opening of a `for` loop. The arguments are these: initialize a variable (`initial-expression`), create a condition to test for (`condition`) and specify an incrementation scheme (`incremental-expression`). (2|3|4)

- `for..in`   Imposes a variable to all properties of an object and executes a block of code for each. (2|3|4)

- `function [name]()`   Declares a function so that it can be referred to or reached by event handlers (or other processes). (2|3|4)

- `if..else`   A structure used to test whether a certain condition is true. `If..else` blocks can contain nested statements and functions (and call these) if a condition is either true or false. (2|3|4)

- `import`   Used in conjunction with the `export` statement. In secure, signed scripts, this enables the developer to import all properties, functions, and variables from another script. New in JavaScript 1.2.

- `label` (`labeled statements`)   Statement that creates a label or pointer to code elsewhere in the script. By calling this label, you redirect the script to the labeled statement.

- `new`   Creates an instance of a user-defined object. (`new` can also be used to create an instance of built-in objects, inherent to JavaScript, such as new `Date`.) (2|3|4)

- `return [value]`   Specifies a value to be returned by a given function. For example, `return x` returns the variable value associated with x. (2|3|4)

- `switch`   Evaluates an expression and attempts to match it to a `case` pattern or label. If the expression matches the `case`, trailing statements associated with that label are executed. New in JavaScript 1.2. (Operates in a similar fashion to the `switch` statement in C Shell syntax.)

- `this`   A statement used to refer to a specific object [2|3|4]. For example,
  ```
  onClick = 'javascript;my_function(this.form)'
  ```

- `var [name]`   Declares a variable by `name`. (2|3|4)

- `while`   Statement that begins a `while` loop. `while` loops specify that as long as (while) a condition is true, execute some code. (2|3|4)

- `with`   Statement that sets the value for the default object; a method that is similar to creating a global variable with a function. (2|3|4)

Operators

- Assignment Operators—See Table E.1, Assignment operators in JavaScript. (C|2|3|I)

TABLE E.1   **Assignment operators.**

Operator	Description
=	Assigns the value of the right operand to the left operand
+=	Adds the left and right operands and assigns the result to the left operand
-=	Subtracts the right operand from the left operand and assigns the result to the left operand
*=	Multiplies the two operands and assigns the result to the left operand
/=	Divides the left operand by the right operand and assigns the value to the left operand
%=	Divides the left operand by the right operand and assigns the remainder to the left operand

- Arithmetic Operators—See Table E.2, Arithmetic operators in JavaScript. (C|2|3|I)

TABLE E.2   **Arithmetic operators.**

Operator	Description
+	Adds the left and right operands
-	Subtracts the right operand from the left operand
*	Multiplies the two operands
/	Divides the left operand by the right operand
%	Divides the left operand by the right operand and evaluates to the remainder
++	Increments the operand by one (can be used before or after the operand)
—	Decreases the operand by one (can be used before or after the operand)
-	Changes the sign of the operand

- Bitwise Operators—Bitwise operators deal with their operands as binary numbers but return JavaScript numerical value (see Table E.3). (C|2|3|I)

TABLE E.3   Bitwise operators in JavaScript.

Operator	Description
AND (or &)	Converts operands to integers with 32 bits, pairs the corresponding bits, and returns one for each pair of ones. Returns zero for any other combination.
OR (or ¦)	Converts operands to integers with 32 bits, pairs the corresponding bits, and returns one for each pair where one of the two bits is one. Returns zero if both bits are zero.
XOR (or ^)	Converts operands to integer with 32 bits, pairs the corresponding bits, and returns one for each pair where only one bit is one. Returns zero for any other combination.
<<	Converts the left operand to an integer with 32 bits and shifts bits to the left the number of bits indicated by the right operand. Bits shifted off to the left are discarded and zeros are shifted in from the right.

Operator	Description
>>>	Converts the left operand to an integer with 32 bits and shifts bits to the right the number of bits indicated by the right operand. Bits shifted off to the right are discarded and zeros are shifted in from the left
>>	Converts the left operand to an integer with 32 bits and shifts bits to the right the number of bits indicated by the right operand. Bits shifted off to the right are discarded and copies of the leftmost bit are shifted in from the left.

- Logical Operators—See Table E.4, Logical operators in JavaScript. (C¦2¦3¦I)

TABLE E.4   Logical operators.

Operator	Description
&&	Logical "and." Returns `true` when both operands are true, otherwise it returns `false`.
¦¦	Logical "or." Returns `true` if either operand is true. It returns `false` only when both operands are false.
!	Logical "not." Returns `true` if the operand is false and `false` if the operand is true. This is a unary operator and precedes the operand.

- Comparison Operators—See Table E.5, Comparison Operators in JavaScript [C|2|3|I]

TABLE E.5   Logical (comparison) operators.

Operator	Description
==	Returns true if the operands are equal.
!=	Returns true if the operands are not equal.
>	Returns true if the left operand is greater than the right operand.
<	Returns true if the left operand is less than the right operand.
>=	Returns true if the left operand is greater than or equal to the right operand.
<=	Returns true if the left operand is less than or equal to the right operand.

- Conditional Operators—Conditional expressions take one form:

  ```
  (condition) ? val1 : val2
  ```

  If *condition* is true, the expression evaluates to *val1*, otherwise it evaluates to *val2*. (C|2|3|I)

- String Operators—The concatenation operator (+) is one of two string operators. It evaluates to a string combining the left and right operands. The concatenation assignment operator (+=) is also available. (C|2|3|I)

- The typeof Operator—The typeof operator returns the type of its single operand. Possible types are object, string, number, boolean, function, and undefined. (C|3|I)

- The void Operator—The void operator takes an expression as an operand but returns no value. (C|3)

- Operator Precedence—JavaScript applies the rules of operator precedence as follows (from lowest to highest precedence):

  Comma (,)

  Assignment operators (=, +=, -=, *=, /=, %=)

  Conditional (? :)

  Logical OR (¦¦)

  Logical AND (&&)

  Bitwise OR (¦)

  Bitwise XOR (^)

  Bitwise AND (&)

  Equality (==, !=)

  Relational (<, <=, >, >=)

  Shift (<<, >>, >>>)

  Addition/subtraction (+, -)

  Multiply/divide/modulus (*, /, %)

  Negation/increment (!, -, ++, —)

  Call, member ((), [])

Installing Dreamweaver and Accessories

F

Dreamweaver System Requirements

In order to run Dreamweaver on a Macintosh, you'll need the following:

- *A PowerPC-based system.* Dreamweaver will run on any PowerPC Macintosh system, but will not run on older 680×0 systems. (Actually, it's pretty darn slow on older PowerPC machines.)

- *System 7.5.5 or better.* As of this writing, the latest version of the Macintosh operating system is MacOS 8.1. MacOS 8 is a commercial release of the Macintosh operating system; MacOS 8.1 is a free upgrade for those who have purchased MacOS 8, and can be purchased by users of previous operating systems. See `http://www.apple.com/macos/8.1/` for details.

- *Video support for 256 colors or greater.* Dreamweaver needs at least 256 colors to run. All of the current Apple Macintoshes in production as of this writing support the necessary number of colors, but there's at least one PowerPC—the one I own, of course—without the proper video hardware, the PowerBook 5300.

- *Lots and lots of memory.* Dreamweaver prefers at least 24MB of memory to run smoothly. MacOS 8 can require 10 to 15MB. That's just to get Dreamweaver started. You will almost certainly want to run a few other applications concurrently with Dreamweaver: Netscape Navigator (the stripped-down version, not Netscape Communicator) requires 7MB, and BBEdit requires about 2MB. Most folks will also want to run Adobe Photoshop, which isn't really happy without 15 to 20MB. Finally, if you set a lot if type for GIFs, you'll probably want to use Adobe Illustrator 7, add 5MB for that. In other words, to be really productive, you'll need about 70MB of memory. Of course, you can use virtual memory if you must, but Dreamweaver and Photoshop will slow to an agonizing crawl if you do. In other words, hie thee to the Micro Warehouse and pick up some RAM.

In order to run Dreamweaver on Windows, you'll need the following:

- *Windows 95 or Windows NT 4.0.* Dreamweaver requires a 32-bit Windows system, and the Win32 crutch libraries for Windows 3.1 just won't make it happen. As fond as we all are of the old Windows, if you want Dreamweaver, you've got to upgrade.

- *Pentium-class 90MHz or greater.* Dreamweaver will run on slower 486 machines, but, between the overhead required by Windows and Dreamweaver itself, life gets bogged down pretty quick. For testing the software, I used a 100MHz Pentium and didn't experience any difficulty.

- *20MB or more free hard disk space.* Depending on how much you install, and how much you plan to do with Dreamweaver, you may need more. If your drive runs at more than 60 to 70 percent full, it's time to get a bigger hard drive.

- *16MB RAM, or more.* This is Macromedia's official statement on the minimum memory required, but let's face it, 16MB is hardly enough to let Windows run smoothly, let alone one or more applications. And with Dreamweaver, you'll be likely to have several editing windows open, the Site window, plus possibly another HTML editor such as HomeSite, and one or more browsers open for previewing. All of this eats up system resources, so the more memory you can afford, the better off you'll be. A base of 32MB is not a bad plan these days.

- 640×480, *256-color display*. This is kind of like the 16MB minimum memory requirement. A 256-color display is more than adequate, but an 800×600 display is much easier to work with, especially when you're dealing with several floating palettes or split site screens at the same time.

Running the Dreamweaver Installer

Installing Dreamweaver is a cinch. To make your life a little easier, the Dreamweaver installer can automatically look for and configure browsers on your computer for previewing pages. Of course, the browsers have to be installed first. If you don't have both Microsoft Internet Explorer 4.0 and Netscape Navigator 4.0, jump to those sections and load them first, and then come back to install Dreamweaver.

Installing Dreamweaver (Macintosh)

1. Double-click the **Dreamweaver Installer** icon.

2. Dreamweaver presents a window that contains the terms of the Dreamweaver license agreement. Read it. If you agree to the terms, click the **Accept** button. If you decline the terms of the agreement, the installer will quit; you can't install Dreamweaver without accepting the license terms.

3. The Dreamweaver Installer dialog box appears. There aren't any interesting options here. Click **OK**, and the installer will put Dreamweaver in its own folder (called "Dreamweaver") on your hard drive.

Installing Dreamweaver is the same as installing any other software package you've installed for Windows. The Dreamweaver CD-ROM is not configured to work with Windows AutoPlay (where you put the disk in and it runs). As a result, you'll have to run the installer manually.

Installing Dreamweaver

1. Shut down any other programs running on your computer, such as word processors and Web browsers. Programs that sit in the service tray (bottom-right corner) are okay where they are—you don't have to close them.

2. Select **Run** from the Start menu. Type the path and file-name to the installer. For my computer, it's E:\setup. Or, you can also browse to the CD-ROM and double-click the setup icon.

3. Dreamweaver presents windows with an introduction and a license agreement. Glance through them, click **Next**, and continue to the first screen of the installation.

4. The first choice is where Dreamweaver should be placed. By default, this is C:\Program Files\Macromedia\ Dreamweaver\. If for some reason you want to put Dreamweaver somewhere else, choose **Browse** and select a new location.

5. Pick the group that is added to your Start button Program menu. By default, this is Macromedia Dreamweaver.

6. The installer confirms your choices and tells you it's ready to start copying files. Clicking **Next** at this point begins copy-ing all the requisite files to your hard disk. When you're done, you can view the Readme files and start Dreamweaver.

Other Stuff on the Dreamweaver CD-ROM

There's a lot of cool stuff on the Dreamweaver CD-ROM. All you really need is the Dreamweaver installer, but I'll run through the process of installing the other goodies that are bun-dled with Dreamweaver.

Installing BBEdit (Macintosh)

BBEdit is a sleek little text editor with some nice HTML-editing tools and none of the RAM-clogging baggage that is included in most word processors. To install BBEdit, do the following:

1. Double-click the **BBEdit Installer** icon in the BBEdit 4.5 folder on the Dreamweaver CD-ROM.

2. The installer presents the Install BBEdit dialog box. There are no fancy choices here; just click **OK**, and the installer will take care of the rest.

Installing HomeSite (Windows)

HomeSite is one of the premiere HTML editing software programs for Windows. It was originally created by a Web author for himself and other Web authors, and the result is a very intuitive, easy-to-use tool. Dreamweaver includes a full-featured copy of HomeSite as part of its Web page editing package. For more information on working with HomeSite, see Appendix B, "HomeSite Quick Reference."

Loading HomeSite

1. Double-click the **Dreamweaver Installer** icon in the HomeSite 3.0 folder on the Dreamweaver CD-ROM. Or, select **Run** from the Start menu, and enter `"E:/Homesite 3.0/homesite3_dw"`. You'll need the quotation marks since there's a space in the Homesite folder name.

2. Move through the introductory and licensing screens to the point where you enter your name, company name, and HomeSite serial number (contained in your documentation). You'll need all three to progress any further.

3. Select a location for HomeSite, or accept the default.

4. Next, select which components to install—the program files, documentation, or both. By default both are installed, which is a good choice.

5. HomeSite is equipped with basic English spell-checking ability. If you need additional dictionaries for your work, including foreign languages or occupational dictionaries, you can add them to the Spell Checker now.

6. Next, choose a program folder for HomeSite to reside in from the Programs list of the Start menu.

7. At this point, HomeSite has enough information to begin. The installer will display your choices and begin copying files after you select **Next**.

Netscape Communicator Installer

Netscape Communicator is a "suite" of network-savvy applications including a Web browser, an email client, a news reader, and a bunch of other geegaws. For the Macintosh, Communicator demands at least 10MB of RAM. Netscape also offers a browser-only product, Netscape Navigator, which only needs about 6.3MB of RAM.

The Dreamweaver CD-ROM contains a free copy of Netscape Communicator 4.0 If you don't have Communicator 4.0 or better installed on your machine already, it's a good idea to install Communicator so you can explore Dreamweaver's DHTML support.

Installing Netscape Communicator (Macintosh)

1. The installer presents a window that contains the Netscape Communicator license agreement. If you accept the terms, click **Accept**. If you click **Decline**, the installer will quit.

2. The installer presents a window that contains release notes and last-minute information for Netscape Communicator 4.0. Read the notes. Really.

3. The installer displays the main installer window. You may chose between Easy Install and Custom Install options using the pop-up menu in the top-right corner of the window. If you choose **Easy Install**, the installer will put all of the modules on your hard disk. If you chose **Custom Install**, the installer presents one last window that allows you to check the components you want to add.

The process to install Communicator on Windows is very similar, with a couple of additional things to watch for.

Installing Netscape Communicator (Windows)

1. If you have a version of Navigator earlier than 4.0, it's a good idea to uninstall it and restart your computer. If you don't, you could end up with more than one entry for

---

Get the latest!

As of this writing, the latest version of Netscape Communicator is version 4.04. (By the time you read this, it's likely that an even newer version will be available.) See http://home.netscape.com for information about upgrading to the latest version of Communicator.

The release notes are important

It's a good idea to print out the release notes. They include valuable information.

Netscape on your installed programs list (a nuisance, but not life-threatening), and Communicator might not install correctly because of inaccessible files in the Netscape folders (bad karma).

2. Browse to the Netscape Communicator 4.0 folder of the Dreamweaver CD-ROM, and then double-click the installation program. For version 4.04, the name is **cp32e404.exe**.

3. You're reminded to close down an active programs.

4. The installer presents a window that contains the Netscape Communicator license agreement. If you accept the terms, click **Accept**. If you click **Decline**, the installer will quit.

5. Next, you're asked where Communicator should be installed, and if you want a Typical or Custom installation. The typical installation is basically a "kitchen sink" install, where every component in the Communicator suite is installed. For your options on a custom install, see the list of components after these steps.

6. After you've chosen which set of components to install, the installer will make sure you have enough disk space. Then, you're prompted for the program group to create for the Start menu.

7. The installer will give one more overview of your choices, after which you can click **Install**, and watch your available disk space fly away.

8. The installer presents a window that contains release notes and last-minute information for Netscape Communicator 4.0.

9. The last step is to restart the computer. This gives Windows a chance to clean up any temporary files and update the system registry with the various entries needed for Communicator.

The only real reason you wouldn't choose Easy (Macintosh) or Typical (Windows) install is to save on disk space. If you've got a sexy new computer with a lightning fast processor and a mega-giga hard drive, go ahead and take the easy route. If your hard

Close down what?

As a general rule, you can just close programs on the task bar and ignore any applications running in the service tray. The exceptions are any programs that are launched into the task bar from the service tray, such as backup utilities. You might want to disable those items if there's a chance they could interfere with your installation.

Keep those notes handy!

It's a good idea to print out a copy of the release notes. They often include valuable information.

drive is full, and you need to delete useful stuff to accommodate Communicator, use Custom Install to avoid installing components you won't use.

If you choose Custom Install, you can choose from the following components:

- *Calendar*. Netscape's calendar is similar to a personal information manager software calendar. Netscape's calendar can be shared by several users over the Internet (or an intranet). This option requires about 5MB of space.

- *Host-on-Demand*. This module allows Communicator to act as a client for applications running on an IBM host machine. (If you don't know what that means, you probably don't need the module.) This option requires about 500KB of space.

- *Netscape Conference*. Netscape's conference module allows users to communicate via voice and eletronic whiteboard over Internet and intranet connnections. This option requires about 5MB of space.

- *Communicator Module*. This is the core of the Communicator package: it contains the Web browser, email client, newsgroup reader, and other basic services. You must install this component; the other modules aren't much good without it.

Microsoft Internet Explorer Installation (Windows)

Currently, Dreamweaver only includes Internet Explorer for Windows. Macintosh users aren't included in this portion of the great browser give-away, so if you have a Macintosh, you'll need to go directly to Microsoft for what you want.

Installing Internet Explorer (Windows)

1. Browse to the Microsoft Internet Explorer 4.0 folder on the Dreamweaver CD-ROM, and double click **Setup.exe** to start the ball rolling.

2. Since it is Windows, and it is Microsoft, you're greeted with a little animation and a short piece of music that's interesting the first time around, and annoying every time thereafter.

After the show is over, you have a list of four choices: install Internet Explorer, install add-ons, browse the CD-ROM, or exit. Click the first choice.

3. As you start clicking **Next**, you'll find yourself at the license agreement. In another new twist, you actually have to click a checkbox that says you accept it, and then click **Next** again.

4. Depending on your needs, you can select a Standard or Full installation. The Standard installation includes the basic necessities: browser, Outlook Express (for mail and news), and multimedia enhancements (ActiveX controls, Dynamic HTML features, and so on). The Full installation adds additional components, including FrontPage Express, NetMeeting, NetShow, Chat, and the Web Publishing Wizard.

   If you have a need for the bells and whistles, you can select the Full install, but Standard is a much more sane choice.

5. The next choice is whether to accept a new feature of Internet Explorer 4.0 that affects the basic user interface on your desktop and everywhere else on your computer, including the Control Panel, Windows Explorer, Help, and every other corner of your computer. Essentially, this turns your computer into one big browsing experience, where every choice and menu becomes a list of hyperlinks, and pages from the Web can be automatically used as wallpaper on your desktop.

   This choice is purely personal preference. Microsoft doesn't force you in either direction.

6. Next, select the country of origin for your Active channels, followed by the location of the Internet Explorer files on your computer.

7. The Active Setup program then prepares to install Internet Explorer on your computer. If a previous version of Internet Explorer is found on your computer, you'll be given the opportunity to update older versions of various components or exit from setup.

You're not in Kansas anymore

Internet Explorer uses a new installation process called Active Setup, instead of the Install-Shield method. This means you may see screens you've never seen before during installation, but that's OK. The end result is the same.

8. When the process is completed, you'll be prompted to restart the computer. This gives the installer a chance to update the Windows Registry and any other tidbits to get the browser ready to run.

Shockwave Installer

Shockwave is a plug-in that allows Web browsers to play Shockwave content. (For the record, Shockwave is a system for optimizing Macromedia Director Presentations for inclusion in Web pages.) Dreamweaver's online documentation contains Shockwave content, so it's a good idea to install the Shockwave plug-in.

Installing Shockwave (Macintosh)

1. Click the **Shockwave Installer** (PPC) icon in the Shockwave folder on the Dreamweaver CD-ROM.

2. The installer presents a window containing the Shockwave license agreement. If you accept the terms, click **OK**. If you decline, the installer will quit.

3. Dreamweaver presents a dialog box that asks you to chose between the Netscape Communicator and Microsoft Internet Explorer Web browsers. Check the checkbox next to your preferred browser. (I recommend that you install the plug-ins for both browsers, so we'll come back later and install the plug-in for the other browser.)

4. The installer displays a new, unlabeled window that shows which browser (if any) it has found that matches the browser you picked in step 3. There are four different possibilities at this point:

- Click **OK** if the installer has found the browser you had in mind.
- Click **Try Again** if the installer has found the wrong browser. For instance, if you have both Netscape Communicator and Netscape Navigator installed, the installer may find Navigator, while you want Communicator.

Checkboxes versus radio buttons

Because the Choose Browser dialog box uses checkboxes next to each Web browser's name, you might expect that you'd be able to check both browsers' names and install the plug-ins for both in one bold stroke. Alas, you can't. The checkboxes in this particular dialog box think they're radio buttons, and checking one box un-checks the other.

- Click **Browse** to manually lead the installer to the Web browser that you want to use. The installer will provide you with a standard file dialog box you can use to navigate to your preferred browser.

  - Click **Cancel** when you can't seem to find the browser, the installer can't find the browser, and you're ready to bail.

5. The installer presents another dialog box that reminds you that use of the Shockwave plug-in will increase the browser's memory requirements. The installer offers to adjust the amount of memory the browser requests when it launches. I suggest that you accept the installer's offer—one of the main reasons why Netscape browsers crash is that they have run out of memory.

6. The installer installs the plug-in files. When the installer is finished, it asks if you want to quit the installer or continue with other installations. Click **Continue**.

7. Repeat steps 3–6 to add the plug-in to the browser that you didn't choose during the first pass through step 3.

For Windows, you also need to run an installer to load the plug-ins. However, this only loads the files needed for Netscape browsers. If you want to install Shockwave for Internet Explorer, see the paragraph after the instructions.

Installing Shockwave plug-ins (Windows)

1. Browse to the Shockwave folder of the Dreamweaver CD-ROM. Double-click the **Shockwave_Installer** icon to start the installation.

2. After the standard introduction and acceptance of the license agreement, the Shockwave Installer looks for your Netscape plug-in directory. It's a good idea to use the directory the installer finds, unless you have a real good reason not to.

3. Once you've confirmed the directory, click the **Install** button to copy the files.

4. After copying the files, you can restart your browser to load the new plug-in.

The install process is a little different for Internet Explorer, which relies on an ActiveX control that's automatically installed when needed. To load it ahead of time, start Internet Explorer and find your way to the Macromedia Web site (http://www.macromedia.com). From there, click the **Get Shockwave** button, and follow the instructions on the screen.

Index

formatting text, 69
frames
  naming, 239
  referencing nonexistent
    frames, 241
  thumbnails, 242
  Library items, 121
  tables, 183
  text boxes, 147

**proprietary HTML,
437-439**

**proxies, transferring files
through, 35**

push
  frames, 342
    frameset contents, 343-344
    headlines file, 347
    reload time, 348
    timeline reload,
      345-347
  LAYER tag
    base page, 348
    content, 350
    timeline reload, 351-353

Q - R

Q tag, 483, 490

QuickTime, 136

quotations, 483, 490

radio buttons (forms),
152-154

rectangular hotspots, 167

referencing, styles, 513

refreshing images, 111

relative size (fonts), 518,
524

relative URLs, 83

reloading, push pages, 348

remote servers, uploading
files, 392

Remote site, 12

remote sites
  configuring FTP, 34
  file check-out, 36

**Remove Tags command
(BBEdit), 453**

revision marks
  controlling, 37
  DEL tag, 481, 488
  INS tag, 482, 489

rollovers, 279, 356
  anchors, 362
  base image, 359-361
  button images, 357-359
  mouseout, 365
  mouseover, 362-364
  sizing, 358

round hotspots, 168

Roundtrip HTML, 43

**Row command (BBEdit),
453**

rows
  colors, 201
  number of, 183

rules, 477

S

S tag, 492, 499

SageProv, 487

SAMP tag, 483, 490, 497

sample output, 483, 490,
497

sans-serif fonts, 517

saving
  framesets, 232
  scripts, 282

**Script command (BBEdit),
449**

scripts, 278-280
  browser support, 281
  creating, 281-283
  downloading, 282
  event handlers, 287
  for non-script browsers, 435
  gatekeeper, 439
  hiding, 436
  HTML Editor, 287-289
  JavaScript/VBScript, 281

limitations, 280
linked, 286
local, 284-286

scrollbars (frames), 242

seamless images, 114

sections (layers), 256

selecting tables, 182

selectors, 513
  classes, 513
  contextual, 514
  first-letter values, 514
  first-line values, 514
  separating, 514

**semicolons (;), style sheets,
514**

serif fonts, 517

server-side imagemaps, 164
  creating, 172

servers
  layers, 261
  receiving forms, 155

Shockwave, 129-130
  installing, 600-601

sidebars, 212-213

single-celled tables, 224

site
  Gallagher Design, 259
  saving files to, 33-36

**Site Information dialog
box, 29, 390**

site management
  archiving, 393
  design, 384
  easy updates, 391
  files, 392
  folders, 393
  frames, 392
  libraries, 388-390
    strategies, 390-391
  style sheets, 385-387
    custom, 387
  uploading site, 394

Site Manager, 28

Site window
  adding pages without edit-
    ing, 31-33
  organizing files, 10